GOD'S OWN COUNTRY

Also by Stephen Bates:

A Church at War
Asquith

GOD'S OWN COUNTRY

Tales from the Bible Belt

STEPHEN BATES

HODDER

Copyright © 2007 by Stephen Bates

First published in Great Britain in 2007

The right of Stephen Bates to be identified as the Author of the Work has been asserted
by him in accordance with the Copyright, Designs and Patents Act 1988.

1

British Library Cataloguing in Publication Data
A record for this book is available from the British Library

ISBN 978 0340 909263

Printed and bound in Great Britain by
Clays Ltd, St Ives plc

The paper and board used in this paperback are natural recyclable products made
from wood grown in sustainable forests. The manufacturing processes conform to the
environmental regulations of the country of origin.

Hodder & Stoughton
A Division of Hodder Headline Ltd
338 Euston Road
London NW1 3BH
www.madaboutbooks.com

For my dearest of American friends, Nicholas A. Ulanov and
Cynthia Hostetler
and
Jef McAllister and Ann Olivarius

Contents

Foreword

It is, of course, presumptuous for any non-American to write a book like this. My sole qualification is that I have admired the USA, its people, its landscapes and, above all, its history for very many years and have always wanted the chance to write something about them for a wider audience. This, however, will not be a work of heavy scholarship, and especially not of theology, but largely of journalism, which is something I am much better fitted to produce.

The purpose of this book is to try and explain to readers in the UK, and perhaps in the USA as well, a little bit about how America comes to be the sort of religious place it is – an aspect of a society that is so like ours and yet that Europeans find hardest to understand. There is a tendency here, in the secular UK, to write off US religiosity as alien and monolithic when, of course, it is far from that; and to see all US religious people as crazed fundamentalists, when they are not that either. So alienated are many Europeans from the current Bush administration that some assume that its strange deployment of religious rhetoric and its occasional pursuit of religiously motivated policies is some novel aberration in US life. Sometimes my colleagues at the *Guardian* (as well as those working elsewhere in the UK media) – and our readers as well – tend to fall into this trap, especially those who tell us at frequent and shrill intervals that all religion is nonsense.

What I am hoping to show in this book is that US religion's relationship with politics did not start with George W. Bush, or even with the rise of Jerry Falwell, Pat Robertson and the other television evangelists. Indeed, it is quite possible to trace very similar strands in US thought and society stretching right back to the Pilgrim Fathers. These motivations have shaped the USA from the beginning and have very deep roots in the US psyche: in people's sense in that country of being set apart and specially chosen by God, in their self-appointed mission to be a benign beacon to mankind and in their insistence on telling others about it, sometimes to the exasperation of less-favoured mortals.

US styles of worship and religious engagement in democratic politics derive something from the circumstances in which the nation was founded and the nature of its settlement. Its preachers' forthrightness, independence and entrepreneurial zeal derive from the absence of an established Church or a hidebound social order.

Other, less attractive trends in US thought are also evident, arising out of its religious life: its occasional paranoia and bursts of self-righteousness, its suspicion of the outsider and fear of otherness, and its addiction to conspiracies. And, of course, the strand of fundamentalism in some of its beliefs.

Inevitably, this book is largely about the USA's most distinctive religious tradition, its evangelical Protestantism, but it is hard to ignore the influence of Catholicism, particularly in recent years as that religion has entered the mainstream of US life.

Many of the theorists and campaigners of the Religious Right are, in fact, Catholics, and one of the electoral achievements of the movement has been to unite previously mutually suspicious and antagonistic Christian religious traditions in pursuit of a number of issues, most notably abortion.

It is true that US religiosity, and its effect particularly on the current administration, has been strong and sometimes cynically deployed. It would be a great mistake, though, to think that religion will creep away when President Bush leaves office. Whoever takes over now and in the foreseeable future will have to acknowledge a potentially formidable conservative religious constituency which has the power to influence both domestic and foreign policy – and hence to have an effect on the rest of the world. There are clear signs too that US religious conservatives are working to exercise their influence outside the USA's borders, especially in the Third World. Progressives ignore or discount these trends at their peril. In the UK they can already be seen at work in a number of high-profile political campaigns.

There are a great many books published about the Religious Right in the USA – a new one seemed to come out every week while I was researching and writing this book. Many are written by very angry people indeed – and there have also been a number of outstanding studies by academic historians over the years into US religious practice and its evolution. Surprisingly few, however, have married the two together and this is what this book tries to do. There may also be some merit in an outsider looking in on the phenomenon from abroad. And not only a British outsider, but a Roman Catholic one at that.

In the summer and autumn of 2006 I made several trips to the USA, to travel across the country and to meet and interview people, mainly from the Religious Right, along the way. I was met entirely with courtesy and almost invariably with openness by people who really did not need to speak to a journalist from the UK. Very few of those I would have liked to see turned me down – Senator John Danforth, Rick Warren (who does not co-operate, apparently, with other people writing books) and Senator Sam Brownback were too busy, and only Focus on the Family was sniffily dismissive.

On the other hand, I was very glad to have the chance to speak to people such as Richard Land, Rich Cizik, Michael Cromartie, Judge Roy Moore, David Parsons, Michael Farris, Ken Ham, Jim Tonkowich, Tim LaHaye, Luis Lugo, Randy Brinson, Joel Osteen, T. D. Jakes, Jim Wallis, Sister Helen Prejean, Frank Page, Frank Griswold, John Bryson Chane and Gene Robinson.

Many journalists also helped me, of whom I should especially mention Jay Tolson and Dan Gilgoff of US News and World Report, Jane Little of the BBC, Mark Pinsky of the *Orlando Sentinel*, George Conger, Greg Warner of the Baptist News Service, Raymond Arroyo and his colleagues at EWTN and, particularly, Jim Naughton of the Washington diocese of the US Episcopal Church.

I also need to thank my *Guardian* colleagues for their forebearance and support, particularly Nick Hopkins, Harriet Sherwood, Jonathan Freedland, Claire Phipps, Georgina Henry and Deborah Hargreaves, and especially Julian Borger and Carol Keefer in the *Guardian*'s Washington office.

No acknowledgments would be complete without mentioning my oldest and closest American friends, Nicholas Ulanov, a lifelong Democrat, who in the spring of 2007 married his partner Cynthia Hostetler, a member of the Bush administration team, and Jef McAllister, formerly London editor of *Time* magazine, and his partner Ann Olivarius, all of whom have had to endure many hours over the years listening to my enthusiasm for all things American. They have usually been able to set me right. My parents-in-law, Werner and Sheila Thurau of Houston, deserve my gratitude too, not only for the obvious reason, but because their hospitality and friendship sustained and refreshed me at the end of my long and dusty journey through the Bible Belt.

This book came about as the result of a commission by Judith Longman of Hodder and Stoughton, who liked a previous book I wrote called *A Church at War* so much that she bought the paperback rights and encouraged me to write more, this time for Hodder.

Last, but of course not least, I need to thank above all others my wife Alice and my three children, Helena, Timothy and Philip – still good evangelicals all – who have had to endure this strange, arcane enthusiasm of mine for perhaps too long and have put up with my absence with rather disquieting equanimity.

Tunbridge Wells, Kent,
February 2007

1

From Sea to Shining Sea

'What Hath God Wrought!'
Samuel Morse's first telegraph message, 24 May 1844

It is impossible, even today, to drive across the USA without being struck by its immensity and beauty. It is quite breathtaking in its fertile plains and wooded mountains, its vast prairies and mighty rivers, and you can well imagine the wonder felt by its first settlers as they crested the rise and saw the land spread out in endless fecundity before them.

We cannot tell what the original aboriginal inhabitants believed, but we don't have to guess what the first white men thought of the land because they left a written record to tell us. It was 'the most plentiful, fruitfull and wholesome of all the world', two Elizabethan explorers reported back to London from what became the Carolinas. Even if ultimately they were to die there of disease, violence or hardship, still it drew men to its shores in awe. Nearly three hundred years on: 'The views are magnificent, the valleys so beautiful, the scenery so peaceful. What a glorious world God Almighty has given us', General Robert E. Lee wistfully wrote to his wife from West Virginia during the Civil War, 'And how we labour to mar His gifts.'[1]

For these people understood, above all else, that God had laid the land on personally for their benefit and given them special responsibility for its exploitation and stewardship. It was not just any old land, inherited or owned by virtue of birth from time immemorial by someone else – it was *their* land, new, fertile and unexploited (the Indian savages did not count of course), and they were blessed to have it as a mark of God's special favour towards their diligence and endeavour. For religious people, coming to the New World to escape persecution and establish their own society under their own rules, there could be no other explanation.

As John Winthrop, leader of one of the first great Puritan

migrations, told his followers in probably the most famous sermon ever preached about the New World, aboard the *Arbella*, before they even stepped ashore in 1630: 'If the lord shall be pleased . . . he shall make us a praise and glory. For we must consider that we shall be as a city upon a hill, the eyes of all people are upon us; so that if we deal falsely with our God in this work we have undertaken . . . we shall be a story and a byword through all the world.'[2] This, of course, was a conscious echo of the Sermon on the Mount: 'You are the light of the world,' Jesus told his followers. 'A city that is set on a hill cannot be hidden.'[3]

Most Americans still feel that their country is a beacon to mankind: not just a geographical entity, but a moral and spiritual symbol to the rest. This image infused the rhetoric of Ronald Reagan and it still resonates, like a peal of distant thunder around the peaks and valleys of the Catskills on a summer afternoon. With it comes a wider sense of being a chosen people and a larger understanding of a special destiny, so obvious that, nearly two hundred years after the term was first coined and 100 years after they spread across the continent, it remains manifest.

Despite such divine approval, however, the USA's Christians are in a febrile state. Even though they form the overwhelmingly dominant faith group in a country famous for its religious observance and respect for Christian belief, many of them believe they are fighting a war to the death, and one they fear they cannot be certain they will win. Moreover, it is a battle on two fronts: internally against secularism, liberalism and godless sexual immorality, and externally against the forces of an alien religious creed, militant Islam, that wishes them nothing but evil. Such fears, in the heartland of the richest and most powerful nation the world has ever seen, may seem exaggerated, may even be what the distinguished historian Richard Hofstadter famously once described in relation to an earlier crisis as 'the paranoid style in American politics'; but these fears are not entirely groundless either. US society is both the most overtly religious and aggressively secular in the modern, Western world. And, even separated by thousands of miles of ocean from its most virulent enemies, it has found itself vulnerable to terrorist attack of the most ostentatious and devastating sort.

God, indeed, does seem to intervene an awful lot in the activities of individual Americans, as well as the state itself, in big things and in small. To him is ascribed success in the examination, the election to office, the cure from illness, the escape from Hurricane Katrina, even when others, equally Christian, did not survive. 'The Lord is on our side,' politicians tell the electorate, but sometimes He's there for them; and sometimes He's not.

'Nation after nation, cheered by our example, will follow in our footsteps till the whole earth is freed,' said Lyman Beecher, the sober-sided nineteenth-century Yankee Presbyterian preacher and campaigner for the abolition of slavery, who participated in one of the earlier Great Awakenings of the USA's religious conscience, in the 1840s.

'God did not make the American people the mightiest human force of all time simply to feed and die,' exclaimed Albert J. Beveridge to the Union League Club of Philadelphia in February 1899, some time before the USA was indeed the mightiest force on the planet. 'He did not give our race the brain of organization and heart of domination to no purpose and no end. No! He has given us a task equal to our talents . . . He has made us the lords of civilization, that we may administer civilization.'[4]

That is a doctrine that has become steadily more marked and even more overtly clad in religious rhetoric in the last one hundred years and perhaps increasingly widely resented abroad as US power and influence have grown more incontrovertible. Its self-conscious piety, so obvious to Americans, is not always so evident to foreigners, not only in the old countries of Western Europe that share and were the source of the USA's Christianity, but also across the countries of the developing world on other continents that have ancient religions of their own. What is perceived as US sanctimoniousness has irked Europeans before, as when Woodrow Wilson descended on the Versailles peace conference after the First World War to lecture the Europeans on the virtues of peace, democracy and self-determination, but then the USA was at least perceived as something of a saviour, the New World fortunately having redressed the balance of the Old to the allies' advantage. Now the Americans' sense of moral superiority is more than ever aggravating to Europeans. To them it comes across often as arrogant, hubristic, even imperialist, and sometimes as naïve and simplistic – maybe even hypocritical, given some of the US military's actions in Iraq, as well.

We come from common stock and Christian religious heritage, speak the same language, share much of the same history, watch the same television programmes and films, hear the same music and use the same appliances. The sidewalks of New York and Los Angeles are as familiar to us from cinema and television, even if we have never visited them, as if we walked them every day. And yet, to invoke a phrase much in use in current theological disputes, in one respect we seem to be walking farther apart than ever. We don't 'get' their religion and they don't 'get' ours, or lack of it.

The more it puzzles us, however, the more we need to understand it and appreciate its wellsprings. We have to know what motivates a country so powerful and so close in many of its instincts to our own. It won't do either to dismiss the US religious impulse as mad or malign, or to assume that the country's leaders are simplistic know-nothings merely because they profess to believe in a form of Christianity that many of us find particularly strange and inimical. In a world where religion motivates so many of the most dynamic as well as the most destructive and terrifying forces in global politics, we need to understand our friends as much as our enemies.

We need to do so not least because, however strange some strands of US religious politics appear to us in our highly secular culture and society, that does not mean that we ourselves are entirely immune from their influence. There are groups in UK society that would dearly like to import US-style partisan campaigns on moral issues such as abortion and gay partnerships and to censor those who oppose them by bullying and threats. And, more insidiously, there is evidence that some of the wealthy backers of US religious campaigns on such issues are also secretly funding UK pressure groups. They are presumably not doing this for entirely philanthropic reasons, but instead for what changes they hope to achieve beyond their shores.

The sheer alien-ness of some aspects of the US religious culture struck home to me one Sunday morning in May 2006, as I was driving through the Cumberland Gap, between the far southwestern tip of Virginia and Tennessee, the route first pioneered by Daniel Boone and now traversed by an interstate highway carrying vast lorries trundling towards Knoxville and on the long haul to Nashville, Memphis and the West. The road passes now through pleasant, rolling farmland and wide, verdant valleys, dotted with small towns. It had been a long morning's drive and I felt the need for some spiritual refreshment, or at least the company of a human voice.

Turning the dial on the radio of my hire car, I came across an arresting one. 'Would to God our children grew up to be virgins,' it said startlingly, in a thick and rasping Tennessee twang. 'I would rather put my .38 pistol in my child's room than have a computer or a television set in there. You watch enough of that sit-com nonsense, that *Desperate Housewives* – not that I do – and you know the Devil's crowd is working how to get to your children.'

I had to pull over to listen and take notes. 'Satan is out to destroy your children. Yes sir, I do believe that. You gotta strike him and rescue them from Hell. If they don't fear you, they won't fear God. You gotta make them more scared of you than they are of Satan,' the preacher said.

Then, clearly gesturing to his congregation, he asked: 'Anyone got a baby out there?'

Judging from the pause, followed by a shuffling sound, a couple brought a child forward. It turned out to be a six-month-old girl, held by her proud parents. 'Cute baby, very cute,' said the preacher almost seductively before adding: 'But that cute baby is a Child of Perdition. Ya gotta beat it out of her. Now you don't need a big stick to do that, a 12-inch ruler like you get in school'll do . . .'

The reason for the sermon became apparent as he went on to describe in some detail and with no little relish how he'd beaten a three-year-old boy with just such a ruler when his parents had visited him in his office for advice about their son's recalcitrance. Clearly the retribution had been as much a pleasure as a duty.

It was Mothering Sunday. Brother Richard Emmett was giving his considered views on child-rearing. The announcer said he'd be back next week with another service and more thoughts. Phew, I thought, I don't believe I've ever heard a more terrifying sermon. It certainly wasn't anything like *Thought for the Day*, the cosy little homilies the BBC broadcast for two and a half minutes each morning on Radio 4 and that stir up so much controversy from non-religious folk back home.

All across the nation that Sunday people were heading for church, or listening at home or in their cars to the sermons and thoughts of priests and clergy, ministers, pastors, bishops and radio evangelists, before taking their ageing moms out to celebratory lunches for a different sort of nourishment. Very few of the homilies, I hope it is safe to say, were as ferocious as that of Brother Emmett, though the fact that his words were broadcast at all, and would be recorded again the following week and for all I know the week after that, indicated that at least he had a following. For me, his words emerged from a hubbub of sermons around the radio dial that day merely because they were so extreme.

For a Briton, coming from a nation where regular churchgoing is a declining habit – maybe 3 to 4 million people a week out of 60 million – and where Christian religious contributions to the national debate tend to be corralled, sanitised and de-fanged so as not to cause offence, it is hard sometimes for a foreigner to appreciate the ubiquity, passion and occasional ferocity of the Christian voice beamed out across the USA.

It is a country with 200 Christian television channels and 1,500 Christian radio stations. There is always one nearby. It's there in the phone-in shows where, as I heard, a discussion about stem cell research carried the assumption that only Christians could have moral views. It's there in the roadside signs proclaiming 'Jesus Reigns!' And it's present, of course, on the Country 'n' Western Christian channels – my favourite song on my journey through the South was 'Jesus Take the Wheel', a harrowing and hugely popular ditty sung by Carrie Underwood about a young mother whose car skids on a slippery road one dark Christmas Eve until a miraculous force responds to her prayer by intervening to take control of the steering. That Divine intervention again: He does not stop the war in Iraq, or the attacks of 9/11, but He's perfectly capable of correcting a skid on a lonely road.

Every green hillock and suburban highway seems to have its neat, clapperboard and be-steepled church or chapel, advertising a warm welcome and fellowship each Sunday. Most small towns have many more churches than bars. Sometimes they line up along a strip beside the main road as if competing for business like supermarkets, which actually they are. You can avoid religion: one large police patrolwoman, leaning her stomach companionably against the reception desk at a country motel in the deep South as she chatted to the receptionist, said to me: 'Ah jest turns the rock station up louder.' But its presence is hard to escape completely.

The statistics bear that out. Some 95 per cent of Americans say they believe in God, compared with 76 per cent in the UK, 62 per cent in France, and only 52 per cent in Sweden. Three out of four Americans say they belong to a church and at least 40 per cent go at least once a week (in England the figure is about 5 to 7 per cent and falling). This indicates at the very least a much higher proportion of religious adherence than almost anywhere else in the Western, developed, world. Actually, US religious observance is at similar levels to many other parts of the world. It is in Europe that Christian allegiances and the hierarchy's moral authority have slumped. When US conservatives say that Europeans are the ones out of step on religion, they do have a point, though their extrapolation that Europeans are thereby ceasing to be Christian and becoming Islamicised instead is sufficiently far-fetched as to be either obtuse or mischievous.

The US census does not ask questions about religion and has not done so for over fifty years, but estimates and extrapolations by polling organisations more or less agree that between three-quarters and 82 per cent of the USA's adult population of 207,980,000 in 2001 described themselves as 'Christian'. This would amount to at least 160 million people. That inevitably dwarfs all other religious, spiritual and other allegiances. For comparison, the next largest identifiable group is those who say they are non-religious: just over 13 million or 7.5 per cent, and the second largest religious group – the Jews – come in a distant third at 3.1 million or 1.8 per cent.

Six out of ten Americans say religion plays 'a very important part' in their lives and 39 per cent say they have been 'born again in Christ'. Nearly two-thirds of Southerners claim to have had a religious experience that changed their lives (only about half of non-Southerners believe they have had the same) and a quarter of households say they have at least five Bibles in their homes.[5]

Now these figures cover a multitude of Christian religious practices and observances, not to mention definitions. The proportion of Southerners who say they attend church at least once a week – 41 per cent – is exceeded by the proportion of Southern households that admit to owning a gun (44 per cent), though of course there will be a cross-over here, with religious, gun-owning families. And furthermore there's even some evidence to suggest that religious adherence is falling slightly: the City of New York Graduate Center's US religious identification survey found that the proportion of Americans identifying themselves as Christians has dropped in recent years from 86 per cent in 1990 to 77 per cent in 2001.[6] If four in ten attend church weekly, that still leaves six who stay in bed or head for the shopping mall each Sunday, whatever the dire warnings about their eternal destiny. Of course, only half of the electorate votes in its presidential elections too.

There may be Christian radio and television stations aplenty, but *Sex and the City*, *Will and Grace* and *Desperate Housewives* offer a radically different, networked, view of US life and culture, and every cheap motel still offers its guests a choice of adult-viewing channels on the television in their room. The word 'fuck' is apparently to be heard on average once every 38 seconds on Home Box Office channels.

When I visited the Southern Baptists' annual convention in North Carolina, my walk each morning along High Point Road to the Greensboro Coliseum, where the Christians were gathering, took me past a dismal windowless concrete pillbox, complete with fake Grecian columns and set in the middle of a parking lot. It was called the Players' Club and proudly advertised 'The Finest Ladies in Greensboro' on its sign. It did, however, seem to be closed for the week, or maybe I just wasn't passing by at the right time of day.

Gambling too is a growth industry in the USA in defiance of all religious warnings. Dying towns and cities across the South and Midwest – the most overtly religious parts of the USA – are replacing their clapped-out, rust-belt factories with casinos and licensed gambling dens. The riverboats tethered to the banks of the Mississippi offer employment to those in need of work, but also an easy means of relieving their mostly poor and working-class punters of their hard-earned cash. And they are thriving with scarcely muted criticism from religious pundits who are otherwise so quick to inveigh against the moral degradation of the nation.

In your search for Christian worship in the USA, you can find gay-friendly churches and the most severe of fundamentalists; high church Anglicans and low church Presbyterians. Up in the Appalachians there are men and women who wave poisonous rattlesnakes around their heads and drink cyanide during services as proof of their virtue and God's saving grace, in loyal obedience to a misreading of an erroneous verse in the Gospel of St Mark.

There are mega-churches that attract tens of thousands of worshippers each weekend and little, quiet chapels off the beaten track, such as the Union Christian Church in the hamlet of Plymouth Notch, Vermont, where President Calvin Coolidge was born and grew up, that seem so dusty and deserted that it is as if they have not been entered in a century.

You can attend foot-stomping, arm-waving, black inner-city Pentecostal services and ancient Spanish mission churches looming over Native American pueblos, perched on top of the mesas in the West.

There are old faiths: users of the ancient Latin rites in Catholic churches and also Protestant chapels where the King James translation of the Bible is used, not because it still sounds so good, but because the worshippers believe it is clearly written in the idiom that God originally spake, the Deity obviously being an Anglophone if not necessarily an Englishman.

And there are US-made religions. The Shakers, founded by an Englishwoman but once flourishing in New England, have now almost died out – down to four survivors in Maine at the last count – in proof of the efficiency of their celibate living arrangements. But the Mormons flourish in demonstration of the fecundity of theirs. As do the Amish, whose gentle rejection of those parts of the modern world they find unbiblical and inconvenient in most circumstances, such as electricity, the horseless carriage, television and the safety razor, was dreadfully shattered in October 2006 by that outside world at its most ghastly, perverse and nightmarish, when a local man burst into one of their schools in Lancaster County, Pennsylvania and executed several girl pupils.

Of other significant sects, the Jehovah's Witnesses still emerge from their secretive and repressive kingdom halls to proselytise the unwary, usually without troubling to divulge their weird and malign views on blood transfusions and the satanic wickedness of the UN. The Christian Scientists retain their suspicion of doctors and the Scientologists continue to believe in interplanetary travel and L. Ron Hubbard. And that's before you reach all the other religions available in the USA: the Muslims and Hindus, Jews and Buddhists, who taken together comprise 4 per cent of the population.

Although Christian fundamentalism – a belief in the literalness of the Bible – tends to dominate foreign fascination with US Christian practice, it is worth recalling that the largest single denomination in the USA remains Roman Catholicism, which has between 50 and 60 million adherents, about a quarter of the entire adult population, though only about 11 per cent of churchgoers in any given week. Some way behind come the Baptists (33.8 million or 16 per cent of the total, but 8 per cent of churchgoers), followed by the Methodists, Lutherans, Pentecostals, Presbyterians, Mormons and, even further down the list, the Episcopalian-Anglicans. Taken together, all the Protestant groups just about outweigh the Catholics, but none of these groups is politically homogeneous. In 1996 it was calculated that there were 19 separate Presbyterian denominations, 32 Lutheran, 36 Methodist, 37 Episcopalian (Anglican), 60 Baptist and 241 Pentecostal. Los Angeles has the widest range of Buddhist organisations in the world and each week its newspaper, the *Los Angeles Times*, publishes a directory of services that takes in over 600 denominations.

This is entered as a caveat at the start for those who tend to believe that American religion is all of one variety: white, middle-class and politically conservative, inimical to and intolerant of the outside world. You can find plenty of evidence for that too, but also an enormous and eclectic range of beliefs and practices among evangelicals, Episcopalians, Baptists and the rest of the Protestant reformed tradition.

Having made that point, though, poll findings do seem to indicate a literalist turn of mind that is growing among US Christians. When a *Newsweek* poll in December 2004 asked its sample audience whether they believed the Bible to be literally accurate, 55 per cent said yes. The figure rose to 83 per cent among evangelical Protestants, though it sank to 47 per cent among non-evangelical Protestants and 45 per cent among Catholics. Polls conducted during the same year for Gallup and Fox News recorded over three-quarters of those questioned saying they personally believed in God, in heaven, in angels and hell, dipping to just 70 per cent who said they believed in the devil. When in February 2004 a poll for ABC *Prime Time* asked whether the Bible's descriptions of certain events were literally true, 60 per cent of respondents said they believed in Noah's Ark, 61 per cent in God creating the Earth in seven days, and 64 per cent in God parting the Red Sea for Moses. A CNN/*Time* poll in 2002 found 59 per cent of Christians saying they believed the events in the Book of Revelation would occur in the future (against 33 per cent who said they would not), a figure rising to 77 per cent among born-again, fundamentalist and evangelical respondents. When *Newsweek* in 1999 asked whether the world would end in a battle of Armageddon between Jesus Christ and the anti-Christ, evangelical Protestants responded 'yes' by 71 per cent against 18 per cent saying 'no', while among other Protestants and Catholics only minorities held that view. No one can misread the data, says the former Republican strategist Kevin Phillips in his recent book *American Theocracy*, the world's leading economic and military power is also the world's leading Bible-reading crusader state, immersed in an Old Testament of stern prophets and bloody Middle Eastern battlefields.[7]

It is the Religious Right, practitioners of politicised, partisan and Bible-based evangelicalism supported by a growing number in some Episcopal, but mainly nonconformist and non-denominational, churches, that this book will focus upon. Even if some mainstream denominations are losing members, the evangelical churches are not. At a time when the Catholic hierarchy has been battered, discredited and distracted by paedophile scandals among the priesthood and Episcopal bishops are falling out among themselves over the Church's accommodation of homosexuality – just, in other words, when mainstream, established religions are losing influence and authority – it is the churches without hierarchies that are gaining a more prominent and political role in the wider society. In the mid-1980s, 33 per cent of those polled told Gallup they had been 'born again' – the mark of an evangelical. Now the figure is nearing 40 per cent and rising.

This is not a new phenomenon that pitched up with the election of President George W. Bush, an overtly born-again Christian, to the

White House in the autumn of 2000. As this book is intended to show, it reflects many long-term trends in US life, stretching right back to the Pilgrim Fathers, at the very dawn of white immigration to the continent, which have coloured significant parts of the nation's character ever since.

The word 'evangelical' itself covers a wide range of worship styles, theological priorities and practices in the USA, as in the UK and other countries across the world. Its adherents, just as in other communities in US society, have a range of political and ethical views. You may come across political conservatives such as the televangelists Pat Robertson, Jerry Falwell – who died in May 2007 while this book was in production – and James Dobson, but also Jim Wallis, of the Sojourners Network, who is unashamedly on the Left and believes fervently that his faith teaches him to be so.

These are men who would agree on very little and who can barely bring themselves to sit in the same television studio together. When, a couple of days after the terrorist attacks that brought down the World Trade Center in New York on September 11th 2001, Falwell chuntered on during Robertson's 700 Club television show about the attack being the responsibility of abortionists, feminists, gays and lesbians and the American Civil Liberties Union – 'all of them who have tried to secularize America – I point the finger in their face and say "you helped this to happen"' – many thousands of US evangelicals were rightly outraged and disgusted. Partly because of this and other equally bizarre outbursts, Robertson and Falwell have lost some influence, though they retain their television platforms and are still courted by politicians – Senator John McCain, a Republican presidential hopeful, paid a visit to give a speech at Falwell's Liberty University in the spring of 2006. But, ageing as they are, if they are on the wane, others are queueing up to take their places on the public circuit.

Evangelicalism is not a political creed, still less a partisan one. What evangelicals share in common, however, is a belief in the Bible as the essential, central pillar of their faith – though they may differ in their interpretation of it, or even, so far as some are concerned, whether it is permissible to interpret it at all. Following on from that, evangelicals also believe in the importance of personal conversion: being 'born again', turning deliberately and specifically towards Jesus Christ as their personal Saviour. This is no inherited faith handed down institutionally from time immemorial, but a highly specific and deeply individual commitment. And finally – and most importantly for the political tenor of this book – evangelicals believe that, having been converted themselves, they have an absolute imperative to proselytise others, to spread the Good News: in a word, to evangelise.

This noble and often altruistic impulse has historically given evangelicals a political engagement and dynamic energy for involvement in secular society that other religious groups lack. Their emphasis on personal change has shaped not only US individualism – that feisty attribute that shows itself in so many areas of life, from business practice to sport and from attitudes to government to health insurance – but also to a suspicion of the collectivism and social co-operation that is so prized in 'old' Europe.

It is these born-again Christians and their vociferous leaders who have become increasingly politically engaged and organised in US politics in recent years, and hence influential beyond their own church doors. It is their brand of hardline, almost invariably reactionary Christianity that the talk-show hosts, local radio stations and national politicians pander to and that outsiders, in the USA but also abroad, find hardest to understand or appreciate. They have been mobilised in a partisan way by a series of moral issues – often misleadingly, even cynically, presented – and by a traditional distrust of government, and they have been shaped into a formidably motivated and almost cohesive political force.

Recently they have become more formidable still by tactically allying with Catholics who share their moral concerns in many areas – over abortion pre-eminently, but also stem cell research – in an alliance of convenience that previously both sides would have shunned. This makes them a formidable electoral force, potentially at least doubling the significance of the religious vote, so long as it remains cohesive. Historically they have been religious enemies, candidates and supporters of one faith tradition despising those of the other. Now, together, they see themselves as the silent majority once spoken of by Richard Nixon, but they ain't silent any more. In fact, they're so noisy it's sometimes hard to hear them think.

Viewed from across the Atlantic, this is a strange and alien phenomenon. It is hard to recognise these business-suited evangelicals as churchmen (they are almost all men) at all. We are much more used to clerics in cassocks and dog-collars who may spout their views but have almost no effect at all. So we find the US evangelists' ostentation and confidence in the certainty of their views hard to understand or accept, and their influence on US society inexplicable.

Who are these people without mitres and titles and accordingly so hard to place in the hierarchy of religious authority? They appear on our more obscure cable channels, but their visibility beyond the shores of the USA is miniscule. Of Christian leaders, only Pope John Paul II has had a similar charisma on our side of the Atlantic these last twenty years and a similar willingness to speak out on issues – though he took care to be largely non-partisan; and anyway he was widely ignored by his European flock, much to his exasperation, when they did not like what he was saying.

These Americans, setting up their own churches and cable channels, holding press conferences to pronounce on the issues of the day and having their views reported instead of routinely ignored, visiting the White House for breakfast and praying with the president, are different. We laugh at their pretensions – Pat Robertson thinking all Scotsmen are gay because they wear kilts, well really! – but we just can't figure them out at all. Are they real? Are they serious? The answer is yes.

To outsiders it often seems a strange and even backward religion, retreating into a thicket of unreason, away from the fresh air and sunlight of modern, secular society. It appears obsessed with a biblical literalism that many others thought had been consigned to the Dark Ages before the Enlightenment and Rationalism and all the other impulses endorsed by the Founding Fathers who shaped the country's Constitution over two hundred years ago.

The paradox is that a society that can put men on the moon and develop the internet, the iPod, air-conditioning and the pop-up toaster – a country that, as Bill Bryson astutely observed, has shaped its inventions towards making consumers' lives more comfortable – also contains a growing number who believe in the face of all the evidence that the Earth was created in seven days only 6,000 years ago.

This, of course, would all just be quaint if it wasn't for the fact that these are the voices that are shaping aspects of US government policy. It may, in fact, be the most successful electoral insurgency of modern times: the co-opting of a government behind a partisan and politicised agenda supported by an electoral minority, based on a number of key moral issues that derive their impulse from an appeal to a previously deeply sectarian religious tradition.

Here's why. The figures, assiduously compiled by the respected and authoritative Washington DC-based Pew Forum on religion and public life, show that in the presidential election of 2004, more than three-quarters of white evangelicals, who make up fewer than a quarter (23 per cent) of the electorate, voted for President George W. Bush. They provided him, almost certainly, with more than the margin of his victory. In its report on the election, Pew stated that they have become 'by far the single most potent voting bloc in the electorate'.[8]

The report adds:

> The 2004 election was the latest in a string of modern presidential campaigns in which candidates openly discussed their religious beliefs, churches were increasingly active in political mobilization and voters sorted themselves out not just by their policy preferences and demographic traits but also by the depth of their religious commitment. In fact, whether a person regularly attends church (or synagogue or mosque) was more important in determining his or her vote for president than such demographic characteristics as gender, age, income and region and just as important as race ... Americans who regularly attend worship services and hold traditional religious views increasingly vote Republican while those who are less connected to religious institutions and more secular in their outlook tend to vote Democratic.

This so-called 'God Gulf' is not strictly accurate since many Democrats are also religious – old, traditional Catholic working-class voters, liberal Episcopalians, Jewish voters and the rest – but the figures are striking: of the 16 per cent of the electorate who told the exit-pollsters that they attend church more than once a week, the margin of support for Bush was 64 per cent to 35 per cent for the Democratic candidate Senator John Kerry, while of the 15 per cent who said they never attended worship services, the figures were almost precisely reversed: 62 per cent to Kerry, 36 per cent to Bush.

The figures are most marked for those identified as religious traditionalists – Catholics as well as those identified as mainline Protestant and evangelical – who voted Republican by a margin of 70 to 20 per cent. Their importance is not only that religious people now make up the majority of the membership of both main parties, but that they are the proportion of the electorate most likely to be motivated to get out and vote. Donald Paul Hodel, a former president of the Focus on the Family organisation and once a member of Ronald Reagan's cabinet, wrote in the *Weekly Standard* in 2003: 'The fact is without the hard work and votes of millions of Christians, there would be no Republican majority in both Houses of Congress, no Bush presidencies, few Republican governors and a small handful of state houses in Republican hands.'[9] They have been well organised too: overtly Christian supporters are now said to be prominent in no fewer than forty-four state Republican committees and relatively weak only in six states, all in the north-east, old New England.

And what gets them going are the so-called moral issues: school prayer, abortion, homosexuality and gay marriage. To those are added stem cell research and immigration. As the conservative activist from Kansas, Tim Golba, told the journalist Thomas Frank: 'You can't stir the general public up to get out to work for a candidate on taxes or the economy. People today are busy. But you can get people who are concerned about the moral decline of our nation. Upset enough to where you can motivate them on the abortion issue, those type of things.'[10]

These hot button topics have been chosen by religious conservatives to inflame and mobilise their supporters and to signal their presence and power. The Pew report says:

Among those with a high level of religious commitment, fully 80 per cent oppose same sex matrimony. Among those with average levels of religious commitment, the opposition drops to 57 per cent and among those with a low level of religious commitment, it drops further to 39 per cent . . . While 52 per cent of all American adults favour embryonic stem cell research, the level of support drops to 34 per cent among those with a high level of religious commitment and it rises to 66 per cent among those with a low level of religious commitment.

This might be more understandable if the Democrats were fielding a godless or aggressively secular candidate, but in John Kerry they had a practising Catholic, and indeed all their presidential candidates in recent years have ostentatiously avowed their Christian religious belief. Jimmy Carter, president in the 1970s, was a Southern Baptist lay preacher and Sunday School teacher who has devoted his life since leaving office to good works; Bill Clinton (admittedly not necessarily a shining example of moral rectitude in his private life) was raised as a Southern Baptist, as was Al Gore, his vice-president and the candidate in the 2000 election. All three come from the largest, fundamentalist and conservative Christian, nonconformist denomination in the country.

'Only in America,' noted the UK *Economist* magazine journalists John Micklethwait and Adrian Wooldridge wryly about the Clinton presidency in their study of US politics *The Right Nation*, 'could a president who attended church every Sunday and began each of his weekly lunches with the vice-president with a prayer be considered irreligious.'[11]

But the Republicans have succeeded in capturing this vote and accordingly winning the moral high ground, despite the fact that a majority – 65 per cent – of the electorate told the Pew Forum in August 2004 that churches should not endorse political candidates. President Bush took not only a majority of white evangelical votes, but also a rising percentage of all other religious voters, though still not a majority among black Protestants or Orthodox Jews. The only religious group whose support for Bush declined between the 2000 and 2004 elections was that of the US Muslims.

In all this, however, the Pew report says: 'White evangelicals are by far the most important component of the GOP coalition. This group makes up nearly a quarter of the electorate and votes Republican by increasingly lopsided margins. The president garnered 78 per cent of all white evangelical votes in 2004, a 10 percentage point increase over what he received four years earlier.'

This, though, may be somewhat out of touch with mainstream US opinion. The Pew Forum's national survey on religion and public life, published in August 2006, found a much higher degree of pragmatism among the public at large than the Religious Right might care to admit. On homosexuality, 54 per cent of those surveyed favoured allowing civil unions for same-sex couples (though only a third said gays should be allowed to marry) and 49 per cent accepted that homosexual orientation could not be changed. Asked about abortion, two-thirds said there should be a compromise rather than an outright ban, as demanded by religious conservatives. Moreover, questioned in the month that President Bush vetoed government involvement in stem cell research, 56 per cent said they supported such research – as did more white evangelicals than opposed it. The overwhelming majority of the survey – 80 per cent – said they believed chemists should not be allowed to refuse to sell birth control pills.[12] It is no wonder that the influence of this raucous section of the electorate over the current administration alarms some Republicans who see it as sectarian and alienating of the wider public.

But they are undoubtedly electorally useful. What we have in the Religious Right is not only a highly motivated and relatively prosperous slice of the electorate, but also a strategically placed one, disproportionately located in the Southern states, the South-west and the suburbs. These are the fastest growing areas of the USA.

Some 30 per cent of the USA – 84 million people – now live in the eleven former Confederate states of the old South. The proportion was much the same (in a much smaller population, of course) in 1861, when the Civil War broke out, but declined thereafter and throughout the succeeding century, in wealth, political influence, social standing and self-confidence.

Now that has all been reversed. It has even been calculated by the US Census Bureau that the geographical centre of the US population is moving south and west at the rate of 3 feet an hour, or 5 miles a year.[13] Indeed, it is Southerners who have largely boosted the population growth of the empty western states, from Texas as far north as Montana. Just as 4.5 million blacks left the South for the northern cities in the first sixty years of the twentieth century, so, at the same time, did 4.6 million whites, heading west.

From the 1960s, the availability of air-conditioning and the convenience of cheaper labour in the Southern states, and accordingly an attractiveness to industry, encouraged an upturn in the South's population: a 19 per cent increase in the 1990s alone. A new self-confidence has seized the region and spread out towards the west.

Professor Ronald Green, director of the Ethics Institute at Dartmouth College, New Hampshire, writing in *Conscience*, the Catholic magazine, in the autumn of 2006, said:

> The real story is in long-term, large-scale demographic and social changes that have increased the reach and strength of conservative Christian attitudes. Traditional southern attitudes have spread throughout the population, Republicans have capitalised on antagonisms left over from the civil rights movement and Catholics who once defined themselves by ethnic-religious affiliation have transferred their loyalty to conservative ideology . . . aspects of southern culture have not only gained status in the new south but have also been exported to the rest of the US . . . With the money and confidence to proselytise, southern based forms of evangelical religion have reached out to conquer new territory – and souls.[14]

Ninety-seven of the USA's 100 fastest growing counties voted Republican in 2004, but more than that, because of the anti-urban bias of the electoral system, the party has an in-built advantage. Each state, however big or small, has two senators, so that the 7 per cent of the population that live in the seventeen least populous states have effective control over more than a third of the Senate. They also have a disproportionate influence within the electoral college that formally elects the president, each state giving all its electoral votes to whichever candidate has obtained a majority in the state on election day. It may be a hundred years since the USA was a predominantly rural country, but the legacy is still felt.

Steven Hill of the Center for Voting and Democracy estimates that the combined populations of Montana, Wyoming, Nevada, North and South Dakota, Colorado, Nebraska, Kansas, Oklahoma, Arizona and Alaska together equal those of New York and Massachusetts and yet they have nine more electoral votes and five times more votes in the Senate.[15] Similarly, California has a population of 36 million, making it the biggest state, and accordingly has fifty-five votes in the electoral college; but the twelve inland states of the Great Plains and the West have only 23 million inhabitants, yet command fifty-nine electoral votes. All twelve were won by Bush in 2004 and he took all their college votes. The voting figures are striking in other elections too: the forty-four Democrats in the Senate before the 2006 elections represented more people and received more votes than the fifty-five Republicans. It is not an imbalance that is likely to be corrected. Essentially, 16 per cent of the population elects half the US Senate. In the USA, says the author Michelle Goldberg, conservatives literally count for more.

Following the 2004 presidential election, there was much talk of the 'blue' states that voted for Kerry, clustered around the east and west coasts and the Great Lakes, and the Bush-voting 'red' states of the South and Centre. This of course is simplistic: plenty of blue staters voted for Bush and many in the red states voted for Kerry. It has been pointed out that Bush won every non-coastal county in California, but still lost the state because of the Kerry majorities in Los Angeles and San Francisco. It may be more true to say that there was an urban versus rural divide and certainly, just as in the UK, there is a sense among rural and small town voters that they stand for a truer, better country, a place of rustic and traditional (superior) Christian values.

The US's Norman Rockwell-like picture of itself, a nation of sanitised habits and traditional customs, may be based on nostalgia for a mythical America that never quite was, and certainly does not really exist now, but it plays directly to the Christian Right's self-image. Wouldn't it be a better country if boys still went fishing in the creek and girls made up their dolls, if teenagers escorted each other chastely to the school prom, if cowboys still walked tall and straight, and every family had a mom and pop sitting down to dinner with the kids around a table groaning with the weight of wholesome food each night? Yes, it would, of course, but it never did and it's not going to happen now.

Instead, in the words of Andrew O'Hehir in an article for Salon.com, there is a new traditional culture:

A friend of mine who grew up in rural Indiana in the '70s and '80s talks about the way his region has been transformed since his childhood. No one in his hometown cared much about country music or stock car racing, he says, until those things became attached to a new conception of rural identity...These days if you're rural and white and you feel OK about those things, you've got an entire nationwide culture waiting for you: Rush, O'Reilly and Faith Hill for the sober folk, Michael Savage, Neal Boortz and Toby Keith for the hell-raisers and outlaws. Jesus, of course, is for everybody.[16]

The modern Christian Right forms an interesting constituency on its own account. It is no longer appropriate, if it ever was, to dismiss it as H. L. Mencken did the Southern rural fundamentalists in the 1920s as the 'booboisie'. Many of its members are articulate, some are affluent, and many are in good jobs. Half are classed as small businessmen: 40 per cent of those earning more than $85,000 a year are regular weekly church attenders, a higher proportion than those earning less than $15,000. Business people are four times more likely to be regular church attenders than those working in the news media, and nine times as likely as those working in television: no wonder the likes of Brother Emmett regard TV folk as a pernicious influence.

A good many of those heading south and west over recent years have not been archetypal Republicans: nor part of the country-club set. They are indeed often ostentatiously anti-elitist. It is one of the triumphs of the conservative insurgency that they have managed to stigmatise several of the groups who would traditionally be regarded as natural Republicans – Wall Street financiers, newspaper and media owners, big business – as somehow unAmerican, effetes and snobs, almost traitors to the country, and certainly trying to subvert it. Big City bankers have often been characterised as enemies of decent, little people – you only have to watch the films of Frank Capra to see that – but they have not usually been regarded as beyond the pale before.

Today's Republican voters may well have come from working-class backgrounds and families that traditionally voted Democratic, though they themselves are unlikely these days to be union members. It infuriates writers like Thomas Frank, author of *What's the Matter with Kansas?*, that their religious allegiances have increasingly caused them to vote against what might otherwise be traditionally seen as their best economic interests. Frank almost explodes with rage and frustration in quoting Blake Hurst, the conservative Missouri farmer and part-time columnist, who insouciantly assured the nation: 'Class consciousness isn't a problem in Red America . . . [people] are perfectly happy to be slightly overweight and a little underpaid.'[17]

For the voters of the Southern states to have gone Republican after more than a century of voting Democratic, with only very rare, localised exceptions, has been a remarkable turn around. Republicans were formerly always associated with the North in the Civil War. They were from the party of the hated Abraham Lincoln and the despised Carpet-baggers of the post-war Reconstruction era. The South was the home of the Yellow Dog Democrats – so solid that if the candidate were a dog they'd vote for it. Kevin Phillips, a former Republican strategist, says in his recent book: 'Party politics in the major western nations offers no parallel to this great reversal.'[18]

Bush secured the votes of only 54 per cent of those earning more than $100,000 a year in 2000. Not that successive Republican presidents have failed that client base. In 1970, it has been pointed out, the top 0.01 per cent of taxpayers earned 0.7 per cent of total income, but by 1998 that figure had become 3.0 per cent: the 13,000 richest families had almost as much as the 20 million poorest.[19]

A Massachusetts Institute of Technology survey based on data compiled in 1990 found that churchgoers have on average an income 9 per cent higher than their non-attending neighbours. Unsurprisingly, they are less likely to be divorced, but they are also less likely to be on welfare. Most are passionate, and I would think all are sincere. What they may be, however, is fearful and insecure. And, like so many of their ancestors throughout US history, just a little paranoid and prey to uncertainty about the present and the future, anxious about those outside, alien forces who would subvert their lives and undermine their security with secret, powerful, unknowable conspiracies.

Americans have always had fears of outsiders in their safe continental remoteness: successively of Native Americans, African Americans, Irish immigrants, east European immigrants, Jews, communists, and now gays and Muslims. Usually those fears have eventually been disarmed and subsumed, the outsiders absorbed into the mainstream. But just because you are paranoid, doesn't mean that terrifying and horrific events such as those on September 11th 2001 won't emerge unexpectedly from a clear blue sky one fine morning to attack you.

It has been well pointed out that US middle-class society now tends to be atomised, with lives revolving round the shopping mall and the church, with contact only with similar families and individuals and access only to others who think the same way as they do. Their houses are bigger and more affluent than those of their parents and grand-parents' generations – average suburban house sizes have doubled since the 1960s – but their social lives are probably less varied and accordingly more impoverished. They don't live in cities any more, but in suburbs, in gated communities and on housing estates whose names are meant to conjure up a more rugged and picturesque American past. Near where my parents-in-law live in Houston are near-identical communities with homes whose varied external architecture – ranch house, hacienda, Gothic, Corinthian, ante-bellum, New Orleans, modern and brownstone – disguise an internal similarity of design. All bear names such as Hunters Creek Village, Piney Point, Bunker Hill and West Oaks, which aim to convey a rustic, rural or historic identity and a charm that otherwise they conspicuously lack. Those good, firm, old, country values again.

Sitting in his consulting room on the fringes of Montgomery, Alabama, Randy Brinson, a doctor and gastrology specialist but also a Baptist and a Republican, spelled it out for me: 'The growth of the evangelical movement is not just a growth of the spiritual message but of social and economic events. In a city like this you have middle class flight into the suburbs, creating their own communities and tax base.'[20]

Montgomery, of course, was one of the bastions of the old, racist South. When de-segregation came in and the Democrats' Great Society civil rights reforms of the 1960s, not only did the whites move out of the city to the suburbs, taking their tax dollars with them, but they also changed their age-old voting allegiances from Democrat to Republican.

Dr Brinson's surgery is testimony to that. It is on a rather charac-
terless suburban estate near the university hospital, an area of con-
dominiums, manicured lawns and SUVs in the driveways. On his
walls are the testimonials of his professional and personal success:
medical certificates, family photographs of sons and children engaged
in energetic and affluent pastimes and, in the waiting room, modern,
romanticised pictures of victorious Confederates winning battles in
the Civil War. Tall and thin, Dr Brinson looks more than a little like
the British actor Hugh Laurie in his Dr *House* persona, but a lot more
genial.

He also has a slightly different take than you might expect. He sees
folk who are insecure, not prosperous, struggling financially to make
ends meet, worried about losing their jobs and scared of losing their
identity. The church gives them a welcome, friendship and a family,
when their own may be far away across the country. It provides their
local circle of support, a community of shared values, views and
understanding to belong to and an outlook that is common: all shared
by people like themselves. They spend their money locally and they
don't want their taxation going elsewhere. They are worried about
their children's schooling, not just what they are taught in the
curriculum but what sort of values they will learn and, if they can,
they'd like to shut out the world completely, beyond the gates of their
housing estates. In the big, bad world beyond, devils lurk: evil men,
other people, different, difficult opinions. Dr Brinson says:

'So many of these are political feelings, and the church becomes
their mantle. It gives them an identity and it meets their need for
community. There's the Monday night visitation, the Wednesday
evening supper, the Bible class, the Sunday service. The church
softball team. It becomes a whole way of life. And it gives them a
strong political message too: you want to pay lower taxes? That's a
Christian message, they're told. I never saw anything about cheaper
taxation in the Bible but that's what they are told and the Democrats
have a hard time combating that.'

Brinson, who set up the internet Redeem the Vote 2004 campaign,
promoting voter registration for the Republicans and – he estimates –
thereby getting 25 million votes out for President Bush, has issues now
with the party. Appalled by the naked partisanship of the Religious

Right Republicans of Alabama and their demonisation of the Democrats, he has started reaching out to the other side, even advising them on electoral strategies to attract Christian voters. For his pains, he says he and his wife have received anonymous telephone death threats.

Social pressures point in one direction. As Wilfred McClay, an evangelical Anglican and humanities professor at the University of Tennessee in Chattanooga, told the *Washington Times* in April 2006: 'There's a way in which churchgoing is woven into the fabric of life. When you move down here one of the first things people ask is: "Where do you go to church?" In parts of the South, you still feel you're in a kind of Christendom . . . This is a world where the normative assumptions are Christian and evangelical.'[21]

The same newspaper article quoted a document on Southern Culture compiled by historians on the staff of Vance-Granville Community College in Henderson, North Carolina:

> Those visiting or moving to the South, especially in the traditional rural areas, would do well to respect the religious traditions of the area. Sunday mornings are for going to church, not mowing the lawn, going shopping (the stores won't be open anyway) or buying liquor or beer . . . If someone in the grocery line finds out you're new in town and asks you to his/her church, go ahead and say yes and enjoy the experience. Southern hospitality surely shows itself best in the willingness of the people to share what is most important to them: their faith.

Their values and views are reinforced not only by their churches, but by the television programmes they watch, the radio stations they listen to, the newspapers they read, and the websites they log on to. Anyone checking out a religious talkboard, even moderate ones, cannot help but be struck by the enclosed, hermetically sealed attitudes many of their contributors display. To take a random example on the Titusonenine, conservative Episcopalian website, in November 2006, as I was writing this: there was a discussion of South Africa's Archbishop Desmond Tutu, which divided between those who thought his opposition to apartheid was worthy of mention and others who believed that meant nothing as he was not sound on the Bible and in particular was tolerant of gays.[22]

These people are continually told, in defiance of all evidence or reason, that the USA is being taken over – or has already been – by a series of malign and powerful liberal, and godless, conspiracies, which appear to be well organised in the way they dominate the media, the universities and the mainstream churches. This is reinforced by the books they read and that weigh down book shelves in airports and city stores, their raucous titles screeching highly partisan messages, often in triple-decker headlines. Among them during a brief trawl of a Washington DC Barnes and Noble last summer: *Treason* by the Republicans' pin-up blonde polemicist Ann Coulter (a follow-up to an earlier best-seller modestly entitled *Slander: Liberal Lies about the American Right*); other titles included *The Global War on Your Guns*; *The Bush Agenda*; *Myths, Lies and Downright Stupidity: Get Out The Shovel – why everything you know is wrong*; and *Can She Be Stopped?*, a book about Hillary Clinton. It is only fair to say that there are plenty of expostulations on the other side too: *Foxes in the Henhouse: How Republicans stole the South*; *Take it Back: Our Party, Our Country, Our Future*; *Jesus is not a Republican*; and *50 Simple Things You Can Do to Fight the Right*. It is impossible to imagine such a range of polemics about British politics or culture in a bookshop back in the UK.

The conspiracy theorists somehow ignore that six of the nine presidential elections since 1968, the year that is regarded by the Religious Right as the acme of dissolution, degradation and depravity, have been won by Republicans from the South and West: two from California, Nixon (who won in 1968, albeit narrowly) and Reagan, and two, at least nominally, from Texas: the Bushes. Republicans lost control of the Senate – narrowly – and the House of Representatives in November 2006, but only after twelve years in charge, and conservatives have a majority – or near majority – on the Supreme Court. They run many states. And yet their supporters are continually warned that all they hold dear is under attack, even though the politicians of both main parties are often virtually interchangeable.

'We are America and those other people are not,' the chairman of the Republican National Committee announced in 1992. 'Democrats,' said Newt Gingrich, 'are the enemies of normal Americans.' Even though they have about half the votes.

The idea that Christianity is about to be submerged or is under attack in the USA is risible and yet it helps fuel a sense of persecution and paranoia. In the spring of 2005 when cadets at the US Air Force Academy in Colorado Springs were reported to be falling under the influence of some fairly extreme Christian pressure – with cadets who would not sign up to born-again Christianity or attend chapel being labelled heathens and one Jewish recruit being told he was a Christ-killer – a Congressional attempt by Democrats to instigate an inquiry was opposed by the Republican Congressman John Hostettler in the following terms: 'The long war on Christianity in America continues today on the floor of the House of Representatives. Democrats can't help denigrating and demonising Christians.'[23]

Or take Katharine Harris, the Republican challenger for a Democrat-held Senate seat in Florida in 2006 (who was, incidentally, a US Congresswoman, as well as being the electoral official who helped secure the state for George Bush and ensure his election to the presidency in the hanging chad debacle of 2000), who claimed: 'If you are not electing Christians tried and true . . . you are legislating for sin.' This may have been a particularly stupid claim to make, given that she was campaigning in a state containing a large number of elderly Jewish voters. In the event, Harris, who had a reputation for eccentricity and had been all but abandoned by the party hierarchy, was soundly beaten in November 2006.

Still, all good knockabout political stuff perhaps, though it would get scornfully laughed out of the chamber if attempted in the House of Commons at Westminster. Some of the rhetoric about liberal threats to the US way of life, though, has more than a ring of UK Europhobia and similarly deep and paranoid wellsprings. There is dark talk of plots and subversion: of how schools and universities are being taken over by dangerous liberals, how churches will not be allowed to preach the gospel by vicious, secular Democrats, and the Bible will be banned. It is a threatened assault on all that good conservatives hold dear, and dire predictions that, as with anti-EU stories, somehow never quite come to pass.

Americans do not have the EU to rail against, but they do have central government and the UN, viewed by some Christian fundamentalists as the Scarlet Beast mentioned in the Book of Revelation, a harbinger of world government ushering in the nightmare of the end of days.

The areas of current electoral strength for the Religious Right have not always been fertile territory for either political or religious conservatives. The Deep South was not regarded as particularly religious before the Civil War – indeed, the campaign for the abolition of slavery was led largely by evangelicals in the North and East whose motivation was overtly religiously based – and the Midwest was once at the centre of national political radicalism. In one of many small ironies, the Religious Right has now even attempted to annex the rhetoric of the abolitionists and the civil rights activists, movements that at the time it spurned.

It makes perfect electoral sense for the Republicans to target such a constituency and Christian conservatives have an absolute right to lobby for their causes and to throw large amounts of money into their campaigns. But what particularly grates is the ostentatious assumption of higher virtue that they display in doing it and their insistence that it should give them a higher priority in the decision-making of the state. There appears to be a degree of cynicism in this, not just among the political classes – you might expect that – but among the leadership of many Right-wing religious lobbying groups.

It may be hubris, but the Religious Right certainly does not hide either its convictions or its objectives. In the words of George Grant in *The Changing of the Guard: Biblical Principles for Political Action* as far back as 1987:

> Christians have an obligation, a mandate, a commission, a holy responsibility to reclaim the land for Jesus Christ – to have dominion in civil structures, just as in every other aspect of life and godliness.
>
> But it is dominion we are after. Not just a voice.
> It is dominion we are after. Not just influence.
> It is dominion we are after. Not just equal time.
> It is dominion we are after.

World conquest. That's what Christ has commissioned us to accomplish. We must win the world with the power of the Gospel and we must never settle for anything less...Thus Christian politics has as its primary intent the conquest of the land – of men, families, institutions, bureaucracies, courts and governments for the Kingdom of Christ.[24]

Scary rhetoric from a man who was formerly executive director of the Florida Coral Ridge Ministries run by D. James Kennedy, one of the foremost conservative evangelical broadcasters of the day.

It mirrors the extreme views of the fringe group known as the Christian Reconstructionists who believe in the creation of a theocratic state ('Pluralism is a myth. God and his law must rule all nations'), no tolerance for other faiths, and the restoration of biblical punishments for malefactors (death by stoning for homosexuals, people who carry out abortions, even recalcitrant children), and it is no nearer coming to fruition now than it was twenty years ago. But what makes such talk worrying is not only that Reconstructionism has been paid lip-service by some extremely wealthy conservative sponsors and prominent telly-evangelists such as Pat Robertson, but it has also had some traction with influential advisers to the Bush administration including Marvin Olasky, inventor of the term Compassionate Conservatism. It is not the sort of language that gets much play in front of broader audiences. But it is certainly used at meetings and conferences of True Believers. And George W. Bush has not been averse to giving the Faithful a nod and a wink in that direction to show that he is with them really.

While waiting for the joyful day when such a country will come to pass, the Religious Right has focused tactically on more immediate goals: targeting particular issues to galvanise their constituency and keep them onside. The issues they have chosen have a degree of calculation and selectivity about them that appears designed to drive a wedge between the elect of the electorate and the rest, to politicise them and to polarise voters. Issues such as abortion and gay marriage have not generally been considered suitable for partisan debate in the UK, or across much of Continental Europe (or, at least, to nothing like the same extent they have been in the USA). Fastidious Europeans view such US debates from afar with distaste and incredulity – as do many Americans of course.

If these are issues that play directly into the so-called culture wars in US society, they are, on the face of it, peripheral matters to choose. If the concern is the promotion of family life and the avoidance of breakdown in relationships, why target gays who want to register the permanence of their partnership and who form a tiny minority within a small section of the population, rather than those who divorce? Divorce, after all, affects millions – the rate has doubled since 1960 and the number of single-parent families has tripled – and it is the cause of much more heartache and damage to relations between adults, and between parents and their children, than is the small number of gays who want to express their commitment to their partners.

Furthermore, divorce is even more roundly condemned in the Bible: Jesus never mentioned homosexuality (or, if he did, his disciples did not trouble to note the fact) but, just a few verses farther on from his city on a hill rhetoric, during the Sermon on the Mount, he specifically anathematised divorce and equated it with adultery. Surprisingly, this is rather glossed over. Evangelicals who devote considerable energy and exegesis to the scattered biblical references to homosexuality find they can quite easily dismiss the unambiguous message of Christ. Leo Giovinetti, pastor of the Mission Valley Christian Fellowship, who led a campaign to secure the prohibition of a gay pride festival in Jerusalem in 2005, can also be found telling his congregation that Jesus's words in Matthew 5:32 'doesn't mean that divorce sometimes isn't a good idea. There are some very good reasons for divorce.'[25]

Surely it cannot be, can it, that divorce affects many more members of the Religious Right's target constituency than homosexual partnerships do and so is a much more inconvenient and uncomfortable issue? It strikes rather too close to home for their target supporters. Or, in the words of Dr Jim Tonkowich, director of the Institute on Religion and Democracy, one of the Christian lobbying groups in Washington that makes gay marriage but not divorce a campaigning issue: 'We have to prioritize. We don't have the resources to tackle everything.'[26]

After all, it is at least possible that many of those who take moral issues as their lodestars in deciding how to vote have met or even know people who have been divorced – members of their own family, possibly even themselves – whereas that may not be the case with homosexuals. By and large, those who are related to gays or have them as friends are noticeably more tolerant of them.

The selectivity is stark. The 2,000-odd mentions of the poor in the Bible never get much of a priority. As Randall Balmer, an evangelical, liberal – it is perfectly possible to be both – and professor of American religious history at Columbia University, says with heavy irony in his book *Thy Kingdom Come: An Evangelical's Lament*:

> I went to Sunday school nearly every week of my childhood . . . but I must have been absent the day they told us that the followers of Jesus were obliged to secure even greater economic advantages for the affluent, to deny those Jesus called 'the least of these' a living wage and to despoil the environment by sacrificing it on the altar of free enterprise. I missed the lesson telling me that I should turn a blind eye to the suffering of others, even those designated as my enemies.[27]

But the other defining feature of these wedge issues is that they are never quite won. They create an atmosphere of outrage which is left simmering, to keep the constituency motivated. Somehow, despite the rhetoric, despite the majorities in Congress, despite the incumbents in the White House, abortions continue, gays don't go away, affirmative action is not dropped, stem cell research continues. This is put down to the hidden power of liberals, or at least to a supposedly liberal majority on the Supreme Court, rather than to a more general and pragmatic consensus among the population at large.

The themes that currently drive the Religious Right and the manner of campaigning are recurrent ones throughout the nation's history. They exploit the fear of outsiders and acknowledge the potency of moral panic. They promote the demand for interventionist action from a government whose powers are otherwise both constrained and regarded with suspicion, particularly by people on the Right. And, not least, they attempt to win control, or at least supremacy, for a particular religious constituency.

Presidents and their administrations have always responded to such movements. Europeans have often found it strange that the USA, a country that so adamantly insists on the separation of Church and state and a scrupulous constitutional system of checks and balances, to prevent the creation of an overweening executive, should not only be so religious in practice and observance, but that religious influence should play such a prominent part in its political life.

In Europe, political movements have been inspired by reaction against – or defence of – religious authorities, but rarely in the last half-century by a desire to impose a partisan theological agenda. In the UK in particular we have always found religiosity puzzling.

But in the USA it has always been a powerful political force, even in the background but often in the foreground too. Alexis de Tocqueville, first and greatest of European observers of the US political scene, reported as far back as 1835: 'Religion never intervenes directly in the government of American society [but it] should be considered the first of their political institutions . . . Christianity reigns, without any obstacles, the universal faith.'[28] 'Hmpph', said the Catholic (and conservative) writer G. K. Chesterton a century later, 'the United States: a nation with the soul of a church'.

In the USA too it is true to say that many, even among those who are devout in their religious observance, find the Religious Right's agenda irksome, with its assumption of moral superiority, its casual contempt for those who do not share its philosophy and its blithe disregard for inconvenient truths. There is more than a whiff of hypocrisy about much of its campaigning – not that that would be unique in political life, but the religious do claim to adhere to higher virtues. Those who do not share the Religious Right's self-righteousness occasionally find themselves constrained to point out that in the supposedly superior red – Republican – states it is objectively true that rates of murder, illegitimacy and teenage pregnancies are all higher than in the supposedly decadent and effete blue – Democrat – states of New England and the far West. And that the supposedly corrupt and spiritually dying blue states subsidise the dynamic and righteous red ones to the tune of $90 billion a year through federal funding.[29]

What makes this current debate in the USA different is the skill with which the Religious Right constituency has been mobilised and pointed in one direction to vote and the ostentatious readiness of this president and this administration to accommodate it. For the religious agenda appears to be winning: it would be unthinkable now for a candidate for election not to profess some religious affiliation or allegiance, certainly if they hope to win. The drift to the Right has been scrupulously tracked by the American Conservative Union since 1972, basing its statistical analysis on how each member of Congress votes each year, awarding points out of 100 largely on the basis of (ACU-defined) moral issues of the sort that obsess the religious constituency. In 1972 the average Republican score was 63 per cent. By 2002 that figure had climbed to 91 per cent.[30]

Religious imagery has always infused political discourse in the USA, perhaps more openly and candidly than in the rest of the Western world. Few presidents have been indifferent to Christian belief or reluctant to deploy its imagery to illustrate their own religious allegiances in a way that has not been the case abroad, among, say, British prime ministers.

Tony Blair, perhaps the most avowedly engaged Christian to lead a British government since Mr Gladstone in the nineteenth century, was famously told by his adviser Alastair Campbell that 'we don't do God' when he wanted to end a televised statement on the eve of the Iraq war in 2003 with the words 'God Bless'. Blair took Campbell's advice and did not use the phrase, advice that it would have been both inconceivable for a presidential adviser to offer, or for an US president to accept, in such circumstances.

It seems true, however, that US presidents are becoming more avowedly religious. It is hard now to imagine a president of the USA saying, as Eisenhower once did in the 1950s: 'Our government makes no sense unless it is founded on a deeply-held religious faith – and I don't care what it is.'[31] The first bit would be all right, but the second half would be almost impossible for a man running for office to say today if he wanted to get elected – even if he had been a war hero – and would be quite incomprehensible to the Religious Right. They know precisely the only religious faith worth having and any president pledged to pluralism, except in the most perfunctory sense, would be regarded with the deepest suspicion.

This new presidential religiosity is a trend that started with Jimmy

Carter in the mid-1970s (and which persuaded a majority of evangelicals to vote Democrat in the presidential election of 1976), mirroring the social and indeed psychological changes in US society that were underway by the mid-1970s. Carter's religiousness did not prevent evangelicals being urged by their self-appointed leaders to abandon him in 1980, however, in favour of a genial, divorced, former Hollywood screen actor, Ronald Reagan, whose church attendance was perfunctory at best. It has now reached an apogee with George W. Bush, who has skilfully used his mid-life conversion to Methodism (from the Episcopalianism of his childhood) as a political weapon. His undoubtedly sincere religious faith has been crucial to his political career, though it has been somewhat less evident in the playing out of policy, where more pragmatic considerations have applied. The rhetoric has been electorally useful, but the delivery has been disappointing to many evangelicals.

Michael Cromartie, vice-president of the Washington DC conservative evangelical think-tank the Ethics and Public Policy Center, said to me: 'The president's personal story, of his struggle with alcoholism, and his religious conversion makes him instinctively a non-judgmental person.'[32] That may be true, but he certainly also knows how to walk the rhetorical walk that tells evangelicals that he is on their side: the messianic rhetoric of moral words such as 'evil' has largely been directed outwards.

We Europeans may not quite understand or appreciate the Religious Right or its current and future pull on the US government, but we also have many misconceptions about its real effects: is it a passing fancy or a wellspring that is likely to grow stronger under Democratic as well as Republican presidents? Either way, we need to know more about it, so that we can try to comprehend what is going on inside the world's most powerful nation; in other words, why somewhere so similar in so many ways as the USA is walking to a different drummer in one, crucial respect.

2

Men of God

'If society lacks learning and virtue it will perish . . . The nation with the greatest moral power will win.'

President Calvin Coolidge

The Revd Dr Richard Land sat on a raised circular dais in the middle of the exhibition hall at the Southern Baptists' convention in Greensboro, North Carolina, looking like a sleek but enormous sealion. His comfortable frame filled the small armchair that had been provided for him. He shot the cuffs of his brilliantly white shirt and munched reflectively on a protein bar while waiting for his audience to arrive at the scheduled time for his address. His dark hair was slicked back and around his wrist was a chunky watch, glittering as it caught the light. A small microphone was clamped to his resolutely square jaw and he amiably solicited questions from the small crowd that had gathered around the dais – rather, one imagines, as the Oracle of Delphi once did.

The lure was irresistible. I had come to the convention to see the gathering of the largest nonconformist denomination in the USA in their annual session and Dr Land is their representative in the halls of Mammon: the church's spokesman in Washington DC, president of the Southern Baptists' Ethics and Religious Liberty Commission, and probably its most prominent public figure. A glossy booklet about his career – Princeton *magna cum laude*, Oxford doctorate – sang his praises and showed why President Bush had made him a member of something called the United States Commission on International Religious Freedom. Dr Land, the booklet said, speaks passionately and authoritatively on the social, ethical and public policy issues facing the USA. His weekend phone-in programme *Richard Land Live!* is syndicated on the Salem Radio Network and his latest book identifies timeless principles from God's word for changing the USA from the inside out, one family at a time. His proudest achievement, it added, is his thirty-year marriage to a psychotherapist, and their three children.

At the back of the booklet curiously, apart from endorsements by prominent conservative figures such as James Dobson, Charles Colson ('a gifted leader who well understands the cultural crisis of our age and eloquently addresses the solution') and William Bennett, formerly Ronald Reagan's Secretary of Education, there were also odd little encomiums from the secular media. They sounded more like appreciations of a spin doctor or PR man than a religious paragon, but, of course, that's exactly what Dr Land is. *Atlantic Monthly* described him as a 'very quotable fellow', the *Boston Globe* wrote: 'Huge number of quotes – can't use them all!' The *Los Angeles Times* added: 'We want to be able to call him again', and the *New York Times* said: 'He's always helpful'. The *Washington Post*, more ambiguously, had: 'Interesting guy'. I tried to think of a UK religious figure – the Archbishop of Canterbury, say – putting out similar praise for himself, but gave up.

The Southern Baptists have over 16 million members, which makes them the second-largest Christian denomination in the USA after the Catholics, though the separate National Baptists have only slightly fewer. It is a highly fissiparous church: there are more than fifty separate Baptist sects in the USA alone, though five of those cover most of the membership. It is easy to see how one in five Americans claims to be a Baptist.

Although rooted firmly in the South (and originating in a pre-Civil War split with abolitionist Baptists), the Southern Baptists' 43,000 churches are now spread across almost the whole of the USA. This is a rapidly expanding church. According to their annual report, over 370,000 people were baptised into the church in the USA in 2005 and 450,000 overseas: one baptism every thirty-eight seconds. They launched 1,717 new congregations in the USA, which is an average of 4.7 new churches every day. They have six seminaries and 251 theological schools, which means that one in five US theological students is a Southern Baptist. More than that, the church sends out 5,000 missionaries around the world, mainly to US spheres of influence, such as Guam and Puerto Rico. It also has chaplains serving in Iraq and Afghanistan.

All, it must be presumed, share the same fundamental acceptance
of the Bible. As its statement of belief says:

> The Holy Bible was written by men divinely inspired and is
> God's revelation of Himself to man. It is a perfect treasure of
> divine instruction. It has God for its author, salvation for its end
> and truth, without any mixture of error, for its matter. There-
> fore, all Scripture is totally true and trustworthy. It . . . is and will
> remain to the end of the world . . . the supreme standard by
> which all human conduct, creeds and religious opinions should
> be tried.

The Southern Baptists are, says their literature, people of deep beliefs
and cherished doctrines.

This makes them, in perception at least, and because of the
reputation and high public profile of their leaders such as Dr Land,
politically conservative and hence a vital constituency for Republicans
to attract. Conservatives gained a grip on the Southern Baptists' annual
convention in the late 1970s, just as the backlash against the permissive
Sixties was getting under way, and they have never relinquished it. It is
only a couple of years since the Southern Baptists separated themselves
(and their money) off from the rest of the world's Baptists because they
deemed them too liberal on social issues.

President Bush beamed in a supportive message to the convention
direct from the White House, and Condoleezza Rice, the Secretary of
State, though not a Southern Baptist herself (when she was growing
up in Alabama she would not have been able to join, because she is
black), came in person to praise the Southern Baptists' sacrifice,
courage, faith and moral leadership. This was not something the
administration troubled themselves to do the following week when the
more liberal Episcopalians met at their convention in Columbus,
Ohio. After all, the Episcopal Church is an eighth of the size of the
Southern Baptists and full of gays and liberals – and that's only the
bishops.

'We stand for ideals greater than ourselves, not as masters of others
but as servants of freedom,' Ms Rice told the Southern Baptists. 'Our
world needs America's leadership more than ever. If not for America,

who would rally other countries to the defence of religious liberty?'
They cheered her to the rafters for that and were led by the
convention's president, the Revd Bobby Welch, in a fervent prayer,
heavy with biblical cadences and Southern oleaginousness: 'Thank
you, Lord, for this sweet lady. Send a band of angels to camp over her
presence. We have long yearned for such a one as this.'

Back on his dais in the nearby exhibition centre, Dr Land had been
expatiating on Washington and the political process to a somewhat
baffled audience. One man asked why President Bush only seemed
interested in religious people's views at election time and why he had
supported a constitutional amendment defining marriage as between
a man and a woman during the electoral campaign and then lost
interest in it once he had won? This was five months before the
midterm Congressional elections.

Dr Land was having no backsliding from potential voters. He
wanted to stiffen their spines:

'The only president in my lifetime who would have supported the
marriage amendment is George Bush. Ronald Reagan would've
wanted to, but Nancy would've talked him out of it,' he said
confidentially, as if spilling beans. 'In all the president's staff, the only
person who agrees with us is the president himself. I think he's getting
really bad advice and I've told him that. Listen, we are living under the
best president we will see in our lifetime.

'If you want to impeach the president of the United States, go
ahead and vote Democrat. Within your circle of influence you should
do everything you can to get the right people elected. You should
know, if you get involved in someone's political campaign, when you
get elected and you call their office in Washington, your call is on
steroids. It's worth ten times as much. If you were a donor as well, that
quintuples your influence.'

About the Clintons, Dr Land could find it in himself to be less
charitable, even though Bill Clinton is himself a Southern Baptist. 'I
can pray for anyone who's married to that woman, but some day he'll
have to answer to higher authority,' he told the audience. 'If John
Kerry had won in 2004, Hillary Rodham Clinton would be parking her
broomstick outside the Supreme Court for the next thirty years as
chief justice.'

Another questioner wanted to know why one Southern seminary had hired ground-keepers and plumbers whom it knew to be gay. Dr Land put on a serious face:

'Unfortunately, we have been on the defensive while the other side has been pressing to change the status quo. I agree that too often we have behaved with hostility towards people, not targeted their behaviour . . . but, one of the cruellest things the Devil has ever done is to get that lifestyle called gay. I've never seen sadder people. Everything we need to know about homosexual people is written in the Bible. Homosexuality is not only a sin, it is unnatural. The Bible is nowhere as crystal clear on women and blacks as it is on homosexuality: it's comparing oranges and apples.'

And he had an awful warning for the respectable folk in front of him: pornography was everywhere, even in their churches. The man sitting beside me shifted uncomfortably as Dr Land continued:

'This is life-destroying stuff. We must do everything to wrestle it to the ground. It's spiritual and emotional toxic waste! Pornography is preventing the boy becoming the sort of man, father, husband we want him to be. Hard core porn is corrosive. It's like putting cobalt under your child's bed. I don't want that sort of temptation in my life but . . . make no mistake, hard core pornography is in your church. If you have fifty people in your congregation, you will have it, that's why insurance companies are sweeping church computers for pornography to avoid child abuse suits.'

He swept on via a bizarre aside – 'When God watches sport, he watches American football' – to take on abortion: 'We have killed 47 million American babies, a third of a generation'; and stem cell research: 'The Bible says the embryo is human, Psalm 139. The next Billy Graham may be frozen in a fertility clinic somewhere. We're saying we will kill someone against their will on behalf of someone bigger than them. It's biotech cannibalism.' And finally Darfur: 'Nothing will be done about it unless the US takes a stand. The only way the genocide will stop is if we go in. It would take two battalions of US marines to rip the oppressors to bits.'

By now, Dr Land had been speaking for more than an hour and his voice was beginning to crack as it competed with the rousing sound of gospel singers down the hall. He mopped his brow and the audience respectfully moved away. It occurred to me that I had not heard him mention Christian charity once.

Later in the press room, he came among the religious correspondents, shaking hands, slapping backs, laughing and joking, nodding sagely and telling stories, like any politician. And he agreed to sit with me: 'I used to read your newspaper when I lived in Britain.' It turned out we had been at Oxford together at the same time, mid-1970s, coincidentally the same years as Tony Blair. Dr Land had been studying for his doctorate in seventeenth-century English Puritanism and ministering in a Baptist Church in South Oxford, which may have been one of many reasons why our social circles had not coincided.

He was keen nevertheless to reminisce:

'Britain has fallen for so-called modernity and it has become less religious. That's true in western Europe and Canada, but not in the US: we started out from a higher base-point of belief. I think it is the UK and Europe that's out of step. If you didn't live in pre-Thatcherite Britain you can have no idea how she changed your country. I am a big fan: a great stateswoman, second greatest after Winston Churchill. Winston would have been proud of her.'[1]

Dr Land had a demographic take on US conservatism: Republicans were outbreeding Democrats because the latter were aborting their children, and therefore the younger people coming out of Republican families were demonstrably more conservative in outlook and morality:

'America is certainly getting more religious. I believe the explanation for that is not susceptible to the usual human answers. It is because of Divine intervention. The percentage of adult Americans who have accepted Jesus as the Son of God since 1983 has gone up from 31 per cent to 46 per cent now. That's 77 million out of 200 million people who claim to be born-again Christians. We've got 20 million revolutionaries in their twenties and thirties absolutely committed to lives of religious obedience. Younger people are more conservative – it's in the demographics.

'What we have here is the liberal baby-bust. It's their weakness, their Achilles heel, their catastrophically low birth rates. What has happened since '64 is that people who are more socially conservative have got married and had more children. People who are liberal and secularist have tended not to get married and had fewer children. Bluntly, Republicans have aborted less than the national average and Democrats more. The eighteen states with the lowest birth rates voted for Kerry. Married people with children voted 59:40 for Bush, single women voted 62 for Kerry, single men 59 for Kerry.

'The liberals are losing the future. I tell you, the Democrats are going to have to become more conservative on social issues. And another thing, the next Republican presidential candidate, whoever he is, is going to look a lot like George Bush. This is a long-term historical force.'

The words came out in a confident torrent, brooking no argument. It seemed accepted that God was on the Republicans' side. After all, hadn't George Bush won in 2000? I pointed out that he had scarcely received a mandate: 'He got more votes than Bill Clinton in 1996 so I wouldn't say Clinton got a mandate either.'

So that was it: the future was cut and dried, no space for electoral disillusion with a president perceived to have abandoned Religious Right issues, or to have got the Iraq campaign wrong. And no sense either that some Southern Baptists indeed do still vote Democratic. Or that the children of religious households might decide to kick over the traces and vote differently from their parents, just as their parents in turning to vote Republican had abandoned the old Democratic allegiances of their parents before them. 'He really knows his stuff,' says the *Toledo Blade* in its appreciation at the back of Dr Land's booklet. Well, he certainly talked a good game.

The Coliseum centre in which the Southern Baptists were meeting had an enormous indoor arena, more usually used for sporting events such as basketball matches, with banks of seating stretching in tier after tier up from the convention floor. There were 10,000 messengers, as the Southern Baptists call their delegates, attending the convention, but even so the stadium seemed to swallow them up. These were the loyal foot soldiers of Southern Baptistry, three-quarters of them pastors and their wives, elected by their own congregations. They sat placidly in their seats, overwhelmingly white, mostly middle-aged or even elderly, smartly dressed in suits and ties for the men and summer dresses for the women. Greg Warner, a religious journalist (and a Baptist), told me down in the press room: 'They'd be pretty much into biblical inerrancy, seven days of creation, that sort of thing.'

The stage on which the hierarchy of elders sat seemed very far away – they were little more than distant dots as far as the messengers were concerned, with the large video screens showing their giant-sized images only emphasising the distance from the rank and file of the congregation.

It was clear that there was something of a grass-roots revolt going on. For the first time in more than a decade there was actually a contest over who should be the convention's next president. In normal times the good old boys on the platform choose from among their number the next pastor in line to take the year-long presidency, but this time their candidate faced not one, but two challengers – the first time such a contest had been held in fourteen years – each promising not radical reform, but something different. The platforms were discreet and cloaked in the language of spiritual renewal and winning souls for Christ, but the dissatisfaction was obvious. Everything had been stitched up for too long. There was much muttering about how little the establishment candidate, the Revd Ronnie Floyd's First Baptist Church of Springdale, Arkansas and its congregation of 16,000 people, had given for the work of the Southern Baptists nationally: less than $500,000. In response Floyd tried to induce a spirit of mild panic: 'We are at a critical hour. The greatest need we have is for a mighty spiritual movement of God to take place among us, the kind of movement that's biblically based, Jesus-centered and Holy Spirit-controlled.'

Paul Pressler, a retired Houston judge, said: 'I think this shows the maturity of our movement. We don't have to walk in lock-step with each other. The time that there were threats from liberals is gone. We don't have to guard ourselves as carefully.'

And indeed not: the main insurgent candidate, the Revd Frank Page of Taylors, South Carolina, actually won. He did not look too radical to me: fifty-three years old, grey-haired, rimless spectacles, dark suit and blue tie. 'As God is my witness, I never sought this,' he said, blinking and smiling in the spotlight after his election was announced. There would be a different tone, he said, oh yes, the landscape had changed, younger pastors would be brought on. 'I pray I will speak the truth in love,' he said. To try and understand just how radical he was, I asked him where he stood on the biblical fundamentals. He didn't pause: 'I believe in the historicity of the Genesis account of creation. It is literal and it is true.'

This would have chimed perfectly with the messengers thronging the exhibition hall – anything else and they would have been worried.

The Southern Baptists had brought in Fred Luter, a black pastor from New Orleans, to wake them up after lunch and he was in rhetorical overkill, fortissimo: 'We're goin' to win. You have new purpose. You *shall* be witnesses unto *meeee*. Once you been empowered by the Spirit of God you gotta new purpose. Not Islam, not Buddha, but *Jesusssss*. It's not about the pastor it's about the *power*.'

Not a great deal of this made sense to me, nor apparently to the messengers wandering past in search of a hot dog and fries. It was too glib and frenzied, slabs of phrases bolted together devoid of meaning, depth or sense. Most of them would have been born in the era of segregation and they showed few signs of listening to the ranting figure. As he drew to a breathless stop, Mr Welch, the president, said genially: 'You white guys try that and your vocal chords'll be shot for the next six years.'

The exhibition hall contained stands for a host of Southern seminaries and colleges and also a bookstall with the biggest display of Bibles that I had ever seen. Each side of a hollow square of tables was at least 10 yards long. In fact, it sold only Bibles: there were King James Bibles, keyword study Bibles, student Bibles, women of faith Bibles, Bible navigators' Bibles, super-giant-print Bibles, Bibles especially for firefighters ('something happened on September 11th that changed our perception of firefighters . . .'), even a sportsman's Bible, with a man carrying a rifle, waiting to shoot ducks, on the cover: this last was for those with 'a passion for the great outdoors and the God who made it'.

Nearby was another bookstall, filled with 'improving' books and instruction manuals, many written by the same small coterie of authors. *Boundaries with Teens: When to Say Yes, How to Say No* was written by Dr John Townsend, who also popped up as co-author of a nearby book called *Rescue Your Love Life*. They were clearly aimed at an audience of worried folk, evidently mainly men: *Parenting Isn't for Cowards*, by James Dobson, *Six Battles Every Man Must Win*, *Straight Talk to Men* (Dobson again), *No More Christian Mister Nice Guy*, *No More Excuses: Be the Man God Made You to Be*, *The Exemplary Husband*, *Maximized Manhood*, *Prepare Your Son for Every Man's Battle*, *A Look at Life from a Deer Stand* (clearly for hunters waiting for their prey to show up after they had finished reading their sportsmen's Bibles). There were nowhere near as many books aimed at mothers, so perhaps the publishers knew where their best customers stood. There are plenty of things in my life that need straightening out, but somehow I could not see any of these books doing the trick.

It was while I was in the convention centre's Gents, of all places, that I experienced the one attempt to proselytise me that I had in the whole trip. A small, genial, elderly man with greased grey hair, a shiny face and a garish tie introduced himself to me. 'I am seventy-nine years of age and I have been a Christian for eighty years,' he chuckled with what was obviously a well-worn paradox. 'My mommy was a churchgoer, see?'

He engaged me earnestly in conversation about my immortal soul with an idiom so thick I could barely understand it. When he heard my accent he told me he had done exactly the same for Princess Diana (clearly without resounding success) during a visit to London. His name was Paul Strickland, he came from LaCenter, west Kentucky, and his mission in life was to distribute Gideon Bibles wherever he went.

A simple photocopied sheet of paper, in English and Spanish, explained his mission in bold type and a rush of words:

Plan of Salvation to get to Heaven:
May I ask you a question or rather questions which I ask hundreds of thousands of people across the world? I have asked priests, ministers, missionaries, doctors and pretty well everyone I meet from all walks of life. I even asked Princess Diana in London, England. She squeezed my left hand and said how sweet you are, Paul, that you are sharing Jesus Christ with us in London. Then she hugged and kissed me on the left cheek. Have you invited Jesus Christ into your heart, received and

accepted him as your personal Saviour, knowing for certain that if you were to die tonight that you would spend eternity in Heaven and not in Hell for ever and ever separated from our Heavenly Father? Have you been Spiritually Reborn or Born Again? Have you actually done that? This is the most important thing in life, nothing could be more important.

Then, to emphasise the point, the typeface changed to bold:

God loves you and wants you in Heaven. I love you and want you in Heaven. And you certainly want to be in Heaven also when you DIE, don't you?

Accompanying cuttings from Mr Strickland's local newspaper, *The Advance Yeoman*, detailed other evangelising trips that he, with his wife Lou Nelle, daughter Suzie Nutt and granddaughter Paige Harper, had undertaken as far away as New York. They had even appeared on national television where a wind blew their scriptural tracts into the audience: 'It was God's work,' Strickland was quoted as saying with a smile. Everything was God's work: another cutting from the same paper told of an occasion when Strickland, who because of a heart condition was not allowed to lift more than 5 pounds at a time, was ferrying Bibles in relays from his car into a meeting when he came across a young woman crying with joy because she had just been led to Christ. 'They had just prayed for a Bible. God sent me there, and there I was with a Bible,' he said.

God's interventions in his life had indeed made for a happy soul. It seemed far-fetched that He had sent us into the Gents together, but you never know, and it was good to meet someone so cheerful in his work and with so simple a faith. 'I been to England,' he said as we parted. 'Did I tell you I met Princess Diana? Any time you want me to preach the gospel in England, you let me know – I'm ready.'

Out in one of the corridors of the convention centre I came across Keith and Joy McMinn, from Salem Baptist Church at Crozier, Virginia, and their six-month-old baby, Jonah. Keith, the church's music pastor, did the talking: 'I became a Christian at the age of ten,' he told me. 'It all centers on the gospel of Christ. It satisfies my soul and gives comfort in suffering. This is my third convention. We come because the preaching is good and we get encouragement about sharing the faith of fundamentalism. I don't have a doubt about the word of God. Without a doubt, it's true.'

The Institute on Religion and Democracy (IRD) is one of a number of more or less raucous lobbying organisations based in Washington with a clearly partisan conservative agenda and an ostensibly religious purpose. I had come to see its new president, Jim Tonkowich, at the IRD's offices in a smart block in the middle of downtown Washington.

On the face of it, Tonkowich was an unlikely choice to head an organisation whose speciality is to attack, carp and snap at the heels of the liberal national leadership of mainstream US churches, particularly the Episcopalians, Methodists and Lutherans. A former television producer for the Watergate plotter turned conservative Christian evangelist Charles Colson, Tonkowich did not actually belong to any of the main churches, but to the small breakaway Presbyterian Church of America, which split off from the main denomination in the 1970s because it deemed it too liberal in its support for ecumenical relations through the National Council of Churches and for women's ordination.

The IRD claims to be non-partisan and is incorporated as a tax-exempt charitable organisation, and it is indeed true that it is an ecumenical body, in that it will attack anyone so long as they are liberal. It is a small, though well-funded, organisation and, although its ostensible purpose is 'to promote spiritual renewal within the church and to work for more balanced and responsible discussion of foreign policy issues', its attacks all seem to be one way. Flick through its magazine, *Faith and Freedom* ('Reforming the Church's Social and Political Witness'), and the slant of every article is critical of any churchman voicing an even vaguely progressive opinion. Thus, summer 2005, a fairly typical report on the National Council of Churches' statement criticising the war on Iraq, written by the IRD's chief polemicist Mark Tooley, begins:

In not untypical fashion, the faithfully left-leaning National Council of Churches has issued a poisonous little July 4 greeting to the American people. The statement . . . is not a celebration of two centuries of American democracy and religious liberty, with gratitude to God. It is instead a screed against the 'dishonourable' war in Iraq . . . although comprised of denominations totalling over 40 million mainstream Americans, the NCC has for 40 years been a voice for unending 1960s-style radical protest.

The article concluded that withdrawal from Iraq would equal the horrors of thirty years before when Indochina was liberated from US influence 'thanks to policies advocated by the NCC', as if the unmentioned Republican administrations of Richard Nixon and Gerald Ford had had nothing to do with it. The message was that churches should keep their noses out of causes of which the IRD disapproved.

In January 2007, the IRD was snapping at the heels of the National Council of Churches again, producing a report called 'Strange Yokefellows', claiming it was funded by 'Left-leaning' organisations such as the National Religious Partnership for the Environment and the Ford Foundation. The report's researcher John Lomperis said: 'Several of these groups that the NCC has turned to for financial and other forms of support are so blatantly partisan that they can be accurately described as . . . the shadow Democratic Party.' Mr Lomperis admitted that the report was written as a response to criticism of the IRD's own funding by Right-wing groups.[2]

In fact, there is little other than polemics in the IRD's publications. Its website, ird-renew.org, also contains action plans to use against mainline churches. It courts disaffected church members and offers manpower and financial support to conservative groups, such as the American Anglican Council, which is seeking to oust the leadership of the Episcopal Church. It also seeks to place its board members and their views in prominent sections of the media.

Tooley came to shake my hand, wanly, as I waited to meet the president. A sallow, slightly cadaverous man, he is viewed with some suspicion and not a little derision on more liberal church websites, both for his zeal and the lack of proportion of some of his attacks on opponents. Tooley had earlier in 2006 made small headlines by criticising gay families for showing up to the traditional egg rolling contest for children which is held at the White House each Easter. He denounced them as 'sad' groups that were exploiting a 130-year-old children's party to make a political statement, presumably overlooking the fact that he was doing the same by denouncing them. This seemed to be rather par for the IRD's course.

Dr Tonkowich himself, only a few weeks in post, was small, courteous and grey-haired with a tendency to lose his thread as he voiced the party line. Several times he told me he had three points to make and then could not remember what they were. It had been, he said, a busy weekend:

'It's issues rather than denominations that we go for. We bear a social witness against the churches that have very large footprints on public policy, so when we attack the churches' stance on homosexuality the issue for us is one of worldview: how do we know right from wrong, truth and falsity? Did Jesus physically rise from the dead? Some people say it doesn't matter, but we think it does. I just can't understand these folks who are progressives and revisionists who want to change things completely. We just point this out.

'But we never encourage people to leave their churches. We encourage them to stay and change them from within. We work for change within denominations.'[3]

I asked why the IRD had not tackled the Roman Catholic Church, rather than picking away at smaller denominations. He replied: 'Half our board are Roman Catholics but . . . we've got enough on our plate already, we can't cope with more at the moment.'

The Institute seems to go for soft targets. It is obsessed by gays: gay Anglicans, gay Methodists, gay Lutherans and the churches' attempts to accommodate them. But worst of all was gay marriage, which just happened to be one of the focuses of the president's and the Republican Party's assault in the culture wars. He said:

'Where homosexuality is accepted, the family degenerates. We have not campaigned on divorce. I think it has become very accepted . . . you don't hear a lot of pastors talking about it. There is no question marriage has become very vulnerable. Once you have redefined it as not being between a man and a woman you have created a real problem: why not three people together, or four people?

Why not polygamy? Orthodoxy and the evangelical faith need to be supported and defended.

'I think we make a difference. We shine a light on things that the churches want to keep hidden. The fact that we cause them embarrassment is proof that we are doing something right. It's one of the most effective ways of doing journalism: you ask questions, you quote the answers and let the chips fall where they may.'

Dr Tonkowich made it all sound like a high-minded public service, which indeed, if it were not so partisan, it might be. Founded in the early 1980s, the Institute boasts a number of prominent neo-conservative polemicists and religious writers on its board and it receives substantial funding from a small number of extremely wealthy supporters: people whose names crop up again and again as sponsors across a network of religious-lobbying organisations.

The IRD's board includes Fred Barnes, former editor of the conservative *Weekly Standard* but now with Fox News; Michael Novak of the American Enterprise Institute; Richard John Neuhaus, formerly a Lutheran pastor, now a Catholic priest, founder of the Institute on Religion and Public Life; and George Weigel, a Catholic writer, and author of an enormous, hagiographical biography of Pope John Paul II and member of the Ethics and Public Policy Center (EPPC). Working for the IRD as treasurer is Mary Ellen Bork, contributor to the *Asian Wall Street Journal*, daughter of the conservative judge and folk hero of the Religious Right, Robert Bork. Their paths intertwine: Weigel, Neuhaus and Novak sit on the boards of the IRD and the IRPL, and the EPPC and the IRD also share board members with other similar bodies such as Empower America, Project for the New American Century and Foundation for the Defence of Democracies.

Their backers tend to be the same people too: the Ahmansons, heirs to a multi-million Californian real-estate fortune, who also give money to other conservative groups, the Coors brewery family, the Olins, the Scaifes and the Smith-Richardsons. The National Council of Churches responded to the IRD's attack on their funding in January 2007 by pointing out that it was much more open in detailing its sponsors than the IRD was. Dr Tonkowich admitted that about 60 per cent of the IRD's revenue came from individuals and 40 per cent from conservative foundations such as the Scaife, Bradley, Coors, Ahmanson and Smith-Richardson family charities.

In the last twenty years, the IRD alone has acknowledged receiving nearly $5 million from five families' foundations. Neuhaus's Institute on Religion in Public Life received more than $8 million in donations between 1989 and 2005, and the Ethics and Public Policy Center Institute nearly $12 million between 1985 and 2003. These are not negligible sums.

Dr Tonkowich told me:

'The conspiracy theories would be comical if they were not so sad. We are a small organisation. We cannot be blamed for churches losing members. We have no way of causing that. All these churches need to do is read their own statistics: the churches which are growing are almost entirely orthodox and conservative.

'We are a donation-based organisation. The Ahmansons have been very generous. They give to us because they like what we are doing. We tell them how they are going to use their money and it is their decision whether they go on giving to us.'

The Ahmansons support Republican candidates but also provide money to the creationist Discovery Institute, the Christian Reconstructionist Chalcedon Foundation, and the conservative American Anglican Council (AAC), which is seeking to undermine the liberal national leadership of the US Episcopal Church and get it expelled from the worldwide Anglican Communion. The AAC, which for a time shared office space with the IRD, is secretive about its funding, but receives over $400,000 a year in donations, ten times what it receives in membership subscriptions. It is difficult to believe that its backers are doing it entirely out of philanthropy, rather than seeking to make a decisive difference to the church.

They have also provided funding in smaller amounts in recent years for the evangelical lobbying organisation within the Church of England, Anglican Mainstream, which has received at least $60,000, the Church Missionary Society ($27,000) and the Oxford Centre for Mission Studies (OCMS), an academic body helping theology students ($7,000).[4]

The Ahmansons also gave substantial sums to a body called INFEMIT, the International Fellowship of Evangelical Mission

Theologians, which is based in Washington at the offices of the EPPC, and in the UK at the Oxford Centre. The OCMS, whose director Vinay Samuel sits on the board on INFEMIT, received over $350,000 from the International Fellowship between 2000 and 2004. Samuel's former colleague at OCMS, Chris Sugden, now runs Anglican Mainstream and pops up posing as a journalist and lobbyist at Anglican Church meetings around the world.

These are complex institutional-relationships. It is like watching a series of interconnected spiders' webs with busy little figures crisscrossing them, interacting, sitting on each other's boards and receiving funding from the same small group of wealthy sponsors.

Across town from the IRD, in an office in a converted cinema in a more downbeat part of Washington, sits Jim Wallis of the Sojourners Movement, on the opposite end of the political spectrum from Dr Tonkowich. Indeed the IRD's magazine is accustomed to describe him as a 'liberal activist and self-described evangelical', as if there might be some doubt about the matter, insinuating that he flies under bogus colours.

While the preaching style is somewhat similar, earnest and Bible-based, to those on the political Right, the content is a mirror-image. Wallis would say he just reads the Bible differently. A prolific author and regular speaker on both sides of the Atlantic – rather more consulted by Labour ministers in the UK than he is by the administration back in Washington – Wallis insists that the political Right has tried to hijack religious people purely for their votes. Wiry and energetic, he is married to an English woman, who is always alleged to have been the model for the *Vicar of Dibley* television character, following her ordination in the 1990s.

The Sojourners, a mailing network of liberal Christians, receive regular weekly newsletters combining exhortation and exegesis. It makes frequent appeals for cash to keep going, rather in the way of National Public Radio. The offices look familiar: more like a by-election constituency headquarters or a classy student union than the bookish headquarters I'd become familiar with among the Religious Right organisations. The pictures on the wall commemorated progressive heroes too: Martin Luther King, Nelson Mandela, even William Jennings Bryan.

In a recent book called *God's Politics*, which sold more than 250,000 copies in a year in the USA, Wallis argues:

> Religion has been lifted up for public life in two different ways . . . One invokes the name of God and faith in order to hold us accountable to God's intentions – to call us to justice, compassion, humility, repentance and reconciliation. Abraham Lincoln, Thomas Jefferson and Martin Luther King perhaps best exemplify that way. The other way wrongly invokes God's blessing on our activities, agendas and purposes. Many presidents and political leaders have used the language of religion in such ways and George W. Bush is falling into that same temptation.[5]

The book does have its messianic (as well as repetitive) moments as it tries to wrest God back from the conservatives, and Wallis has been accused of resorting to low tricks similar to those used by the conservatives while he seeks to gain the moral high ground. As the former British Conservative MP (and agnostic) George Walden noted in his recent book *God Won't Save America*:

> These are not God's Politics, which by their nature are inscrutable, they are Wallis's . . . in this respect between Wallis and the Christian Right there is little to choose. His conviction that he is a vehicle for the expression of the Almighty's views on the relief of child poverty is on the same level of presumption as the fundamentalists' claim to know what the Bible would have said on abortion and stem cell research, had the scientific data been available earlier.[6]

This is a little harsh, since Wallis is largely pointing out what the Bible actually says about poverty – one gets the impression that Walden is grateful to have found someone on the Left in the USA he can get his teeth into since there are so few of them about – but it does contain a grain of truth.

When I met Wallis six months before the midterm elections and long before criticism of the administration's handling of the Iraq war came to be openly voiced by its senior commanders, he was in an upbeat mood, buoyed by a recent visit to university campuses where his message had apparently gone down well. 'The Religious Right are losing, they're on the way out, their time has come and gone,' he said, not noticeably with the air of one whistling in the dark. 'I just got a tremendous response when I spoke in Omaha. They've got very high negatives: Falwell and Robertson are among the most unpopular people in the country.'[7]

Wallis continued: 'They have lost control of the agenda: the environment and climate change are not Religious Right issues and yet they are tremendously important to an increasing number of young evangelicals. They care much more about world poverty than they do about gay marriage, and in that they are firmly rooted in the nineteenth-century radical evangelical tradition. It's James Dobson and people like that who are the heretics – the prosperity gospel is an American heresy.

'The Right narrows morality down to two issues: gay marriage and abortion, and they ignore the 2,000 verses in the Bible that are about poverty. People like Rick Warren know that. They can't keep it pinned down to two issues and ignore all the rest. Can you imagine Jesus Christ turning up here on Sunday with 3,000 children dying every day and saying: "I am here to talk about same sex marriage"? Can you imagine that?

'The leaders of the Religious Right are into a secular political agenda. The smell of political power has reached Dobson's nostrils. As for Falwell, he's just an enormous ego. What he wants to be is king-maker to the next president. You know these guys' movements are just clones of the political right. They are tremendously impressed because they sit in on Karl Rove's conference calls. It is not an indigenous movement at all – they and their grievances are being exploited for reasons of power. Their foundations are political and they are just part of the conservative strategy, just as Fox News is.

'But now they are losing to religion. They are losing to Jesus. They have caricatured faith for too long and they are losing the next generation. Falwell is so repugnant to these people; they want to say: "Jerry, you don't speak for us." You know, these guys, I've seen them in the television studios. They are totally obsessed with suits and steaks. You'll see Falwell and Al Sharpton in the studio together and they're knocking spots off each other and then they'll chat about where's a good place for dinner. They have been corrupted by political power. Sharpton and Falwell: two peas in a pod.'

Wallis, who has advised the Democratic Party in the past, was convinced however that they could not wait for the Religious Right to collapse of its own accord as a result of its own internal feuds and contradictions. As an evangelical he believed the Democrats must move in to fill the vacuum by offering religious folk a different vision rather than trying to win without them. The answer had a particularly traditional ring to it:

'What we've got to do is organise and create an infrastructure, mobilise on the issues. We've got 250,000 Sojourners out there. We've got to mobilise like we did in the '60s against Vietnam. It's not been done yet but we've got to begin. John McCain is taking a risk dealing with these people: he has to get the Republican nomination and unless he gets these people's endorsement from the Religious Right, he has no chance. But the Democrats have been seen as a secular party, unwilling to be the creature of any religious figure – well, you are going to see a change there.

'White evangelicals make up 22 per cent of the electorate: half Religious Right, half moderate or progressive: and half of 22 per cent is a considerable constituency to go for. If the Democrats get religion in a way that is transparently false, then that will hurt them, but they cannot allow that potential constituency to sit at home: if it costs a winnable candidate victory, what benefit is that? In 2004, the Democrats got out 105 per cent of their vote and they still lost. They cannot afford to be written off by that part of the electorate.'

God's Politics argues:

The religious and political Right gets the public meaning of religion mostly wrong – preferring to focus only on sexual and cultural issues while ignoring the weightier matters of justice. And the secular Left doesn't seem to get the meaning and promise of faith for politics at all – mistakenly dismissing spirituality as irrelevant to social change . . . It is indeed time to take back our faith . . . from religious Right wingers who claim to know God's political views on every issue, then ignore the subjects that God seems to care the most about . . . It is time to reassert and reclaim the gospel faith – especially in our public life. When we do we discover that faith challenges the powers that be to do justice for the poor instead of . . . supporting politicians who further enrich the wealthy . . . The Democrats should be much more willing to use moral and religious language in defence of economic fairness and justice.[8]

So no escape from religion on either the Left or the Right in US politics. Both sides need to capture its adherents in order to win. The problem is in the Right's successful annexation and prioritisation of precise moral issues: for that to change, voters would have to switch off from the Republicans for other reasons. I asked one religiously active progressive what he thought of Wallis. 'He's just a general without an army,' he retorted.

3

And This Be Our Motto –
'In God Is Our Trust'

'Without religion this world would be something not fit to be mentioned in polite company, I mean Hell.'

John Adams to Thomas Jefferson

It was surely a sign of Divine providence – and certainly of enormous luck – that after the Pilgrim Fathers struggled ashore at Plymouth Rock in December 1620 and barely survived their first winter, the Native American who first befriended them just happened to speak excellent English. When Tisquantum of the Patuxet tribe, known as Squanto because the Englishmen could not even get their tongues round his name, emerged to greet them out of the forest, he not only knew England probably as well as they did, but had actually lived in London for more than a decade as a domestic servant. Indeed, he had only just returned home a few months earlier. His friend Samoset, who was actually the first to meet the new settlers, also spoke English. Without this stroke of luck, the Pilgrims would never have been able to communicate sufficiently with the local inhabitants, to learn how to plant their first harvest with local crops or where best to catch fish, and accordingly to survive long enough to establish their religious colony on the shores of Massachusetts.

Squanto is remembered as the friendly Indian, but his linguistic facility is often overlooked – he almost certainly spoke a bit of Spanish as well, having been sold as a slave by an English ship's captain to Catholic friars in Malaga – yet his story is worth telling to show not only that the first English-speaking religious group to seek escape in the New World were entering a land that was not entirely unknown (even Plymouth had been named by Captain John Smith before they arrived) but that the society they were trying to establish was heavily dependent on the goodwill of others who they would regard as lesser beings. Squanto had originally been enticed aboard an English ship fifteen years before, in 1605, by Captain George Weymouth and taken back to England to show financial backers the sort of specimen that was to be found in the New World. One of the entrepreneurs was Sir Ferdinando Gorges, who employed Squanto as a servant as well as a curiosity and then hired him out as a guide and interpreter for other explorers, including Captain Smith.

By the time the Pilgrims arrived, Squanto had crossed the Atlantic several times himself, as free man and slave, and had experienced both friendly white men and rogues. He was undoubtedly the Native American who had more to do with establishing a British presence on the east coast than any other single figure and he certainly knew their ways. When Squanto died in November 1622, Governor William Bradford recorded that he had desired him 'to pray for him that he might go to the Englishman's God in Heaven', which was certainly what Bradford would have wished to hear.

Despite the national myth that the immigrants were fleeing religious persecution to establish freedom of worship in the New World, the first settlements in the New World were repressive theocracies of the like-minded. Down the coast, where the first English settlers had arrived about a decade before the Pilgrim Fathers, the first charter of Virginia, signed by James I for the commercial company set up to exploit the land, expressed the pious hope that the settlers would carry 'the Christian religion to such people as yet live in darkness and miserable ignorance of the true worship and worship of God', but the company's central aim in the words of Captain Smith 'was nothing but present profit', chiefly in the form of finding gold, silver and copper just as the Spanish had done farther south.[1] The colonies were primarily business ventures.

But as soon as the Virginia settlement faltered, the new governor Sir Thomas Gates set about establishing a set of 'Laws, Divine, Moral and Martial' – in that order – to restore discipline, exacting savage punishments on those who failed in their religious observance. It was a three-strikes-and-you're-dead policy: those who broke the Sabbath or failed to attend church three times faced being hanged, as did those convicted of sodomy, incest, rape and adultery, imposing the old world's scale of punishment on the new.

The Pilgrims came with loftier motives, wishing to separate themselves from the Church of England, rather than purify it by staying at
home and working on it from within. Their was the continuation of the
Reformation's theological struggles by other means. They saw themselves founding a society of saints, composed only of those who
thought precisely like themselves: the elect, pre-chosen by God, unlike
all the rest who were doomed to hell. It would be a place where, in the
words of Thomas Shepherd in 1636, 'there are no enemies to hunt you
to heaven'.

But that did not mean that they sought to overturn an established
social hierarchy of the sort they had known in England. In fact, they
planned to replicate it in the New World, except in so far as all – from
the king back home in London downwards – were equally subject to
the will of God. After all, as Winthrop told the faithful in his famous
sermon on board the *Arbella*: 'God almighty . . . hath so disposed of
the condition of mankind as in all times, some must be rich, some
poor, some high and eminent in power and dignity, others mean and
in subjugation . . . The rich and mighty should not eat up the poor nor
the poor and despised rise up . . . and shake off their yoke.'[2] That
applied to masters and their servants, but also certainly to husbands
and their wives, who must be subservient to them in all things. No
Leveller nonsense for them. It was God's will to place them as he
wished. It was inconceivable that the Divine Word as revealed and
transcribed by the styluses of ancient men in far-distant societies
should ever be questioned. As Cotton Mather said: ''Tis the last advice
we have had from heaven for now sixteen hundred years.'

Although the Puritans made up only one strand of the many
religious groups that would settle in the New World, their ethic,
perhaps more than any other, continues to infuse US society. Their
stress on individual virtue and personal development as a sign of
worth, hard work as an indication of merit and material success as the
reward for diligence, remains central to many Americans' sense of
their country's strengths. This is a remarkable tribute to the theocratic
ethos that the Puritans self-consciously attempted to create for
themselves in their new country, even 300 years after they had to
accommodate themselves to a wider society.

Having established their exclusive colony, the Pilgrim Fathers did not welcome immigrants of other religious persuasions: theirs was to be a pure commonwealth – others 'shall have free liberty to keep away from us' – and to make sure it stayed that way they instituted laws that stipulated that only Puritans of their sort could have the vote or hold office. Any non-members visiting their settlements must attend their religious services and were, furthermore, to be obliged to help pay for the preaching in the expectation that it might ultimately lead to their conversion.

The Pilgrims saw themselves as being in a covenant with God. The Deity would promise redemption to his chosen, special people, infusing them with grace, and they in turn would give him their allegiance and await his revelation. As Puritan settlements spread across New England, individual towns drew up compacts of their own. Charlestown, on the north shore of Boston harbour, promised its inhabitants would 'bind ourselves to walk in all our ways according to the rule of the Gospell and in all sincere conformity to all his holy ordinaunces and in mutuall love and respect each to other, so neere as God shall give us grace', and Dedham's warned: 'we shall by all means labor to keep off from us such as are contrary minded'. Self-control was necessary, but it must be backed up by institutional power and sanctions. Mutual love within the community, says the historian James Morone, expulsion for anybody who might be contrary minded, a sentiment that has echoes down to today.[3] In March 2004 one Tennessee county contemplated banning homosexuals from living within its borders altogether, a plan that foundered only on impracticality and after a national outcry. The Puritans would fully have understood the impulse.

Opponents might denounce the Pilgrims' idea of such contracts as fantastical and impertinent – placing an obligation on God – but it had an awesome daily reality for those who felt bound by it on earth in the New World. It meant they had to follow God's word, as they understood it, to the letter and also ensure that everyone else did too, whether they were saints or not, by interfering with their freedoms and their behaviour if necessary (and it would be necessary) in order to ensure unquestioning social conformity to his will. In this lies the origins of those repressive, disapproving, indeed puritanical, societies that are so associated with this Calvinistic religious observance, so intolerant of diversity and contemptuous and fearful of difference: a mindset that has surfaced repeatedly throughout US history, whether taking on alcohol drinkers or communists. It is a mentality prone to doctrinal splits and purity tests to an almost secular political degree, an attitude that, as H. L. Mencken famously remarked, boils down to the haunting fear that someone, somewhere might be happy. Or, as Lord Macaulay put it in his *History of England*: 'The Puritan hated bear-baiting, not because it gave pain to the bear, but because it gave pleasure to the spectators.'

Some historians now insist that the Puritans were not as grim as painted: that they tolerated alcohol (though they had not much alternative given the quality of the water supply), that they enjoyed sex (strictly within the confines of the marital bed), and that they were interested in science (in order to improve their God-given talents). But it is hard to overlook their attempt to enforce a strict social and religious uniformity while they controlled a large proportion of the white Anglo-Saxons in the New World.

The early Puritans, the first Anglophone religious group to establish themselves in America, wanted to establish a God-fearing and conformist society. Despite the American foundation myth, there was to be no freedom and latitude so far as they were concerned; as a contemporary Bishop of Salisbury noted: 'Every party cries out for Liberty and toleration, till they get to be uppermost, and then will allow none.' The irony was that the Puritans were fleeing a society in England that was becoming slowly less religiously repressive, one that allowed a range of Protestant worship by the mid-seventeenth century. Eventually London would force the saints in Massachusetts to allow in Anglicans and stop killing Quakers.

The covenant idea continues to influence US society, most notably in the Constitution. The Founding Fathers took their ideas from the social contract originally proposed by the Whig philosopher John Locke, but he in turn derived his thoughts from the Puritans' covenants. Their ideas would help to provide a religious underpinning for the challenge to the king when it came to seeking independence 150 years after the Puritan settlement. Even King George III was to be subject to the rule of God if he broke his covenant with men.

And everyone ultimately did fail the Divine test of course, bringing down God's wrath on sinful man for undermining the just order of things, as preachers – then and now – felt themselves constrained to point out in apocalyptic terms. These repeated admonitions to the faithful have rung down through history as jeremiads: warnings of the dire consequences of backsliding and the inevitable downfall of a sick society. And the sins they pointed out and condemned with most prurience were those that specifically undermined the social order – and especially those that related to sex.

The clergy synod of 1679 was particularly ripe in its denunciation of moral shortcomings: children and servants were not kept in due subjugation ('parents especially being sinfully indulgent towards them . . . most of the evils that abound among us proceed from defects as to family government', just the sort of thing Brother Emmett in twenty-first-century Tennessee was saying on my car radio), there was too much pride shown in the wearing of strange apparel and ornaments ('the poorest sort of people are notoriously guilty in this matter'), drinking, debauchery, adultery, false hair, naked necks, arms, even uncovered breasts, dancing, gaming, sinful company, idleness, high prices, declining schools, soaring lawsuits, greedy business practices – an endless list of depravity of a sort familiar to moralists even today. 'We have forgotten the errand upon which the Lord sent us hither . . . we are a perishing people if we reform not.'

But how could the established order be maintained? In a dynamic, developing society it was and remains a conundrum: the reconciling of individual initiative with maintaining social discipline. At first the solution was to restrict individual development – something that the Catholic hierarchy has often tried: in the words of Governor Sir William Berkeley: 'I thank God there are no free schools nor printing and I hope we shall not have them these hundred years, for learning has brought disobedience and heresy and sects into the world and printing has divulged them and libels against the best government. God keep us from both.'

But such a solution was unsustainable. If men bettered themselves by hard work and diligence, was that not a sign of divine pleasure with them? If every one fell short in some way, soon the elect would be a very small and vulnerable group indeed. The answer was that God's purpose was that the world would get better: 'If we get well through, we shall soon enjoy halcyon days with all the Vultures of Hell trodden under our feet,' exclaimed the most famous preacher of them all, Cotton Mather. It was a truly American and enduring vision: the bright tomorrow, achieved through hard work, application and devotion to God's will.

The Puritans' world-view was not without challenge from within their own community. One of the first to do so was Roger Williams, the pastor of Salem just north of Boston, who proclaimed that there ought to be a division between the conduct of the state and those of the religious communities within it. In this he foreshadowed the Founding Fathers 140 years later in their desire to build a wall between Church and state.

Williams's argument was that just as the Church had its own distinct spiritual values and should not compromise them in order to conform to the desires and dictates of the state, so the state itself had no right to dictate how its citizens should, or should not, worship. This arose not from a lofty view of the state or of the equal value of others' beliefs, but because of his conviction that to impose oaths on 'unregenerate' men was to take the name of God in vain. The government could not compel its citizens to be good Christians, nor coerce them through 'oaths, tithes, times, days, marryings and buryings in holy ground'. Williams even took his views to London to argue them in the middle of Oliver Cromwell's Commonwealth. A self-proclaimed 'Christian' nation was a violation of non-Christians' liberty of conscience: 'Papists and Jews . . . ought freely and impartially to be permitted their several respective worships, their ministers . . . and what way of maintaining them they freely choose.'[4] Good Christians only became so of their own spiritual volition. Persecution for conscience's sake was therefore 'heretical, blasphemous, seditious and dangerous to the corporal, to the spiritual, to the present, to the Eternal Good of men'. With opinions like that, Williams was banished from Massachusetts on his return and went off to found the colony of Rhode Island, where his principles could be put into practice, albeit with limited success.

Another of those to fall foul of the established order by challenging its rulings was a woman, Anne Hutchinson, a midwife who established something of a following in Boston in the mid-1630s and whose preaching in her own home proved both popular and deeply subversive because it undermined what ministers were telling their congregations. It did not help that she was female; as with the early Christian Fathers, there was a terror among the elders of what a woman could do to besot, bewitch and seduce: 'There are few controversies where a woman is not at the bottom of them,' warned Mather. Hutchinson does not have much in common with Hillary Clinton, but both are equally threatening to anxious men. Thus we get the Revd Jerry Falwell in September 2006 expatiating on another Clinton candidacy for president: 'I certainly hope that Hillary is the candidate . . . because nothing would energize my [constituency] like Hillary Clinton. If Lucifer ran, he wouldn't.' There's an authentic whiff of ancient sulphur there, right down to conjuring up the devil.

Hutchinson's message was that salvation was absolutely in God's hands and there was nothing anyone could do to change it. This too was an argument rife during the Reformation. So there was no point in the damned trying to save their souls through good works because it wouldn't do them any good. Hence the Puritan moral codes made no difference: you could not force the hand of God. It was placing human purposes over divine grace and hence the heresy of Arminianism: the idea that you could make a difference to your eternal destiny through good works (something that still divides a certain sort of Christian: the Southern Baptists were debating it at their convention in June 2006). Hutchinson, the uppity woman, was preaching danger: a subversive zeal for a direct and personal relationship with God, unmediated by ministers and unaffected by a man-made system of rules. She was dangerously undermining the secular diligence and moral piety that the authorities wished to instil in the community; Governor Winthrop declared: 'Most of her new tenets tend[ed] to slothfulness and quench all indevour.'

Ministers were being heckled in their pulpits in Boston, the heartland of Hutchinson's supporters. The dissidents were accusing other ministers of being 'enymeys to the Lord, not only paganish but anti-christian . . . we must kill them with the word of the Lord . . . breake them in peeces as shivered with a rod of iron . . . there is whoredom in Ehraim, Israel is defiled' – and these were fellow Puritans! The tone is familiar to anyone who has stumbled across the

arcane disputes of modern Protestant sects, or Trotskyist factions for
that matter.

Anne Hutchinson was duly arraigned in the Fall of 1637 before
Winthrop and the local magistracy in the colony's general court, with
various ministers queueing up to offer testimony, to interrogate and
then, edgily, to denounce her. The accusations were that she had
encouraged sedition, held meetings 'not comely in the sight of God or
fitting for her sex' and, worse, had 'disparaged all ministers in our
land'. If they expected to confound the midwife, they were mistaken.
The transcript shows she largely got the better of her accusers. You can
hear their exasperation:

> 'We are your judges and not you.'
> 'I deny it because I have brought more arguments than you
> have.'
> 'Why, this is not to be suffered . . .'[5]

She threw the court into consternation on its second day by
demanding that her accusers give testimony against her under oath –
and taking the Lord's name in vain was a sin. The clergy havered and
it seemed as though the case was collapsing before their eyes. Then
she overreached herself, claiming as justification for her demand that
God himself had instructed her. It was one thing to claim a covenant
with the Lord, another that he spoke directly to a woman. Winthrop
ordered her expulsion from the colony. 'I desire to know wherefore I
am banished?' she asked plaintively. 'Say no more,' he famously
replied, doubtless with relief. 'The court knows wherefore and is
satisfied.'

Hutchinson tried to recant but it was too late and did her no good.
She and some of her followers were banished down the coast to
Rhode Island where, when she suffered a miscarriage six months later
– 'innumerable distinct bodies in the form of a globe, not much unlike
the swims of some fish . . . confusedly knit together by so many
strings', a doctor reported back to Winthrop gloatingly – the
'monstrous birth' was taken as a sign of God's condign punishment.
When she and her family were murdered during an Indian raid while
they were living in what is now the Bronx six years later, this too was

ascribed to the Divinity. 'These people had cast off ordinances and churches,' sniffed Winthrop.[6] They deserved all they got.

God was in everything and he could be vicious. After a man who had worked building a mill dam on a Sunday lost his five-year-old daughter the following day when she drowned in a well, he was told that it was no more than the work of 'the righteous hand of God for His profaning His holy day against the checks of his own conscience', and he and the congregation accepted it.

But others were sailing into Boston harbour to challenge the Puritan order. Quakers started arriving in the 1650s with their subversive resistance to authority, in the Church and in society: 'They preached not Jesus Christ but themselves, yea they preached the Lord Jesus to be themselves.' Sometimes they walked naked through the streets, at others they smashed bottles in church to demonstrate that the preachers were empty vessels. Extraordinarily, they even allowed women to preach during services – not even Anne Hutchinson had done that – they proclaimed religious tolerance, they criticised the settlers' treatment of the Native Indians and they even attacked the practice of slavery. All 'damnable heresies . . . abominable idolatrys to the scandall of religion, hazard of souls and provocation of divine jealousie'. Quakers were banished and at least four were whipped to death in the colony until the English king, Charles II, eventually intervened to put a stop to it: a measure of toleration imposed from England.

It was in this dank and arid commonwealth, surrounded by the darkness of the forest, the scourge of disease, the regular threat of harvest failure and starvation and the incursions of predatory Indians, a society suffocating with superstition and stifled by religious and intellectual obscurantism, filled with fear and scared of divine anger, that the most notorious and – some would say archetypal example – of early American paranoia occurred: the Salem witch trials of 1692.

Witches were particularly terrifying because they were hidden and powerful. You couldn't see them coming, they disguised themselves in all sorts of ways, and they were everywhere among you, hideous women, wreaking destruction, seducing you from your Christian allegiance, sometimes using their sexual wiles and always secretly proselytising for Satan. They did all the things that the covenant with God was supposed to prevent: 'They swarm about us like the frogs of

Egypt, even in the most retired of our chambers,' exclaimed Cotton Mather.

'Are we at our boards? There will be devils to tempt us into sensuality. Are we in our beds? There will be devils to tempt us unto carnality. The devil is come down in great wrath. Awake, awake then I beseech you,' Deodat Lawson preached in Salem.

The scare began in Salem Village, the poor, rural and isolated end of the town of Salem, outside Boston, where Roger Williams had once been pastor, when Betty, the nine-year-old daughter of the local minister Samuel Parris, and her eleven-year-old cousin Abigail Williams, probably assisted by other friends and possibly aided by the family's long-serving Amero-Indian, Caribbean slave called Tituba, began to relieve the boredom of a dark winter's day by playing at fortune-telling to predict what sort of husband they would have. It was something they knew to be wicked and dangerous, but they did it anyway. They broke an egg into a bowl of water to see what shapes the white made and were scared when it apparently assumed the shape of what they took to be a coffin.

The girls began to complain that they had seen witches and evil spirits and were being tormented by them. When they saw Tituba they burst into fits and terrifying screams, claiming she had baked a witch cake – rye mixed with a girl's urine – and fed it to the Parrises' dog, which was evidently now satanically possessed. The slave, who was probably a light-skinned Arawak Indian and had been purchased in Barbados fourteen years earlier, has, interestingly, through the course of history, come to be described as black. In the nineteenth century, historians routinely took to describing her partner John Indian as a common law husband.

Fingers, says Morone, first pointed towards women who were emblematic of every witch hunt: the poor, the deviant, the member of a foreign tribe. Under interrogation, Tituba cracked and admitted to hurting the children, seeing the devil's book, and even riding to Boston with other witches on a broomstick. Following leading questioning, she confirmed all her interrogators' worst fears.

The girls' hysterics and, as they developed, their denunciations terrified first Mr Parris and then his credulous congregation and, in gathering numbers, local women and some men were pointed out as witches and imprisoned – sixty-six within three months, twenty-three of them also accused separately of sexual crimes – until the jail was so full it could not hold them all. Demons were everywhere: a little yellow bird, a large white dog which unaccountably followed a preacher, cats, a hairy-faced, long-nosed figure, even Old Nick himself in the shape of 'a black man with an hat'.

The girls were implicitly believed, even when the court realised they were lying and even as some began to notice that they were able to turn on their hysterics at will.

Modern historians point to the fact that the community was living in a time of plague and uncertainty. At the start of the year, Massachusetts was without a governor and its inhabitants were fearful of being absorbed into a much larger dominion of New England where saints did not necessarily prevail. The colony's population was growing increasingly diverse and the villagers of Salem appear to have been a particularly truculent and introspective lot. They were both resentful of being controlled from Salem town and in continual warfare with the ministers such as Parris who had been sent to officiate over them.

The witch fear may even have provided a fortuitous opportunity for local Puritan ministers to reassert their control over their unruly flock by generating supernatural fears, though there is no reason to believe they did it particularly cynically, for they too believed in the reality of demonic possession and were as credulous as their parishioners. If they did attempt to manipulate the crisis, it was a strategy that backfired spectacularly, ultimately discrediting the Puritans and undermining their authority.

The girls' hysteria must have been terrifying to watch, especially for those at the receiving end of their accusations. The preacher Deodat Lawson recorded:

Sometimes in their fits they have had their tongues drawn out of their mouths to a fearful length, their heads turned very much over their shoulders and while they have been so strained in their fits and had their arms and legs etc. wrested as if they were quite dislocated, the blood hath gushed plentifully out of their mouths for a considerable time together . . . I saw several together thus violently strained and bleeding in their fits to my very great astonishment that my fellow mortals should be so grievously distressed by the invisible powers of darkness. For certainly all considerate persons who beheld these things must needs be convinced that their motions in their fits were preternatural and involuntary.[7]

Anyone who has seen *The Exorcist* probably has some idea of what it was like.

The hysteria may have been an example of group psychosis, or possibly prompted by a fear of being found out as the crisis developed. In the late 1990s when I was a journalist in Brussels, a sudden panic about the safety of Coca Cola swept Belgium and France after media reports that groups of teenage girls in several vicinities had claimed to have been poisoned by the drink one after the other. Tests eventually showed that there was absolutely nothing wrong with the composition of the cola, at which point the scare immediately subsided. It could also be of course that the Salem girls implicitly believed the allegations they were making, and certainly only one of them is ever recorded as having expressed remorse.

The accusations flowed almost entirely from girls living in the poorer, rural end of Salem and were aimed almost entirely at women who lived in the more prosperous part of the settlement. Elderly, bedridden women were accused, as was a five-year-old girl named Dorcas Good, whose mother Sarah was one of the first to be hanged. Dorcas's fate is almost unimaginably cruel and inhumane: she was carted off with the rest to be thrown into the basement jail in Boston where she was chained to a wall, in the dark and the cold, for the next eight months. Her father later said she 'was so hardly used and terrified that she hath ever since been very chargeable, having little or no reason to govern herself'. By that he meant that for the rest of her short life he had to pay for her to be looked after.

Sarah Good herself was regarded as pugnacious and recalcitrant, though she was probably just feisty. She was a woman whose family had once been relatively prosperous – her father had been an innkeeper – but who by the time of the trial was married to an out-of-work weaver and had been reduced to begging. She had Dorcas and was pregnant with a baby who would die while in custody with her. Professor Morone says: 'She is usually described as the perfect stereotype of a witch – a quarrelsome, pipe-smoking hag. Another modern stereotype might fit even better – "welfare mother".'[8]

It was clear from her interrogation by John Hathorne (a successful merchant and community leader who was an ancestor of the novelist Nathaniel Hawthorne) both that Sarah was utterly bemused by the allegations against her, and that he explicitly believed from the outset that she must be guilty as charged. The transcript says:

> 'Sarah Good, what evil spirit have you familiarity with?'
> 'None.'
> 'Have you made no contract with the devil?'
> 'No.'
> 'Why do you hurt these children?'
> 'I do not hurt them. I scorn it.'
> 'Who do you employ then to do it?'
> 'I employ nobody.'
> 'What creatures do you employ then?'
> 'No creature, but I am falsely accused.'

The transcript adds that Hathorne then turned to Good's four child accusers and asked them if she was the person who had been hurting them: 'so they all did look upon her and said this was one of the persons that did torment them', and 'presently they were all tormented'.

When, some months later, Good and four other women were dragged to the scaffold, surrounded and harried all the way by jeering villagers and the women's accusers, still screaming and writhing, the executioner Nicholas Noyes called on her to repent and confess. Even as he twitched the rope around her neck, Noyes told Good that she was a witch and she knew it. She shouted back: 'You are a liar. I am no more a witch than you are a wizard and if you take away my life, God will give you blood to drink.' This came to pass, according to local tradition, when Noyes died some years later of an internal haemorrhage, with blood spewing from his mouth.[9]

Twenty suspects were executed that summer and a further four died in jail before sceptical questions began to be asked about why

Salem suddenly seemed to be filled with witches. There were also concerns that some obviously good people, all swearing their innocence, had been executed while others, including Tituba, who confessed to being witches, were allowed to go free – in her case to be sold on to another owner by Minister Parris. Even by the standards of the seventeenth century, there seemed to be a degree of naïvety going on, with the word of accusers being implicitly accepted without corroboration. But when their accusations came to be directed at the wife of the governor of Massachusetts, Sir William Phipps, newly arrived from England, it was time to call a halt.

The Revd John Hale wrote: 'Those that were concerned grew amazed at the numbers and quality of the persons accused and feared that Satan by his wiles had enwrapped innocent persons under the imputation of that crime. And, at last, it was evidently seen that there must be a stop put, or the generation of the children of God would fall under that condemnation.'[10]

The girls attempted one last bout of hysterics: their fits directed towards an old woman they met while crossing a bridge but when they were ignored, they abruptly stopped. The preacher Increase Mather, father of Cotton, sagely noted in his pamphlet *Cases of Conscience Concerning Evil Spirits Personating Men*, circulated that autumn: 'Better that ten suspected witches should escape, than that one innocent person should be condemned.'

Governor Phipps consulted the local clergy about what he should do but, when they urged continued prosecutions, ignored them and quietly reprieved the remaining condemned. It was, the mid-twentieth-century historian Perry Miller said, the last time that a governor of Massachusetts would in an hour of hesitation, formally and officially, ask the advice of the churches.[11] Indeed, ministers like Cotton Mather and his father soon found themselves, to their outrage, covered in ridicule. One pamphleteer, Robert Calef, added insult to injury by reporting that Mather had suggestively touched up one of the girls, Margaret Rule, while she was having a fit. He had 'rubb'd her stomach (her breasts not covered with the Bed-clothes) and bid others to do so too'. It was, exclaimed Mather, 'a lie contrived . . . to make people believe a smutty thing of me'. He tried suing Calef for libel, but ultimately did not show up in court.

Calef's conclusion – 'And now to sum up all in a few words, we have seen a bigoted zeal, stirring up a blind and most bloody rage, not against enemies or irreligious profligate persons, but . . . against as virtuous and religious as any' – has been generally endorsed by history. He added: 'The accusations of these, from their spectral sight, being the chief evidence against those that suffered. In which accusations they were upheld by both magistrates and ministers, so long as they apprehended themselves in no danger.'

It may have been too much to expect ministers like Cotton Mather to express contrition (though the controversy dogged him for the rest of his career), but one of the girl accusers, Ann Putnam, did, many years later as an adult:

> I desire to be humbled before God . . . that I then being in my childhood should by such a providence of God be made an instrument for accusing of several persons of a grievous crime whereby their lives were taken away from them, whom I now have just grounds and good reason to believe they were innocent persons and that it was a great delusion of Satan that deceived me in that sad time, whereby I justly fear I have been instrumental with others though ignorantly and unwittingly to bring upon myself and this land the guilt of innocent blood.[12]

The witch hunt was a grave embarrassment: 'Salem superstition and sorcery . . . not fit to be named in a land of such light as New England is . . . ages will not wear off that reproach and those stains,' these being the contemporary words of the Boston merchant Thomas Brattle.[13]

The crisis in Salem helped to undermine the authority of the Puritan ministers who had tried to establish the first community of saints in New England and it was the last time that witches were ever sought out in the English-speaking world. But it was far from being the last witch hunt in American history. And only four-score years later, a new generation of young men, the finest intellectual flower of the Enlightenment, would attempt to establish a wholly new Constitution with a view of the place of God that would have scandalised their forebears.

4

No King but King Jesus

'We formed our Constitution without any acknowledgment of God; without any recognition of His mercies to us, as a people, of his government, or even of His existence. The Convention by which it was formed never asked even once His direction, or His blessing upon their labors. Thus we commenced our national existence under the present system, without God.'

The Revd Timothy Dwight, Yale College Chapel, 1812

Asked why the Constitution did not mention God, Alexander Hamilton replied: 'We forgot.'

Judge Roy Moore, former Chief Justice of the Supreme Court of Alabama, I was told, would be pleased to give me an interview. He was currently running for the Republican nomination for state governor, so I'd have to catch him on the stump, but if I could make it to his Wednesday lunchtime campaign stop, he'd surely give me a few moments of his time. I'd find him at the Po' Folks Restaurant in the town of Enterprise, addressing the members of the Coffee County Republican Women's Club.

Enterprise was not exactly where I wanted to go, being diametrically at the opposite end of the state from where I was in Birmingham. It was 180 miles away, down in the south-east corner, near the Florida border, but a chance to meet the judge was too good an opportunity to miss. I set out early, driving through the early summer morning heat, across the flat farmland of Alabama shimmering in the haze, through villages of neat bungalows and trailer homes, past barrack-like churches, fenced-in social housing estates like prison camps and deserted gas stations.

Judge Moore was a key man to find. He had been the judge who made headlines around the world a couple of years before after insisting on placing in the foyer of his court a two-and-a-half-ton marble block whose top was carved in the shape of an open Bible incised with the Ten Commandments. This ostentatious proclamation of faith, which he had paid for, was in open defiance of America's long-established doctrine of separating Church and state, and, after Moore had repeatedly defied judicial attempts to order him to get rid of it, he had eventually been removed from his position by the Supreme Court.

In the circumstances, there was little chance of him going quietly. Outside the courthouse in Montgomery, Christian groups from as far away as California and Illinois gathered in their hundreds to preach, pray and expostulate against the iniquities of secularists and liberal judges. National politicians and leaders of the Religious Right such as James Dobson, head of Focus on the Family, had flown in to offer their support. Dr Dobson told them: 'The liberal elite and the judges at the highest level and some members of the media are determined to remove every evidence of faith in God from the entire culture. They are determined to control more and more of our private lives and it is time we said enough is enough.'

The crowds stayed through the night and one wheelchair-bound elderly woman named Karen Kennedy was arrested after she attempted to chain herself to the granite. 'In the face of all our travails Americans can take hope that God has given us men like Roy S. Moore,' proclaimed the Right-wing polemicist Ann Coulter.

Judge Moore saw himself igniting a godly insurrection: 'The sparks of hope and faith from those impromptu rallies on the steps of the Alabama Judicial Building ignited a fire that continues to burn across this land. Those who came to Montgomery to protest the removal of a monument were witnesses to another movement, a movement of God . . . I had stood for the God who never loses and the law I had stood to uphold.'[1]

He even wrote a paean of praise to the Founding Fathers for creating the birthright of every American. There could be no doubting its fervour, though its metre left something to be desired:

So with a firm reliance on Divine Providence for protection,
They pledged their sacred honour and sought His wise direction,

They lifted an appeal to God for all the world to see,
And declared their independence forever to be free.

I am glad they're not with us to see the mess we're in,
How we've given up our righteousness for a life of indulgent sin,
For when abortion isn't murder and sodomy is deemed a right,
Then evil is now called good and darkness is now called light.

While truth and law were founded on the God of all Creation,
Man now, through law, denies the truth and calls it 'separation',
No longer does man see a need for God when he's in full control,
For the only truth self-evident is in the latest poll.[2]

Judge Moore's defiance did not impress the Supreme Court in Washington, which decided he had violated the Alabama Canons of Judicial Ethics and, as he had given no assurance that he would not do it again, ordered his removal from office. The state ethics panel duly ruled: 'Any person who undertakes a solemn oath to carry out a public trust must act in a manner that demonstrates both respect for and compliance with established rules of law of the institution that person serves. Here, however, we are faced with a situation in which the highest judicial officer of this state has decided to defy a court order'.[3] Even so, there were some in the state court who wanted him to stay.

Judge Moore's monument was also, eventually, removed but not put into storage. Irreverently, it became known as Roy's Rock and it toured the country with its owner, like a holy relic on a flatbed truck, to be exposed before the faithful at churches and even in supermarket parking lots. Videos extolling the judge and his stand for Christ were sold through evangelical outlets. 'The Ten Commandments judge' embarked upon the conservative lecture circuit to lucrative effect, becoming what one Alabamian political scientist described as 'a rock star of the Christian Right'.[4]

Just why Judge Moore, unlike all other Christian judges in the previous 200 years, felt he needed to make such a defiant proclamation of faith when he did, at such a risk to his career, remains slightly unclear, even from his book, characteristically entitled *So Help Me God: The Ten Commandments, Judicial Tyranny and the Battle for*

Religious Freedom. This is by turns legalistic ('The only thing I ever said I would do again was to acknowledge God') and moralistic ('I disobeyed because I was ethically bound to do so by my oath of office that forbade me from following an unlawful order').

What is clear was that he believed Christianity was under attack. Michelle Goldberg quotes him telling an audience in Tennessee: 'For forty years we have wandered like the children of Israel. In homes and schools across our land, it's time for Christians to take a stand. This is not a nation established on the principles of Buddha or Hinduism. Our faith is not Islam. What we follow is not the Koran but the Bible. This is a Christian nation.'[5]

In any event, Judge Moore had achieved martyrdom and the Christian Right had gained a victim of the forces of liberal secularism. Now, with polls registering double-digit leads, he was stomping his home state to address his supporters – possibly the most famous Alabamian since George Wallace. To gain a new platform, he was running for Wallace's old office: standing to be the Republican Party's candidate for governor in the state primary against the incumbent, Bob Riley, himself a former US Congressman and a Christian conservative. The governor had already been sufficiently rattled to make an unscheduled appearance on the US version of *Pop Idol* to endorse a local Alabama contestant in order to show how 'with it' he was.

Enterprise, home of the Boll Weevil Monument rather than the Ten Commandments, proved to be a pleasant, anonymous town, spread out along the highway and lined with chain restaurants, of which the Po' Folks was one. It was a folksy, self-consciously Southern sort of place, built like a barn, adorned with old tin advertisements and ancient farm implements and decorated with archly badly spelled messages. Tucking into their ribs and hamburgers out at the front was the normal clientele in farm dungarees and polyester business suits, while in a backroom, gathering around tables covered in gingham cloths, queueing for their iced teas and southern fried chicken and awaiting the candidate, were the Republican ladies and their spouses.

They were definitely not themselves po' folks. They had driven up to the parking lot in large sedans and shiny SUVs and had come in their Sunday best, as if for a church meeting. Almost all of them were white, all were resolutely middle class, and a fair proportion were elderly. The accents were 'wha' ah *do* declaire . . .' They whiled the time away listening to candidates for various local political offices, all promising to do better than whoever was doing the job at the moment.

The candidate himself was an hour late. It turned out he had come from even further upstate than I had, driven in a heavy Lincoln sedan by his bodyguard Leonard Holyfield, cousin of the more famous boxer, who would be the only black man in the room during the meeting, and accompanied by his trusty press officer, a former local radio presenter named Jack Holland. Dressed in a blazer and seersucker shirt, a small replica badge of the Ten Commandments on his lapel, Holland was part PR man and part evangeliser. 'I felt God was telling me to do this,' he told me confidentially.

Up at the top table Judge Moore was getting into his stride. He had received a strong but not overwhelming ovation. His message was that of insurgent candidates everywhere: his rival had been sucked into corrupt politics and been suckered up by special interest groups in the big city in Montgomery, evidently a place not unlike Gomorrah, while he himself was going to stand up for the working people of the state. He did not have the governor's money for his campaign, but people were placing him in their hearts. There were too many illegal aliens being let into the country – they should just close the borders – and why should driving tests be conducted in different languages? Somewhat illogically: 'If you can't read "bridge" in Persian, you gotta problem.' The judge was not the most fluent of speakers and his answers to questions were perfunctory. 'The people of Alabama are going to get the truth and we're goin' to do everything to bring it to them if God wills it.'

Afterwards, as folk milled round the candidate, I asked one, Perry Hooper, son of the chief justice who had preceded Moore, whether he would be voting for him. Hooper smiled wryly and said: 'I don't know, I ain't made up my mind yet', though with every indication that he had and that he would be sticking with the incumbent.

I had expected a few moments with the judge, but Jack Holland suggested they would find somewhere for lunch and I could tag along behind. This was easier said than done. The judge's sedan roared out of the parking lot and down a slip road, then on to the main highway, crossed it and turned left, then doubled back at high speed, leaving me trailing in its wake. It crossed into the slip road on the other side of the highway and then did a U-turn on that as well. Either the judge was trying to lose me, I decided, or he was a victim of chronic indecision about his luncheon arrangements. Eventually we pulled up at a steak house diametrically opposite the Po' Folks.

The judge got out, adjusting his sun-glasses. 'Kept up then?' he said. I tried jocularity: 'Takes more than that to lose me,' I said. He grunted disdainfully. I had the impression that he regarded me rather as he might a stain beneath his shoe. I was certainly glad I was not appearing before him on some ungodly charge. He was, after all, the judge who had placed three children in the custody of an abusive father in preference to their lesbian mother because her homo-sexuality was 'abhorrent, immoral, detestable, a crime against nature and a violation of the laws of nature and of nature's God upon which this nation and our laws are predicated . . . The state carries the power of the sword, the power to prohibit conduct with physical penalties, such as confinement and even execution. It must use that power to prevent the subversion of children towards this lifestyle, to not encourage a criminal lifestyle.' One might tremble before such certainty.

Judge Moore was lean and leathery with, I guessed, little sense of humour or small talk.[6] In Vietnam where he had served in the Military Police, he had earned the nickname Captain America – 'they did not mean it as a compliment' – because of his habit of patrolling round camp at night armed with a sawn-off shotgun in search of marijuana smokers. Later on, he had been a professional kick boxer and worked for a time on a farm in Australia before returning home to resume his legal career.

His entry into politics had been providential – 'I am not really a politician' – just as his birth had been: 11 February 1947, which just happened to be the day after the Supreme Court handed down its judgment in *Everson* v. *Board of Education of Ewing Township*, an early ruling endorsing the constitutional separation of Church and state.

In that landmark case, which concerned the legality of using public funds to pay for the bussing of children to Church schools, actually a

Roman Catholic school in New Jersey, the justices had repeated their belief that taxation should not be used for religious purposes.[7] 'No tax in any amount large or small, can be levied to support any religious activities or institutions, whatever they may be called, or whatever form they may adopt to teach or practice religion,' wrote Justice Hugo Black, coincidentally an Alabamian and a Southern Baptist, in enunciating the court's ruling, unaware that in his home state a small boy named Roy Moore was about to be born, who would one day rise up to challenge that distinction. 'I don't think that's chance,' Moore told me gravely.

Clearly God was havering too since, despite his declaration, Justice Black had ruled in favour of state funding for transport to religious schools.

Judge Moore's profound Baptist faith really came to him, he said, following defeat in a murky campaign to be elected district attorney in 1982. 'I was done wrong by the political system. We were not an ultra religious family before, but after I ran for public office I came to a closer relationship with God. I had hard feelings towards people and I prayed about that. God touched my heart and made me forgive them.'

The steak house's teenage waitress, who had been suspiciously eyeing the immaculately dressed bodyguard Mr Holifield as he sat with us at the table, now sidled up and asked nervously about the gun sticking out of his holster. The judge waved her away impatiently. 'He's with me,' he said.

As we sat sucking our diet sodas and iced water in the steakhouse, Judge Moore suddenly started reciting large chunks of the writings of William Blackstone, the eighteenth-century British judge whose commentaries were influential for many years in shaping the common law both in England and America. Long cadences, pronounced in the judge's Alabama drawl, rattled the baseball photographs on the wall. He had evidently learned them by heart, though he was occasionally assisted in remembering them by a little booklet he had written called *Our Legal Heritage*, adorned with pictures of George Washington and the Stars and Stripes on the cover.

Blackstone was very much a man of his time, a tad reactionary even for some of his contemporaries, with his support for the reasonable physical chastisement of wives by their husbands ('the courts of law will still permit a husband to restrain a wife of her liberty in case of any gross misbehavior') and a distinctly ambiguous attitude towards slavery, but his commentaries still endured in the mind of the judge.[8] It was, of course, particularly his attitude to God that appealed: 'This law of nature, being coeval with mankind and dictated by God himself is of course superior in obligation to any other. It is binding over all the globe, in all countries and at all times; no human laws are of any validity, if contrary to this; and such of them as are valid derive all their force and all their authority, mediately or immediately, from this original.'

I was at somewhat of a disadvantage here, disgracefully having only the haziest notions of who Blackstone was or even when he lived, nor knowing that his commentaries were written in the years shortly before the American War of Independence. So I asked the judge whether he had ever been to England, or met an English lawyer. No, he had not. It would not have mattered if he had. He was in full flow by now: 'All law comes from God. Man's laws are bound by God's law. Human laws are of no validity if they are contrary to these foundations. Politicians think they are above that now. They put themselves in the place of God.'

He might not know England but he knew where it was going, with the USA following in the same direction. I asked him whether he really believed America was heading for perdition. 'That's it. We're going the same way England is now, without God. Read Blackstone: there is no law without God, no truth without God. America is watching Alabama in this and the world is watching America. The truth will spread.' Sitting in Alabama, where nine out of ten inhabitants call themselves Christians, where half are Baptists and where just 1 per cent of the population belong to non-Christian faiths, here was the judge telling me he was living in a godless country.

A quick burst from the Epistle to the Romans followed – 'read it, 1.21: that's what the Bible says will happen and it is happening' – and then there came a rumination: 'I am not running because of ambition: I am running to serve the will of God. If he judges that is not the place I serve him, well, I will probably be happy.' There was a pause before he corrected himself: 'I *will* be happy.'

I told him what Perry Hooper had said at the meeting. He almost spat: 'Pah! I know Perry Hooper's never goin' to vote for me. Do you know his father swore me into office as chief justice? They're not going to vote for me, ever.'

John Giles, head of the Christian Coalition in Alabama, told the journalist Ray Suarez: 'I would say at the outset of this election, I've always maintained it was [Moore's] to win and his to lose. When he started off he was at 29 per cent. And that was a core solid vote . . . He hasn't increased that.'[9]

The judge called for a pen and inscribed both his autobiography and the Legal Heritage booklet for me before sweeping out of the restaurant. I was left with my half-eaten and now cold hamburger and fries, watching as the sedan pulled out of the car-park on the next stage of its long haul to do the Lord's work. In the booklet he had written in a large and flowing hand: 'To Stephen, May God grant you wisdom and understanding of His law and our own!'

Three weeks later, Governor Riley won the primary easily. He would go on to win re-election in November 2006. God had obviously spoken.

By the early decades of the eighteenth century it has been calculated that over 60 per cent of the British settlers living in the New England and Chesapeake Bay areas were believers, or living under the control of the descendants of the Puritan ascendancy, and despite the fact that there was little access outside the cities to a range of different churches, there was already a diversity of worship across the colonies as a whole.

In such circumstances, none could claim absolute precedence. Catholics could make for Maryland – whose ruling family before the Glorious Revolution back home in 1688 allowed religious toleration – Quakers could settle in Pennsylvania where there was also tolerance and Baptists, and other dissenters found welcome surroundings in the settlements of Rhode Island and later in North Carolina. Your local choice might be limited, but settlers thrusting westwards into the Appalachians could take their own religions with them.

More importantly, although the Church of England became the state church by law established in the colonies after 1700 – just as it had back home after the overthrow of the Catholic James II in 1688 –

it never quite managed to become the establishment religion. Some states legislated for their own denominations, but without lasting success: Massachusetts being the last to disestablish its official, Congregational, church in 1833.

The Anglican Church's reach was too limited – there were too few clergy – and it had difficulty imposing itself anyway among so many colonists who were themselves dissenters. One of the reasons many of them had left home was to get away from conformity with the Church of England and to be able to worship as they wished. In America, the established Church lacked both the aristocratic social superstructure and the bolstering framework of legal obligations and penalties for failing to observe the rites that it had in England. It also lacked the authority to punish dissenters or put them to death, as the governments of Catholic Europe were doing at this time. Nonconformism in America sometimes carried social penalties, but legal ones such as execution were not among them. Sects could be open, proselytise for new members and thereby flourish.

When men pushed westwards therefore, few of them took an allegiance to the Church of England with them into the wilderness, but instead it was muscular Presbyterianism and small-scale Congregationalism, sects that did not require the formal panoply of mitred and bewigged bishops, but placed priority on the individual's piety as leading to his own salvation. This was both convenient and useful. Nor, confronted by the warlike Iroquois, Creeks, Seminoles and Cherokees in the forests, did the early settlers generally retain their Quaker pacifism.

This lack of a religious establishment was and has remained one of the most significant features of US religiosity. Americans change their religious adherence and choose their churches much more easily than their ancestors could back in England and Europe. Allegiances shift; churches and parishes rise and fall; churchmen must become much more entrepreneurial to attract worshippers and cannot rely solely on custom and habit to maintain their congregations.

The Bushes are a case in point: the family is Episcopalian – Anglican – in background and upbringing and, when they are in town, President George H. W. Bush and his wife Barbara still attend St Martin's Church in Houston as good White Anglo-Saxon Protestants

tend to do. But President George W. Bush himself is now a
Methodist, following his conversion and renunciation of alcohol in
the mid-1980s while his brother Jeb, governor of Florida, is a
Catholic. These denominational differences in one family mirror a
tension that has existed more widely throughout US society for 300
years. The disparities of style between Bush *père*, president Number
41: patrician, haughty and slightly dessicated, diligent but ineffectual,
absorbed by foreign rather than domestic policy, and Bush *fils*,
president Number 43: folksy, demotic, self-conscious, electorally
astute and wily, may be remarkable in a father and his son, but they
echo the traditional edginess between High Church Episcopalianism
and Low Church Nonconformity down the generations in US society.

This personal freedom of denominational choice was already
evident in the eighteenth century and played a significant part in the
development of religious and consequently of political thought in the
colonies. John Adams, the second president, son of a church deacon
and descendant of English Puritan settlers, was a sturdy Congregationalist, but he saw no problem in attending the services of a
number of religious denominations. While he was a member of the
Massachusetts delegation to the Congress in Philadelphia in 1776, a
town that had no Congregationalist chapel, his journal reports him
whiling away his Sundays by attending services in Anglican,
Methodist, Baptist, Presbyterian, Quaker, German Moravian and
even Catholic churches – though the latter admittedly only out of
'curiosity and good company'. He did not like the Mass much, but
approved the priest's 'good, short, moral essay' to the congregation
and decided the experience was awe-ful and affecting.[10]

This was pretty ecumenical of him, as well as showing an intellectual
curiosity, but it was not entirely unusual. In the words of the historian
Professor John Murrin of Princeton University (itself founded in the
mid-eighteenth century as the country's first non-denominational
college to train both Presbyterians and Episcopalians): 'Because it
lacked the fixed structures of European societies, people could try out
in the wilderness a whole range of ideas and experiments impossible to
attempt in Europe. Some had a liberating vision that we still find
bracing. The Quakers of west New Jersey drafted and implemented a
constitutional system that was as radical as anything yet tried by

Europeans. Other novelties could be extremely repressive . . . [such as] the resurrection of chattel slavery on a gigantic scale.'[11]

This relative intellectual adventurousness and religious freedom helps to explain how it was that within a lifetime – though admittedly an unusually long one for the period – the American colonists could proceed from hanging women as suspected witches to adopting one of the most sophisticated, secular, philosophical and political documents ever devised by man, the newly independent country's great Constitution, an instrument of government that has now survived the evolution of America for over two hundred years. It has done so, much to the frustration of some recent neo-con evangelicals, without even a passing mention of God and only a perfunctory reference to religion.

Even before the War of Independence, one of the most striking examples of the burgeoning religious liberation of colonial American life was the so-called Great Awakening of the 1730s and 1740s, an outpouring of fervour and revivalism that has periodically repeated itself once or twice a century ever since. Something similar happened in England at the same time. In England it gave rise to Methodism. In America it helped to shape the coming revolution.

The first Great Awakening provoked hysteria and rioting and a frenzy of competing sects and preachers across New England. Arguably, the unsettling vision it provoked – of the imminence of heaven and the desperation for salvation – foreshadowed the political upheaval that followed as the colonies sought their political independence from Britain a few years later.

The revival began as a manifestation of frustration and discontent with the complacent ministers and the uninspiring preaching to be heard in the old sects. It was sparked in the town of Northampton, Massachusetts, in 1734 by two unexplained deaths that came to be seen by a younger generation of ministers as a manifestation of divine frustration with the lewdness and general worthlessness of the population. The theme was given voice and urgency by the local preacher Jonathan Edwards in a series of characteristic and compelling jeremiads: hell was gaping, the flames were gathering, and all the benighted population had to preserve them was the 'uncovenanted, unobliged forbearance of an incensed God'.

Edwards told his congregation in a peculiarly low, though evidently compelling, monotone – perhaps he would have been better suited to the conversational style of the modern televangelists – that they needed God's saving grace: 'You have an extraordinary opportunity . . . Christ has thrown the door of mercy wide open and stands crying with a loud voice . . . God [is] gathering in His elect . . . Awake and fly from the wrath to come . . . look not behind you.'[12] They could make all the difference to their own eternal destiny. They individually could save themselves. With only small modification, similar words and identical sentiments beam out from some evangelical broadcasts today.

In the 1730s, the congregations laughed and screamed and sang and spoke in tongues when they heard such ideas. And when the charismatic English preacher George Whitefield arrived at about the same time on one of his regular speaking tours, people walked miles to hear him – 'he was strangely flocked after by all sorts of persons', sniffed Charles Chauncy, the president of Harvard, who was not a fan. When Whitefield got to Boston, five people were killed in the crush and his farewell sermon on the common attracted 20,000 people, considerably more than the entire population of the city.

Once again, as with Anne Hutchinson a century before, though with a different perspective, the revivalists were preaching a subversive gospel: that their audiences did not need preachers to get to heaven. God's grace would sweep them up in a wave of emotion and bliss. It was a message that was both ecumenical and undermining of the long-established ministers with their tedious textual analysis and disapproval of any departure from their narrow paths of self-righteousness. It undermined both the established order and the idea of an elect covenant of saints. 'What can be expected but confusion, when church members will forsake their own pastors for every passing preacher?' demanded Chauncy.[13]

One of the most extraordinary of these local passing preachers was James Davenport, a graduate of Yale, whose 'wild, angry and emotional' sermons often anathematised the shortcomings of other ministers in a manner calculated to make him deeply unpopular with them, if not necessarily with their congregations. His outpourings were interrupted by his occasional forays into the crowd and by their spontaneous outbursts of singing. The songs were apparently often repetitive and trite, a phenomenon not unknown among some evangelicals even today.

In New London, Connecticut, Davenport lit a bonfire and urged his followers to burn their vanities. They incinerated books and tossed cloaks on to the blaze. Then Davenport became entirely carried away and pulled off his trousers preparatory to hurling them into the flames too, until he was stopped by a colleague so he did not 'strutt about bare-arsed'. That was quite enough. The authorities decided he was mad and threw him into jail instead.[14]

Such wild passions were hugely alarming and out of control as far as the magistracy was concerned: not only was no work getting done, but people were questioning the established order and getting ideas above their station. Even women were preaching, and some, it was suggested, were allowing other, even more disreputable, passions to get out of hand. A hostile contemporary cartoon of the boss-eyed Whitefield, preaching with a suggestively large bag of cash in his hand, has the women in his audience exclaiming in speech bubbles ecstatic remarks such as: 'I wish his Spirit was in my flesh' and 'Lift up ye horn of thy salvation unto us'.[15]

'What is now seen in America and especially in New England may prove the dawn of a glorious day . . . so often foretold in Scripture,' wrote Jonathan Edwards enthusiastically. God's intention was that this would be the beginning of something vastly great.

And so it came eventually to pass. Where people could start by questioning the *bona fides* and integrity of their ministers and measuring their own opinions against them, they could go on to question other things that were part of the established order, such as taxation. Partly as a result of the Great Awakening, new young men – 'New Lights' – were coming forward and new schools were being established to educate them: Princeton (where Edwards was president), Brown University in Rhode Island for Baptists, Rutgers and Dartmouth. From following new preachers it was a short step to endorsing new politicians (sometimes they were the same people) and mobilising to challenge the authorities over political issues.

When the British government imposed the Stamp Act in 1765 – the first spark on the road to the War of Independence – the imposition was meekly accepted by the old lights represented by the governor and the upper house of the state of Connecticut. Both promptly found themselves turfed out of office by the new lights. Insurgency could work; new, diverse voices could make themselves heard and get their way.

The religious allegiances of those who fought in the American War of Independence, which finally broke out into warfare in the spring of 1775 after several years of developing tension, have tended to be overlooked except by the most specialist of scholars. They have found, however, that supporters of the American Revolution were drawn from precisely those Calvinist denominations that had endorsed the Great Awakening: the Baptists, the Congregationalists and Presbyterians, while their Loyalist opponents, supporters of British rule and those trying to remain neutral, tended to be Anglicans, Quakers and Methodists who had not.

The descendants of the Puritans who fought the war against the British naturally saw its outcome, the defeat of the mightiest power on earth, as a sign of God's favour towards them, a proof that they had divine approval for their actions. Such an argument was propounded by the most intellectually distinguished minister in the colonies, the Scottish-born divine John Witherspoon, who was the contemporary president of Princeton and ultimately one of the signatories of the Declaration of Independence. Their liberty was God's gift, in recognition of their religiousness: 'So in times of difficulty and trial, it is in the man of piety and inward principle that we may expect to find the uncorrupted patriot, the useful citizen and the invincible soldier. God grant that in America true religion and civil liberty may be inseparable and that the unjust attempts to destroy the one may in the issue tend to the support and establishment of both.'[16] There are some who sense the continued working out of God's principle incarnated in George W. Bush today.

The British eventually departed, their band playing 'The World Turned Upside Down', following the surrender at Yorktown in October 1781, leaving the institutions of the new country to be shaped almost from scratch. But this had not been a revolution to overturn the existing order. The men who had led it were landowners, businessmen and lawyers and they had absolutely no wish to upset the social hierarchy when they were already the beneficiaries of it. Nor did they remotely consider trying to change the way people thought by establishing a new religion as some of the revolutionaries they inspired in France would attempt to do a few years later.

On the contrary, the men who drew up the Constitution certainly by and large endorsed the view that citizens should think for themselves and be guided by their own consciences. In this they were influenced more by the Enlightenment and secular philosophers such as John Locke rather than by ancestral or religious pieties, even though the Constitution undoubtedly drew on the Puritan tradition of the contract. This, however, would be a social and political contract, not a theological one. All religious observance was to be protected, not just that officially sanctioned by the state. Indeed the state was not to be allowed to discriminate: it would be officially secular, allowing each citizen the freedom to choose their own form of worship. This was a remarkable innovation, especially beneficial to minority sects.

What is striking is not just the phraseology of the Constitution's ringing and unambiguous first amendment – 'Congress shall make no law respecting an establishment of religion or prohibiting the free exercise thereof' – but the fact that the Constitution of 1787, which was largely shaped by the future president James Madison, makes no mention of God or Jesus Christ. Nor does it use the circumlocutions favoured by some of the states in drawing up their individual constitutions at the same time, such as Supreme Being. This was not an oversight but quite deliberate. Equally remarkably, there was very little opposition at the time to this absence of references to God, and such as there was was unsuccessful.

The Federal Convention that drafted the Constitution in Philadelphia during the summer of 1787 consisted of fifty-five delegates from twelve states, Rhode Island having declined to attend. They were all men, of course, and most of them were strikingly young. They were also drawn, naturally enough in the circumstances of the time, from the very classes that the modern Religious Right tends to view with the deepest suspicion in the Washington of today. Two were college presidents, three had been professors, twenty-six were graduates (several of them had been educated at Princeton under Witherspoon), nine were foreign born, and four had been trained in the law in London. Five were under the age of thirty and most of the rest were in their thirties or forties: Madison himself being thirty-six. There were only four members aged over sixty and Benjamin Franklin was by far the oldest at eighty-one.[17]

Absent from their number was Thomas Jefferson, who had drafted the Declaration of Independence eleven years before, with its resolutely unpuritan assertion of 'self-evident', i.e. natural truths, that all men are created equal and endowed by their Creator with certain inalienable rights among (which) are Life, Liberty and the Pursuit of Happiness. He was Ambassador to Paris in 1787. But there is no doubt that he was kept as closely informed as it was possible to be in the late eighteenth century, and his extensive correspondence with his friend Madison survives. In any event, his influence was clear and he remains an iconic figure in the birth of America.

In their writings, many of the leading Founding Fathers were scathing about religious institutions. 'Christianity is the most perverted system that ever shone on man,' wrote Jefferson; 'light-houses are more useful than churches,' said Franklin; and Madison opined that the fruits of Christianity were 'pride and indolence in the clergy [and] ignorance and servility in the laity'. Lest there should be any doubt, John Adams, the second president, signed a treaty in 1797 which explicitly stated: 'As the Government of the United States of America is not, in any sense, founded on the Christian religion . . .' It is hard to believe he did not really mean it.

These, then, were the Founding Fathers, America's secular saints. Professor Murrin writes: 'Jefferson and Madison along with George Washington, John Adams, Benjamin Franklin and nearly all the Founding Fathers claimed to be Christians; but, by virtue of any standard of doctrinal orthodoxy, hardly any of them was. They demanded the right to think for themselves on the most sensitive questions of faith, doctrine and morals but they did not try to impose their conclusions on others by force.'[18] There seems to have been only one genuine evangelical Christian, who could claim to have been 'born again', among them, Richard Bassett of Delaware – Roger Sherman of Connecticut may have been another – but Bassett never spoke during the convention.

What at least some of the key leaders were was Deists, believers in a Creator who started the universe off and then stood back to let men get on with it. They had doubts about aspects of the Bible, particularly the unverifiable bits such as Jesus's miracles, and an extreme reluctance to bow the knee to a church hierarchy or to give it a special, privileged place in the life of the nation. They saw this as a means of safeguarding religious and individual freedom, removing the threat of oppression or coercion over worshippers, not as an attempt to remove religious belief altogether and, by and large, the theory has worked.

It was to be a liberation for both churches and individuals, a decisive break with the established, authoritarian regimes of old Europe. Jefferson wrote: 'History, I believe, furnishes no example of a priest-ridden people maintaining a free civil government. This marks the lowest grade of ignorance of which their civil as well as religious leaders will always avail themselves for their own purposes.' In drawing up the 1786 Virginia Act for Establishing Religious Freedom, he wrote: 'The opinions of men are not the object of civil government, nor under its jurisdiction . . . truth is great and will prevail if left to herself.'

This did not mean that the Founding Fathers were not fascinated by religion, or did not see themselves as Christians. Long into his old age, Jefferson sat up late at night at his hilltop home in Virginia, Monticello, cutting out those bits of the Gospels he believed to be untrue and pasting the rest together in his own expurgated version, leaving just the passages he believed to be credible. The work he eventually published was called *The Life and Morals of Jesus of Nazareth*. Yet the bits he excised are among those considered most indispensable by Bible believers to this day: there was no virgin birth, no Holy Ghost, no Holy Trinity, no miracles, no resurrection, no assertion that belief in such matters would bring salvation.

As Jefferson's biographer E. M. Halliday says: 'Jesus had turned out to be, of all things, what today would be called a secular humanist – one indeed of great wisdom, sensitivity and eloquence, but on the whole a man with a close intellectual resemblance to Thomas Jefferson.'[19] The man himself wrote: 'I am a Christian in the only sense he [Jesus] wished anyone to be; sincerely attached to his doctrines, in preference to all others; ascribing to him every *human* excellence; and believing he never claimed any other.'

In office as the third president, Jefferson displayed a sort of benign pragmatism towards the Church. He allowed the Capitol building to be used every Sunday for services – something that would not be allowed today – and was an attender at services. In one incident, recorded by the Revd Ethan Allen, he was apparently accosted by a friend one morning with a prayer book under his arm. The friend could not believe he was actually going to church – 'you don't believe a word of it' – but was told by the president in no uncertain terms: 'Sir, no nation has ever yet existed or been governed without religion. Nor can be. The Christian religion is the best religion that has ever been given to man and I, as chief magistrate of this nation, am bound to give it the sanction of my example. Good morning, Sir.'[20] In other words, he saw the social utility in religious belief, even if he was not prepared to accept it uncritically.

It is pointed out that Jefferson did not actually admit he was a believer. Such revisionist, even liberal, sentiments would never win him political election in the USA today. But long in advance of Darwin, still further away from Intelligent Design theorists, men with doubts and questions like Jefferson were, in the opinion of the preacher Jonathan Edwards, no better than 'professed infidels [and] heretics . . . they deny the whole Christian religion . . . any revealed religion, or any word of God at all; and say that God has given mankind no other light to walk by but their own reason'.[21]

This God-shaped hole has given modern members of the Religious Right, keen to assert America's Christian origins, something of a problem in recent years. The separation of Church and state, something the founders were so keen to assert, is precisely what people like Pat Robertson do not wish to admit when they call Americans back to what they assure them are their old religious allegiances. So they have been forced to resort to partial quotation, misquotation, misinterpretation and, when all else fails, what look suspiciously like direct falsehoods to prove their point. It works for those who don't know the history of the Constitution backwards – like most of their congregations – but it is still demonstrably false.

The irony is that it was the Baptists, the forebears of many of today's Religious Right, who were most wholehearted in supporting the separation of Church and state, to enable them to practise their own religion without interference from others. In the words of John Leland, an early and influential Baptist, in 1790: 'The notion of a Christian Commonwealth should be exploded for ever. Government should protect every man in thinking and speaking freely and see that one does not abuse the other.' It has indeed hitherto been one of the denomination's proudest boasts. Here is George Washington Truett, pastor of the First Baptist Church in Dallas and president of the Southern Baptist convention between 1927 and 1929, in a speech on the steps of the Capitol in Washington DC in May 1920:

> The supreme contribution of the new world to the old is the contribution of religious liberty . . . the chiefest contribution that America has made thus far to civilisation [which was] pre-eminently a Baptist achievement.
>
> It is the consistent and insistent contention of our Baptist people, always and everywhere, that religion must be forever voluntary and uncoerced and that it is not the prerogative of any power, whether civil or ecclesiastical, to compel men to conform to any religious creed or form of worship.[22]

Yet it is often Baptist Religious Right leaders now who insist that the division was never meant, or is artificial, or has been dreamed up by wicked liberals. And they will distort the record to prove it. One case in point is the occasion on 28 June 1787 when the convention was deadlocked and Benjamin Franklin – otherwise a notorious free-thinker: of Jesus Christ he said 'I have some Doubts as to his Divinity' – stood up to make a famous and impassioned call for the delegates to summon clergy to offer daily prayers for a solution to the impasse. David Barton, the revisionist polemicist, writes in his 1992 book *The Myth of Separation*:

> Franklin's admonition – and the delegates' response to it – had been the turning point not only for the Convention but also for the future of the nation. While neglecting God, their efforts had been characterised by frustration and selfishness. With their repentance came a desire to begin each morning of official government business with prayer . . . [only] after returning God

to their deliberations, were they effective in their efforts to frame a new government?[23]

Former Senator Jesse Helms used to cite the occasion frequently in speeches supporting school prayer, as did Judge Moore in his booklet *Our Legal Heritage*.

Barton, incidentally, is a graduate of the fundamentalist Oral Roberts University, a former maths teacher, and the president of WallBuilders, a Texas-based organisation devoted to remaking the USA as a Christian nation – WallBuilders being nothing to do with the doctrine of separation of Church and state, but an Old Testament reference to the rebuilding of the walls of Jerusalem.

The writings of David Barton have been marketed by groups such as Focus on the Family, the Christian Coalition and Coral Ridge Ministries, so have reached mainstream evangelical audiences. But he has also in the past, according to Michelle Goldberg, addressed meetings of Far Right Christian Identity groups (who believe Anglo-Saxons are the true children of Israel, that blacks are 'mud people', and that Jews are the spawn of Satan) and has shared platforms with Holocaust deniers and neo-Nazi sympathisers. That did not prevent him becoming a vice-chairman of the Texas Republican Party in 1997.[24]

Unfortunately, what actually happened on that June day in 1787 was nothing like what Barton suggests. Franklin's proposal was objected to by other delegates, including Alexander Hamilton who opposed it on the grounds that there was no money to pay chaplains and the matter was dropped. Franklin himself noted: 'The Convention except for three or four persons, thought prayers unnecessary.' There was never a vote on the matter, still less a mass conversion to the efficacy of prayer to resolve political disagreements.

Judge Moore's booklet quotes Franklin's speech to the convention at some length and with approval: 'the venerable Benjamin Franklin commanded the respect of all present as he reminded them that without God nothing would be accomplished', but curiously then omits to mention that they took no notice of him whatsoever.

The grey, sickly and diminutive 'withered little applejohn' James Madison has also been creatively reinterpreted, despite his frequent, outspoken and authenticated recorded remarks about the need to separate Church and state, which date back at least to his early twenties when he expostulated against religious persecution as 'that diabolical, hell-conceived principle'. Barton again, as specialist of choice, claimed to have found a quotation in which Madison was alleged to have said: 'We have staked the future of all of our political institutions upon the capacity of each and all of us to govern ourselves ... according to the Ten Commandments of God.' That would do nicely for the Christian revisionists except that there is no record of Madison ever saying it. The University of Virginia searched through his papers and could not find it and Barton himself now admits that he can't put his finger on the source.

Jefferson remains problematic, a figure almost above criticism, yet indisputably religiously unorthodox. His views were controversial even in his own day. Jefferson's Federalist opponents tried to use his supposed atheism against him in the presidential election of 1800: they asked, would the nation choose God and a religious president, or declare for Jefferson and no God? In a pamphlet called *The Voice of Warning to Christians on the Ensuing Election*, preacher John Mason of New York hyperventilated that Jefferson was an infidel 'who writes against the truths of God's word; who makes not even a profession of Christianity; who is without Sabbaths; ... without so much as a decent external respect for the faith and worship of Christians', a description that might seem a touch over the top even in modern elections. 'Murder, robbery, rape, adultery and incest will all be openly taught ... the air will be rent with the cries of the distressed, the soil will be soaked with blood and the nation black with crimes,' warned the *Connecticut Courant*.[25] It ultimately made no difference: Jefferson was elected, albeit narrowly, and then re-elected by a landslide four years later, the earth not having turned black.

In these circumstances, the revisionists usually resort to denying that Jefferson had any influence on the Constitution or the First Amendment because he was in Paris, not Philadelphia. Unfortunately, his work on the earlier statute on religious freedom for Virginia, and a later letter that he wrote to the Baptists of Danbury, Connecticut, when he was president on 1 January 1802 do not help their case.

The revisionist line is that the Founding Fathers were all Christians, in a country of Christians, that they shared the Christian views of today's Religious Right, that they assumed Christianity was central to national life and that therefore they simply did not conceive of the need for a separation between Church and state. This in turn gives rise to the 'original intent' doctrine that some conservative jurists such as Robert Bork – rejected after being nominated for the Supreme Court by Ronald Reagan in the 1980s – and current Supreme Court Justice Antonin Scalia propound in attempting to perceive the founders' original intentions and then sticking to them in their interpretations of current cases.

Scalia says: 'I look at a text. I take my best shot at getting the fairest meaning of that text and where it is a constitutional text, under-standing what it meant at the time it was adopted.'[26] This doctrine has its most profound effect in the justices' interpretation of the death penalty. It becomes an attempt to set in aspic for all time what the men of the eighteenth century thought they were legislating. Thus, the Constitution permits the death penalty, but not 'cruel and unusual punishment', which in the minds of the framers meant torture such as the use of the rack and thumbscrews. They also enjoined that only 'idiots' could be excused culpability for their crimes, defined as persons who 'cannot account or number 20 pence, nor can tell who was his father or mother, nor how old he is etc., so as it may appear he hath no understanding of reason'.

Despite all the advances in psychiatry and the understanding of mental illness in the last 200 years, that is still the definition preferred by justices such as Scalia, and we know that is so because he quoted that reference with approval in the judgment *Atkins* v. *Virginia* in 2002 after the court ruled to the contrary, that it was unconstitutional to execute someone who was mentally handicapped. In Scalia's view, the founders did not limit the death penalty and neither should the modern court, even if some states interpret the law differently or even capriciously. He is against what he sees as the excessive use of mitigating factors and has pointed out that in the eighteenth century boys as young as fourteen could be executed for stealing.

Unfortunately for those who believe that the Constitution was an explicitly Christian document, Jefferson for one did entirely conceive of the likelihood of a multi-religious society. He first put forward the

Religious Freedom Bill in the General Assembly of Virginia in 1779 and it was finally passed in January 1786. The Bill described it as 'sinful and tyrannical to compel a man to furnish contributions for the propagation of opinions which he disbelieves and abhors'. More importantly, Jefferson and his supporters insisted that the law must protect all religious practitioners in the face of attempts by their opponents to limit its provisions only to Christians. Their amendment, Jefferson wrote in his autobiography, 'was rejected by a great majority, in proof that they meant to comprehend, within the mantle of its protection, the Jew and the Gentile, the Christian and Mahometan, the Hindoo, the infidel of every denomination'.[27]

The conservative revisionists are correct to say that the words about separation of Church and state do not appear in those terms in the Constitution or its amendments. They do, however, occur in President Jefferson's letter to the Baptists of Danbury. They had written to him in October 1801 to complain that they were being persecuted by Connecticut which was making it extremely hard for them to avoid paying taxes to support the state's established Congregational Church. They knew very well that the president would not approve of such coercion and they laid it on with a trowel: 'our hopes are strong that the sentiments of our beloved president, which have had such a genial effect already, like the radiant beams of the sun, will shine and prevail through all these states and all the world till Hierarchy and Tyranny be destroyed from the earth'.[28]

Jefferson's considered reply came back three months later and might be thought a clear and definitive statement of his views. It has usually been thought so:

> Believing with you that religion is a matter which lies solely between Man and his God, that he owes account to none other for his faith or his worship, that the legitimate powers of government reach actions only & not opinions, I contemplate with sovereign reverence that act of the whole American people which declared that their legislature should 'make no law respecting an establishment of religion, or prohibiting the free exercise thereof,' thus building a wall of separation between Church and State . . . in behalf of the rights of conscience.[29]

Mr Barton and others have asserted in the past that the letter had a very limited purpose. Chief Justice William Rehnquist, nominated by Ronald Reagan to head the Supreme Court in 1986, described it as 'a short note of courtesy' which was only meant to protect the Church from the state. Rick Scarborough, one of Judge Moore's firmest supporters (like him, a Baptist), head of the Texas-based Vision America organisation and a former preacher in Houston, claims in a booklet called *In Defense of Mixing Church and State* that those who support separation 'have resorted to extracting nine words from a private correspondence to validate their views, which is foreign to the constitution's original intent'.[30] Separation, he states, is a 'lie introduced by Satan and fostered by the courts. Unfortunately it is embraced by the American public to our shame and disgrace and that lie has led us to the edge of the abyss.'

For good measure he informed the *Houston Chronicle* in 2005: 'The whole concept . . . is a myth propagated by liberal judges.' So much for Leland, Truett and all former Baptists such as those at Danbury – perhaps they could not read plain English, or were just deluded.

Of course, Jefferson knew his letter to the Danbury Baptists would not remain private. That is why he consulted colleagues and revised his draft before sending it. The revisionists suggest that Jefferson added that 'Christian principles' should always guide government, but that somehow this was dropped off the end. Even though they devote some attention to debunking it, the Religious Right also claims that the letter was either dashed off without thought, or that anyway it was unimportant and so can be ignored.

Thus, in his dissenting verdict to the Supreme Court's 1985 judgment on school prayer, Rehnquist argued that government could indeed aid religion as long as it did not give one denomination preference over others. 'The "wall of separation between church and state" is a metaphor based on bad history, a metaphor that has proved useless as a guide to judging. It should be frankly and explicitly abandoned,' he announced, putting Thomas Jefferson firmly in his place.

This is part of the wider effort, as in Judge Moore's case, to push the judiciary in a more avowedly Christian direction by asserting that the nation has always been based on its religious principles and that they should take priority in its secular judgments.

In this, the judiciary are regarded as dangerously out of control and in need of being reined in if they exercise any independence of view. Hence the battle to control the Supreme Court and the argument that courts should be ignored or overruled if they make decisions that are not religiously approved.

Not even Jefferson is quite safe from conservative revisionism, despite the bright clarity of his prose and the care he took to elucidate precisely what he meant, as if he knew that future generations might come to question him or to subvert what he and the other Founding Fathers were trying to do.

Perhaps the attempt to reinterpret Jefferson's words and so reclaim him for a religious society of the sort he explicitly and repeatedly opposed is a tribute to his continuing monumental status in US life: carved in stone on Mount Rushmore and commemorated in a neo-Greek Temple, across the Potomac tidal basin from the White House in Washington DC. Incidentally, when the architects of the Jefferson Memorial built it in the 1940s they found it expedient to misquote him as well. Around the interior frieze runs the slave-owning Jefferson's stirring reflection on the future of black Americans: 'Nothing is more certainly written in the book of fate than that these people are to be free'. The designers then carefully omitted the second half of the sentence: 'nor is it less certain that the two races, equally free, cannot live in the same government'.[31]

Jefferson had a short way with judges who allow their religious beliefs to infiltrate their secular judgments and, unfortunately for them, his words survive, from a letter written in 1824, two years before his death. Of the idea that Christianity was part of the Common Law, he wrote brusquely: 'The proof of the contrary . . . is controvertible; to wit, that the common law existed while the Anglo Saxons were yet pagans, at a time when they had never yet heard the name of Christ pronounced, or knew that such a character had ever existed.' He challenged 'the best-read lawyer to produce another script of authority for this judicial forgery . . . What a conspiracy this, between church and state!'[32]

Would Jefferson be gratified to know that his metaphor still has the power after more than 200 years to cause conniptions? Or would he regard the current debate with deep depression? Judge Moore's verse springs back to mind: 'So with a firm reliance on Divine Providence for protection/They pledged their sacred honour and sought His wise direction.' They could have done. But they didn't.

5

A Fiery Gospel, Writ in Burnished Rows of Steel

'We have it in our power to begin the world over again.'

Thomas Paine

The America that emerged from the Revolution and was formed by its godless Constitution became an increasingly religious country. Its nineteenth-century society would be shaped not only by another Great Awakening, but by a series of political crusades that were explicitly religiously motivated. The fight for the abolition of slavery, which culminated in the Civil War between 1861 and 1865, was led over several decades by church ministers or those inspired by them (and, equally, opposed in the South by other clergy using biblical texts of their own) as were, later, the struggle for women's rights, campaigns for sabbatarianism and prison reform, and ultimately the long fight for the prohibition of alcohol.

And these were radical evangelical movements for political change, not reactionary or conservative ones. They were campaigns arising squarely out of the evangelical tradition: the promotion of individual change and personal improvement – a self-betterment available to everyone, not just the elect – through the high-minded reform of institutions. Thus the abolition of slavery was seen not only as the remedy of an injustice and the ending of a social evil, but also a way of ameliorating the moral standing of the nation and elevating the behaviour of its citizens.

It was a transformation that began with the self and then moved on to society and the state. In the words of one of the early evangelical revivalists, Charles Finney, his conversion had come in 1821 while he was studying law in New York: 'The Holy Spirit descended on me in a manner that seemed to go through me, body and soul. I could feel the impression, like a wave of electricity, going through and through me.

Indeed it seemed to come in waves and waves of liquid love . . . It seemed like the very breath of God.' This then moved on to become a mission to convert others, first singly and then across society, in Finney's words: 'The great business of the church is to reform the world – to put away every kind of sin.' The faithful then were 'bound to exert their influence to secure a legislation that is in accordance with the law of God'.[1]

America's white population was expanding hugely, even faster than Britain's at the same time during the height of the Industrial Revolution. In America, it grew from 2.5 million at the time of independence in the 1780s to 20 million by the middle of the next century, many of them arriving from Europe in the 1840s. Three-quarters of the early immigrants were Protestants, mainly from the British Isles. In the 1820s there were about 15,000 immigrants a year, but by the mid-1840s there was suddenly a flood. The Irish potato famine and political and economic upheavals in the German states shifted the balance, with suddenly more Catholics arriving to transform the Protestant, Anglo-Saxon hegemony, at least in the great cities and the farmlands of the Midwest.

There was what Protestants saw as 'a tidal wave of pauperism, ignorance and degradation' among the 3 million who arrived within a decade during the 1840s. This created a source of conflict and riots in cities such as New York and Philadelphia and, incidentally, led to the long association of the Irish and Catholics with the Democratic Party, which was much more welcoming to them than their opponents, the nativist Whigs, predecessors of the Republican Party – a traditional, even hereditary, allegiance that is only now changing some 160 years later.

The Catholics' arrival certainly complicated the fight against slavery. They voted for the pro-slavery party, their gangs fought the Protestant abolitionists in the streets, and their whole belief system was alien to the nativist tradition. The long-established Protestants saw the incoming Catholics as being in thrall to a foreign potentate, the Pope in Rome, and to their superstition-riddled priests, who threatened the fundamental American commitment to the liberty and democracy of the nation. They were the new outsiders.

It did not help that the denominations that were growing among the local population were the nonconformist ones, those most suspicious of the Catholics, and it was their New England leaders who both voiced the moral outrage against Southern slavery and fostered the campaign in the North to abolish it.

Expanding particularly quickly were the Baptists – a tenfold growth in the thirty years following the war of independence – and the Methodists, whose membership reached a quarter of a million by 1820, had doubled by 1830 and doubled again to top a million by 1844, partly due to the energetic organisational skills set in place by its early bishop, Francis Asbury, who was sending circuit riders and preachers over the Appalachian mountains to convert the settlers on the far side as early as 1782. The church groups were often fissiparous and ever ready to split over differences of doctrine and practice. But they grew exponentially until they made up nearly 70 per cent of the Protestant churches in the USA and two-thirds of its ministers.[2] Where there had been 1,800 Christian ministers in 1775, by 1845 there were 40,000. The Freewill Baptists alone had more clergy than the Episcopalians and the Antimission Baptist ministers outnumbered both Catholic and Lutheran priests.

These were vibrant, young churches, proselytising fervently, building their own schools, leading their own revivals and preaching a zealous and democratic message of personal salvation and individual responsibility. Their ministers by and large were young too, often setting up their own congregations and not beholden for their appointments on squires and aristocrats, Oxbridge colleges or bishops and prelates, as they would have been in England. They were instead drawn from the ranks of those to whom they were preaching. As a consequence, they were also not under any obligation to teach a message of social order and knowing one's place. They were not a privileged or educated class, but men with zeal and a conviction that theirs was the true divine revelation. And they had the official sanction and freedom to say it.

Their congregations wanted plain speaking and down-to-earth interpretations of the Bible from local men who laced their shows with excitement and action, not high-falutin' and impenetrable jargon ('all hic, haec, hoc and no God in it,' as one said), passing ponderously over their heads from the pulpits of lofty and remote divines disengaged from everyday life. The parishioners wanted to join in too, express their own thoughts, beliefs and feelings, and they saw no reason why they should not do so.

Their ministers spoke the same language they spoke, bluntly and straightforwardly, and addressed them and their fears and aspirations directly. This demotic style has remained a striking feature of evangelical preaching in the USA, deployed by all the most successful evangelists ever since, from Billy Sunday to Billy Graham. Watch their successors preaching on television any Sunday now and you can see it in action: simple words and often simplistic thoughts, but fervently and usually sincerely expressed.

All these young preachers were convinced that they were building a new nation whose success rested on their own Christian belief and their mission to convert others. They had swallowed the rhetoric of liberty: for themselves in their worship and for their country in its wider life, and it was a central and hugely important feature of their thought and their world-view.

The historian of the movement, Nathan Hatch, quotes one Sidney Rigdon, son of a poor farmer, about a revival meeting in a log cabin in 1830: 'I met the whole church of Christ in a little log house about 20 feet square…and we began to talk about the kingdom of God as if we had the world at our command, we talked with great confidence and talked big things, although we were not many people we had big feelings . . . we began to talk like men in authority and power – we looked upon men of the earth as grasshoppers…we saw by vision a thousand times larger.' Rigdon became a Mormon that year, joining the most successful of the new religions emerging out of the Midwest.[3]

This passion was a feature of the Second Great Awakening, the evangelical movement that swept through New England, across New York state and then spread south, through the Cumberland Valley, generating huge energy as it went into the first third of the nineteenth century. The revival found a ready audience among hard-bitten settlers and farmers, living harsh, lonely, poverty-stricken and precarious lives while they pushed the boundaries of the frontier out into the wilderness. All around them these folk could see moral decay and human weakness. There was huge, rough alcohol consumption (an average of 5 gallons of 90 per cent proof alcohol per person, per year;

this is at least three times levels today). Grain was cheap and plentiful and alcohol was poured down the throats of babies and children to pacify them as well as imbibed by their parents to deaden their tedious days. Violence and sexual licence were rife – one in three brides was said to be pregnant at the time of marriage – and in the circumstances it was no wonder that there was a hankering for spiritual improvement of a non-alcoholic kind. In a land lacking most other uplifting diversions and entertainments, such revivalism was hugely popular, but it must also have been both frenzied and exhausting.

Families travelled for many miles – as they still do today to similar gatherings – to attend camp meetings, listening to preachers who were often vehement in their denunciations and passionate in their preaching. These men issued anathemas and hurled jeremiads about the fearsome and terrifying future of their country and the frightful fate of the backsliders, the drinkers and the fornicators in their congregations. They shouted and they screamed, they whispered and they shook, and their congregations followed suit. They sang and they danced. They told jokes and stories.

And more than that, they also offered fellowship, identity and membership of a common family, just as their successors do today. As one Methodist convert put it: 'I now found myself associated with those who loved each other with a pure heart fervently, instead of being surrounded by those with whom friendship was a cold commerce of interest.'[4]

The most famous revival meeting, the start of the new awakening, took place at Cane Ridge, Kentucky, in 1801, attracting up to 25,000 people – a tenth of the white population of the state – to a week of frenzy. It was evidently quite a show, described by one preacher who attended like this:

The noise was like the roar of Niagara. I counted seven ministers all preaching at one time, some on stumps, others in wagons . . . People were singing, others were praying, some crying for mercy in the most piteous accents while others were shouting most vociferously . . . A strange supernatural power seemed to pervade the entire mass. At one time I saw at least 500 swept down in a moment, as if a battery of a thousand guns had been opened upon them and then immediately followed shrieks and shouts that rent the very heavens.[5]

The most celebrated of these preachers was Lorenzo Dow, a gaunt Methodist with the long flowing beard of an Old Testament prophet, a fiery eye and a manic delivery, who could induce his listeners to break into shaking, dancing, barking like dogs, running and singing – sometimes all at the same time – and also so-called jerking exercises which left many of them writhing on the ground. Dow was quick-witted and funny too. When a heckler shouted to him to explain Calvinism he shot back:

> You can and you can't,
> You will and you won't
> You'll be damned if you do
> And you will be damned if you don't . . .

He claimed to have walked 10,000 miles in 1804 alone – getting on for 30 miles a day, every day, if true – and to have preached at 500 meetings, and his message was a stridently democratic one: 'You may support your distinction and feed your pride, but in a religious point of view, all men are on a level . . . Christ gave himself for ALL. A-double L does not spell some, nor few, but ALL.' No wonder the Methodist hierarchy back in England would not let him preach when he crossed the Atlantic.[6]

The South shared in the growth of evangelicalism. In the words of W. J. Cash in his seminal 1940s study *The Mind of the South*: 'What our Southerner required . . . was a faith as simple and emotional as himself. A faith to draw men together in hordes, to terrify them with Apocalyptic rhetoric, to cast them into the pit, rescue them and at last bring them shouting into the fold of grace.'[7] One contemporary observed: 'They tended to be of lower social and economic status, exhibited much less interest in an educated ministry and extended westward by means of farmer-preachers.'[8]

Back east in Puritan New England, the preaching was less excitable but more severe, and the congregations more middle class, better educated and also more politically focused. Nathaniel Bangs,

Methodist preacher in charge of New York City's congregations, was contemptuous of the 'spirit of pride, presumption and bigotry, impatience with spiritual restraint and moderation, clapping of the hands, screaming and even jumping, which marred and disgraced the word of God'. No shouting for them: when the dour Presbyterian Lyman Beecher's congregation got over-excited he sent them home to cool down. There was to be no 'poor, uneducated, reckless mass of infuriated animalism' because all that would be left afterwards would be utter desolation, spiritual cold turkey.

Instead they organised charitable organisations: Bible and tract societies, Sunday schools and missionaries; they did this, in the words of Professor Morone, to fight sin. Their fund-raising, petition-signing, rally-holding and campaigning transmogrified into political organising, and eventually into the fight against slavery and for other campaigns. Many of those involved in the fight would be women, the wives of the newly prosperous urban middle-class families, extending their sphere of moral authority outside the home to causes elsewhere. They taught their children the alphabet from the Abolitionist Primer ('A is an abolitionist/A man who wants to free/The wretched slave and give to all/An equal liberty;/B is a Brother with a skin/Of somewhat darker hue,/But in our Heavenly Father's sight,/He is as dear as you . . .', etc.), but they also organised and attended meetings and even braved brickbats and other violence to speak at them.

The most famous of these women were Lyman Beecher's daughters: Catharine, a campaigner for female education, and Harriet, wife of a Congregational clergyman and author of the single most influential book in the entire anti-slavery struggle, *Uncle Tom's Cabin*, which sold 2 million copies in America in its first decade after publication in 1852. Henry James called it 'that triumphant work, much less a book than a state of vision'. It squarely hit its evangelical target audience. 'So you're the little woman who wrote the book that made this great war,' said Abraham Lincoln on being introduced to the author in 1862.[9] It is ironic that the name of Uncle Tom, the Christ-like, ever patient and forbearing figure at the heart of the story, has now become a byword for cringing black submissiveness to white supremacy.

This female campaigning voice caused enough trouble to those evangelicals who believed a woman's place was in the home – 'would any sensible man who loves truth and reason follow the guidance of women and children?' asked one William Sullivan, an anti-abolitionist from New Hampshire[10] – but black slavery became an even more urgent issue for them as indignation spread out from New England. Black Christians posed a considerable dilemma for the evangelicals: should they be taught to accept their lot, or should they be led out of slavery? The Bible offered both solutions: there was Exodus, but there were also plenty of verses (much relied upon by preachers in the South, serving the interests of the plantation owners, the farmers and the social order) enjoining servants to obey their masters.

In the North ministers like Beecher and William Lloyd Garrison began pronouncing jeremiads and their printed sermons were passed subversively among the black preachers of the South. Garrison, the editor of a paper called the *Liberator*, certainly saw the abolition of slavery as only part of a wider crusade to convert the nation: 'to emancipate all men from the bondage of sin and to create a perfect world under the dominion of God, the control of an inward spirit, the government of the law of love and . . . the obedience and liberty of Christ'.[11]

Below the Mason-Dixon Line, evangelical preachers and their white congregations feared 'niggers taking over the country', especially after Nat Turner's revolt in Virginia in 1831, when a slave who had convinced himself that he was the Messiah and others that he had a divine mission, rose in rebellion and, with his followers, murdered sixty-one whites, including his master's family, before he was captured and executed. The revolt was a ferocious and terrifying experience that convinced the state's legislators that it was too dangerous to allow slaves to be taught to read, even the Bible, so they made it illegal.

They also found an ingenious solution to prevent the dissemination of abolitionist tracts, using the newly established federal bureaucracy of the national postal service to block the distribution of literature. This was a useful means of circumventing the Constitution's guarantee of free speech, even though it was an ironic tool for the defenders of slavery to use, given that they were shortly to revolt against the whole system of federal government. Blocking the mail, however, would become a standard means of closing down liberal social impulses or reformist campaigns over a whole range of issues in the years ahead.

Southerners became ever more ingenious and contorted in their attempts to justify slavery to their consciences. They took to marrying principle to expedience, and enlisted biblical sanctions to justify injustice and to implement a form of social control based on naked racism. This convinced even some devout Christians who might otherwise have opposed slavery, such as Thomas 'Stonewall' Jackson, who would become one of the Confederacy's most heroic generals. His wife, Anna, wrote after his death – and after the war – that her husband 'would prefer to see the negroes free, but he believed that the Bible taught that slavery was sanctioned by the Creator himself, who maketh men to differ and instituted laws for the bond and the free. He therefore accepted slavery . . . not as a thing desirable in itself, but as allowed by Providence for ends which it was not his business to determine.'[12] This was undoubtedly also convenient, as the Jacksons owned six slaves themselves, but he did at least teach them to read, in defiance of the law, at the Sunday School he ran for local black children near his home in Lexington, Virginia.

Defenders of slavery also wrote novels about happy slaves to counter the influence of the saintly Uncle Tom, but the 'peculiar institution' caused increasing fissures, especially among the Christian denominations.

As early as 1845 the Northern Baptists told their Southern counterparts that they could 'never be a party to any arrangement that would imply approbation of slavery'[13] and the movement split, leading to the creation of the Southern Baptist convention. The Southern Baptists were enthusiastic supporters of the Confederacy and flooded its armies of farm boys with over a hundred religious tracts during the course of the war: 50 million pages or more of hymns, Bible readings and improving literature. 'The history of the world,' the Baptists of Virginia claimed afterwards, 'we presume, reports no instance of an army so thoroughly under the influence of the gospel as was our noble southern army.'

Episcopalians also opposed slavery, an early example of the social liberalism that not only bought it some black and many Native

American members, whom it proselytised with missionary zeal on the tribal reservations of the West, but which now over a century later brings it to grief – and hardening internal divisions – over its non-judgmental acceptance of the homosexuals in its midst, especially among its clergy and even among its bishops.

Before the Civil War, the two religious arguments batted to and fro, North and South, in mirror images of each other. Slavery debauched and enfeebled Southern society, said the abolitionists, making it lazy and licentious. On the contrary, retorted the South, slavery protected the social order, preserved the (white) race and promoted harmony.

It was an argument I once heard offered by a white woman in Natchez, Mississippi, 130 years after the Civil War, sitting on the porch of the house that had been owned by Confederate president Jefferson Davis's in-laws: "Course we don't object that we *lost* the war,' she drawled as if hostilities had finished only the day before. 'We just didn't like what they did to *our country*. We looked after our slaves then because they were our property. And they appreciated that.'

Slavery was even used to justify the sexual abuse and rape of black women by white men, as if it were a sort of social safety valve for the frustrated, to be exercised on a sub-human species. As one notorious pre-war apologist, W. Gilmore Simms, put it: coloured women, who had 'no consciousness of degradation', filled the place that had to be taken by white women in the North by acting as outlets for the natural lusts of red-blooded white men: 'It scarcely affects the mind of the negro and does not materially affect his [sic] social status.'[14] So really it was performing a useful purpose: staving off divorce, rape, sexual assault and feminism, leaving white women pure and unsullied and, importantly, maintaining the hierarchy of society.

It was said that slavery was the kindest and most Christian way to organise a stable and civilised society. It would even work, the theorist George Fitzhugh asserted, for the 'toil worn, half fed, pauperised population of England' – the best remedy for their 'complicated evils, would also be to ENSLAVE the whole of the people of England who have not property'. This sublimely wrong-headed assertion has a similar whiff to those conservative US bloggers who like to argue these days that the UK has become 'spiritually dead' because its population is not as devout as they believe they should be.

The abolition debate was becoming a hugely moral fight, and not just between North and South, but within the North as well. Few Northerners, however, thought of black people as brothers, still less that all men really were equal. Indiana, Iowa and even Lincoln's Illinois all passed laws in the 1850s refusing to allow the immigration of any blacks, free or slave. 'The white race is the master race and the white man is the equal of every other white man . . . the negro is the inferior race,' the Alabamian William Yancey told a sympathetic Northern audience in 1860. Such people needed to be kept down.

Morone insists that is a common characteristic in American life:

> The struggle to curb dangerous others – clamping on our own controls rather than (as Tocqueville thought) escaping from European controls – shapes American political thought and culture in every era. Enforcing the lines between us and them turns American politics into their distinctive forms: a first-world laggard in traditional welfare programmes, an international leader in government efforts to control (or improve or uplift) its people. That is how we get 2 million Americans – overwhelmingly black and Latino – stuffed into prisons and jails.[15]

In such overwrought circumstances, some could readily believe themselves to be above the man-made law and instead to be motivated by a higher calling. One such was John Brown, the man who would eventually seize the small federal armoury at Harpers Ferry, Virginia, in October 1859 in a woefully misconceived, amateurish and unsuccessful attempt to foment a general slave uprising. 'Without shedding of blood there is no remission of sin,' he declared apocalyptically. The first casualty of the attack was a freed black man named Hayward Shepherd, the local railroad station baggage master, who had come to see what all the fuss was about and was caught in the cross-fire.

Looking at the early photographs of Brown it is impossible to avoid the unmistakable glint of manic and self-righteous fanaticism in his eye. Brown's belief in direct action, the purifying nature of violence and his wilful ignoring of laws he considered from his superior virtue to be morally wrong, has more than a hint of those modern fundamentalists who target abortion clinics and threaten violence against their staff. His biographer Stephen Oates says Brown, a Calvinist and Congregationalist, enjoyed quoting the Old Testament 'from one end to the other' and regularly preached from the sermons of Jonathan Edwards, the originator of the First Great Awakening a century before, on subjects such as the Eternity of Hell Torments, the Evil of the Wicked Contemplated by the Righteous and Sinners in the Hands of an Angry God. When a stranger moved into town, it was said, Brown made a point of calling and asking 'whether he was an observer of the Sabbath, opposed to slavery and a supporter of the Gospel and common schools. If so, all was right with him, if not he was looked upon with suspicion.'[16] This too has a familiar ring to it as far as some modern evangelicals are concerned. Brown also had a very modern eye for the power of the symbolic sacrifice: 'I am worth inconceivably more to hang than for any other purpose,' he told his brother before his execution. And, of course, two years later Northern troops marched into battle singing 'John Brown's Body'.

Both sides went off to war in 1861 believing they had God on their side. Indeed, the Confederates even had a general, Leonidas Polk, who had been a missionary Episcopalian bishop though he was apparently a rather ineffectual soldier, described by one contemporary as 'a gentleman and a high church dignitary, more theoretical than practical'. A portly figure and so a large target, he was cut in half by a cannon shell at the battle of Pine Mountain, Georgia, in June 1864, apparently because he took cover at too stately a pace, hands clasped behind his back and deep in contemplation, when he came under fire.[17]

Defeat in the Civil War produced long-term resonances in the South, not least a sense of victimhood and a confirmation, rather than a questioning, of religious values: as the authors of *Religion and the American Civil War* conclude: 'In the mythology of the Lost Cause, the southerners became like the Israelites of the Old Testament. They remained God's people, who would enter the promised land if they kept his commandments and covenants, among which was fealty to their noble cause.'[18] The historian James McPherson in the same anthology says: 'Like Job, many southerners concluded that God was testing their faith as a preparation for reformation and deliverance; as

a southern woman put it, "The Lord loveth whom he chasteneth." '
God was in charge and he would see them right, evidently without the
need to repent or even revise his followers' views on segregation. The
Southern Baptist convention spoke of proselytising black members,
but it denied their churches membership of its all-white organisation.

And so it remained for a century. The civil rights movement of the
1950s and 1960s drew its moral strength from the leadership of black
clergy such as the Revd Martin Luther King, but it did so almost
entirely without the support of Southern white ministers. Quite the
reverse: in a remark he has subsequently disowned, Jerry Falwell in
1965 was condemning the movement: 'Believing the Bible as I do I
would find it impossible to stop preaching the pure saving gospel of
Jesus Christ and begin doing anything else – including fighting
Communism or participating in civil rights reform.'[19] He also preached
that integration would mean the destruction of the white race. Falwell
later insisted that his Thomas Road Baptist Church in Lynchburg,
Virginia, desegregated early when he recalled that he baptised a black
family in 'probably' 1960 or 1961. Unfortunately, local records suggest
it actually remained segregated until 1968, more than a decade into his
ministry there, and that the first black baptisms did not occur until
1971.[20]

Like Falwell, many white religious leaders – and not only in the
South – explicitly endorsed the existing social order and condoned
segregation. There is even evidence that the original motivation for
Religious Right activism in the South did not come from its organisers'
reaction to the Supreme Court's ruling on a woman's right to abortion
in the celebrated *Roe* v. *Wade* case in 1973, as they now like to claim.
Only the Catholic Church protested against that ruling at the time and
indeed it was accepted, sometimes quite enthusiastically, by
evangelicals.

On the contrary, the first modern attempt to mobilise Protestant
religious conservatives arose out of an entirely separate issue: the
defence of racial segregation at the fundamentalist Bob Jones
University in its battle to maintain tax exemption as a charitable,
educational institution.

The Internal Revenue Service's challenge to the university in 1975
followed a Supreme Court ruling in an earlier case than Roe, that of

Green v. *Connally* in 1972, which decided that institutions practising discrimination could not by definition be considered charitable and so could not claim that status in order to avoid paying tax. At that time the university's statutes forbade interracial dating and it was only just beginning to enrol unmarried black students.

The Right, when it admits this now, tends to claim that the IRS's action was a result of vindictiveness by the Democrat Jimmy Carter's administration, conveniently overlooking the fact that the IRS challenge took place before Carter was elected, during the presidency of the Republican Gerald Ford. By the time the university's appeal came before the Supreme Court in 1983, however, there was indeed another Republican administration in place – Ronald Reagan's – and that gave the university's appeal its backing.

The IRS's action was seen as an attack on religious schools as well as the right to discriminate, and it was a much more potent issue than that of women's abortion rights at the time. Randall Balmer quotes Ed Dobson, a former associate in the pressure group the Moral Majority that Falwell founded in the late 1970s, as saying: 'The religious right did not start because of a debate about abortion. I sat in a smoke-filled back room with the Moral Majority and I frankly do not remember abortion ever being mentioned as a reason why we ought to do something.'[21]

The abortion issue was a later addition to the platform and *Roe* v. *Wade* now forms a central plank in the Religious Right's campaign against Judicial Activism, targeting judges who do not share its views on social issues. Not the least of their hypocrisies is the fact that some on the Religious Right now declare themselves to be the 'new abolitionists', attempting to annex for themselves the rhetoric of the anti-slavery campaigners of the 1850s and the civil rights protesters of the 1960s, whose movements their predecessors resolutely opposed.

The overtly religiously defined sense of self – and self-esteem – among white Southerners shaped their politics and gives it its flavour to this day. 'We are a different people, a different blood, a different climate, a different character, different customs and we have largely different work to do in this world,' as one North Carolinian put it in 1899. The sense of superiority that this implies remains, and continues to fuel a self-conscious Southern destiny.

And their evangelicalism endorses the status quo rather than challenging it: progress and prosperity are due to individual effort and ability, not social or government action. Southern evangelicalism was never infected by Northern radicalism because it was defending the relatively privileged social system of its members, not questioning it. The Southern sociologists Emerson and Smith argue that 'white evangelicals lopsidedly believe that if blacks don't get ahead, it is because of black culture or lack of initiative: explanations that pivot on individual responsibility. Under evangelical theology social structures are not the real problem and government action . . . rarely the solution.'[22] That Puritan and conservative ethic, having spread southwards from New England, has now also spread back across the nation, propagated largely by Southern preachers.

In the North, the great mission for abolition – the sort of fervour pronounced by Julia Ward Howe in the Battle Hymn of the Republic with its rhetoric about seeing the glory of the coming of the Lord and trampling out the vintage where the grapes of wrath are stored – seeped away after the Civil War was won and the Southern states had returned to the Union. The Northern churches did not exactly welcome blacks into their congregations – indeed some banned them altogether, leading to the establishment of separate black congregations and churches, even where they were part of the same denomination.

That was also true when the national body sought integration. When the Episcopal Church's Province of Sewanee, covering the dioceses in the Deep South, voted in 1883 to create a 'coloured missionary district' with its own (white) suffragan bishop, so that black worshippers need not be admitted to white churches, its proposal was defeated in the national general convention that year. The province still went ahead and created the separate, parallel church anyway. The last meeting of its black convention was held as recently as 1954.

Victory in the war was its own redemption and reconciliation with the Southern whites, rather than the passage of equal opportunities for blacks, was the priority. As Lincoln said in his second inaugural a few weeks before his assassination: 'With malice towards none; with charity for all; with firmness in the right, as God gives us to see the right . . . let us strive to do . . . all which may achieve and cherish a just and lasting peace among ourselves.' The president was killed, possibly fortuitously for his historic reputation, at the end of the war, but there is no real evidence that he would have substantially altered the situation of black people: he had been rather drawn to shipping them all off to fend for themselves on an island far away, such as Madagascar.

In the periodic revivals of popular interest in the Civil War, which occur about every thirty years, the moral dimension of the fight is often overlooked these days in the interests of celebrating reconciliation. General Sherman's estimation that the Southern cause was the worst for which men ever fought is long forgotten. Everyone was just good chaps together and the war is, euphemistically, the Late Unpleasantness. Some other opinions do remain, however. 'You know,' said one of my Yankee friends, gazing up at one of the magnificent war memorials commemorating the courage of regiments from individual states that litter the Civil War battlefields such as Gettysburg, 'I can't get over the fact that they were just plain wrong.'

Instead, in the decades after the Civil War, as America changed – grew industrialised, became urbanised, its population more diverse and infinitely expanded in size and origins, its disparities of wealth more enormous, its politics more corrupt and less principled – the country's social and moral reformers turned in different directions. They had got slavery out of their system and now they quested for virtue in crusades, seeking to exert political pressure and to achieve civic and national piety through targeting individuals' vice. Their attention turned to campaigns against sex and licentiousness, immoral books and immoral people such as prostitutes and their procurers, a movement that would reach its apotheosis with the prohibition of alcohol after the First World War.

It was impossible to overlook the changes that were occurring in American society, particularly in its burgeoning factories and its booming (and periodically busting) stock exchange. But, in keeping with Puritan tradition, some Christians saw the enormous wealth some tycoons amassed in the Gilded Age not as a burden or an opportunity for philanthropy, but as a reward from God, in proof of their hard work and virtue. They might inveigh against gambling and could not entirely ignore the personal peccadilloes of some of the more egregious crooks who made fortunes, such as 'Jubilee Jim' Fisk ('I was born to be bad'), but on the whole, and aided by their pious donations, they could forgive them.

And, of course, there is a long tradition among the USA's more virtuous tycoons to see their wealth both as a gift and as a chance for giving, targeting high-minded causes and institutions of their own choosing, rather than those wider social purposes selected by the state. 'He who dies rich dies dishonoured,' said the steel magnate Andrew Carnegie as he spent his vast wealth on building libraries across the world, and Mellon Foundations, Getty Museums and the like have generally been predicated on developing opportunities for individual self-improvement and edification rather than providing more general social services or ameliorating the material condition of the poor and disadvantaged. It is the praiseworthy American way, and in this, Bill Gates, devoting a portion of his riches to eradicating malaria, is continuing a long tradition.

Henry Ward Beecher, Lyman's son and the brother of Catharine and Harriet, who became the most influential and famous New York preacher in the 1860s and 1870s, indeed one of the first transatlantic celebrity preachers, attacked Fisk as a mountebank 'absolutely devoid of moral sense as the Sahara is of grass'. He was an early preacher of what came to be known as the social gospel. But Beecher also gave the clearest indication of where he thought virtue lay: 'No man in this land suffers from poverty unless it be more than his fault – unless it be his sin.'

Beecher was a charismatic and thunderous speaker with an affable manner. He wore fine clothes, had a mania for shopping ('It is astonishing how one's necessities multiply in the presence of the supply'), epicurean tastes and a proclivity for reclining expansively on sofas. He was for a time, in the words of his latest biographer, the most famous man in America,[23] as well as a star of the British lecture circuit, and his earnings were prodigious.

He was more than happy to extol the 'men of Wall Street – brokers and bankers – who stand near the heart of God and who are pouring out their means in a way which gives evidence of a Christian manhood in them'.[24] The well-heeled flocked to hear him at his Plymouth Congregational Church in Brooklyn Heights as a consequence, at least until 1874 when he was accused of adultery with a newspaper editor's wife and, although the case remained unproven, lost much of his social standing and some of the less devoted members of his congregation. In this, of course, he was by no means the last celebrity preacher to be accused of impropriety.

As Beecher's star waned, he was supplanted by new preaching sensations with grander razzamatazz and manipulation techniques, passions and emotions – such as Dwight Moody, the former shoe salesman from Chicago, and his colleague, the hymn writer Ira Sankey, who toured England to great acclaim and set the style for the revivalist preachers of the following century. When Moody waved his Bible and called for people to step forward for conversion at the end of his first meeting in London, 400 did so. In the words of the historian Sydney Ahlstrom,[25] Moody's message was 'a simple and relatively innocuous blend of American optimism and evangelical Arminianism': eternal life was theirs for the asking, 'they had only to "come forward and t-a-k-e. TAKE!" He told them: "Join some church at once". Any church. As he famously said: "God has given me a lifeboat and said to me: 'Moody, save all you can'." '

It was also a fundamentalist message – Moody, who was never ordained, has some claims to being the Father of modern American fundamentalism – but it largely lacked the rancorous partisanship that came to characterise the movement. Moody was a pragmatist and shuddered at sectarianism and controversy. Shortly before he died in 1899 he said: 'Couldn't they agree to a truce and for ten years bring out no fresh views, just let us get on with the practical work of the kingdom?'

Moody's and Sankey's campaigns raised money from business, used railroads to criss-cross America and filled giant arenas. Theirs was a sober, middle-class form of revivalism: 'As he stood on the platform,' wrote one admirer. 'He looked like a businessman, he dressed like a businessman; he took the meeting in hand as a businessman would.' Moody's message was unthreatening and conservative: that individual repentance and conversion would provide salvation and the multiplication of the saved would in turn improve and so rescue society. Good works were not good in themselves, but only as they touched individuals and then converted them. Sermons were only worthwhile in so far as they converted, and Moody eschewed hellfire and brimstone: 'Terror never brought a man in yet.'

This, says Ahlstrom, served to convert the traditional message of Protestant Christianity 'into something dulcet and sentimental'. The collection of his sermons advertised that they contained: 'living truths for head and heart, illustrated by . . . thrilling anecdotes and incidents, personal experiences, touching home scenes and stories of tender pathos'.[26] It is a tried and tested technique that any televangelist would recognise today.

By contrast, in the face of the extraordinary disparities of wealth that were being spawned and the appalling social conditions in which many workers lived, some religious folk concluded that their poverty was not necessarily either of their own creation or a result of their own moral turpitude. The more liberal of them began preaching a new, social, gospel, that called for group action against the ills of society with the imperative of public service rather than the priority of individual salvation. The poor could be improved in their lot if society was ameliorated. It is a debate that continues, though the morally self-righteous currently have the upper hand, the social gospel having faltered in the licentiousness that followed the social and civil rights reforms of the 1960s.

Such social action was always an anathema to evangelists like Moody because it distracted from individual moral improvement. He frequently visited the poor, but in order to convert them rather than to assuage their material needs: 'If I had the Bible in one hand and a loaf in the other, the people always looked first at the loaf; and that was just contrary of the order laid down in the Gospel,' he said. In the Puritan tradition, they must avoid the sins of the world: breaking the Sabbath, pandering to the lusts of the body, telling vile stories and enjoying worldly amusements such as the theatre. A line should be drawn between the Church and the world 'and every Christian should get both feet out of the world'.

One of the longest of the reformist campaigns, in America and in Britain, concerned the role of women, a backlash that grew more serious after the Civil War. Up until then, women could be ridiculed as Amelia Bloomer was for wearing her eponymous trousers, or revered or ridiculed for their part in the abolition crusade. After the war the question was asked what they wanted with education – 'why spoil a good mother by making an ordinary grammarian?' – or a job, when they should be at home, breeding a family. Or why they wished to have the vote for that matter.

They were frivolously abandoning the high and sacred duty of motherhood – to go shopping (not unlike Beecher, though he tended to be mocked rather than excoriated for it). As the *New York Times* put it in 1881: 'The awful prevalence of the vice of shopping among women is one of those signs of the time which lead the thoughtful patriot almost to despair of the future of our country.'[27] They were being encouraged by dangerous, radical ideas of equality that were seducing them from their household responsibilities. Some even wanted to divorce their abusive husbands – this was just 'liberal obscenity mongering'. A book entitled *Cupid's Yokes* by the socialist free-thinker Ezra Heywood, arguing in favour of free choice and mutual respect in marriage, was banned by the courts as 'obscene, lewd and lascivious'.[28]

The sweet and fragile wife and devoted mother was being replaced by uppity harridans. State legislatures started making divorce more difficult, not less. Contraceptives and abortion had both been relatively freely available at the time of the Civil War. Recent studies suggest the barely credible statistic that in the middle of the nineteenth century there was one abortion for every six live births and condoms sold for six cents apiece in the 1870s.[29] But now both were increasingly restricted.

Such practices were seen as affronts both to male authority and female dignity: 'Ladies boast to each other of the impunity with which they have aborted, as they do of their expenditures, of their dress, of their success in society . . . [few dare] publicly or privately to acknowledge . . . the . . . first, highest and holiest duty of her sex to bring forth living children,' said Horatio Storer, the vice-president of the American Medical Association, in a publication entitled *Why Not? A Book for Every Woman*, issued in 1866.

The problem of this feminist thinking was regarded as both serious and urgent because the patriotic home-born mothers of America were being outbred by the flotsam of the underclass of immigrants flooding ashore. Americans were told they were indulging in too much pleasure and not enough breeding. J. H. Kellogg, the health faddist and inventor of the ubiquitous breakfast cereal, declared that the fault lay with excess indulgence: 'Too frequent emissions of life-giving fluid and too frequent excitement of the nervous system', with contraceptives to blame as 'accessories of evil'.

What was worse, the immigrants were not only bringing with them their alien cultures, lack of English, lazy and dirty habits and ignorance of American customs and civilisation. They were also bringing with them immorality, vice and diseases that would enervate the character of the nation. The vilest practices were being imported from effete old Europe. They seduced women and enticed them into white slavery, locked them away and subjected them to unspeakable crimes, all aided and abetted by corrupt city governments, backed in office by Catholics, Irish, Radicals and Free-Thinkers. That was where the real degradation lay. Preachers reported hearing piteous cries from barred upper windows and locked rooms as they walked the late-night city streets: 'My God, if only I could get out of here!'

This abduction of white women produced a moral panic and legislation was rushed through Congress. The Mann Act of 1910 was intended to stamp out white slaving by prohibiting the transportation of women across state lines for immoral purposes, and was passed with the support of Southern politicians because, as Representative Mann said, the traffic was 'much more horrible than any black slave traffic ever was in the history of the world'. The Act was an early and ostentatious example of legislation adopted in haste by the executive and legislative branches of government because of a moral fright. As such, the Congress and president trampled, seemingly without noticing, over other traditional rights, including those of individuals and of the states to regulate their own borders – states' rights, over which America had gone to war fifty years before, were forgotten in an attempt to legislate for a transient scare story. It would not be the last time that such a localised panic would produce such a sweeping federal solution.

In all this, it was only a minor inconvenience that researchers sent out to investigate the slave trade could find no evidence whatsoever that it was being carried on. A researcher for a commission in New York in 1913 reported back: 'I have entered at least 2,500 houses of ill-repute and talked face to face with possibly 15,000 of these women and I . . . do not hesitate to tell you that they are wedded to their ways and that they laugh and make fun of those who try to help them.' A more pressing imperative, the commission found, was that a prostitute could earn five times as much as a stenographer, twelve times as much as maid servants, and twenty times more than factory workers.[30]

It did not matter. A federal bureau of investigation was established to track down the white slavers. In due course its remit widened, and it became known by its initial capitals: the FBI.

In this climate of insecurity and moral fear, none was more influential than the plump and bewhiskered figure of Anthony Comstock, the archetype and progenitor of a whole series of righteous crusaders after virtue. Comstock, a dry-goods clerk from Connecticut, who had been shocked as a young man in the Union army by the profanity of his comrades (and, worse, by their ridiculing him about it when he complained), became in 1873 the guiding force behind the formation of the New York Society for the Suppression of Vice.

He started off with an energetic lobbying campaign against 'vile books' such as birth control literature, which convinced a sleepy House of Representatives, at a late hour, in the concluding minutes of a legislative session, without debate, to forbid the transportation of 'every obscene, lewd or lascivious and every filthy book, pamphlet, picture, paper, letter, writing, print or other publication of an indecent character' through the post. Furthermore, Congress appointed Comstock himself as a postal inspector so he could be the regulator of his own legislation (though he retained his day job in dry goods), interpreter of the Act and, effectively, the definer of what obscenity was for the nation. It was the same control mechanism used by the Southern opponents of abolition years earlier, and not only did it effectively prohibit the dissemination of information about birth control, but it also took in a whole range of other material that Mr Comstock deemed to fall within his purview. This included anatomy textbooks, sex education, contraceptives, the Louisiana lottery, and eventually even the text of George Bernard Shaw's play *Mrs Warren's Profession*.

Comstock was zealous in his work and highly political. Armed with sanctions under the Act that made provision for fines up to $5,000 and prison sentences of up to ten years, he prosecuted not only pornographers, but also persecuted those who could best be described as people who disagreed with him. Thus he went after the feminist campaigner and spiritualist Victoria Woodhull – the first woman ever to run for president – for distributing obscene material when she published the allegations of adultery against Henry Ward Beecher (she had done so, incidentally, not to censure the preacher's hypocrisy, but to praise his 'immense physical potency' and to celebrate his apparent conversion to free love).

Comstock was personally brave in confronting his opponents, though his bulk – '210 pounds of muscle and bone...Atlas shoulders and a chest of prodigious girth' – probably helped. His raids were, after all, good publicity and he was often accompanied by reporters. Sometimes he went in disguise or pretended to be drunk, and he was not above entrapping his victims by soliciting material from them. In his pockets he carried rubber toys to distract the children of those he came to arrest. His luxurious sidewhiskers were grown to hide a scar inflicted by a disgruntled victim and he received acid bombs and smallpox scabs from ill-wishers in his own mail.

He was, of course, totally undiscriminating in his seizures of material, aided by the fact that juries usually did not get to examine it before reaching their verdicts when the cases he brought came to court, having to accept judges' word that it was too lewd to be seen by ordinary men. The obscenity could even reside in a single word or phrase in an otherwise blameless document. No wonder Shaw was enraged when his play was banned. He fulminated: 'Comstockery is the world's standing joke at the expense of the United States . . . Europe likes to hear of such things. It confirms the deep-seated conviction of the Old World that America is a provincial place, a second-rate country-town civilization after all.'[31]

That worried Comstock not at all. He had an immense influence in the prudification of America, instilling terror into legitimate publishers and doctors as well as crooks, cranks, quacks and pornographers. The fact that at least a dozen of those he persecuted committed suicide was merely, he felt, a condign sign of God's judgment on them. He provoked opposition (though not usually in the press) and by the end of his long career had become a figure of fun – a cartoon of the time shows him hauling a bedraggled young woman before a judge with the caption: 'Your honor, this woman gave birth to a naked child!' – but by then he had had his effect.

Comstock kept a precise tally of his achievements: 15 tons of books destroyed, 284,000 pounds of printers' plates, 4 million pictures and 3,750 people prosecuted, $237,134.30 levied in fines and imprisonments totalling 565 years, 11 months and 20 days imposed. Towards the end of his forty-two-year career, he punctiliously boasted to an interviewer: 'I have convicted persons enough to fill a passenger train of 61 coaches . . . 60 containing 60 passengers each and the 61st almost full. I have destroyed 160 tons of obscene literature.'

A few months before he died in 1915, Comstock gave an interview to a woman journalist named Mary Alden Hopkins from *Harper's Weekly*. She wrote:

'Does it not,' I asked, 'allow the judge considerable leeway in deciding whether or not a book or a picture is immoral?'

'No,' replied Mr Comstock, '. . . what he has to decide is whether or not it might arouse in young and inexperienced minds, lewd or libidinous thoughts.'

If at times his ban seems to some to be too sweepingly applied it is because his faith looks forward to a time when there shall be in all the world not one object to awaken sensuous thoughts in the minds of young people.

I was somewhat confused at first that Mr Comstock should class contraceptives with pornographic objects which debauch children's fancies, for I knew that the European scientists who advocate their use have no desire at all to debauch children. When I asked Mr Comstock about this, he replied – with scant patience of 'theorizers' who do not know human nature: 'If you open the door to anything, the filth will all pour in and the degradation of youth will follow.'[32]

If his methods sound vaguely familiar, that may be because they greatly impressed a young Washington lawyer just starting to make his way in the public service, J. Edgar Hoover, who would shortly employ them when he took charge of the FBI, during the course of an even longer career invigilating the private morals of the public.

By the time Comstock died, the moralists were about to win their longest-awaited and most surprising victory, with the prohibition of alcoholic drinks, a reform that was supposed to usher in the kind of virtuous society that Protestant campaigners had long hoped for – sober, diligent and high-minded – but that actually produced the reverse – hedonistic, corrupt and pervasively criminal. It is perhaps understandable that today's successors to the prohibitionists, wishing to impose their own moral standards on others, enforced by law, tend not to mention it. Prohibition remains, however, the US government's most sweeping – and unsuccessful – attempt to invade the rights of its citizens and legislate to make them good. Nor was it an entirely reactionary campaign. Many progressives supported abolition as a means of improving the lives of the poor and elevating their condition.

Various campaigns for abstinence had been conducted throughout the nineteenth century, led largely by Christians, in an attempt not only to restrict the amount that was being drunk, but also overtly to create a better society: a community of saints shorn of a wide range of vices. Visitors to America often commented on the amount of alcohol being drunk: 'many of them drink spirits almost the moment after they get out of bed and also at frequent intervals during the day; . . . but excessive drinking is rare,' noted one visitor in 1818. But that was too much: as early as 1784, an influential pamphlet by Dr Benjamin Rush set the tone with *An Inquiry into the Effect of Spirituous Liquors upon the Human Body and Mind*. Preachers emphasised the moral depravity that even a single drink could bring: here's the Revd Nathaniel Prime of Long Island in 1811: 'Drunkenness and lewdness go hand in hand . . . few who have drunk a gill of ardent spirits can be exposed to . . . small temptation without becoming adulterous in the sight of God.' Or the Revd Dr Heman Humphrey of Amherst College: 'All who embark on this flood are in danger of hellfire.'

The lower classes were infected by the habitual use of spirits such as whisky, gin and particularly the demon rum, from which they needed to be weaned. If it could be done, a sparkling prospect opened: there would be no need for any prisons, or lunatic asylums, workhouses, maybe even of police, and Americans would become a race strong in body, clear in mind and industrious in habits.[33]

More ruthlessly, if the working population could be persuaded off their drinks of choice, especially by taxing them so highly that they could no longer be afforded, and persuading them on to beer or cider instead, then those who insisted on drinking spirits would rapidly succumb to a poverty-stricken death, leaving America in the possession of the virtuous. In pursuit of such a strategy, Elkanah Watson, the man who invented the idea of the county fair, established the Berkshire Agricultural Association in order specifically to encourage farmers to plant more apple trees and hopvines.

Just as the abolitionists and women's activists did – often they were the same people – the temperance activists campaigned and organised, if necessary, to close the saloons down street by street, town by town and state by state.

They issued pamphlets, they wrote books (*Ten Nights in a Barroom* by T. S. Arthur was regarded as the movement's *Uncle Tom's Cabin* with its message: 'For every [moderate drinker] who restrains himself, ten will rush on to ruin'), they wrote songs, and they formed Temperance Unions, Anti-Saloon Leagues, Women's Christian Temperance Unions and children's Cold Water Armies. They pointed out what was true: that saloons and bars were often dirty and disreputable places, run yet again by foreigners. The social reformer Jacob Riis estimated that, south of 14th Street, Manhattan, there were 111 Protestant churches and 4,065 saloons: 'there are easily 10 saloons to every church today. I am afraid too that the congregations are larger by a good deal; certainly the attendance is steadier and the contributions the more liberal the week round, Sunday included.'[34] The local inhabitants were 'Italian, German, French, African, Spanish, Bohemian, Russian, Jewish . . . the one thing you will ask for in vain in the chief city of America is a distinctively American community,' said the Baptist Missionary Society in 1906. They were, in short, in the words of the *Saturday Evening Post*'s Kenneth Roberts: 'human parasites [who would produce] a hybrid race of good-for-nothing mongrels'.

The roll-call of bar owners in New York City told the virtuous all they needed to know: Cross-Eyed Murphy, Moustache Ike Witkoski, Slippery Johnny Leipziger, Max Hahn, Stitch McCarthy and boxers such as John L. Sullivan and Tom Sharkey. Such men in the big city took your money and cheated you. And they got their friends elected to office.[35]

The industrialists behind such bars were not much better: the brewers were Germans and the distillers were Irish. They were also Catholics. The temperance activist Alphonse Alva Hopkins worked up a fine head of steam:

> Besodden Europe, worse bescourged than by war, famine and pestilence, sends here her drink-makers, her drunkard makers and her drunkards . . . with all their un-American and anti-American ideas of morality and government; they are absorbed into our national life but not assimilated; with no liberty whence they came, they demand unrestricted liberty among us, even to license what we loathe and through the ballot box, flung wide open to them by foolish statesmanship . . . they dominate our Sabbath; they have set up for us their own moral standards, which are grossly immoral; they govern our great cities . . . foreign control or conquest could gain little more through armies and fleets . . . Foreign conquest is rapidly making us un-Christian, with immorality throned in power.[36]

The tentacles were spreading: as immigration peaked in the first decade of the twentieth century, the USA was becoming an urban nation. By 1920, the year the Volstead Act ushered in prohibition, the US census showed for the first time that more Americans lived in cities than in the country. In such circumstances, the temperance movement took off. Whereas in 1904 only a minority of states and counties had banned alcohol (clustered almost exclusively in the South and Midwest and Maine in the far North-East, which had been the first to ban alcohol), by 1917 the picture was reversed. Only California, the area around New Orleans and up the Mississippi, the Great Lakes and a swathe from New York up to the Canadian border remained wet. By then, twenty-seven states were entirely dry.

If the message in the North was that drunken foreigners were diluting the blood-line, in the South, despite the fact that many black churches supported temperance, campaigners fostered fears about out-of-control, drunken negroes.

The force of the evangelical campaign was thus directed against outsiders: sinners, people regarded as inferior, degenerate and subversive of American values and its way of life, rather than at any wider cause that might have driven them to drink in the first place, such as their living conditions, their impoverished lives and lack of alternative entertainment. The social gospel played very little part in the campaign. Samuel Gompers, the trade union leader, said that temperance could be achieved without legislation by 'increasing wages, establishing a shorter work day, affording better aspirations and higher ideals which the better standard of living . . . will bring'. Professor Morone, who quotes him, adds: 'Eradicating poverty never unleashed anywhere near the same prolonged, fervent, millennial reformation as fighting drink.'[37]

It was US participation in the First World War, its first world-power intervention in a foreign conflict, that finally made prohibition possible. The brewers were Germans, they had opposed the war, and it was their beer that was holding up the war effort, so that drinking it was almost treasonable. Businesses hoped that the reform would eradicate their workers' hangovers on 'blue Mondays' and the argument that for sobriety to be made to work it was necessary to ban drink state by state gained acceptance. Prohibition therefore suddenly became a patriotic duty, a moral imperative and a panacea for the nation's ills. The brave new post-war world would require clear sight and minds purged of befuddlement.

Republicans, with their solid rural and Protestant constituency, supported prohibition; Democrats were more split, between the temperance South, still voting solidly for them, and their supporters in the boozy cities of the North: a division that would cause them some lively, prolonged (and ultimately unsuccessful) presidential nominating conventions throughout the 1920s. It was to be the Democrat president Woodrow Wilson's desperate search for votes in a hostile Congress, for US participation in his plan for a League of Nations, that would ultimately swing his support behind prohibition.

Frederick Lewis Allen in his brilliant book about the 1920s, *Only Yesterday*, published in 1931 when the title really was true and prohibition was still in force, says: 'Nothing in recent American history is more extraordinary, as one looks back from the 1930s, than the ease with which – after generations of uphill fighting by the drys – prohibition was finally written upon the statute books. The country accepted it not only willingly, but almost absent-mindedly.'[38] The 18th Amendment which presaged the reform was passed by the Senate in 1917 after thirteen hours of debate and by the House of Representatives in a single day. The Volstead Act, which enforced the amendment, was passed even more quickly. Only two states, Rhode Island and Connecticut, refused to ratify. And, sensing that the long promised Utopia had arrived, the Anti-Saloon League believed that Congress's appropriation of $5 million a year would be quite enough to secure enforcement. That must rank as one of the biggest miscalculations ever.

6

A Book Dropped Out
of Heaven

'Heave an egg out a Pullman window and you will hit a Fundamentalist almost anywhere in the United States today.'

H. L. Mencken

Very early one morning in the Fall of 1888, after a long railroad journey back from making a speech at a town by the biblical name of Chadron in the desolate windswept wastes of northwestern Nebraska, an ambitious twenty-eight-year-old local politician named William Jennings Bryan crept into his bedroom back home in Lincoln, the state capital, and woke his wife. Sitting on the edge of the bed, he told her: 'Mary, I have had a strange experience. Last night I found that I had power over the audience. I could move them as I chose. I have more than usual power as a speaker. I know it. God grant that I may use it wisely.' And he fell on his knees in prayer.[1]

He had indeed. It was a voice like a bell and the ringing power of his oratory that brought him fame. Within eight years Bryan was running as the Democratic Party's candidate for president – at thirty-six in 1896, the youngest man ever nominated by one of the two main parties – and he would run again twice more in 1900 and 1908. He was, perhaps, the most radical politician ever to be a candidate for the highest office with a chance of actually winning it. Although unsuccessful each time he ran for the presidency, he would eventually become a revered – and reviled – elder statesman of his party. His campaign in 1896 was the first to take on a modern style as he crossed the country by railroad, making speeches at every whistle-stop as no presidential candidate had ever done before. He would also, ostentatiously, be the first national politician to declare his evangelical religious beliefs as the prime motivating factor in his politics. 'Much as I am interested in government,' he would declare, 'I am more interested in religion. Anxious as I am too that man will vote right, I am more anxious that man shall live right.'[2]

Bryan is indeed in many ways a recognisably modern politician, although he is largely forgotten today, long disowned and ignored by those on the Religious Right who might otherwise be expected to revere him for his beliefs. But he espoused a form of religion-based politics that is largely alien to them. It is likely that no other single politician in American history has supported quite so many socially progressive reforms: women's suffrage, federal income tax, railroad regulation, currency reform, state referendums, campaign fund disclosure, improved factory conditions, public holidays, urban parks, as well as opposition to capital punishment. 'Probably no other American, save the authors of the Bill of Rights, could rightly claim credit for as many Constitutional amendments as the Great Commoner,' says the historian Edward Larson.[3]

Bryan regularly outlined for audiences another constant theme of his career, based on his religious principles, pacifism: 'The day will come when the world will see the folly of the doctrine that you can justly settle a difference of opinion by shooting the man who may differ from you,' he told an audience in Havana in the early 1900s. In 1910 in New York, he added that the USA should 'tell the world that it did not believe in war, that it did not believe that it was the right way to settle disputes, that it had no disputes that it was not willing to submit to the judgement of the world and, if this nation did it, it not only would not be attacked by any other nation on the earth, but . . . it would become the supreme power in this world.'[4] In 1913, as a reward for support and in recognition of his influence over the party, Woodrow Wilson made him Secretary of State, but Bryan grew increasingly disenchanted and resigned two years later, after Germany's sinking of the *Lusitania*, in protest at the pressure mounting for the USA to enter the First World War on the allies' side. There is more than a hint that Wilson and his other colleagues found him a tad sanctimonious, and his parading of his religious conscience insufferable. When he resigned, the Springfield Republican described him, curiously, as having suffered a 'mad mullah outbreak'.[5] Bryan of course lived in a world before Al-Qaeda, but it is possible to suspect that modern Religious Rightists would have issues with his view of the world and his Christian imperatives.

All this was in the future as Bryan self-consciously seized the nomination for president at the Democrats' 1896 convention in Chicago with one of the most famous and barn-storming speeches in US political history. It was a call for the American currency, at that time based on the gold standard, to be modified to allow silver coinage as well, so that the amount of money in circulation would increase, in the hope of boosting commerce and spending.

This dilution was a populist solution to the economic depression of the mid-1890s and it found favour among those hardest hit by it: factory workers, thrown out of work, small farmers and, not least, the silver miners of the West. On the other side, the undermining of the currency was viewed with horror by the industrialists, bankers and middle classes of the east, as economically illiterate and recklessly inflationary. Bryan, with the Nebraska delegation at the convention, was naturally on the farmers' side, in favour of 'free silver' and the loosening of the currency. But the way he made his case and swept the convention was with a speech couched in ostentatiously religious terms – he was a lay preacher – and the reaction he obtained had all the fervour of a revivalist meeting. More than a century on, it remains probably the most famous speech in the history of US political conventions.

Like that other great American political speech, Martin Luther King's 'I have a dream' civil rights oration on the steps of the Lincoln Memorial in 1963, the cadences of Bryan's remarks echoed those of preachers down the ages. It was a great evangelical sermon, laden with biblical resonances.

Early recordings of Bryan's voice show him to have had a pleasant, well-modulated and resonant baritone. It was one which could fill a hall and thrill an audience.[6] He was at this stage of his career also a strikingly handsome man of a sort that would make him perfect candidate material even today, with dark hair, chiselled features, a gimlet eye and a winning smile. He had not come as one of the party's favoured candidates, but as he spoke, applause and cheers repeatedly echoed round the stiflingly hot convention hall. He seized the moment with calculated messianic zeal. One farmer delegate was observed repeatedly striking his chair exclaiming: 'My God! My God!'

Bryan told them: 'You tell us that the great cities are in favour of the gold standard. Burn down your cities and leave your farms and your cities will grow up again. But destroy your farms and the grass will grow in every city of the Union.' Men must choose between two theories of government; one that 'if you will only legislate to make the well-to-do prosperous, their prosperity will leak through on those below', the other, Democratic, idea was: 'if you legislate to make the masses prosperous, their prosperity will find its way up through every class which rests upon them'. Trickle-down economics is evidently nothing new.

Then, the famous peroration: 'Having behind us the producing masses of this nation . . . we will answer their demands for a gold standard by saying to them: "You shall not press down upon the brow of labour this crown of thorns, you shall not crucify mankind on a cross of gold." ' [7] As he said this, Bryan raised his hands to the sides of his head and slowly lowered his fingers on to the sides of his temples. It was electrifying. The audience could almost imagine the thorns piercing his skull and the blood trickling down his face. With the final phrase he extended his arms wide as if he were himself hanging from a cross.

No wonder that, as he resumed his seat and they realised he had finished, following a few seconds' silence, the convention erupted. The ovation lasted twenty-five minutes, men danced in the aisles and, on the wave of emotion, Bryan swept the nomination. 'The audience,' Bryan wrote later, 'acted like a trained choir – in fact I thought of a choir as I noted how simultaneously and in unison they responded to each point made.' Others were less impressed: 'For the first time I can understand the scenes of the French Revolution,' said one. Another delegate turned to Clarence Darrow, the Chicago lawyer who twenty-nine years later would be Bryan's nemesis, and said: 'I have been thinking over Bryan's speech. What did he say anyhow?' But it did not matter about the content, the fervour won. [8]

In presidential elections at that time, it was customary for candidates not to campaign themselves, but to remain at home and graciously receive delegations there while sitting on their front porches. They left the murky business of electioneering and deal-making to business managers and cronies and duly rewarded them if they won office. William McKinley, Bryan's Republican rival, was no exception; dozens of groups travelled to his home in Canton, Ohio, on a daily basis, to be rewarded by seeing him wave and murmur platitudes to them.

But Bryan – the 'Boy Orator of the Platte', the 'Silver Knight of the West', 'the Great Commoner' – took to the railroads himself to make his case directly to the electorate. He had his shoes specially reinforced to stand the strain, bought his own tickets and travelled by scheduled services, making speeches from the rear platforms of carriages wherever the trains stopped on their long, slow, jolting, hot and dusty journeyings. In three months he travelled 18,000 gruelling miles, made 600 speeches – sometimes 20 a day – and addressed an estimated 5 million people. Although he was a teetotaller, he reeked of gin 'like a wrecked distillery' because, in pre-air conditioning and anti-perspirant days, as the train travelled onwards he would strip down and rub himself with alcohol to eliminate the smell of sweat, apparently innocently oblivious of the alternative impression he might give.

In his campaign, he gave the Republican Party managers an enormous fright. Some employers were reduced to warning their workers that if they voted for Bryan they would be out of work the next day. But ultimately the power of money told and McKinley won narrowly, but by a clear 600,000 votes out of 13.6 million cast. The Republicans carried the North, the Middle West and some of the Far West, while Bryan won the South, the western plains and the mountain states. McKinley won the upper and middle classes, the prosperous, large farmers and the urban workers; Bryan won the small farmers and the dispossessed, those uncertain of their place in the modern world and baffled by the changes being remorselessly wrought in their lives. He brought a utopian, radical but impractical message to deal with old fears and modern uncertainties. But the economic depression was lifting and the USA was becoming an urban country, the Republicans had powerful press support – the *New York Times* called Bryan 'an irresponsible, unregulated, ignorant, prejudiced, pathetically honest and enthusiastic crank' – and employer pressure probably told too.

And yet he still nearly won. Even the wife of the Republican senator, the fabulously wealthy, patrician Henry Cabot Lodge, was impressed. She wrote to the British ambassador: 'A disorganised mob, out of which there burst into sight, hearing and force, one man, but such a man! Alone, penniless, without backing, without money, with scarce a paper, without speakers, that man fought such a fight that even those in the East can call him a crusader, an inspired fanatic – a prophet! It has been marvellous. Hampered by such a following, such a platform . . . he almost won.'

Bryan had brought revivalist rhetoric and messianic conviction to a presidential campaign for the first time. He never got as close again. In 1900, campaigning as the Democratic candidate on the same platform, though with added anti-imperialism, he lost to McKinley once more, this time by 860,000 votes, and in 1908 he lost again, this time to William Howard Taft, by more than a million votes, receiving a little less support than he had twelve years before, even though the size of the electorate had increased.

For his third attempt, Bryan still carried his Bible with him but his opponent Taft, a portly Republican lawyer who had been Theodore Roosevelt's vice-president and was a somewhat unwilling candidate for the presidency, kept his religious views firmly to himself. This was unsurprising as Taft was a Unitarian, a disbeliever in the concept of the Trinity and denier of the divinity of Jesus Christ, and so therefore a heretic to many Americans, then and now.

It is a denominational allegiance that would almost certainly make any such candidate impossible to elect a century later. Roosevelt, the man who had relished the 'bully pulpit' of the presidency, advised him not to mention his religious views during the campaign: 'Will, I would simply say that you decline to permit any such gross violation of the first principles of our government as an effort to make you subscribe to any given principles of dogmatic theology before counting you as eligible to receive votes . . . the same attack was made upon Lincoln as being a non-orthodox Christian as upon you, and far severer attacks on Jefferson.'

The retiring president added publicly:

If there is one thing for which we stand in this country, it is for complete religious freedom and for the right of every man to worship his creator as his conscience dictates . . . It is an emphatic negation of this right to cross-examine a man on his religious views before being willing to support him for office. Is he a good man and is he fit for office? These are the only questions which there is a right to ask ... In my own cabinet there are at present Catholic, Protestant and Jew – the Protestants being of various denominations. I am incapable of discriminating between them.[9]

In time Bryan grew fat, old and bald and became something of an embarrassment to his party, though he ostentatiously continued to deploy his religious conscience. His political ambitions thwarted, he took to spreading the message by writing syndicated articles – for which he earned the not insubstantial sum for those days of $20,000 a year – and advertising real estate prospects in Florida, the state to which he and his wife retired. And the Great Commoner moved increasingly into the maelstrom of evangelical fervour, devoting his later years to preaching (and earning money) on the religious lecture circuit. This was not such a strange progression, for Bryan's political message had always mirrored his religious one: the nobility of mankind, particularly Americans, and the moral leadership of the USA. His populist rhetoric chimed well with his religious outpourings. He had, it was said, 'a persistent faith in the essential goodness of Man, who would respond immediately and wholeheartedly to the truth once he was made to see it and understand it'.[10]

Bryan made a fine figurehead and a popular orator, but he was no great thinker or intellectual. He came from a Presbyterian background and a devoutly religious Illinois family, in which his lawyer father Silas led prayers three times a day and hymn-singing sessions around the family piano every evening. After a brief personal struggle with the new doctrine of Darwinism while he was at college, Bryan never again questioned his faith and in due course decided that God had indeed called him to use his oratorical gifts as a politician rather than a church minister. Thereafter, even at the height of his career, he made it his business to patrol the country, preaching an old-time religion that he saw as under attack from the forces of an aggressively secular modernity. It is a characterisation that, more than eighty years on, remains potent and is still constantly deployed.

Indeed, in a lecture that was actually entitled 'The Old Time Religion', delivered to the Winona Bible Conference in 1911, he outlined the view that religion must not change to meet the conditions of the day, but should hold firm to its received, biblical message; 'it is better to raise the temperature than change the thermometer . . . [and] in the abundance of our wealth, we have surrounded ourselves with material comforts until the care of the body has absorbed our thought and the saving of the soul has become a secondary matter'.[11] It is a strikingly similar message to that deployed nearly a century later in the debate over homosexuality that is dividing evangelicals in both the UK and the USA: how far secular society has abandoned its Christian roots and ignored the constant teaching of the Bible.

It was probably the politician in Bryan that caused him to enliven his audiences of believers by regularly proposing a trial of strength with the forces of secularism. He saw it in biblical terms, similar to the contest between Elijah and the prophets of Baal in the Old Testament, to see whose God was stronger: 'Let the atheists and the materialists produce a better Bible than ours, if they can . . . use to the full every instrumentality that is employed in modern civilisation, let them embody the results of their best intelligence in a book and offer it to the world . . . Have they the confidence that the prophets of Baal had in their god?' This not only underestimated the opposition – besides presuming that they were also actuated by quasi-religious impulses – but confirmed him in his opinion that his views were unchallengeable.

For Bryan showed very little interest in thinking more deeply about his faith, or engaging intellectually either with modern science or progressive theology – 'if we will try to live up to that which we can understand, we will be kept so busy doing good that we will not have time to worry about the things that we do not understand,' he said to applause. And, in a very American train of thought – one again echoed in some modern reactions to Islam and towards those 'old' European countries that were hesitant in supporting the war in Iraq ninety years later – Bryan added that he had found that 'in the countries where other religions and philosophies prevail, except where they have borrowed from Christianity, they have made no progress in 1,500 or 2,000 years'. This wilful and determined ignorance was eventually to receive its come-uppance in the most humiliatingly public way.

Yet there were many who heard Bryan and rallied to him because of the uncertainties of the day. Just as the farmers of the South and West had feared for their economic futures in 1896 and become his most loyal supporters, so, as the twentieth century dawned, many others whose living was precarious and seemingly under threat supported him too. In a religious society, they sought the comfort and security of the Bible as a refuge from the ruthlessness and mechanisation of modern life. Indeed there was something to fear from the survival of the fittest theories preached by secular Social Darwinists, which would eventually spin on from justifications for ruthless capitalism into altogether more murky arguments for eugenics and the elimination of the medically, intellectually or racially 'inferior'.

These uncertainties gave birth to both fundamentalism, a belief in the literal and inerrant truth of the Bible as the direct, unexpurgated word of God and to an entirely new religious form, Pentecostalism, which would eventually towards the end of the twentieth century grow exponentially to become one of the world's largest Christian denominations, especially among the poor and dispossessed. Both sprang to prominence in the USA in the first decade of the century.

How this religious movement transmogrified out of an essentially progressive philosophy of social concern and political activism into what became a deeply conservative and introspective creed – what some have called the Great Reversal – is a question in which Bryan played an unwitting part.

The answer seems to lie in the fact that social Christianity became increasingly associated with political liberalism, while many, if not most, Protestant evangelicals were inherently conservative. They were suspicious of Progressivism and not at all sure whether they wanted to be part of it, or even whether religion had a role to play in politics at all. Mostly they were white, mainly they were struggling to maintain economic security and respectability, and many of them were new arrivals from the country into the godless and burgeoning cities of a rapidly industrialising America. It was becoming an alien country to them, devoid of the old Protestant certainties and values, filling up with alien immigrants: Catholics and Jews, who to their minds espoused heretical, even satanic, cultish views. The universities were pouring out pastors of their own denominations who no longer seemed to believe in the old traditions of the Bible. This was a destabilising experience that only increased their need for certainty in their lives. Again, the parallels with the lives of their great-grandchildren in modern, suburban America are striking: the insecurity, the isolation and the fear. These concerns played directly and neatly into the vital, ongoing internecine dispute about the priorities of evangelicalism: was it meant, bluntly, to transform individual lives, or to change the world?

The conservative faction suspected that for liberals it was too much the latter. Indeed some progressive Christians were beginning to suggest that the important element of their mission was to alter society through the deployment of the social gospel and that what directed that impulse ultimately did not really matter. In the words of the historian George Marsden: 'The social gospel emphasised social concern in an exclusivistic way which seemed to undercut the relevance of the message of eternal salvation through trust in Christ's atoning work . . . Traditional Christian belief seemed to be at stake. The social gospel was presented as equivalent to the Gospel itself.'[12] Similar arguments were deployed by conservative evangelicals against their liberal opponents a century later during the course of the debate about homosexuality: that liberals were accommodating the world and its gay inhabitants at the expense of the eternal truths of the Bible.

In a way, this debate reached right back to the Pilgrim Fathers, but what was to happen in the early twentieth century was a positive withdrawal by many evangelicals from engagement with the political process altogether. This retreat was to be accelerated by the First World War when the power of hideous modern technology and its ability to demoralise, crush and destroy the human spirit, as well as the human body, became all too apparent. Marsden says that funda-mentalists emerged in the 1920s, fixated on a set of views that had been characteristic of middle-class Americans in the last years before the crisis occurred: 'Their social views were frozen at a point that had been the prevailing American opinion around 1890, save that the fundamentalists of the 1920s had forgotten the degree to which their predecessors – and even they themselves – had earlier espoused rather progressive social concerns.' They wanted certainty and they distrusted intellectuals with their new-fangled ideas – and fundamentalism reassured them that they were right. Anti-intellectualism has been the curse of evangelicalism ever since. As the US theologian Mark A. Noll has it in his book *The Scandal of the Evangelical Mind*: 'The scandal . . . is that there is not much of an evangelical mind.'[13]

This ferment occurred in parallel to an internal theological dispute that to outsiders might appear both arcane and bizarre – as indeed it is – but that continues to animate many fundamentalists even today. The debate over what is called dispensational premillennialism and the rival theory of postmillennialism remains vital and goes to the heart of different strands of American evangelicalism, informing and influencing its adherents' views of society, of the outside world and of their own destiny. The fact that millions of Americans now have a view of the world and its fate that shapes their attitude to a range of institutions, such as the UN, and also to issues such as the environment and climate change, based on their view of how the world is going to end, makes what otherwise would seem to be highly artificial and inward-looking theological disputes of continuing importance.

Postmillennial theories had been around for quite a while before the late nineteenth century. Based on a reading of supposed prophecies in the Book of Revelation, these postulated the imminent defeat of the anti-Christ (usually identified as the Pope, as head of the main false religion, but also including other faiths such as Islam) and the arrival of a 1,000-year, millennial, golden age. During this period the Holy Spirit would be poured out and the gospel would spread around the world in advance of the return of Christ at the end of the period (which might not be 1,000 years of 365 days as such – a lot of ink was spilled defining how long the period might actually last in practice). This, surprisingly enough, was an optimistic world-view that foresaw the inevitability of human progress and the vanquishing of evil. The abolition of slavery in the 1860s was taken as a particular sign of the defeat of wickedness and the changing of the culture for the better, as were technological and scientific advances, which were to be welcomed. Some postmillennialists came to believe that the era had even already dawned, in which case perhaps the Bible could take on new meanings as it was already being fulfilled. Of course, the USA would lead the march of humanity towards the sunlit uplands, any day, so that the theory combined both social progressivism and a sense of national righteousness.

Premillennialism by contrast was much more pessimistic and doom-laden and took the Bible's prophecies even more literally. The world was not going to get any better before Christ came. Indeed, it would only get worse. The theory was actually given its original force by an Englishman, John Nelson Darby, a disillusioned former Anglican minister who had been convinced that the mainstream churches had become too worldly, so that their message was corrupted and dissolute. He joined the harshly fundamentalist Plymouth Brethren instead, as the only pure Church, and, finding its message rather unpopular in England as well as too emollient, first established the breakaway Exclusive Brethren and then spent much of his time preaching the pure, unadorned Word in the USA, where his reception was much better.

Darby's was a gloomy vision, as shown by a lecture he gave in Geneva in 1840: 'Instead of permitting ourselves to hope for a continued progress of good, we must expect a progress of evil; and that the hope of the earth being filled with the knowledge of the Lord before the exercise of His judgement and the consummation of this judgement on the earth is delusive. We are to expect evil, until it becomes so flagrant that it will be necessary for the Lord to judge it.'[14]

Darby believed the Second Coming was imminent all right, but he also believed that Christ was coming with fire and the sword to settle the struggle against evil once and for all, rather than waiting for the eventual triumph of Goodness. The premillennialists believed absolutely and explicitly in the inerrant word of the Bible and held that even its most metaphorical allusions, such as those in Revelation, should be taken entirely seriously as the literal truth. Nowadays, there are those who believe that the hallucinations, visions and prophecies of St John the Divine as recorded in the last book of the Bible have more to do with the magic mushrooms he would have found to eat on the Greek island of Patmos than with a blinding flash of insight, but this is clearly only the malicious invention of those who would denigrate the inerrant word of Scripture.

To the premillennialist every biblical word is precisely and accurately true, however obscure and metaphorical it might appear, otherwise it would not be divinely ordained and the theory on which their belief is built would be undermined. They constructed a fantastically complicated and minutely precise story about the end times, based on readings from Revelation and the Book of Daniel – New Testament combining with Old to define a common and coherent plan – about the circumstances of Christ's return. The process is divided up with mathematical precision into seven ages, or dispensations, but at its culmination lies a seven-year period at the start of which the anti-Christ appears as a false prophet, the Beast of Revelation, a world leader who creates a new Roman empire and facilitates the return of the Jews to the Promised Land, but then persecutes them. This brief period of seething warfare, chaos and violent hatred and persecution (allegedly predicted in Matthew 24) is known as the tribulation, at the end of which an angry, judgmental Christ and his armies will arrive and defeat the Beast and his earthly powers in an apocalyptic battle in the Middle East at Armageddon. True Believers would escape this awful period at the outset by being carried safely up to heaven, a transfiguration known as the Rapture when they will meet Christ in the air. The defeat at Armageddon will be the signal for his 1,000-year reign to start.

As a story this is quite fantastical and bears all the hallmarks of those who in other circumstances believe the world can be defined through the configurations of tea leaves, the conjunctions of the planets, or statues weeping blood. But believers thought they saw the signs of the imminence of the End Times in the 1870s as the theory first took off, as they viewed what they took to be the growing wickedness of society and its rejection of God, as exemplified by growing secularisation and the continuing popularity of other religions. They believe it even more so now, identifying the Beast, preposterously, with the UN or the EU, or Iran or Islam, and pointing to events in the Middle East as a practical working-out of the prophecy. The great strength of the theory is its infinite flexibility and its apparent ability to be made applicable to events and circumstances arising long after it was first developed. True believers, of course, would assert that this only demonstrates its veracity.

Darby's theories became influential in the USA, a society

categorised for its sunny and optimistic view of the benignity of God and the inevitability of human progress, partly because it was indeed counter-intuitive and seemed to explain the moral decay and corruption his hearers saw around them (they still do), partly because it played into the neo-Puritans' view of themselves as an elect who would be saved by refusing to be contaminated by the rest of mankind, but mainly because he had a ready outlet to proselytise his message, which he had lacked in Britain. Darby was a success on the lecture and revival meeting circuits, just as men like Dow and Whitefield had been before him – he too could certainly preach jeremiads – and he gathered influential disciples to share his vision.

Although the two theories are similar in their creation of a view of the ending of the world, they are quite different as to how it will come to pass. The premillennialists in particular have created a hermetically sealed and impervious model of what is going to happen and which world events can be wrestled into fitting. With such a fatalistic view too of what will happen and who will be saved, there is less incentive to save the world or to work for its improvement. If the end is nigh, there is little point in trying to reform mankind, who are doomed anyway unless they convert. So the priority is living a holy life yourself and convincing others of the urgency of changing their lives, not embarking on irrelevant schemes to improve society, ameliorate injustice, or even to save the planet by husbanding its resources.

Indeed some premillennialists such as the Jehovah's Witnesses withdraw from the world altogether, refusing to vote or take part in civil society at all. The rigidity of the belief system was shown as recently as 2000 when the leadership of the Witnesses, who had privately excoriated the UN for years to their members as the Scarlet Beast of Revelation, were discovered to have secretly affiliated to it for years in order to secure the advantages of official recognition that affiliation made available to charitable groups. Found out, the Watch-tower, as the Witnesses' worldwide headquarters in Brooklyn is known, immediately disaffiliated, claiming they'd only done it to get access to the UN library. As the library is open to all *bona-fide* researchers, this seemed an odd explanation for an action that might otherwise seem hypocritical.

The *Watchtower* magazine had long illustrated its view of the coming apocalypse with lurid depictions of the destruction of the skyscrapers of New York, especially the UN building, but also the Twin Towers of the World Trade Center, so when on 9/11 they really did fall, the Witnesses were faced with a dilemma. Was this now a literal working out of God's judgment, using Muslims as his instruments, and were the drawings, which had proved only too prophetic, now, actually, in rather bad taste? The organisation quietly dropped them.

The premillennialists' chilly and exclusivist world-view gained ground in the latter decades of the nineteenth century, aided by the conversion to Darby's ideas of several leading evangelicals. Among them was the great evangelist Dwight Moody ('I don't find any place where God says the world is to grow better and better, I find that the world is to grow worse and worse and that at length there is going to be a separation'), but there were others as well, such as James Brookes, a Presbyterian minister from St Louis who was one of the organisers of the influential Niagara conferences that attracted evangelical ministers from across the USA. Darby, whose fierce doctrines had already split the Plymouth Brethren,was disappointed that these followers did not automatically abandon their own sects, by and large, and follow him. The Brethrens' regime was too harsh and joyless for that. But they certainly took up and spread his ideas.

The divergent views in the US evangelical world led naturally enough to splits and schisms among the elect and a self-absorption that was intense. They also gave rise to fierce introspective debates about biblical prophecies and textual readings. And, ultimately, to the new movement known as fundamentalism.

There were several strands to this idea, a term that is now sprayed about liberally to apply, often erroneously, to just about all evangelical Christians and indeed adherents of other religions. But it had its real origins in the premillennialist movement and specifically in a set of twelve paperback booklets published in America in the years before the First World War. These were indeed called The Fundamentals and were conceived and paid for by two South Californian oil millionaires named Lyman and Milton Stewart, who put up $250,000 for the project.[15]

The pamphlets were written by a group of American, Canadian and

British Bible teachers and evangelists between 1910 and 1915. The purpose was to combat the spread of secularism, but more particularly modern theologians' views of the meaning of the Bible, known as the 'higher criticism'.This was based on the belief that the Scriptures were not necessarily literally true and indeed could be fruitfully interpreted, which originated in Germany in the 1860s – coincidentally at about the same time as publication of Darwin's *The Origin of Species* in England. The higher criticism had now spread to many scholars in America itself.

Such views naturally threatened the evangelical mindset and The Fundamentals were intended to counteract them with clear expositions and explanations of what the Scriptures actually said. By so doing they would affirm the authority of God to waverers as well as to true but confused believers.

Certain beliefs were non-negotiable: the inerrant truth of the Bible, the virgin birth, Christ's atonement for the sins of the world, his resurrection, the authenticity of his miracles – and dispensationalism. The priority for these booklets and the guiding force behind them was not to change the world, but to secure the triumph of correct doctrine.

Three million copies of the booklets were produced, enough to send a set free to every pastor, missionary, professor and student of theology, YMCA and YWCA secretary, Sunday school superintendent and religious editor in the English-speaking world. Disappointingly, the initial response to the volumes was said to be cool, with relatively little notice being taken by the recipients, as if they were already imbued with the current theological scholarship.

Despite fundamentalism's later reputation for being hardline and doctrinaire, the booklets were actually rather moderate and intellectual in tone, as though infected by the prevailing religious culture. The authors who wrote the eighty articles the booklets eventually contained came from a variety of denominational backgrounds. There were Presbyterians, Southern Baptists, even the contemporary Anglican Bishop of Durham.[16] Marsden, the historian of fundamentalism, says they represent the movement at a transitional stage before it was reshaped and pushed to extremes by the intense heat of controversy. Some articles in the books defended Scripture and traditional questions such as the nature of the Trinity, others attacked rival creeds, such as Romanism, Mormonism and Eddyism – the Christian Science movement – and still others concentrated on evangelism.

The emphasis, given in personal testimonials, was on individual conversion and scarcely at all on political or social activism. Secular crusades, such as prohibition, were avoided, but, remarkably, one author, while stating that the Church should steer clear of politics, was able to maintain that the profession of Christianity was compatible with a personal advocacy of socialism. Salvation, one contributor, Robert Seer, said, would help to free mankind 'from want and disease and injustice and inequality and impurity and lust and hopelessness and fear'.

The authors even maintained that scientific and historical inquiry was justified: 'one of the noblest instincts in the intellectual life of man', and biblical criticism was 'not only a legitimate but a necessary method for all Christians, for by its use we are able to discover the facts and the form of the Old Testament Scriptures'. But this had its limits and should not be an excuse for mere hypothesising or speculation.

Christianity was an historically proven fact and 'true science does not start with an a priori hypothesis that certain things are impossible, but simply examines the evidence to find out what has actually occurred'. Thus scholars should accept the miraculous and super-natural stories in the Bible as true and, in doing so, they would find that what was said in the Bible was quite compatible with science and rationality.[17] The argument had a certain circularity to it; as one of the authors said, 'The supreme proof to every Christian of the deity of his Lord is then his own inner experience of the transforming power of his Lord upon the heart and life.' Philosophy not grounded in common sense was mere speculation and the experience of divine trans-formation was as real to Christians just as 'he who feels the present warmth of the sun knows that the sun exists'.

With that confidence in individual certainty, the Bible could easily be seen as 'the absolute transcript' of God's mind: it was therefore a 'book dropped out of heaven', but that did not necessarily preclude some limited latitude: the creation of the Earth in seven days might not necessarily mean seven days of twenty-four hours. The important thing was that it had been directed by God. It was ten years after the books' publication that the term 'fundamentalism' was coined, but it has been hardening into stone ever since. By the side of modern-day US fundamentalists, some of whom, as we shall see, insist that when Genesis talks of seven days, it means twenty-four-hour days, the original authors of The Fundamentals can appear positively liberal.

The Fundamentals were only one of a number of similar books and series of about the same period. Of equal importance was the publication by Oxford University Press in 1909 of the *Scofield Reference Bible*, named after its editor, Cyrus Ingerson Scofield, a former Confederate soldier turned lawyer who had moved to St Louis and fallen under the influence of James Brookes and his premillennialist views. Scofield became a Congregationalist minister in Dallas and gradually honed and refined the definition and timescale of the Dispensations. His Bible, with its elaborate cross-references and expositions of scriptural meanings, has been in use in conservative churches and their Sunday schools ever since. In the words of Randall Balmer, 'for generations of fundamentalists . . . the Scofield Bible has served as a kind of template through which they read the Scriptures.'[18] It has been a very successful, if unobtrusive, earner for the OUP too, selling anywhere between 30 million and 50 million copies since 1909, 85 per cent of them apparently in leatherbound editions. The word of Scofield may not be quite as inerrant as the word of God, but it has been almost as influential for many millions of Americans in the last one hundred years.

This was not a movement confined to one denomination either. It had an appeal to several Protestant groups, not only Congregationalists and Southern Baptists, but also to the myriad non-denominational sects whose churches dotted the heartland.

The convulsions between evangelical Protestants also spread to the Methodists, who were themselves split in the aftermath of the Civil War, not only because the conflict had itself divided the denomination North and South, but also because there was a widening division over worship styles between the staid traditionalists and the more exuberant devotees of what became known as the Holiness Revival. This latter group was more receptive to the fundamentalism of the evangelicals and to the doctrine of premillennialism as it developed, but it also embraced a belief in the transforming power of the

Pentecostal story, when the disciples were infused with the galvanising effect of the rushing mighty wind and illuminated with tongues like as of fire, as predicted by the prophet Joel: 'And it shall come to pass in the last days, saith God, I will pour out of my Spirit upon all flesh; and your sons and your daughters shall prophesy and your young men shall see visions, and your old men shall dream dreams' (Acts 2:17).

And lo, it came to pass, first to a female student called Agnes Ozman at the Bethel Bible College in Topeka, Kansas, who experienced the gift of the Spirit on 1 January 1901, when she suddenly found herself transformed and able to speak in tongues – indeed, unable to speak English again for another three days. 'At times,' she reported, 'I longed for the Holy Spirit to come in more than for my necessary food and at night a desire was felt more than for sleep and I know it was the Lord.'

Other students followed, as did the head of the college, Charles Parham, the next day, though he had to wait six hours, between 9 a.m. and 3 p.m. – coincidentally, he noticed, the very hours Christ had spent on the cross – for it to happen to him. Grant Wacker, the historian of Pentecostalism, points out wryly: 'at that point Ozman was 30, unmarried, unsettled, drifting from one experimental community to another. The pentecostal experience provided a desperately needed mooring – at least for a while, for Ozman, like others, apparently wandered in and out of the movement for years before making a firm commitment.'[19]

No matter. The new converts seemed able to exercise gifts of healing, as well as speaking in languages they did not understand, and the movement spread, notably to a black mission in Azusa Street, Los Angeles, in 1906, where the pastor William J. Seymour became an inspirational convert, codifier and leader of the new movement as it sought to recover the experience of the original disciples at the time of the first Pentecost following Christ's resurrection. Pentecostal churches, with a strong belief in healing and personal transformation in the Holy Spirit, together with a conservative, largely premillennialist theology, sprang up right across the USA in denominations such as the Assemblies of God. Tales of personal redemption featured large, as they still do – congregations and television audiences love stories of sinners repenting, lives transformed, and prayers answered as visible manifestations of God's powers of direct intervention in individual human affairs. By the late 1940s there were eight Pentecostal denominations with a membership mainly in the USA of more than a million people. Now, one hundred years after the first fires were lit, Pentecostalism is thought to have over 500 million members around the world, mainly in developing countries, and to be gaining converts at the rate of more than a million a year, making it the second largest Christian denomination, after Catholicism, and the fastest growing in the world. One Christian in four is now what is called a Renewalist: a Pentecostal or a charismatic.

To illustrate the growth and penetration of this US-inspired movement, in the autumn of 2006 the Pew Forum opinion polling organisation in Washington commissioned a ten-country survey. The countries it looked at were: the USA, Brazil, Chile, Guatemala, Kenya, Nigeria, South Africa, India, the Philippines and South Korea – several of which would normally be thought of as deeply Catholic or Anglican countries. Pew found that in every nation except India, at least 10 per cent of the population could be described as Renewalists, and in Brazil, Guatemala and Kenya the figure rose to 50 per cent. In the USA the figure was 23 per cent: 3 in 10 Protestant Americans and over 3 in 10 Catholic Americans said they were charismatic.

Most said they shared their faith with non-believers at least once a week, at least half said they had witnessed or experienced divine healing or speaking in tongues, or prophesying, and about three-quarters of those questioned expressed their view that belief in Jesus Christ is the only way to be saved from eternal damnation: these are very intense forms of worship.

In 9 out of 10 of the countries surveyed, at least half of the Pentecostals and charismatics said that religious groups should express their views on day-to-day social and political questions. This rose to 79 per cent in the USA, compared with 61 per cent in the population as a whole. More than half of US Pentecostals said that the government should take special steps to make the USA a Christian country, compared with only 25 per cent among Christians overall. The Forum quoted John Green, its analyst of politics and religious affairs, saying: 'Pentecostals were once thought of as non-political, at least in the US. That does not seem to be the case any more.'

And the views of these Christians are deeply conservative: 64 per cent of respondents in the USA believed abortion could never be justified in any circumstances (in the Philippines that figure rose to 97 per cent). Majorities in 9 of the 10 countries – except the USA – said that drinking alcohol was never justified. In three countries – Guatemala, Kenya and South Korea, though not the USA – majorities believed that AIDS is God's punishment for immoral sexual behaviour.

Luis Lugo, Pew's director, said: 'Pentecostal beliefs and practices are literally reshaping the face of Christianity throughout the developing world and with religion playing an increasingly prominent role in global affairs, we need to pay closer attention to Pentecostalism – arguably the most dynamic religious movement in the world today.'[20]

At the same time as Pentecostalism was starting, so was another conservative denomination, the Churches of Christ, a fissiparous offshoot of the earlier Disciples of Christ, finding its strongest roots among poor whites in the rural South, in areas in the words of the historian Sydney Ahlstrom 'where a piano was a snobbish luxury [and] they were unspoiled by either middle class manners or a seminary educated clergy . . . going their own way without cooperation, consultation or coordination with anyone but themselves'.[21]

There was indeed a revivalist ferment. In chapels and halls, tents and theatres and in the open air across the USA, preachers strode and barked their messages to willing audiences with the verve and panache of showmen. None more so than the former baseball player, Billy Sunday, a self-made, largely uneducated, man from a poor family out in the Midwest state of Iowa. At the height of his fame in the first two decades of the twentieth century he could compete with Barnum and Bailey, take on the burlesque travelling shows, and fill huge halls across the USA. When he conducted a ten-week crusade in New York in 1917, 1,443,000 people attended and 98,264 of them were listed as converting. As always, how many of those responding on what he himself called the Sawdust Trail *stayed* converted was an open question.

Sunday had been a professional baseball player, and a relatively successful one. But his career with the Chicago White Stockings was stalling when, after a drinking session with team mates one Sunday

evening in 1886, he caught the sound of the band from the Pacific
Garden Mission and his life was changed. He had a conversion
experience: 'Nell,' he wrote to his fiancée, 'If I could lift the mantle
that God has spread over my sins and allow you to look, you would see
sins that would almost put Satan to shame.'[22] He started attending a
local Presbyterian church, then gave up his professional sporting
career and went to work for the YMCA in Chicago instead at a much
reduced salary. This was where his preaching skills were first
discovered and honed.

His skill was in barn-storming. 'Frenetic' doesn't begin to do it
justice. It was simplistic, resolutely unintellectual and direct: 'I don't
know any more about theology than a jack-rabbit knows about ping-
pong, but I'm on the way to glory,' he would say.[23] He relied mercilessly
on his reputation for sporting prowess. Sunday would stalk the stage
swishing a baseball bat, signing autographs or catching balls that were
tossed to him in mid-sermon. Sometimes he would even hurl himself
across the platform, sliding up to the pulpit on his stomach as if
stealing home base in a ballgame. God was 'the great umpire of the
universe' and Satan could pitch with the best of them, 'with a spit ball
that spits fire' – you had to be in peak condition to fight him off.
Sunday would throw himself about as if wrestling with the devil
himself and sometimes stamped so hard on the floorboards of the
stage that the nails would spring out. It was quite a show.

Grown men would faint as he vividly described the wickedness of
sexual promiscuity and its accompanying diseases (some of his
sermons were for men only), masturbation was a vile demon, and
drink was a destroyer of men. One of his specialities was his so-called
Booze Sermon, preached for years around the circuit. 'Lord save us,'
he would cry, 'from off-handed, flabby-cheeked, brittle-boned, weak-
kneed, thin-skinned, pliable, plastic, spineless, effeminate, ossified,
three karat Christianity.'

Strings of adjectives were common; drinkers were 'dirty, low-down,
whisky-soaked, beer-guzzling, bull-necked, foul-mouthed, hypocrites'
and more moderate Christians were 'hog-jowled, weasel-eyed,
sponge-columned, mushy-fisted, jelly-spined, pussy-footing, four-
flushing Charlotte-russes'. It was no wonder that his peak of
popularity coincided with the campaign for prohibition.

Impressed, one reporter wrote: 'There is none of the puffed-up Pharisee about him.' Sunday himself said: 'I put the cookies and jam on the lower shelf so an audience don't have brain fag when they sit and listen to me.'

Understandably, crowds loved his folksy style and the music and magic tricks of his chief chorister Homer Rodeheaver – who played 'Onward Christian Soldiers' on the trombone – and they flocked to his extraordinary meetings. But they were also quite calculated and calibrated gatherings. At the height of his fame, Sunday could impose conditions on organisers who wanted to attract him to their town: all local evangelical ministers must agree to support his mission and underwrite its costs, the meeting tent must be designed to his specifications and, especially, no other evangelist should be allowed to perform anywhere in the neighbourhood while he was there. He made a lot of money and gave some of it away.

There is absolutely no evidence that Sunday himself was not sincere, but his style was the model for almost every depiction of hick preachers ever since. Indeed, many would-be biblical tub-thumpers sought to emulate him, and some, in pale imitations, succeeded. If the stereotype of the ranting demagogue can be traced right back to the Mathers, Jonathan Edwards and Lorenzo Dow, it is Billy Sunday whose entrepreneurial success paved the way for the modern televangelists. Toned down for television, he would surely be a great success on the God channels today.

Sunday's was not a subversive message, it was a deeply conservative one: 'God calls men to business' he said, and 'some of the noblest men and women I have ever met have been men and women of wealth'.[24] Nor did he have any time for wishy-washy nonsense about the social gospel – 'cream-puff religion' and 'godless social service nonsense'. He said: 'It is a Christian act to give a down-and-outer a bath, a bed and a job, but the road into the kingdom of God is not by the bathtub, the university, social service or gymnasium.'[25]

He was blatantly politically partisan: those wrecking America were foreigners, Bolsheviks, dissenters, radicals and evolutionists: 'virtually anyone . . . who did not espouse a rigid Republican party line, which he explicitly regarded as the appropriate political and economic position for true Christians'.[26] When America went to war in 1917 he gleefully laid into the Kaiser. 'Christianity and Patriotism are synonymous terms and hell and traitors are too'; Germans were 'a great pack of wolfish Huns whose fangs drip with blood and gore' and, again, 'If you turn Hell upside down you'll find "Made in Germany" stamped on the bottom.'[27] During the Red Scare that precipitated deportations of communist sympathisers after the end of the war, he announced: 'If I had my way with these ornery, wild-eyed socialists and IWWs [members of the International Workers of the World trade union] I would stand them up before a firing squad and save space on our ships.' He wanted 'to fill the jails so full…that their feet would stick out of the windows'. As for Darwin's theory of evolution, it was no more than 'bunk, junk and poppycock'.

Clearly, Billy Sunday's technique could teach Pat Robertson a thing or two about invective. Eventually his influence waned, not helped by family scandals involving his three sons, but he had created a new benchmark for some evangelists: loud, raucous, clear in his message, if shaky on his theology. But, above all, exciting.

Of course, not all American Christians were like this, by any means. The Catholics were a community largely of immigrants, set apart and scorned by right-thinking Protestants. The Episcopalians were not seduced by premillennialism. And nor were very many evangelicals, who were bemused and baffled by the sectarianism on display and contemptuous of the know-nothing, primitive, backwoods creeds of men like Sunday. They carried the torch for biblical interpretation, Darwinism, progress and a future that did not involve terrifying people into virtue.

In 1922, one of their leading spokesmen, Harry Emerson Fosdick, spoke forcefully at the Baptist Convention in New York on the theme 'Shall the Fundamentalists Win?' He charged that if they did so they would drive out of Christian churches all consecrated souls who did not agree with them on some matters of doctrine. They were majoring in the 'tiddlywinks and peccadillos of religion' and guilty of an 'almost unforgiveable intolerance'.[28] These remarks – again echoed eighty years later by church liberals – naturally were regarded as no better than socialism; indeed it was heresy to the fundamentalists. Fosdick, although a Baptist, was also associate pastor of the First Presbyterian

Church in New York (where he delivered his famous address). Following a long campaign against him he was eventually forced to relinquish his pulpit, though Henry Ford, the motor magnate, built him another church nearby.

Ahlstrom says: 'After 1865 the problems of Reconstruction, urbanisation, immigration, natural science and modern culture destroyed the great evangelical consensus, leaving a situation wherein dissenters were merely angry and frustrated. Increasingly, conservatives and liberals simply lost contact with each other, both culturally and religiously.'[29]

One of the leaders of the attack on Fosdick at the Presbyterian General Assembly in 1923 was the fundamentalists' champion and candidate for moderator, William Jennings Bryan, who had often spoken on platforms with Billy Sunday.

The Great Commoner had finally associated himself with a faction that shared none of his political views. Accused by a modernist of siding with the neanderthals, he retorted from the assembly platform:

> Did you do more than I did to put across women's suffrage? Did you do more than I did to put across the election of senators by direct vote of the people? Did you do more than I did to levy an income tax so that those who had wealth would have to pay for it? There has not been a reform for 25 years that I did not support and I am now engaged in the biggest reform of my life. I am trying to save the Christian Church from those who are trying to destroy her faith.[30]

Bryan did not know that he would narrowly lose the vote for moderator, or that his greatest fight would not only set all his previous career at naught, but that it would also destroy his reputation for ever. And maybe it even cost him his life.

7

Monkey Town

'I believe in part of evolution but I don't believe about that monkey business.'

Dayton schoolboy, 1925

Dayton is a pleasant small town nestling in a valley between Knoxville and Chattanooga just in the western lea of the Appalachian Mountains. The road down from Rockwood is filled with villages littered with neat single-storey ranchhouses on the crests of the ridge above the highway, mobile homes, gas stations and what appear to be dumps for rusting cars. And always there are modern brick and clapperboard churches with little spires and improving messages beside their parking lots: 'Here's Hope! Jesus Cares For You!'

The centre of Dayton itself has changed relatively little in appearance since the events that occurred there over ten days in the sweltering July of 1925 propelled it into headlines and ridicule around the world. As you stand outside the ugly Victorian red-brick courthouse in the square in the middle of town you can easily imagine that not much has altered in eighty years. Downtown, many of the buildings are the same as then; and some of the attitudes too. For it was here that a handsome twenty-four-year-old schoolteacher named John Thomas Scopes was tried in the courthouse for the crime of teaching Darwin's theory of evolution in defiance of state law.

Even at the time, the case seemed bizarre to much of the outside world and it has remained so ever since. When I first visited Dayton in the early summer of 1995 to research an article for the *Guardian* on the seventieth anniversary of the trial,[1] it was still, just, possible to believe that the court case was a curiosity of history. The issues seemed so cut, dried and quaint. Certainly Jerome Lawrence and Robert E. Lee, the authors of *Inherit the Wind*, the 1950s play and subsequent film notionally based, largely inaccurately, on the so-called Monkey Trial, thought so, as did many historians for decades afterwards.

Lawrence and Lee believed they were tackling the themes of McCarthyism and intolerance, not some thirty-year-old joust over the settled issue of evolution. Even just a few years after the trial it could be claimed that Bible-based fundamentalism had lost and accordingly been consigned to history. So declared Frederick Lewis Allen confidently in his book *Only Yesterday*, published just six years after the trial.[2] Many Bible-believing Christians, scientists, historians, commentators and journalists shared that view for years afterwards.

They were too quick off the mark. It is now possible to see the Monkey Trial as a pivotal event in modern US history: the earliest, and still the most politicised, legal clash between the forces of religious conservatism and those of science and secular modernity. What seemed until recently merely a quaint historical event, redolent of the Jazz Age and sepia-coloured photographs, straw hats and galluses – 'the end of the age of Amen and the beginning of the age of Oh yeah!' in the journalist Gaius Glen Atkins's colourful phrase in 1932 – with arcane arguments and vehement clashes between mutually uncomprehending views of the world, now seems merely a forerunner of a continuing debate, still conducted in much the same terms eighty years later.

Nearly a century on, in a much more sophisticated world, Darwin's theory of evolution remains for many US Christians as insidious and dangerous and its defeat as vital as it did to their grandparents in 1925. School boards battle to get the Genesis account of creation on to the curriculum and supposedly scientific institutes seek to disprove or ridicule Darwin's ideas 150 years after they were first published. A whole new theory of so-called Intelligent Design has sprung up to provide a secular-friendly version of the Bible story. Who would have thought that a twenty-first-century US president would say that the creationists have a point, as George Bush has done? The president told Texas newspaper reporters in August 2005 that Intelligent Design should be taught alongside evolutionary theory: 'Both sides ought to be properly taught . . . so people can understand what the debate is all about.'[3] In fairness, he was following in the intellectual footsteps of Ronald Reagan who announced in 1980, when he was running for president, that there were 'great flaws' in the theory of evolution.[4] Not even Calvin Coolidge, the Republican president at the time of the original trial, did that.

Dayton has been known as Monkey Town ever since 1925, the repository of rustic ignorance, superstition and backwardness. It aggravates some – they no longer put 'Monkey Town' on car licence plates – but over the last ten years the town has come to accept its fate. The little museum in the basement of the courthouse has been expanded and updated and is now a little less dusty and deserted than it was the first time I visited. And outside stands a brand-new statue of William Jennings Bryan, erected in 2005, the politician who agreed to defend biblical literalism at the trial. The statue is a poor likeness and it shows him looking fit and dynamic, not the ill, bloated, perspiring and ageing figure he actually was by the time he got to Dayton. Of his protagonist, the atheist lawyer Clarence Darrow, who had once been one of Bryan's political supporters and who defended Scopes, not a trace remains and there is certainly no statue.

Dayton had its five minutes of fame and the monkey label has stuck. Yet, as with several other aspects of the trial, the irony is that the town was not really like its image then. Its reasons for wanting to stage the trial, which was always more a media event than a serious legal dispute, were the precise opposite of the way they are now depicted. In fact, you could say Dayton is probably a more fundamentalist town now than it was then.

The story starts with Tennessee's state legislature up in Nashville, passing a law in the spring of 1925 making the teaching of Darwin's theory illegal even though by then it was pretty well universally accepted by scientists and academics. Tennessee was not the only state considering such a move at the time – Florida and Oklahoma adopted similar resolutions and other states were making Bible reading compulsory in their schools – but it was the first legislature to treat teaching evolution as a crime, punishable by criminal sanctions.

The legislation made it unlawful for any teacher in a state-funded school 'to teach any theory that denies the story of the divine creation of man as taught in the Bible and to teach instead that man has descended from a lower order of animals'.[5] It was the brain-child of a state legislator called John Washington Butler, a farmer and member of the Primitive Baptist Church on the other side of the state, who had grown alarmed to hear from preachers that young Tennesseans were going away to be educated at college and coming back believing in evolution but not in God. This was shocking: Butler, not unlike Judge Roy Moore three-quarters of a century later, believed the Bible was the foundation of civil government and that accepting Darwin's theory meant rejecting the Bible's account of creation and therefore Christianity itself, not to mention the government of the USA. Such wicked theorising was the work of dangerous liberals and subversives, out to destroy the established order of things; in Billy Sunday's words: 'If this radical element could have their way, my friends, the laws of nature would be repealed, or they would reverse them, oil and water would mix, the turtle dove would marry the turkey buzzard, the sun would rise in the West and set in the East; chickens would crow and the roosters would squeal; cats would bark and dogs would mew; the least would be the greatest; a part would be greater than the whole; yesterday would be after tomorrow if that crowd were in control.'[6]

But Butler's Bill was by no means universally supported even in Tennessee where thirteen Methodist and Presbyterian ministers condemned it, both for attacking academic freedom and for being unnecessary, and it was also criticised editorially in the state's largest newspapers. The state judiciary committee initially rejected the measure, but its supporters pushed ahead. There was little public outcry or discussion of the law's potential pitfalls. It shot through both houses of the state legislature in less than a week and was signed by the state governor, Austin Peay.

Governor Peay was himself a progressive Democrat who had improved state spending on schools as well as hospitals and roads. But he needed rural votes to secure re-election and the Butler Bill seemed an easy, cost-free, way of doing so. It had the desired result too, for he was re-elected the following year.[7]

Not for the first or last time, a purely symbolic political gesture had unforeseen consequences, however. Apart from anything else, the state legislature had rendered the biology textbook used in its own schools illegal, because George William Hunter's *A Civic Biology* included an approving section on Darwin and natural selection. It was, it said, 'the theory on which we today base the progress of the world'. Hunter's book – very much a work of its time – also approved eugenics to prevent 'intermarriage and the possibility of perpetuating . . . a low and degenerate race' and described Caucasians as the highest type of humanity 'represented by the civilised white inhabitants of Europe and America', but no one ever appears to have objected to that.[8]

Governor Peay later said he would never have signed the Butler Act if he had thought it was ever going to be tested in court, and described the law as absurd. He believed the legislation only covered anti-biblical doctrines and 'nothing of that sort is taught in any accepted book on science'. He told reporters: 'Nobody believes it is going to be an active statute.'[9]

Active or not, once the statute was passed, criticism and ridicule rained down on Tennessee. Nicholas Murray Butler, the president of Columbia University, in words as temperate as those used these days by Richard Dawkins, accused the state government of 'violently affronting the popular intelligence and [making] it impossible for a scholar to be a teacher in that state without becoming at the same time a law-breaker'. New barbarians were storming the citadels of learning: 'Courage is the only weapon left by which the true liberal can wage war upon all these reactionary and leveling movements. Unless he can stand his ground and make his voice heard and his opinions felt, it will certainly be some time before civilisation can resume its interrupted progress.'[10] The very vehemence and condescension of such attacks by Northern elitists, then as now, only served to convince the Bible-believers of the South that they must be right.

Governor Peay might have been correct about the statute being merely symbolic, but that was not how the newly formed American Civil Liberties Union – later also to be the bête noire for Judge Moore and his Ten Commandments – saw things in its offices up in New York. The ACLU was just five years old and needed high-profile cases to establish its reputation. It also wanted to stave off any more reactionary laws being passed in other states so it offered to support a test-case to challenge the Tennessee law in court and it was this that prompted Dayton to offer just such a hearing.

It was no surprise that the little town should put itself forward. Far from being a typical Southern town, Dayton was highly unusual and was out of step with much of the rest of the state. It had been the only town in Tennessee to oppose secession in the civil war and it had regularly voted Republican ever since (Governor Peay had never received a majority in the area and would not for his re-election in 1926 either). In a state full of various sorts of Baptists, it was a Methodist town. The reasons for this contrariness dated back to its foundation, peopled by Northerners, around a local ironworks and blast furnace, in the previous century. But by 1925 the area was in economic decline: the furnace had closed and the population was shrinking.

In F. E. Robinson's drugstore, opposite the courthouse, the ACLU offer was read about and discussed around the soda fountain by several bright young boosters: two young lawyers, the brothers Herbert and Sue Hicks (the latter may have been the original of Johnny Cash's song 'A Boy Named Sue': he was apparently so named because it was his mother's name and she had died giving birth to him; Hicks later changed his name by deed-poll: his middle name, Xenophon, naturally, not his first name) and a New Yorker called George Rappleyea who had moved to Dayton to manage the failing ironworks. All of them were outsiders, newly arrived in town. It seems to have been Rappleyea's idea: to show the outside world that Dayton was a progressive, go-ahead, scientific sort of place, not sunk in Southern obscurantism, and so to attract Northern investment.

The brothers Hicks tossed for who should represent which side. They never anticipated it would become a worldwide media event. The real issue therefore was not evolution, but the boosting of Dayton: in the words of local Congressman Foster V. Brown: 'It is not a fight for evolution or against evolution, but a fight against obscurity.'[11]

They approached the principal of the local, newly built high school, W. F. Ferguson, who doubled up as the school's biology teacher, but he was unwilling to risk his job by challenging the law. So they turned to Rappleyea's tennis partner instead, John Scopes, the young football coach who also taught maths and physics at the school. Scopes, who had recently graduated, was another newcomer and had only been in town for a year, but was locally popular: sporty, fair-haired and handsome – a good marriage-catch, it was thought, for a local girl.[12]

Scopes was summoned from a tennis court to the drugstore, shown the ACLU's offer in the paper, told by Rappleyea that it would 'make a big sensation', and duly agreed to be the fall-guy, since he had little to lose and had no idea that the case would be anything but a brief local event. He was an ideal candidate. Certainly no one would view him as a subversive secularist or secret communist. Scopes was vaguely against the new law, but did not know much about it. Indeed he thought it was perfectly possible to reconcile evolution and the Bible. The teacher rather reluctantly allowed himself to be formally arrested by the local constable while a warrant was sworn out by Rappleyea against him and then they both went off to play tennis. It was, Scopes said later, no more than 'a drugstore discussion that got past control'.

The chief difficulty with putting him up for the case was that he was not sure that he had ever taught Darwin's theory of evolution to anyone, though he had occasionally taken the principal's biology class when Ferguson was sick. Later, when the possibility of him testifying in the case became real, four local lads from the school were rounded up and he was sent round town with them in the back of a taxi while he read aloud the offending passage from Hunter's book, so that he – and they – should not perjure themselves if they had to take the witness stand. Even so, one of the lads absconded during the trial when he realised the scale of the fuss and had to be enticed back to town from his hiding place in the woods by Scopes himself, who was no more happy about all the publicity than the boy was.

The planned trial soon spiralled out of Dayton's control. F. E. Robinson was not known as the hustling druggist for nothing, and his wife served as a local freelance correspondent for a number of state newspapers. She sent off news of the wheeze to challenge the law to the *Nashville Banner*, which splashed it across its front page. The local correspondent of the Associated Press then posted a report and within twenty-four hours it was national news. Colonel McCormick, owner of the *Chicago Tribune* and the new radio station WGN, and H. L. Mencken, the columnist of the *Baltimore Sun* and the most celebrated journalist in the USA, both picked up the story and had the same idea. Wouldn't it be great if Clarence Darrow, the great defender and a well-known free-thinking atheist, could be persuaded to defend Scopes, and William Jennings Bryan, the most prominent national figure promoting the Bible, could prosecute? Wouldn't that be a challenge neither could refuse?

Bryan was eager to take part. This would give him a national platform in precisely the sort of circles that were now ignoring him. His candidate for Democratic presidential nominee had been defeated the previous year, despite his strong support, and he had also been rejected as the candidate for moderator at the Presbyterian national assembly. At the 1925 assembly the fundamentalists had won, but his support had been spurned. By now he was also ill with diabetes, his political career was over and his last great populist crusade – that 'biggest reform of my life' he had spoken of at the 1923 assembly – for the Bible was all he had left. The Rock of Ages, he would proudly declare, was more important than the ages of rocks.

Bryan had come only relatively recently to a fundamentalist position, in the previous four years, and he had done so not for strictly biblical reasons. He was opposed, he said, to the teaching of evolution as a proven fact, rather than a hypothesis (modern creationists take this line too) and also because he was concerned with 'protecting man from the demoralization involved in accepting a brute ancestry'.

Bryan also had reservations about using the law to enforce belief. He certainly did not think there should be criminal sanctions: 'we are not dealing with a criminal class' he told the state legislature in Florida when they were considering a similar move.[13] But he also had two ulterior reasons for backing legislation: he believed that tax-payers had a democratic right to determine what was taught in their schools, since they were paying for it, and he also feared the consequences of the application of Darwinian principles to wider spheres of life. Social Darwinism and the deployment of the theory of the survival of the fittest by employers in relation to factory conditions was deeply damaging to workers' health and well-being, he believed. In this, he was thinking of philosophers such as the Englishman Herbert Spencer, who had been a great success in the USA forty years earlier, especially with industrialists, men like John D. Rockefeller who had said: 'The growth of a large business is merely a survival of the fittest. It is merely the working-out of a law of nature and a law of God.'

Spencer himself had told Americans during a visit in 1882 that although their character was not yet sufficiently developed to make best use of the country's Republican institutions, immigration from Aryan nations would produce 'a finer type of man than has hitherto existed' and they could 'reasonably look forward to a time when they will have produced a civilization grander than any the world has known'.[14] With thinking like this, Social Darwinism had already been used to justify eugenics and wars for supremacy between nations.

To Bryan, it was not only unchristian, it was anti-Christian. In a justification written for the trial, he would say: 'Science is a magnificent material force, but it is not a teacher of morals. It can perfect machinery, but it adds no moral restraints to protect society from the misuse of the machine. It not only fails to supply the spiritual element needed but some of its unproved hypotheses rob [society of its moral] compass.'[15]

He would willingly serve without compensation in defence of the state's law, he cabled Hicks. And furthermore, he promised that he would personally pay any fine imposed on young Scopes.

Clarence Darrow, the USA's greatest, or most notorious, defence lawyer and a well-known and outspoken atheist, took a little more convincing to act for Scopes. He had once been a political supporter of Bryan's, shared speaking platforms with him, and had known him for nearly thirty years. Darrow had specialised in defending underdogs, though not necessarily impoverished ones: twelve months earlier he had famously defended two rich college boys named Leopold and Loeb in Chicago and had saved them from the death penalty after they had killed a schoolboy in a misconceived attempt to prove their intellectual superiority over the common herd. In this they included the police who managed to disprove the thesis by quickly catching them after Nathan Leopold left his spectacles at the scene of their perfect crime. Darrow had claimed in court that his clients had been practising the survival of the fittest theory without fully understanding its implications. In Dayton he would argue in favour of the same theory being taught to much younger and less well-educated children than the college boys he had defended the year before.

Darrow too was ageing and in search of a cause, but he was not particularly keen to travel to Tennessee for it. In the end he said: 'Civilisation is on trial. I get no fee in this case. I enlisted like the boys who went to France, for liberty and humanity. We are not attacking the Bible. We are willing to let those who worship it, worship it, or anything else they want, but we insist they must let those who disagree have as much right.'[16] The ACLU was not too pleased at having such a controversial lawyer representing their cause. In fact, the whole defence team was scarcely calculated to be sympathetically received in Tennessee. They were all Northerners and, in Southern eyes, of dubious morals and religious backgrounds. One of Darrow's colleagues, Dudley Field Malone, was a divorced Roman Catholic whose second wife caused scandal by booking into their hotel in Dayton using her maiden name. Bryan's wife Mary noted of the ACLU's own lawyer, Arthur Hays: 'at the end of the line is the Jew Hays, who reeks of East End impertinence. His dark hair is standing Pompadour and his eyes are full of shrewdness and brightness.'[17] Mrs Bryan, wheelchair-bound with arthritis, loyally accompanied her husband to Dayton, even though she was opposed to his involvement in the whole business because she was fearful about its effect on his fragile health. Bryan himself believed the ACLU was made up of communists and unbelievers, which gave him all the more reason for embarking on one more crusade.

The ACLU was outmanoeuvred over its legal team: Mencken, who like Darrow was a Social Darwinist and a Nietzschean – 'The strong must grow stronger and that they may do so, they must waste no strength in the vain task of trying to lift up the weak' – argued that the creationists must be humiliated. 'Nobody gives a damn about that yap school teacher,' he told Darrow. 'The thing to do is to make a fool out of Bryan . . . convert it into a headlong assault on Bryan, not that poor worm of a schoolmaster.'

Mencken was exhilarated – rightly as it turned out – by the propagandist opportunities the trial would produce. His was a slash-and-burn style of journalism, polemical, individual, opinionated and hugely exuberant, of a sort that is still less common in US newspaper reporting today than it is in the UK. In some ways his style was more like the invective of modern US radio and television shock-jocks – Mencken would undoubtedly have become a star of the broadcasting circuit had he lived a few years later – but his rhetoric was more literate and elevated and he would certainly have been robust in his ridicule of their inflated religiosity. Eighty years ago, however, his reporting was both remarkable and influential. In the words of his near-contemporary Frederick Lewis Allen, 'on occasion Mencken could write measured and precise English, but when his blood was up, his weapons were gross exaggeration and gross metaphors. The moment he appeared the air was full of flying brickbats: and to read him for the first time gave one, if not blind rage, the sort of intense, visceral delight which comes from heaving baseballs at crockery in an amusement park.'[18] Bryan, Mencken said, was 'born with a roaring voice [which] had a trick of inflaming half-wits', the inhabitants of Tennessee were 'gaping primates', and they formed 'the anthropoid rabble'. The antipathy was mutual.

Dayton muscled aside other towns competing to hold the trial by arranging an early date for the hearing. It set up its own, significantly named, 'Scopes Trial Entertainment Committee' to arrange accommodation for the visitors it anticipated, produced a brochure promoting its attractions, and the Progressive Dayton Club approved spending of $5,000 to boost local businesses. The local policeman slung a sign saying 'Monkeyville Police' around his motorcycle, and Robinson's drugstore started serving 'simian sodas'. They could not say they did not know what they were letting themselves in for.[19]

And indeed, with such well-known protagonists, the town was inundated with journalists even though the hearing was in the middle of July, a sweaty and sultry time of year to go south in the days before air-conditioning. The trial was the first to be broadcast – by Colonel McCormick's radio station – or filmed for newsreels and more than 200 journalists from all over the USA, and as far afield as Europe, filled the town to cover the sensation. They would telegraph back to their offices alone over 2 million words from the hearing, making it the biggest single news event ever covered in US history to that time.

The small town also filled up with the curious, the Christian and the crazy. Local farmers drove up in their mule carts and Model T Fords, preachers slung banners and held rival prayer meetings, hucksters sold their wares and there were even chimpanzees including one called Joe Mendi, imported from Hollywood and dressed in a three-piece suit, complete with bowtie and trilby hat, to entertain the children, until he succumbed to the heat. Among the evangelists was John the Baptist the Third and one calling himself 'The Absolute Ruler of the Entire World, Without Military, Naval or Other Physical Force'.

The expected tourist invasion of impressed Northerners and potential investors, however, did not materialise. Most visitors were country folk, down from the mountains of eastern Tennessee, and the Daytonian boosters soon discovered that the journalists themselves

were not lavish spenders: their chief expenditure being on taxis to get
the 30 miles to Chattanooga, the nearest place where illicit booze was
available.

When I first visited Dayton, I met Robinson's two elderly children,
who were still living in the family home just down from the drugstore
and directly across the road from the courthouse. They certainly
remembered the trial very well (and especially Joe Mendi) even
though they had been very small children at the time. Sonny Robinson
and his sister invited me to lunch in the family dining-room, just as
their parents had the journalists who covered the trial. Sonny chuckled
at the memory: 'We had Mr Mencken come to the door one day and
say: "I hear you are doing lunches," and my father said to him, "Yes,
but not for you, Mr Mencken", and sent him off. He'd seen what he
was writing about Dayton, you see.'[20]

In fact, Mencken's first impressions of the town were by no means
as negative as he had hoped: 'The town, I confess, greatly surprised
me. I expected to find a squalid southern village, with darkies
snoozing on the horse-blocks, pigs rooting under the houses and the
inhabitants full of hookworm and malaria,' he wrote in his first
dispatch for his paper *The Baltimore Sun* on 9 July. 'What I found was
a country town full of charm and even beauty . . . the houses are
surrounded by pretty gardens . . . the two chief streets are paved curb
to curb. The stores carry good stocks and have a metropolitan air,
especially the drug, book, magazine, sporting goods and soda water
emporium of the estimable Robinson . . . Nor is there any evidence in
the town of that poisonous spirit which usually shows itself when
Christian men gather to defend the great doctrine of their faith.'[21] He
was right and Dayton remains a very pleasant small town.

Mencken soon found what he was looking for, of course, when he
sneaked out one evening to a prayer meeting held by Holy Rollers in
the woods outside town, a tale retold in a classic piece of reportage:

There followed a hymn, led by a somewhat fat brother wearing
silver-rimmed country spectacles. It droned on for half a dozen
stanzas, and then the first speaker resumed the floor. He argued
that the gift of tongues was real and that education was a snare.
Once his children could read the Bible, he said, they had

enough. Beyond lay only infidelity and damnation. Sin stalked the cities. Dayton itself was a Sodom.[22]

Mencken was fascinated: women jumped in the aisles, swaying and tossing their hair while others writhed moaning on the ground 'grunting in the grass in great convulsive gasps'.

The trial itself was somewhat less gripping. It was, says Garry Wills, 'a nontrial over a nonlaw, with a nondefendant backed by nonsupporters. Its most famous moment involved nontestimony by a nonexpert which was followed by a nondefeat.'[23] In fact, the ten days of hearings became exactly what Mencken always intended and his highly coloured and partisan reporting helped to make them so: a battle between North and South, town and country, rich and poor, Christian against agnostic and atheist, science against faith: enlightened and deluded. Since the defence acknowledged that Scopes had taught evolution, their real challenge was to the Tennessee law, which they hoped to show breached the state constitution, which talked of 'cherishing literature and science'.

The hearings actually devolved into a series of bad-tempered spats between the lawyers packed together in the crowded and sweltering first-floor courtroom. The court, still in use today, was so overcrowded that people were even perching on the lawyers' desks. Up to 1,000 people a day squeezed into the hearing. Mencken himself stood on a table to get a view. The newsreel cameras whirred, telegraph keys tapped, and the lawyers spoke into a heavy, primitive microphone, set on a column in the middle of the court. Around the spectators' legs dogs rootled and occasionally barked and scrapped and babies in arms screamed in the background. The three electric fans in the court were trained on the judge and the prosecution team – Scopes's defence found themselves placed so that they were sitting in full sunlight for some reason – and through the open windows wafted the smell of barbecues cooking meat outside.

The jury of local farmers included six Baptists and a Methodist, one Disciple-of-Christ and only one non-churchgoer. They might have expected to have had a ring-side seat, but instead spent most of the trial out of the room while legal arguments were batted to and fro. As soon as John Raulston, the local judge hearing the case, ruled that prayers could be said without prejudice at the start of each day's session and that expert scientific witnesses, who had been summoned from all over the nation – but mainly from the North – by the defence to give evidence about the truth of evolution, were irrelevant to the case, Scopes's defenders knew that the trial was lost. Actually, since Scopes had admitted the charge of teaching evolution, there could be no other outcome.

Darrow had to make the best case he could, arguing that the law violated free speech:

> If today you can take a thing like evolution and make it a crime to teach it in the public schools, tomorrow you can make it a crime in the private schools and the next year you can make it a crime to teach it in the hustings or in the churches. At the next session you may ban it in books and in newspapers. Soon you may set Catholic against Protestant and Protestant against Protestant and try to foist your own religion on the minds of men ... Ignorance and fanaticism are ever busy and need feeding ... After a while, your Honor, it is the setting of man against man and creed against creed until with flying banners and beating drums we are marching backward to the glorious ages of the 16th Century when bigots lighted fagots to burn the men who dared to bring any intelligence and enlightenment and culture to the human mind.

A woman leaving the court was heard muttering 'The damned infidel' and when the following night a storm brought down the town's electricity supply there were some who blamed it on God's wrath at Darrow's heresy.[24]

The Scopes team concentrated on ensuring that the case went to appeal, so that the constitutionality of the Butler Act could be tested by the state Supreme Court, but meanwhile Darrow had one more trick up his sleeve. As the trial was winding down, he suggested to Bryan a strategy whereby they could both present their cases to the public: Bryan would take the stand as an expert witness on the literal truth of the Bible and be cross-examined by Darrow, and then Darrow would witness to evolution and be cross-examined by Bryan. It would give them both the platform they sought. Bryan agreed, as he could scarcely not. If the aim was to discredit Bryan, Darrow succeeded.

By this time, on Monday 20 July, Judge Raulston, fearing that the courtroom floor would give way under the weight of the crowd, had moved the trial outside to a small wooden dais against the courtroom's outside wall, with the crowd sprawled out on benches across the surrounding grass lawn. Many journalists, including Mencken – whose reports had made him highly unpopular – had already left town, concluding that it was nearly over, and most of those who remained were either enjoying a long lunch or sleeping it off, so that they missed the trial's most dramatic ninety minutes: the cross-examination of William Jennings Bryan.

Imagine both men in their shirt-sleeves, wringing with sweat in the sticky afternoon heat: Darrow sticking his thumbs in his blue galluses as he loomed over the seated Bryan. Darrow played the village atheist trick of asking Bryan about the veracity of the Old Testament stories and, as it is not hard to do in such circumstances, made something of a monkey out of him.

Worse, Bryan for his part tried sarcasm and condescension in return, his palm-leaf fan shaking increasingly agitatedly as the examination went on, his face getting redder and redder and his pince-nez spectacles steaming up. Although he certainly did not lose all the exchanges, he was clearly tiring by the end. What was much worse from his supporters' point of view was that Bryan finally admitted that the literal truth of the Bible was conditional; that it could be interpreted. Some have still not forgiven him for selling the pass: they take a more fundamentalist position now than he did then.

Thus, Darrow, asking about Jonah: 'When you read that the whale swallowed Jonah . . . how do you literally interpret that?'

Bryan: 'I believe in a God who can make a whale and can make a man and make both of them do what he pleases.'

Darrow: 'You don't know whether it was the ordinary run of fish or made for the purpose?'

Bryan: 'You may guess, you evolutionists guess.'

Darrow: 'But when we do guess, we have the sense to guess right.'

Bryan: 'One miracle is just as easy to believe as another.'

Darrow: 'It is for me . . . just as hard.'

And the date of the flood?
Bryan: 'I never made a calculation.'
Darrow: 'What do you think?'
Bryan: 'I don't think of things I don't think about.'
Darrow: 'Do you think about things you *do* think about?'
And the serpent in the Garden of Eden:
Darrow: 'Do you think that is why the serpent is compelled to crawl upon its belly?'
Bryan: 'I believe that.'
Darrow: 'Have you any idea how the snake went before that time?'
Bryan: 'No, sir.'
Darrow: 'Do you know whether he walked upon his tail or not?'
Bryan: 'No sir, I have no way to know.'[25]
Applause from the crowd gave way to whoops of laughter from the press bench.
And, worst of all, on the six days of creation in Genesis:
Darrow: 'Does the statement, "The morning and the evening were the first day," and "The morning and the evening were the second day," mean anything to you?'
Bryan: 'I do not think it necessarily means a 24-hour day.'
Darrow: 'Now if you call those periods, they may have been a very long time.'
Bryan: 'They might have been.'
Darrow: 'The creation might have been going on for a very long time?'
Bryan: 'It might have continued for millions of years.'[26]
And Darrow: 'Have you any idea of the length of these periods?'
Bryan: 'No I don't.'
Darrow: 'Do you think the sun was made on the fourth day?'
Bryan: 'Yes.'
Darrow: 'And they had evening and morning without the sun?'
Bryan: 'I am simply saying it is a period...'
Bryan's supporters gasped in disbelief. He was cornered. He had been forced to defend the literal truth of the Bible and, in doing so, admitted that it might not be strictly accurate. He waved away his colleagues on the prosecution team as they tried to stop the rout. Then he lost his temper. Shaking and banging his fist, he shouted: 'I am

simply trying to protect the word of God against the greatest atheist or
agnostic in the United States. I want the papers to know I am not
afraid to get on the stand in front of him and let him do his worst . . .'

And finally: 'The only purpose Mr Darrow has is to slur the Bible
but I will answer his questions.'

Darrow was shouting now: 'I object to your statement. I am examining your fool ideas that no intelligent Christian on Earth believes.'

Both men were standing, shaking their fists at each other and that
was the moment that Judge Raulston finally adjourned the trial for the
day. Bryan slumped back in his seat, alone and deserted, muttering:
'slurring the Bible, slurring the Bible', to himself. A few weeks later,
Darrow wrote to Mencken: 'I made up my mind to show the country
what an ignoramus he was and I succeeded.'[27] Scopes himself helped
those journalists who had not bothered to attend the afternoon
session to file their stories that evening. He even wrote some of them
himself.

Bryan never did get his chance for revenge by cross-examining
Darrow, or even to make the closing statement on which he had
worked so hard. The following morning, back inside the courtroom,
Raulston ruled that Bryan's testimony should be stricken from the
record as it had no bearing on the case and Darrow forthwith asked
the court to bring back the jury and instruct them to find his client
guilty. They took nine minutes to do so, without even bothering to sit
down in the jury room. 'The peach crop will soon be coming in,' said
one, relieved that it was all over. They left it to Judge Raulston to set
the fine on Scopes at the maximum: $100. Mencken's *Baltimore Sun*
said it would pay.

The rest of the world was incredulous at the whole event. George
Bernard Shaw, back in England, wrote: 'Let America look to it and let
the newspapers and pulpits of Tennessee rally to their duty lest their
state become a mere reservation of morons and moral cowards. They
can put a stop to this monstrous nonsense in a single Sunday if they
have the courage of their profession and no Sunday in America can
ever be better spent.'

Bryan occupied the next few days pottering around Dayton,
putting the finishing touches to the 15,000-word speech he would
have made, had he had the chance to do so at the trial, and negotiating

with a printer in Chattanooga to get it published. It warned in terms remarkably similar to those used by the Religious Right today: 'A militant minority, made up of atheists, agnostics and other dissenters from orthodox Christianity is seeking to use the courts to compel the majority to pay teachers to undermine the religious faith of the children of the taxpayers who employ teachers.'[28]

He appeared largely oblivious of the debacle of his evidence, though he did admit that because he had spent so much time during his career on political, economic and social problems, it was unfair to expect him to be an expert on science as well. Meanwhile, liberal Christians were creeping quietly away, appalled at the undignified spectacle that they had just read about in the press, and fundamentalists were outraged by Bryan's sell-out. The lesson they took from the trial was not to abandon their beliefs, but to retreat in on themselves so that they were not exposed to the ridicule of outside unbelievers.

On the Saturday, four days after the trial finished, Bryan, having inspected the site of a Christian college which would be named after him on a hill overlooking Dayton, made a speaking tour of eastern Tennessee by railroad. He and his wife were entertained to lunch by Judge Raulston and, on his meandering way back to the town, his train stopped at wayside and village halts so he could address the crowds who gathered to see him: an estimated 50,000 of them did so during the course of the day. On the Sunday morning he – of course – attended church and led prayers before returning to the house where he was staying. There Bryan ate a hearty lunch. He joked with Mary that a recent medical check-up had shown he was well and had several more years to live. If so, his doctor was wrong. After lunch he retired for a nap and died in his sleep. It was the sixth day after the cross-examination.

Told the news that Bryan had died 'of a broken heart', Darrow murmured: 'Broken heart nothing – he died of a busted belly'.

Back home in Baltimore, Mencken exulted: 'Well, we killed the son of a bitch', before sitting down to write one of the most vicious obituaries ever penned. There had been, he wrote, a vague, unpleasant manginess about Bryan's appearance at Dayton:

. . . the hatred in the old man's burning eyes was not for the enemies of God, it was for the enemies of Bryan . . . If he was pathetic he was also disgusting. Bryan was a vulgar and common man, a cad undiluted. He was ignorant, bigoted, self-seeking, blatant and dishonest . . . It was hard to believe, watching him in Dayton, that he had traveled, that he had been received in civilized societies, that he had been a high officer of state. He seemed only a poor clod . . . full of an almost pathological hatred of all learning, all human dignity, all beauty, all fine and noble things. He was a peasant come home to the dung-pile. Imagine a gentleman and you have imagined everything that he was not.[29]

So outraged was reader – and advertiser – reaction that, after the first edition, the paper stopped the presses and Mencken himself was required to excise the more insulting phrases. He did so with ill grace.

By and large, though, it was Mencken's view of the trial that prevailed. In due course the Scopes verdict was sent to the Tennessee Supreme Court where it was quashed on the technicality that it should have been for the jury, not the judge, to set the amount of the fine. This neatly sidestepped any question of arguing the constitutionality of the law, which remained on the state's statute books until 1967, though it was never again tested in court.

Scopes himself gave up teaching – he left Dayton the day after the trial – and became an engineer in the oil industry instead, achieving the obscurity and anonymity that he had always wanted.

'I hate the name Monkey Town. I want to get that monkey off our back,' exclaimed Dr Hollis Green to me when I drove out of Dayton to see him at the college he was building piece by piece on a wooded hillside near the town. Hollis, a former PR man, has now realised his dream of constructing a mini graduate school in Tennessee modelled on Oxford, but he had to think twice about building it somewhere so notorious for ignorance and bigotry. As it was, what he built was a sort of ersatz Oxford college: fake beams and stained glass windows, like no college I've ever seen in the real thing.[30]

On an opposite hill the other side of Dayton sits Bryan College, on the site the old boy visited and pronounced to be good on the day before he died. There they still train Baptist teachers and pastors under strict rules: compulsory Bible study, no sex or drugs, no alcohol, no wearing shorts in class, no smoking or watching X-rated films. And they teach creationism, of course.

Richard Cornelius, the college's English professor and a Christopher Marlowe scholar, sat in his crowded study lined with classic texts: Dickens, Joyce, Hawthorne and, incongruously, W. C. Fields, and told me: 'Bryan was laughed at and ridiculed, but he ended up more nearly right than some of the eminent scientists. Some of them believed in the Piltdown Man after all and that has now been shown to be a hoax. It is still not settled. Actually, there is not as much evidence for evolution as people think there is. We tend to be creationists here.'

Did he think that God created the Earth in seven days? 'It is surprising. The more I read – and I am not really a scientist – increasingly, when I hear some of these things, there is not a whole lot of evidence for the Earth being so old. I believe it might be only 7,000 years old.'

'My goodness,' I said, that put him in agreement with Archbishop Ussher, the seventeenth-century divine who calculated the precise date for the creation of the Earth – 22 October 4004 BC – by working his way back through the Bible. 'Well, I don't think Archbishop Ussher was so far wrong,' he assured me gravely.

Cornelius introduced me to his colleague Kurt Wise, a Harvard-trained geologist, dressed in battered corduroys, sorting slides in his chaotic laboratory. Wise is one of the bright men of the creationist movement. He told me the Grand Canyon could have been created in less than a year, because nature works much faster than she is given credit for: 'I approach this from my scriptural knowledge. Even if it could be shown that the rocks were much older, I do not think I would accept it. It is perfectly possible that this was created as the Bible tells us. I teach theistic evolution and Creation theory. Many of our students would not accept it without mention of the Bible. They think evolution is wicked.'

Dayton High School as such no longer exists. It was renamed Rhea County High School after amalgamation with other local schools twenty-odd years ago and is now sited some miles out of town, up the valley, in what can best be described as redbrick US institutional bunker architecture. On the school board it says that the school is 'Home of the Golden Eagles' football team and there is no obvious mention anywhere of its role as a footnote in history.

When I visited, the school did not bother to teach its pupils about the trial, even though it was the most significant thing ever to happen to Dayton: 'I doubt whether many of our students have even been down to the courthouse to see the museum,' said Jim Rankin, the deputy principal. The school taught both evolution and creationism as theories, not facts, but Joe Wilkey, the biology teacher – a descendant of one of the clergymen who led prayers during the trial – was himself a creationist.

I asked Patrick Conner, then the principal, since retired, what he believed but he did not wish to say. Could he be a secret evolutionist? There was a half nod and a wry smile. Then he added: 'I don't think it is worth my job to tell you what I think. There are some things you can't change and religion is one of them.'

These days you can find creationists and Bible literalists all over Dayton and indeed Tennessee. The would-be boosters soon left the town. Its ironworks is long gone. Nowadays it is an agricultural region.

It is said that, many years after the trial, Darrow passed through Dayton once more and saw a new church being erected. He murmured: 'I guess I didn't do much good here after all.' If he were to return today, he would see very many more.

8

Creation Men

'A mere concept of God in the human mind is no help at all because a God created by human philosophy is just another idol.'
Phillip Johnson, *The Wedge of Truth*, 2000

'Bryan let our movement down,' said Ken Ham reflectively. 'He let the whole team down. The trouble was he was influenced by scientists and he was just plain wrong.'[1]

Eighty years on, Bryan's performance at the Monkey Trial still causes fundamentalists to wince. They have spent most of the last century trying to live it down and to construct an alternative story that will convince not only the true believers, but also a sceptical, even cynical outside world. For them, faith is not enough, they must somehow demonstrate that not only *might* the biblical account of creation be true, or that they believe it to be true, but that it actually, demonstrably, *scientifically* is so, so that non-believers accept it as well.

I had come to see Mr Ham, perhaps the world's best-known creationist proselytiser, at his pet project, the Creation Museum in Kentucky, whose mission will be to convince visitors that God's word as transcribed inerrantly in the Bible actually happened. Blessed are they that have not seen and yet have believed, but evidently that is not quite good enough for the true believers.

The museum is just off the interstate, a couple of junctions down from Cincinnati's international airport, over the state line in Kentucky, so right on the cusp between North and South. When I visited, the finishing touches were being put to an impressive-looking building, girded with pillars and faced with rough-hewn boulders that, on closer inspection, turned out to be made of fibreglass. Like everything else about the Creation Museum, nothing was quite as it seemed.

'I heard of it and I seen it from the road but I ain't never been called to go there,' said my taxi driver as we pulled through the gates flanked by brick pillars on which stood ironwork silhouettes of dinosaurs. Prehistoric monsters play a surprisingly large part in the Creation Museum, almost as if they are a hook to attract the children.

The museum, whose motto is 'Prepare to Believe!', is dedicated to the proposition that the account of the creation of the world in the Book of Genesis is completely correct and it uses all the tricks of modern tourist attractions to convince its visitors, through a mixture of animatronic models, tableaux, video presentations and a strangely Disneyfied version of the Bible story.

No wonder, since its designer Patrick Marsh used to work at Universal Studios in Los Angeles and at various theme parks and the LA Olympic Games, then in Japan, before he saw the light, opened his soul to Jesus and was born anew. He now believes that every word in the Bible is literally and unmistakably true, handed down directly by God himself.

Marsh is a small, intense, middle-aged man with crewcut and glasses. He had been working on the project for five years. It is his vision of what actually happened, tempered by speculation when the whole thing gets too metaphorical for easy factual analysis.

'The Bible is the only thing that gives you the full picture. Other religions don't have that and, as for scientists, so much of what they believe is pretty fuzzy about life and its origins,' he said, eyes shining with enthusiasm. 'Oh, this is a great place to work, I will tell you that.'

So this is the Bible story, as actuality. Apart from the dinosaurs, that is. As we stood in the museum's lobby area – the only part of the building approaching completion when I was there in the Fall of 2006, with six months to go to opening – we were surrounded by extremely lifelike, lifesize models of brontosauruses and the rest, seemingly anatomically correct in every detail, some of them moving slightly, and occasionally grunting as they chewed the cud.

On one side of the lobby was a sylvan glade, with cypress trees, palms and shrubs, a waterfall and a 600-gallon pool in which swam several live turtles, the only living exhibits in the whole place. It looked like a mini, 10-feet-wide Eden, which of course is what it was. Beside the pool, two animatronic brown-skinned children – they would have been dark-complexioned said Patrick confidently – demurely dressed in Hiawatha-like buckskin, gravely fluttered with movement. The girl child was kindly offering a carrot to a model squirrel while the boy poked a stick into the pond.

Behind them lurked two small dinosaurs, only a foot or two away. Pets, of course. 'They are not threatening to the kids,' said Patrick reassuringly. I asked what they were, to be told pityingly that they were Tyrannosaurus Rexes, but not dangerous to little humans at all. This was because they were still herbivores, since the scene predated the Fall of Man and so, presumably, the fall of dinosaurs. I had not realised that Adam and Eve's decision to eat the apple had had such devastating side effects on the entire animal kingdom. It seemed a bit hard on defenceless creatures, but perhaps it was a good job that the little T-Rexes already appeared to have sharp teeth.

Theological scholars may have noticed that there are, in fact, no dinosaurs mentioned in the Bible and here was the creationists' first problem. Since there are undoubtedly dinosaur bones and since the museum's directors believe the world is only 6,000 years old – back to Archbishop Ussher, again – they have to be fitted in somewhere, along with the Babylonians, Egyptians and the other ancient civilisations. As for the Grand Canyon – no problem: that was, of course, created if not quite in a day – that would just be too unbelievable – certainly in only a few months, by Noah's Flood.

But what, I asked wonderingly, about the fossilised remains of early man-like creatures, *Australopithecus* and so forth? Patrick knew all about them: 'There are no such things. Humans are basically as you see them today. Those skeletons they've found, what's the word? They could have been deformed, diseased or something. Just because they had cro-magnon skulls it does not necessarily mean they're not human. I've seen people like that running round the streets of New York.'

Nothing could dent the designer's zeal as he led me gingerly through the labyrinth of rooms still under construction, with bits of wood, and the odd dinosaur head occasionally blocking our path. It was like backstage in a theatre. Front of house, the visitors would move past pictures of Mount St Helens erupting, to show how quickly science can work, past two animatronic archaeologists excavating dinosaur bones in the American desert. One – kindly and bearded – would offer visitors an account of how the bones could have got there from a biblical perspective; the other, younger, hirsuit and be-jeaned, would give the Darwinian, evolutionist case, just to be fair. The creationist scientist would spring up throughout the museum, however, to offer his explanation, while the evolutionary scientist was due to appear just once. 'People say the scientific point of view is unbiased but everybody has a bias,' said Patrick. 'It doesn't take millions of years to create diamonds and coal, you know. We all live in the present. It's all really about interpretation.'

In one little corner rather like a waxworks show, they planned to show life-sized models of the Patriarchs – King David with his harp, Moses, Isaiah – followed by Martin Luther nailing his theses to the door, Archbishop Ussher with his calculations, and even a small representation of the Scopes trial ('Bryan let everybody down,' sighed Patrick). But there was to be no room for an animatronic Charles Darwin. 'He's a significant figure,' Patrick conceded, 'But we're really talking biblical history and he's not a main character in that.'

Further on there was a ghastly warning for parents of the perils of not taking the Bible seriously, graffiti-covered brick walls, abortion clinics, pornographic websites (not shown in detail) and a tableau of two adults arguing about their children while the kids played with videogames; and then the same couple listening to an equivocating, liberal sermon while a giant demolition wrecking ball beat against a church wall and through its stained glass window. It was meant to be a vision of a modern hell and Patrick was in no doubt who was to blame: 'This is happening as a result of the ACLU people fighting against the whole Christian philosophy, saying everything is relative, fighting for homosexuality and multiple relationships, abortion and all those other things,' he said. 'God says this will happen.'

It is not a view likely to be challenged by anyone working at the museum. The light of keenness shone from the faces of the workers as they chiselled out fibreglass mountainsides and worked out where to put the artificial Tree of Life in the section on the Fall of Man. They greeted us cheerily as we passed. They too knew they were doing the Lord's Work and each had signed a contract saying they believed in the Seven Days of Creation theory as a condition of working there. Each morning started with staff prayer meetings in a lecture theatre.

This was not some crazy little hole-in-the-corner project made up of inept cardboard cutouts like a seaside freak show. The museum had cost $25 million and, with six months to go, all but $3 million had already been raised from private donations, three of at least $1 million. Besides the exhibits, there were to be a 200-seat proscenium arch theatre, a 60-seat planetarium, a bookshop and Noah's Cafe, a 150-seat refreshment spot, with a further 200 seats outside. They were expecting up to a third of a million visitors a year. The museum is strategically placed – not in the middle of nowhere, but within a day's drive of two-thirds of the entire population of the USA. It is 5 miles from the international airport – direct flights from the UK, it was pointed out to me – and within range of the South, North-East and Midwest, and yet much cheaper to be there than in a big city.

We passed the site where one day a thunderstruck and fearful animatronic Adam would squat beside the Tree of Life after he had eaten the apple. With the museum's commitment to authenticity, I found myself asking what they were doing about Adam's figleaf. Patrick considered this gravely and replied:

'He is naked but he is down on one knee. He is appropriately positioned, so he can be modest. There will be a lamb or something there next to him. We are very careful about that: some of our donors are scared to death about nudity. Of course, Adam and Eve were nude, but we still cover them appropriately.

'It will be a scholarly, well-researched depiction of the scene but without any absolutes, because we were not there. We are faithful to the scriptures and Adam and Eve were created as adults. We say everything with a caveat.'

The same will go for the scene where Eve is created out of Adam's rib, and parents will be warned that little children may be scared by the authenticity of some of the scenes, such as by now blood-thirsty, post-Fall rampaging T-Rexes. 'Absolutely, because we are in there, being faithful. There are going to be scary things for them to plug into. We don't want to make things so family friendly that you get rid of the story, but we want to let people know there are realistic situations that could be negative to small children.'

A little licence was allowed, however, where the Bible falls down on the details. The depiction of a wall-sized section of Noah's Ark (plywood faced with barge-boarding) was based not on the traditional picture of a flat-decked boat but, proudly, on one designed by US navy engineers, with a keel and bows, which might at least have floated without turning turtle had it ever approached water. 'You can surmise,' said Patrick. Inside there would be computer software telling visitors how they fitted all the animals in too, except, I suppose, the fallen dinosaurs. 'It's sort of like a Pirates of the Caribbean scenario,' said Patrick.

Let no one think this is all made up. The museum's research scientist, Dr Jason Lisle, has a PhD in astrophysics from the University of Colorado at Boulder. He realised he was a Christian while he was a student, but did not advertise the fact: 'People get very emotional about the issue. I don't believe we should ever be obnoxious about our faith. I just kept quiet.' And how did he pass the exams if he did not believe what he was being taught by secular scientists? 'I never lied, but if I was asked a question about the age of the universe, I answered with what they would expect, from my knowledge of the topic, not my beliefs.'

The museum's planetarium is his pride and joy, rather superior to the London planetarium of happy memory. Jason wrote the commentary. 'Amazing! God has a name for each star,' it said, and, 'The sun's distance from Earth did not happen by chance', and again, 'The Moon was created by God to be a lesser light'. There was much more in this vein, but not what God thought he was doing when he made Pluto, or why.

Dr Lisle dwells in an office filled with telescopes and gadgets, part of the management block behind the museum, staffed by the dozens of employees of Mr Ham's organisation, Answers in Genesis. They fill a large, open-plan office, sitting in little cubicles, looking at computer screens as in any modern, high-tech office anywhere. The only difference, maybe, is that among the family snapshots and paraphernalia that staff everywhere use to make individual space their own, there also tend to be biblical tracts and pictures. Around the walls of the office are recording and video studios and broadcasting booths: modern technology in the service of a creationist God. It is the same in the design studios in another part of the building: computer screens filled with graphics, little clay models of dinosaurs and other mystical and fantastic creatures such as you find in fantasy games, life-sized putty-covered casts of bears, deers and a puma-like cat, scale models of scenes yet to be built, even a model monkey dangling from a bookshelf. There are skulls and models of human muscular structures to make sure they get the physiognomy and physiques of Moses and the rest right. The postcards and pictures hanging round their desks are of paintings by the Old Masters such as Leonardo, as if the familiarity of their images guarantees the authenticity of the tableaux in the exhibition. If Moses looks a bit like Michelangelo sculpted him, that must surely be proof of what he really looked like. Probably best not to mention that the sculptor was almost certainly gay.

Then I was taken to meet Ken Ham, the museum's director and its inspiration. Ken is an Australian, a former science teacher – though not, he was at pains to say, a scientist – and he had been working on the project for much of the last twenty years since moving to the USA. 'You'd never find something like this in Australia. There's only 20 million people there,' he said. 'If you want to get the message out, it has to be here, in front of 300 million people.'

Reassuringly for me, on the wall outside his office were three framed photographs of the former Australian cricket captain Steve Waugh, a small god in a green baggy cap – 'cricket's never really caught on over here' – and inside on his bookshelves was a wooden model of a platypus. On top of the shelves was an array of fluffy poodle toys, as well as cuddly dinosaurs. 'Poodles are degenerate mutants of dogs. I say that in my lectures and people present them to me as gifts.'

Ham is a large man with a chin-hugging beard like an Old Testament prophet or an old-fashioned preacher, both of which he is, in a way. He lectures all over the world, including the UK, though when he does, like most creationists, however distinguished, he has to make do with addressing small gatherings of the faithful in obscure parish halls. Creationism remains a distinctly fringe interest in the UK, even for most Christians, though there are a few.

'We want to try to convince people using observational science. It's done very gently but forthrightly. We give both sides, which is more than the Science Museum in London does.'

Then he said something remarkable: 'What we want to do here is to teach people how to think. I am not a scientist but I was trained to be a science teacher and my evolutionist professors decided I was qualified to teach. You have to define what you mean by science. You can have knowledge about the processes – we all agree about that – Darwin was right about natural selection. I was a biology major.'

But here was the nub: 'But when it comes to knowledge about the past origins of beasts or mammals, you have stepped outside observational science. It is one thing to believe in natural selection but to say over millions of years new characteristics develop cannot be proved. We want to teach people how to think.'

On the shelf behind his desk lay several surprising books, including Richard Dawkins's latest. Ham was dismissive:

'I've skipped through it. The thing is, Dawkins does not have infinite knowledge or understanding himself. He's got a position too, it's just a different one from ours.

'The Bible makes sense and is overwhelmingly confirmed by observable science. It does not confirm the belief in evolution. We are in the minority but that's not everything. The majority is not always right.'

'But if you believe in the Bible, why do you need to seek scientific credibility and why are creationists so reluctant to put their theories to peer review?' I asked.

'I would give the same answer as Dawkins. He believes there is no God and nothing you could say would convince him otherwise. You are dealing with an origins issue. If you don't have the information, you cannot be sure. Nothing contradicts the Bible's account of the origins. Isaac Newton, Michael Faraday – they believed in the creator-God of the Bible. Science comes out of a Christian base and God does not change his mind. There are creation legends all over the world and they tend to attest to the creation story of the Bible.

'The more I have studied this over the years, the more I would say we don't have all the answers but the Bible's account not only makes sense, it is also overwhelmingly confirmed by observation. That's why I can say there will be nothing here in this museum which contradicts the Bible's account of the origins. I take the Bible to be the inspired, infallible, inerrant words of God.

'Interpretation just unlocks the door to making anything literally true. You know, interpretation is what puts England where it is today. It's inconsistency. The clergy don't believe any more: they are not standing up for the truth. That's why all those churches are being turned into Sikh temples and call centres. Young people can spot that. You have to have consistency.'

Then he said: 'I am not political. I would not advise anyone how to vote. I would just say that they should look at the world-view of the candidates and choose the one whose views are closest to biblical principles. I just want people to be asking questions, asking teachers what they are teaching. We are shipping out books all the time, pumping out information into the culture. More and more people are questioning evolution. We are getting it out. I am not a scientist but I believe I do have a gift for communication. You haven't seen anything yet.'

We wandered across the reception area, past the browsing pre-lapsarian dinosaurs to the museum's bookshop which, far from being another biblical epic, was done up like a medieval castle, framed with heraldic shields and filled with images of dragons – dragons, you see, being what dinosaurs became. On a wall was a frieze showing St George vanquishing one with the legend: 'Valiant in Battle, he smote the foul beast, struck a mortal blow, rescuing the princess and saving her people', which did not seem to have much biblical content to it.

It was more a fantasy Tolkein or Dungeons and Dragons than Genesis. Like any other museum shop, you could buy sweatshirts bearing the creation logo and school lunch boxes with dinosaurs on them. The shelves were full of books and DVDs with titles such as *The Battle for Truth*, *Infallible Proofs*, *Refuting Compromise*, *The Lie*, *Evolution Impossible* and *The Great Dinosaur Mystery Solved*, and even a DVD entitled *Arguments Creationists Should Not Use*.

Pointing to a stained glass window of a dragon, Mr Ham said: 'It's a bit like an English medieval castle.' Not like one I'd ever seen: I suggested it looked more like Hogwarts. This baffled him as he had not really caught up with the legendary Harry Potter. 'Hogwarts? Hogwarts?' he said bemusedly. I explained the reference. 'Oh yes,' he said, he'd heard of that. Never seen the films though.

As we finished he told me about the museum's website: www.AnswersInGenesis.org. Out of 100 million sites, it ranks 24,000th in popularity, apparently. Someone out there must believe.

And maybe they will travel to Cincinnati to see the museum made flesh. Patrick Marsh said: 'I would say probably 60 per cent are going to be people who believe in creation. Twenty per cent, maybe more, are probably people who believe in some millions of years theory, who are still Christians, maybe who need their faith bolstered. And the rest will be people who are not Christians or creationists. God is going to do all kinds of things here. People are going to change by coming here. Nobody's gone to this much trouble before.'

Stupidly – as if there was any need – I asked him whether he ever had any doubts. Patrick said: 'No, no doubts. You walk outside and look at the birds and the leaves. Everything is full of life. Science is not clear what things are and what life is. Everything works together so perfectly. It is all so intertwined. It doesn't make any sense unless there is a Creator. There's got to be one because otherwise it's all way too complicated. The science community is just guessing: the simple answers make sense.'

As I was leaving the museum, Ken Ham presented me with a book with a glossy cover called *Evolution Exposed: Your Evolution Answer Book for the Classroom*. This was the book he had mentioned being shipped out to schools. Written by one Roger Patterson, a former biology and chemistry teacher in Wyoming who now works for Answers in Genesis, it was a sturdy paperback suggesting to children the questions they should ask their teachers to expose the Darwinians who are subverting the Bible in their midst. There may be a good market in providing a retaliatory book here.

Patterson's book gives a good indication of the hermetically sealed world in which creationists live and the circularity of their arguments, some of which were familiar from my interview with Mr Ham and some of which date back to Bryan's day. What is most striking, however, is the insistence that their theory of creation is just as objectively valid and factually based as the theory of evolution, if not more so. There is a relentless nit-picking of the gaps in the evolutionary argument and a constant questioning of the validity of its evidence – indeed an impugning and carping denigration of it – but a simple, even credulous, recourse to biblical truth to uphold their own sweeping claims, as if that trumps all arguments. Evolutionists have to prove their theory scientifically, while creationists only need to assert their belief without any tedious recourse to proving the existence of God beyond saying He must be true. It is also striking that scientists are always viewed as the enemy, engaged in a relentless conspiracy to subvert Christianity. Some, notably Richard Dawkins, are, of course.

The creationists have a cast-iron defence, proof against all scientific or secular challenge, because it is built on faith rather than objective evidence. Why that means the creationists feel the need to crave academic respectability and scientific respect in addition to their own certainty of belief is at first hard to say, unless it is to find tangible proof of the truth of what they believe, to wave in front of the sceptics and so convert them. Which would rather suggest a certain, unexpected degree of unease and insecurity about their central premise.

Unlike in the 1920s when fundamentalists sought to ban the teaching of evolution, what appears to be sought now is a parity of esteem. This is a much more sophisticated and, on the surface, reasonable argument: as if among rational men there could be a simple difference of opinion. Except, of course, that that is not how they really see it at all. They don't want to balance the scales and they believe that if the Bible's account is put forward, it must win. The consequences of it not doing so are too terrible to contemplate. Unfortunately, science teachers in particular and state schools in general cannot be trusted to teach the creationist view, so they must either be compelled to do so, or fundamentalists must be recruited as teachers – an unlikely prospect in sufficient numbers – or perhaps more parents should be encouraged to teach their children at home, untainted by the school system.

It is curious – or perhaps not – that, despite their quest for scientific acceptance, the creationists and their colleagues propounding Intelligent Design theory have been entirely reluctant to allow their research to be subjected to academic evaluation. Ken Ham says this is because the establishment is biased against them and so is unlikely to accept their evidence. He denied to me that there was a paucity of published research, though he conceded that it was not always given prominence: 'There's definitely a bias against our research but there is a lot of published data there by creationists, though they are not always known as such. There is good material out there.'

However, Michael Behe, a biologist who supports the Intelligent Design theory, conceded at Dover Pennsylvania in 2005 that: 'there are no peer reviewed articles by anyone advocating for Intelligent Design supported by pertinent experiments or calculations which provide detailed, rigorous accounts of how Intelligent Design of any biological system occurred'.[2] How could there be?

Mr Patterson's work begins with the premise that students are being indoctrinated with evolutionary ideas in the state schools and that students who do not accept that should be encouraged 'to ask the questions in a Christ-like manner'. St Paul tells them how to do it in his Letter to the Ephesians: 'speaking the truth in love to defeat the trickery of men in the cunning craftiness of deceitful plotting'. These evolutionists are not unintelligent, the book informs its readers, ultimately it takes just as much faith if not more to believe that only matter and natural laws can explain the universe.[3] Imagine.

That is about as courteous as the creationists get in assuming the good faith of their opponents. Generally, when not alleging a conspiracy of indoctrination, they tend to argue that the Darwinians are guilty of blind faith or that they have no real evidence to support their theory – a startling example of pots and kettles and an exact mirror image of what the scientists say about them.

Patterson calls in aid scientists such as Bacon, Galileo, Kepler and Newton as proof that some great scientists have had a Christian world-view, conveniently overlooking that all those lived long before the theory of evolution was ever developed. He says all four were believers in a recently created Earth and adds: 'The idea that science cannot accept a creationist perspective is a denial of scientific history,' as if the great scientists were all signed up on his side to a debate that did not begin until centuries after their deaths, long after scientific knowledge had outstripped their own. It is as if science has stood still since the Enlightenment which, in a sense, for the creationists it has. 'Creationists can develop theories too, in light of Biblical truth, but they are just not as widely accepted by scientists,' it adds.[4]

Mr Patterson's book argues in some detail that early creatures such as *Australopithecus* could not have been prototype humans because they are too much like apes, citing as evidence that their bone structures meant they could not have walked upright. Lest this reasoning might be thought to endorse the theory that man has indeed descended from ape-like ancestors, the book is at pains to assert: 'Starting from biblical assumptions [sic], we see clearly that God made man in His image and did not use evolution.'[5] It lays heavy emphasis on earlier frauds such as the Piltdown forgery and Nebraska Man to discredit evolutionists. By contrast, the Loch Ness Monster is accepted with complete credulity, despite all the evidence that it was dreamed up as a newspaper stunt in the 1930s:

> . . . stories of large creatures have been present in modern cultures around the world . . . while evolutionists must dismiss all these claims as absurd because dinosaurs have been extinct for 65 million years, there is no reason to doubt that some species of dinosaurs could have survived the 4,500 years since the Flood. Credible accounts of the 'bunyip', 'burrunjor' and 'kulta' among Aborigines seem to fit descriptions of 'prehistoric' dinosaur-like creatures that could have survived in remote regions.
>
> The evidence of human and dinosaur co-existence includes cave paintings that apparently depict dinosaurs, the mention of dragons and behemoth in the Bible and the presence of many dinosaur and dragon descriptions and pictures in Europe and Asia.[6]

Thus neanderthal bones must be a hoax because they do not match God's design in the Bible, but the Loch Ness Monster is likely to be true because, with the eye of faith, it could be a latterday dinosaur.

The book says that when they ask questions, students should remember they are not alone: God is always with them, and good may ultimately come of their questioning: 'Even if a classmate or teacher does not come to Christ, you may be planting seeds that will sprout some day.'

Then comes the nub: 'Just as evolutionists weren't there to see evolution happen over several billion years, neither were creationists there to see the events of the six days of creation. The difference is that creationists have the Creator's eye-witness account of the events of creation, while evolutionists must create a story to explain origins. Just because a majority of scientists believe the story does not make the

story true.'[7] Note the ellision from eye witness account to creating a
story:

> Scientific theories must be testable and capable of being proven
> false. Neither evolution nor biblical creation qualifies as a
> scientific theory in this sense, because each deals with historical
> events that cannot be repeated. Both evolution and creation are
> based on unobserved assumptions about past events. It is incon-
> sistent to say that evolution qualifies as a scientific theory while
> creation does not. Both have scientific character by attempting
> to correlate scientific data within a certain framework.
>
> Since the Bible is the eyewitness account of the Creator of
> the Universe, it is the best starting point for interpreting past
> events . . . If someone expects you to argue that the Bible or
> creation is true without using the Bible as evidence, they are
> stacking the deck in their favour. They are insisting that facts are
> neutral and that truth can be determined independent of God.
> Facts are always interpreted and the word of God is absolutely
> trustworthy.[8]

Too much of this sort of thing can make your head spin.

When Darwin's *Origin of Species* was first published in the USA in
November 1859, on the eve of the Civil War, its initial print run of
1,250 copies sold out within a day, American Protestants initially saw
no problem in reconciling evolution with the Bible. It was, after all,
just as theologians were starting to question the Bible's literal truth
and suggesting new interpretations for its more problematic passages.
As John Fiske, a Harvard-trained philosopher, wrote: 'Evolution is
God's way of doing things'[9] – a line that many Christians, including
those who happen to be scientists, hold to this day. Darwin's theory
could indeed be reconciled with an almighty God: he might be setting
the wheels in motion and watching them spin.

It was not until the industrial, social and religious uncertainties of
the turn of the twentieth century and the rise of fundamentalism that
questioning of the theory began. By the time of the Scopes Trial, all
respectable scientific opinion accepted Darwin and the reverses and

ridicule that the fundamentalists suffered then drove them back in on themselves. They might never accept evolution, but they also preferred not to venture back into the public square, for fear of ridicule. Into the 1960s and the Space Race, the evolutionary argument had the ground entirely to itself. Technology was king and creationism had no answers for the pace and development of modern life.

Only in the 1970s did the biblical arguments resurface publicly, perhaps not by chance. It was a period of US uncertainty and loss of confidence in both the power of science and technology and in the institutions of government, and it happened coincidentally just as the Right was regrouping and the Religious Right was beginning to get organised to challenge the liberal, progressive state.

As Randall Balmer, professor of American Religious History at Barnard College, Columbia University, one of the most acute observers of the evangelical movement – he is himself an evangelical – has noted: 'The history of the conservative, evolutionist "debate" since the Scopes trial has been in essence the story of adaptation to new legal, social and intellectual realities in order to win validation in educational circles.'[10]

The creationist charge started with isolated legal assaults on the curriculums taught in state schools in the South, beginning with the argument that Bryan himself had used fifty years earlier that there should be democratic accountability for what children were being taught in publicly funded schools. One such couple were Mel and Norma Gabler in Longview, Texas, who began challenging state textbooks in the mid-1970s, arguing that 'the historical origins of humankind [should] be edited, if necessary to clarify that the treatment is theoretical rather than factually verifiable'.

The Gablers were characteristically categorised by the Texan polemical journalist Molly Ivins as 'two ignorant, fear-mongering, right-wing fruitloops . . . doing untold damage to public education'. But they and others gained traction at least in the South and Midwest because they played into wider concerns about standards in schools. They gained influence among the religiously inclined, public-spirited evangelical Christians serving on local school boards. In turn, concerns about what children were being taught prompted more Christians to step forward to serve on boards, some with the express purpose of securing at least equal time and status for the Genesis account of creation.

In addition, the creationists, emerging blinking back into the public sphere, were also acute in their presentation of their case – and lucky to have it taken up by ambitious national politicians. The bland biblical account somehow along the way gained the spurious title of 'creation *science*' as if to give it some academic credibility, even though it lacked the attributes of scientific discovery in being both objectively unverifiable and inherently unobservable. Eventually it also spawned an offshoot called Intelligent Design, intended to distance creationism from its scriptural roots and thus give it a supposed secular impartiality.

The basis of Intelligent Design is that the universe and its species are so complex that they must have been developed by a superior and over-arching intelligence, though usually its proponents fight shy of using the G-word to describe who that being might be, in order not to put anyone off.

Intelligent Design is a fairly recent development in the creationist battle, developed only in the late 1980s, not from some sudden intellectual or scientific insight, but in response to a Supreme Court ruling that the teaching of creation science was unconstitutional since it amounted to the promotion of a religion. Hence its supporters' reluctance to specify too clearly who they believe the 'Intelligent Designer' to be.

The theory has proved difficult for other scientists to deal with, partly because a small number of academics – usually from non-scientific disciplines – have been enlisted to argue its case and partly because believers in evolutionary theory have been slow to take Intelligent Design as seriously as perhaps they should on a populist or political level. It is easy to sympathise: looked at coldly, Intelligent Design is an entirely sterile theory. It is based on a supernatural idea for the origin of life that is entirely unprovable. In the words of the science journalist Chris Mooney: 'ID doesn't have any meat to it. It doesn't provide any details that scientists might confirm or refute through future experimentation. And, most crucially of all, it doesn't *explain* anything or *predict* anything, a key requirement for successful *scientific* theories . . . "an unknown Intelligent Designer did something, somewhere, somehow, for no apparent reason" is not a model.'[11]

But, for its supporters, the alternative, of random development of species and organisms, is just too terrible to contemplate: in the words of Phillip E. Johnson, a law professor at Berkeley and leading proponent of Intelligent Design: to scientists, evolution means 'a purposeless, material process propelled by random genetic changes'. In that case, what would be the point of God? At worst, as usual in US controversy, it would amount to yet another secret and subversive conspiracy, this time to discredit religion. As Johnson has also written: 'Darwinism was not just a theory of biology, but the most important element in a religion of scientific naturalism, with its own ethical agenda and plan for salvation through social and genetic engineering.'[12] It is interesting that he should annex such theological language to describe the secular agenda he alleges.

As Balmer says:

> The Religious Right has chosen a peculiar strategy: they set about constructing a Trojan horse by cloaking creationism in the guise of science . . . Intelligent design advocates seek to substantiate their claims that a designer stands behind the creation process by all manner of argumentation, including mathematical probability calculations . . . [They] are notoriously reticent about claiming publicly that God is responsible for Creation, for that would give the movement's critics too obvious a reason to dismiss intelligent design as religion, not science.[13]

But Johnson has also written in his 2000 book *The Wedge of Truth* that, actually, it *is* God who is the great organiser – there is ultimately no mystery about the designer: 'What we need is for God himself to speak, to give us a secure foundation on which we can build . . . when we have reached that point in our questioning, we will inevitably encounter the person of Jesus Christ.'[14]

A series of think-tanks and institutes, usually largely funded by fundamentalist millionaires, and sometimes with links to secular conservative research groups, has grown up to offer some credibility to what remains a case that derives all its authority from the Bible. In fact, virtually all the Religious Right's organisations and leaders from both Protestant fundamentalist and Catholic wings have shown sympathy with the aims of the Intelligent Design lobbyists: James Dobson's Focus on the Family, Phyllis Schlafly's Eagle Forum, the Concerned Women of America, D. James Kennedy's Coral Ridge Ministries, the American Family Association and Alliance Defence Fund have all given it some backing.

Thus the Californian real-estate multi-millionaire Howard Ahmanson, the biggest single sponsor of the conservative insurgency within the liberal US Episcopal Church, has also put his money into a number of such organisations. He and his wife Roberta, a former local journalist, have been keen supporters of the Chalcedon Institute in California, which developed out of the Christian Reconstructionist teachings of their friend R. J. Rushdoony which wants to see the replacement of US civil law with Old Testament biblical laws in all their grisly sternness. The Institute says on its website that it does not appeal 'to modern liberalised, generic Christendom...rather we appeal to those devout, rock-ribbed saints who believe that if the Bible is good enough for the church, it is good enough for the school and state; who believe that if Jesus Christ is Lord of the family, he is also Lord of the laboratory and the board room; who recognise that if Christianity is good enough for them, it is good enough for their great-great grandchildren'.[15]

The Ahmansons also support the Discovery Institute in Seattle, founded in 1990 about the time of the development of intelligent design theory and nowadays a creationist think-tank (Mr Ahmanson sits on its board of directors), which plays host itself to the Center for Science and Culture (CSC) which in turn aims to replace the secular state with one based on religious principles. It seeks, it says, 'nothing less than the overthrow of materialism and its cultural legacies'.[16]

The Discovery Institute has a range of interests, including the environment, tort reform, transport and broadband development. Its fellows are frequent contributors to conservative publications and it has links with other freemarket and conservative lobbying groups both in Washington state and across the country in DC.[17] Its founder, Bruce Chapman, believes: 'certain features of the universe and of living things are best explained by an intelligent cause, not as part of an undirected process such as natural selection'. This is the classic definition of Intelligent Design.

In 1999 a private seven-page Discovery Institute document, entitled 'The Wedge Strategy', found its way on to the web, aimed at appealing to prospective donors. It outlines an agenda to undercut science in order to promote religious goals and argues that there is a need to 'replace materialistic explanations with the theistic understanding that nature and human beings are created by God'.[18]

It adds:

> Debunking the traditional conceptions of both God and Man, thinkers such as Charles Darwin, Karl Marx and Sigmund Freud portrayed humans not as moral and spiritual beings, but as animals or machines who inhabited a universe ruled by purely impersonal forces and whose behaviour and very thoughts were dictated by the unbending forces of biology, chemistry and environment. This materialistic conception of reality eventually infected virtually every area of our culture from politics and economics to literature and art.

As Michelle Goldberg says in her book *Kingdom Coming*, this suggests that the CSC is troubled 'more by the philosophical consequences of evolution than by the fact that it contradicts a literal reading of the Bible'. They present themselves as open-minded seekers after truth, like the scientists of old, being done down by modern liberals and secularists. The CSC earnestly seeks to assert that they have at least a weight of scientific evidence on their side: 'During the past decade new research and discoveries in such fields as physics, cosmology, biochemistry, genetics and paleontology have caused a growing number of scientists and science theorists to question neo-Darwinism and propose Design as the best explanation for the existence of specified complexity in the natural world.'[19] The argument goes that the aim should be at least to ensure that their theory gets equal billing with the evolutionists – or, rather, that the theory of evolution (but not necessarily their own theory) should be sceptically cross-examined.

This is not just academic, they believe that the life of the nation is at stake. The proponents of creationism are sure that evolution has had grave moral consequences that would be removed if students were taught the biblical account of mankind's origins. We are back to the wrecking ball smashing the stained glass window of the liberal church at the Creation Museum.

When Randall Balmer interviewed creationists for a television programme in the mid-1990s, he said he was astounded by their assessments. One told him that evolution was rebellion against God, Phillip Johnson claimed his advocacy of Intelligent Design was intended 'to make it possible to ask theistic questions in the universities', and Duane Gish, another pillar of the movement and member of the Institute for Creation Research, told him that social ills including sex, violence and crime were due to evolutionary theory: 'I believe the major reason these things have happened is that our judges and our educators and our legislators, the leaders in our society, have been indoctrinated in evolutionary theory.'[20] In a curious echo of Darrow's defence in the Leopold and Loeb trial of 1924 – though he would not thank anyone for pointing it out – Tom DeLay, the then Republican majority leader in the House of Representatives, even argued that the Columbine school shootings in 1999 were the result of students being taught evolution.

The CSC's Wedge document argues that the strategy should be to undermine the scientific and educational establishments over five years to restore the 'ideological imbalance', to foster the movement internationally and domestically and to put forward legal reforms based on design theory. Goldberg argues:

> The plan is to undermine the Enlightenment conception of the physical world as a prelude to undermining the Enlightenment's social legacies. What the authors want to discredit isn't just Charles Darwin – it's the very idea that truth can be ascertained without reference to the divine. Religious law makes much more sense when religion is seen as the foundation of reality.[21]

The strategy's second phase is apparently 'to prepare the popular reception of our ideas' by winning over 'our natural constituency, namely Christians'. Thus, Goldberg says, CSC fellows are called to testify about Intelligent Design before school boards, to write commentaries for newspapers, and to offer 'balance' to evolution controversies. It is, she says, the fostering of a deception, the notoriously difficult preposition of a negative argument:

> When truth loses its meaning, all manner of deceptions can be fostered. How do we know the founding fathers *didn't* intend a theocracy? Who's to say there *weren't* weapons of mass destruction in Iraq? Can anyone prove there *isn't* a homosexual conspiracy?
>
> There are two sides to every story, right? Who are you going to believe, your pastor or the liberal media? This kind of psychological climate – at once utterly credulous and sullenly cynical – gives totalitarian movements space to grow.[22]

The creation of uncertainty helps solidify the constituency in other words. Well, yes, but one doesn't have to go all the way with the young journalist and her apocalyptic theories to recognise a certain cast of mind among some creationists, and among the wider Religious Right movement. There have been attempts to get the Intelligent Design theory into UK schools too, though so far with little apparent success. About fifty secondary schools are understood to have accepted ID textbooks, though whether to use them in lessons as the gospel truth, or to show pupils the falsity of the theory behind them, is unclear.

Although creationists have won control of a few school curriculums through being elected to some local school boards and Intelligent Design has managed to give the impression that there should be an academic parity, they have also proved litigious in trying to force equality of treatment for teaching the theory. Between 2001 and 2004, the National Center for Science Education, which was founded to support the evolutionist argument, recorded creationist challenges in forty-three of the fifty states.

But in contrast to Judge Raulston at the Scopes trial, today's judges have so far been highly reluctant to accept evolutionists' attempts to force schools to give their theory equal weight in local curriculums. This is another reason for the Religious Right to hate judges of an independent cast of mind.

A whole series of cases has thrown out the argument that

creationism deserves parity with evolution. For this, evolutionists and progressives have the separation of powers and the absence of religion from the Constitution to thank and the Founding Fathers who ensured that it should be so. In November 2004, the *New York Times* reported that legislators in Missouri were developing a Bill that would require state biology textbooks to include a chapter on alternative theories of evolution and quoted state representative Cynthia Davies startlingly comparing Darwinists to Al-Qaeda terrorists: 'It's like when the hijackers took over those four planes on September 11th and took people to a place where they didn't want to go. I think a lot of people feel that liberals have taken our country somewhere we don't want to go. I think a lot more people realise this is our country and we're going to take it back.'[23] Hitherto, perhaps the only similarity between the retiring Victorian biologist and Osama bin Laden might have been thought to have been the length of their beards. This is clearly developing into a many-pronged attack.

The legal cases date back to *Epperson* v. *Arkansas* in 1968 which ruled that a state law similar to the Butler Act in Tennessee was unconstitutional because the First Amendment to the Constitution does not allow a state to require that teaching be tailored to fit the religious convictions of a particular group.

Then came the Supreme Court's 1987 ruling, *Edwards* v. *Aguillard*, which overturned a Louisiana law mandating the teaching of creation science alongside evolution, on the grounds that the former was a religious doctrine and so violated the First Amendment by promoting religion. Seven of the nine justices supported the decision. No fewer than seventy-two Nobel laureates had earlier signed a statement in favour of overturning the law, arguing that 'teaching religious belief mislabeled as science is detrimental to scientific education'.[24] It was this case that persuaded some creationists to propound the supposedly secular Intelligent Design theory, which first made its appearance in the aftermath of the case.

Peloza v. *Capistrano School District* in 1994 rejected the ingenious attempt at a counter-argument, that evolution is a religion and that the refusal to teach creationism therefore amounted to a violation of the Constitutional right to the free exercise of religion. Then *Freiler* v. *Tangipahoa Parish Board of Education* in 1999 dismissed a call for teachers to be required to read disclaimers before teaching evolutionary theory in order to promote 'critical thought', on the grounds that no other subject had such a requirement.

Most devastatingly – and this is where the liberal judges' theory at least breaks down for now – in the Dover School Board case in December 2005, Judge John Jones, a Bush appointee, threw out a similar attempt to require teachers in part of Pennsylvania to read a statement to students asserting that evolution was 'not a fact' because he said it was an infringement of the separation of Church and state.[25]

The local school board had the year before become the first in the USA to mandate the teaching of Intelligent Design, precipitating a national storm of protest and media attention. The row started when a newly elected board member, Bill Buckingham, who had been made chairman of the curriculum committee, objected to the high school science department's recommendation that the board should buy copies of Miller and Levine's *Biology* for the school as its textbook. Buckingham objected on the grounds that the book was 'laced with Darwinism'. 'This country wasn't founded on Muslim beliefs or evolution,' he said, betraying a certain philosophical confusion. 'This country was founded on Christianity and our students should be taught as such.'

He wanted simple creationism taught instead, but he was soon persuaded to evolve this into Intelligent Design and shortly obtained national political support in the form of the state's Republican (and, incidentally, Catholic) Senator Rick Santorum, who had two years earlier supported similar moves in neighbouring Ohio. He had written in the *Washington Times*: 'If the Education Board . . . does not include Intelligent Design in the new teaching standards, many students will be denied a first-rate science education. Many will be left behind.'

The Dover board initially rejected Buckingham's proposal that the school textbook should instead be a work called *Of Pandas and People*, an Intelligent Design text owned by the Foundation for Thought and Ethics, which is linked to the Center for Science and Culture. It is a book endorsed by Ken Ham's Answers in Genesis as 'superbly written'. But, after heavy lobbying, the board did eventually vote that Intelligent Design should be taught.

A legal challenge was mounted by the ACLU, in support of some parents, amid an atmosphere of increasing divisiveness and not a little acrimony, with local Christians claiming – just as their predecessors had in Dayton eighty years before – that the civil liberties union was an ungodly, communist front. Enthusiasm for the case waned as it became clear that the school board would be faced with a large legal bill if the ACLU won, even though it had secured representation for itself from a pro-bono conservative Catholic law firm called the Thomas More Law Center.

Even the Intelligent Design proponents of the Center for Science and Culture came out against the school board, apparently because it wanted to wait for a better test case and a friendlier Supreme Court. It also saw that, following the earlier rulings, the board was unlikely to win constitutionally.

There was in any event a certain intellectual irony that the Religious Right, having complained about secular moral relativism for years, was now arguing that scepticism should be allowed, indeed mandated, in the case of something they themselves refused to believe in: the theory of evolution.

The CSC was right to be worried about the lawsuit. Judge Jones threw out the school board's Intelligent Design case in particularly scathing terms, criticising the 'breathtaking inanity of [its] decision'. He stated: 'The overwhelming evidence at trial established that ID is a religious view, a mere relabeling of creationism and not a scientific theory . . . the argument of irreducible scientific complexity, central to ID, employs the same flawed and illogical, contrived dualism that doomed creation science in the 1980s.'[26]

For now, Intelligent Design's strategy of securing intellectual and legal credibility as a preliminary to wider acceptance has hit the buffers. But it is much too early to say that the wider war has been won, or lost. In the words of Chris Mooney: 'ID hawkers have clear and ever present religious motivations for denying and attacking evolution. And like creationists of yore, they have failed the only test that matters. They simply are not doing credible science. Instead they are appropriating scientific-sounding arguments to advance a moral and political agenda, one they hope to force into the public school system.'[27]

* * *

If the Intelligent Design row was just an abstruse intellectual or even theological debate, it would, perhaps, be harmless enough, but the groups that have taken up the idea are also engaged in other areas, questioning what they see as an unaccountable, liberal, scientific establishment on other issues, such as stem cell research, global warming and the genetic basis of homosexuality. These are big battles to come, for which they will doubtless some day require a more sympathetic Supreme Court.

In the meantime, there are small victories – the odd district school board requiring teachers to tell their classes that there are other explanations than evolution to explain the development of man, or the occasional resolution to require stickers on textbooks. And, perhaps most notably, there was the decision to approve the sale of a glossy coffee-table book called *Grand Canyon: A Different View* in the National Parks Service's bookstore at the Canyon, arguing that the great chasm was not hollowed out over millions of years from the erosion of some of the oldest rocks on the planet, but caused suddenly by a single catastrophic event – Noah's Flood, of course.[28]

The explanation of flood geology came from the Seventh Day Adventists' George McCready Price who had little scientific training himself, but believed that God had told him to research the 'unworked field' of evolutionary geology. Mooney writes: 'Price's theory basically assumes, based on the Bible, the existence of a worldwide deluge and then fits the facts of the fossil record to that assumption – precisely the opposite of how science should work.'[29] His work contains some basic misunderstandings of how geological strata are actually laid down and has, perhaps understandably, found little favour with scientists. Naturally, Roger Patterson's *Evolution Exposed*, for schoolchildren, insists that all is clear: 'The geologic layers, plate tectonics, radiometric dating and the fossil record can all be explained within the framework provided by the Bible. Starting from the Bible – instead of naturalism – the layers of rock all over the world with billions of dead things in them are the result of the worldwide flood described in Genesis.'[30]

The decision to stock *The Grand Canyon: A Different View* in 2003 caused an immense furore, not least because the Parks Service

operates under a Congressional mandate to promote scientific understanding. While the heads of seven leading geological associations
wrote to the superintendent of the Grand Canyon park to protest
against 'the advancement of religious tenets as science', on the other
side Ken Ham's Answers in Genesis and the Institute for Creation
Research lined up to do battle to keep the book on sale. The
creationists were offered support by the Alliance Defence Fund, a
Christian legal advice body founded by James Dobson of Focus on the
Family and the evangelist D. James Kennedy, with the purpose of
spreading the gospel by litigation if need be. It threatened legal action
if the book was removed and started mobilising the support of
Christian lobbyists. Despite the view of David Shaver, the head of the
Department of Interior's geologic resources division, that the book's
sale in the Park's bookstores 'directly conflicts with the service's
statutory mandate to promote the use of sound science in all its
programmes', *A Different View* remained on sale.

At the same time a document written by the geologic resources
division for Canyon guides, stating that there is no valid scientific data
showing the great rift to be only a few thousand years old, was
permanently quashed.

On 18 February 2004 more than sixty senior scientists, including
twenty Nobel Prize winners, wrote an open letter to President Bush
warning:

> When scientific knowledge has been found to be in conflict with
> its political goals, the administration has often manipulated the
> process through which science enters into its decisions. This has
> been done by placing people who are professionally unqualified
> or who have clear conflicts of interest in official posts and on
> scientific advisory committees; by disbanding existing advisory
> committees; by censoring and suppressing reports by the
> government's own scientists; and by simply not seeking indep-
> endent scientific advice . . . the administration has sometimes
> misrepresented scientific knowledge and misled the public
> about the implications of its policies . . . The distortion of
> scientific knowledge for partisan political ends must cease.[31]

It is indeed hard to believe that Americans would sacrifice their lead as the world's greatest and most technologically and scientifically advanced superpower on the altar of an obscurantist internal, politicised debate. It is hard to see a future generation of US scientists, reared on creationism and Intelligent Design, developing new technologies, new Star Wars, new space stations, a new Microsoft, or even a better mousetrap.

We'll see more about the scientists' worries in discussing the Bush administration's policies. For now, perhaps it is enough to suggest that Clarence Darrow and H. L. Mencken are revolving in their graves.

Monkey Town lives.

9

The Golden Hour of the Little Flower

'Just about the biggest thing that ever happened to radio.'
Fortune magazine about Father Coughlin, 1934

On top of a mountainside surrounded by woodland in rural Alabama, 30 miles outside Birmingham, sits a satellite station whose tall aerials direct the Catholic broadcasting station EWTN, the Eternal Word Television Network (which, despite its name, is also a radio, and now even an iPod service), simultaneously to viewers and listeners in equatorial Africa, Latin America, Europe and North America. It is scarcely situated in the heartland of Catholicism, but the station, started by the elderly Catholic nun Mother Angelica in a converted garage with a budget of $200 in 1981, is now a worldwide brand, broadcasting twenty-four hours a day in English and Spanish, with some programmes in German, to a potential audience in 125 million homes in 140 countries. Its monthly budget of $3.5 million is met through the mostly small and voluntary individual donations of its viewers.

Mother herself lay in her convent bedroom, permanently incapacitated following a stroke on Christmas Eve 2001, when I visited the station in May 2006, but recordings of her programmes in which she sits addressing homilies to devout audiences forever dressed in the fashions of the late 1980s and 1990s were still being beamed out around the Earth twice a week, as are more up-to-date programmes expounding conservative Catholic theology given by a small coterie of US priests. All those who have had a Catholic upbringing will recognise Mother as a terrifyingly familiar sort of nun: gazing out owlishly from behind her spectacles and exuding a slightly chilling air of menace, mouth turned downwards in permanent disapproval, despite occasional flashes of a wintry smile.[1]

Mother Angelica herself was born Rita Rizzo in Canton, Ohio, in 1923 and has spent most of her adult life in a convent of the Order of the Poor Clares, but she has exhibited an entrepreneurial canniness and resolution – some would call it a calculating naïvety – that some media moguls might envy, not to mention institutions such as the wider Catholic Church.

Her mission really started in the mid-1950s when she slipped on a church floor she was polishing and severely injured her back. She was told that an operation could leave her paralysed, but she prayed to God the night before that if she recovered she would found a monastery in the Deep South. She did recover and, in the early 1960s at the height of the racial tensions of the civil rights era, she founded her monastic house outside Birmingham in the USA. Once there, she started publishing devotional pamphlets and appearing on local television programmes. The decision to start her own station only came when she discovered that the local channel she appeared on was about to broadcast a CBS mini-series that she considered blasphemous. It was based on an Irving Wallace novel called *The Word*, about the discovery of a fraudulent papyrus scroll questioning the divinity of Christ, but even the very idea seemed to her to be an undermining of the Lord, raising unwanted questions in the minds of the faithful. When the station refused to withdraw the series, Mother marched out with the celebrated words of the channel's vice-president ringing in her ears: 'You leave here and you're off television. You need us.' Mother replied: 'No I don't. I only need God!'[2]

The EWTN studio, which now has 300 employees, is like no other I have ever visited. It is situated off a side road – barely more than a track – running through pine woods on a back route out of Birmingham. In the grounds there are grottoes and shrines, even an outdoor altar, alongside satellite dishes and aerials. Inside the main building there is a large chapel, together with studios filled with the sort of tasteful sets that are supposed to convey quiet contemplation and deep learning, with bookshelves and holy ornaments. The walls are lined with devotional pictures of Christ, the Virgin Mary and Pope John Paul II.

Each day coachloads of visitors arrive to take part as studio audiences in programmes that are often little more than hour-long scriptural lectures. On the day I was there, there were coaches from as far away as New Mexico, Indiana and Illinois. Each coachload passes through a gift shop near the entrance selling crucifixes, statuettes, books and pictures, and holy water bottles, retailing at $1.20 each.

The message they come to hear is deeply orthodox and unquestion-ing. The output is not designed to display a diversity of opinion even within the parameters of normal Catholic discussion. There is no likelihood of a debate about whether women could become priests or whether celibacy is more than a discipline, for example. Instead its role is to fortify the faith: 'What we like is it's orthodox, straight from the Pope. We're on the same page,' said one couple to me who had travelled all the way from Lake Charles, Louisiana, to visit the studio. Or, in the words of Doug Keck, senior vice-president and a former sports journalist: 'We're not going to use it to beat up the church. Our audience does not want to be harangued. They want to be refreshed. They want to hear somebody stand up for the church.'

Thus, scandals that are too big to be ignored, such as the issue of the Church's treatment of paedophile priests, are approached with kid gloves. On the other hand, Mother has not been averse to dishing it out to those she believes are undermining the faith. She had a celebrated spat with Cardinal Roger Mahony of California over what might otherwise appear the arcane issue of transubstantiation, the real presence of the body and blood of Christ in the communion and whether the cardinal believed in it or not, and at one stage called for the faithful to withdraw their allegiance from him.

On the day I was at the studio, I was just having explained to me how EWTN avoided controversy when on the screen behind the speaker's head flashed a familiar face popping up in a television programme, being reverentially interviewed. It was John Gunn, an Anglo-Irish accountant who made a lot of money in the City of London and now, having refound his faith, runs a tiny ultra-conservative fringe organisation in the UK called the Catholic Action Group which routinely accuses English bishops of heresy and wants the Catholic aid agency CAFOD to be boycotted because it does not entirely rule out the distribution of condoms in the Third World to combat the spread of the AIDS epidemic. Mr Gunn has a convert's – or, in his case a retread's – zeal for unbending, unchanging Catholic orthodoxy, but he is hardly an uncontroversial or mainstream figure. When I pointed this out, I was told blandly that all he was being questioned about was his conversion experience, back to the true faith.

My visit coincided with the release of the film version of *The Da Vinci Code*, which provoked speaker after speaker on shows to condemn the book and the film, unseen, and warn the faithful against going to cinemas showing it. It was the sort of teaching I remember from my upbringing in the 1960s, a fear of allowing any scintilla of doubt or questioning to enter the congregant's mind. There is a sort of paranoia about it all. This from Father Benedict Groeschel, an elderly New York-based priest on a show called *Sunday Night Live*: 'Parents, for Heaven's sake, tell your children this is not a religious book. It's an anti-religious book. Jesus Christ is not another guy with a hot girlfriend. This book is trying to take our religion apart . . . The majority of newspapers and television channels are abysmally anti-Catholic and I am hoping they will drop out of sight with the Internet. I absolutely think you should protest. I am hoping to be on a picket-line [outside a cinema] this weekend.' Working himself into a state, he concluded by comparing the book to *Mein Kampf*.[3]

Fortunately, the makers of the film had already achieved what Father Groeschel could not: they had made a film so bad and so appallingly critically received, even by the abysmally anti-Catholic media, that it quickly vanished from the screens.

Catholicism has not so far featured greatly in this narrative, largely because, although it has been a denomination of growing size, its congregations, made up largely of immigrants – first Irish and Germans in the mid-nineteenth century, then Italians and other southern and eastern Europeans during the great wave of immigration at the turn of the twentieth century – were partially isolated from the social and economic mainstream. Across large parts of the USA Catholics were theologically reviled and socially shunned.

Their political influence was concentrated and localised in a few of the great eastern and northern cities, especially New York, Baltimore, Boston and Chicago. Irish ward captains might serve their clienteles and voters by finding them jobs and housing in return for political support for their candidates individually, and the Democratic Party institutionally, but they tended not to impinge so greatly on national politics, except in a disruptive way, as during periodic tribal urban riots. Indeed, they were rather quarantined from it, and too much open Catholic support for a presidential candidate was regarded as a distinct vote loser for those campaigning for the Protestant vote in the country at large. There were anti-Catholic politicians and parties throughout the nineteenth century, most spectacularly the so-called Know-Nothings of the 1850s, secretive and nativist, which is why they answered that they knew nothing to questioners.

The only successful Democratic presidential candidate between 1860 and 1912, Grover Cleveland, who won in 1884 and again in 1892, was a governor of New York state, but was widely perceived to be someone who had bucked the Catholic Tammany Hall spoils system of the big city and, accordingly, had incurred the opposition of city bosses such as 'Honest John' Kelly. 'We love him for the enemies he has made,' said General Edward Bragg, seconding Cleveland's nomination at the 1884 party convention.

But in the culmination of that campaign it was ironically the Irish Catholic voters of New York who probably secured Cleveland's narrow electoral victory. They were incensed by remarks made by an elderly clergyman named the Revd Samuel Burchard at a rally for Protestant clergy organised on behalf of the Republican candidate James Blaine in New York City just a few days before polling. Burchard blurted out: 'We are Republicans and don't propose to leave our party and identify ourselves with the party whose antecedents have been Rum, Romanism and Rebellion. We are loyal to our flag. We are loyal to you.' 'Did you get that?' the Associated Press reporter asked along the press bench. 'Bet your life – the old fool,' came the reply. The remarks, which Blanchard insisted later were 'a mere rhetorical flourish', were sedulously disseminated throughout the city by the Cleveland campaign and newspapers friendly towards it.[4]

Blaine himself either did not hear the remarks, though he was on the platform, or calculated they would do him no electoral harm. He did not trouble to repudiate them until a few days later, by which time Cleveland had won New York by 1,149 votes, and with it secured the state's electoral college. Since Cleveland won the election by a majority of just 23,000 out of 10 million and the electoral college vote by 219 to 182, Blanchard's remarks may well have turned out to be on the counter-productive side.

There were other reasons for Blaine's defeat, but it is likely that the Catholic vote decisively tipped the result against him. He himself thought so, having believed he had the New York vote sewn up, including the Catholics, 'but for the intolerant and utterly improper remark of Dr Burchard which was quoted everywhere to my prejudice and in many places attributed to myself, though it was in the highest degree distasteful and offensive to me'. He told a friend: 'I should have carried New York by 10,000 if the weather had been clear on election day and Dr Burchard had been doing missionary work in Asia Minor or Cochin China.'[5]

As it was, it was not until 1928 that a Catholic candidate ran for the presidency and it would not be until 1960 that John F. Kennedy did so successfully – and he has so far been the only one. In 1928 Al Smith, the popular Democratic governor of New York, a product of Tammany Hall and a devout Catholic, went down to heavy defeat, not least because of his religious adherence. It may have been doubtful that he could ever have won that year in the midst of the 1920s prosperity boom, but the campaign against him, because of his Catholicism, was virulent and vicious, especially in the traditionally Democratic South, where the anti-Catholic Ku Klux Klan was enjoying a resurgence. As Governor Smith travelled through the Southern states on campaign that autumn, all along his route he could see from the windows of his railroad carriage fiery crosses burning in the fields.

It was little use Smith telling voters 'no power in the institutions of my church [could ever] interfere with the operations of the Constitution of the United States',[6] credulous voters were told that the Vatican would be excavating a tunnel straight into the White House. The Klan openly campaigned for Herbert Hoover, the Republican candidate, and Hoover's wife Lou declared: 'There are many people of intense Protestant faith to whom Catholicism is a grievous sin. And they have as much right to vote against a man for public office because of that belief . . . that is not persecution.' It did not help to win evangelical support that Smith was avowedly a 'wet', opposed to prohibition, still one of their dearest causes, but that was merely an additional reason not to vote for him.

Each of the three Catholic candidates for the presidency – Smith, Kennedy and, in 2004, Senator John Kerry – has had to declare that he would not be influenced by the Pope if he became president. Each faced the traditional smear of a corrupt and sinister (but influential) papal conspiracy, allegations dating back at least to the early nineteenth-century publication of a famous shocker called *The Awful Disclosures of Maria Monk*. This book purported to relate the true but secret tale of rapes, beatings and sexual perversions between priests and nuns as told by an escaped victim. It was in fact penned by a Protestant clergyman called the Revd J. J. Slocum. These and other similarly lurid works – with sensational titles such as *Secrets of Female Convents Exposed*, *Thrilling Mysteries of a Convent Revealed* and *The Moan of the Tiber* among them – had a considerable effect in their time and sometimes even occasionally surface in new editions today.

In the cases of Smith and Kennedy, there was no truth in the allegation of prospective Vatican interference. But in 2004 as Kerry sought to defend himself against similar charges, several US Catholic bishops chose to intervene and warn they would indeed deny him communion if he defied Catholic Church teaching to sustain the long-standing policy of allowing abortion. This was precisely the sort of religious interference that Protestants had always warned that a Catholic president would face if he did not bow to the Church's wishes. Indeed, the US Catholic bishops, meeting in Denver in June 2004, voted heavily, by 183 to 6, in favour of a motion describing support for the right of abortion as a grave sin and therefore a cause for withholding communion. That their resolution was not even stronger was attributed to an assertion by Cardinal Thomas McCarrick of Washington DC that he had received a confidential letter from Cardinal Ratzinger, shortly to become Pope Benedict XVI, saying that other life issues were also important and that the Church should not become politically partisan in its teaching. This in itself became a matter for dispute when the contents of Ratzinger's letter were subsequently leaked, showing that the cardinal did indeed believe that abortion was in a moral class of its own, along with euthanasia, and there could not be any diversity of opinion about their sinfulness.[7] So the man who is now head of the Church himself believes no Catholic politician can uphold the right of even non-

Catholic women to abortion. Incidentally, an ABC News poll taken in June 2004 among rank and file Catholics found that they heavily opposed their bishops' stance by 72 per cent to 22 per cent.[8]

The difference from earlier campaigns was that by 2004 Protestant evangelicals of the Religious Right, whose forebears would have had nothing to do with Catholics, were quite prepared to make common cause on such an issue in order to discomfort the Democratic candidate. By then, of course, the institutional US Catholic Church was itself discredited, not least with many of its own flock, because of the widespread paedophile scandals among its priesthood that had only too visibly corrupted it, a different sort of sexual perversion to those alleged by the Revd J. J. Slocum in *Maria Monk* more than a century and a half earlier, but a deeply disreputable, distasteful – and unfortunately largely true – record nonetheless. By 2004 the old Catholic allegiance to the Democratic Party had long fractured, although Catholic voters appear these days to be fickle in their voting patterns, with many of them not yet reliably or consistently in the Republican camp.

Apart from their difficulties with Catholics doctrinally in the early decades of the twentieth century, those evangelicals who believed in the priority of individual conversion and salvation had little congruence with individual Catholics' social activism. At one level, this was no more than papist city bosses exploiting their constituencies to secure their votes, but the outspokenness of some priests about the conditions in which their poverty-stricken parishioners lived also had some background in their faith. They could point to Pope Leo XIII's 1891 encyclical *Rerum Novarum* or *On the Condition of the Working Class*, which although it is now remembered as a diatribe against socialism also stressed the need for the reform of industrial capitalism, both as a tactic to fight and defuse radical and ungodly movements, and as a means of securing a more just, moral and hence religious society. Thus Cardinal James Gibbons of Baltimore, the Church's leading figurehead in the USA during the early twentieth century, quietly resisted conservative Catholic attempts to ban participation in trade unions and encouraged social activists among the clergy.

It was into this atmosphere in the late 1920s that Father Charles Coughlin sprang, to become the loudest and briefly most influential

Catholic voice on the Continent. Father Coughlin was priest of the Shrine of the Little Flower of Detroit and brought partisan politics of an increasingly virulent and sinister kind to the microphone.

He was a Canadian by birth, but had received his training in the USA and by 1926 had moved to a working-class parish in the suburbs of the car-manufacturing city of Detroit. One of the first things that happened was that the Klan burned a cross on the doorstep of his new church. Coughlin promptly resolved to build a bigger building with 'a cross so high . . . that neither man nor beast can burn it down' and, in an attempt to draw publicity and so raise money, he approached the Catholic manager of a local radio station called WJR to ask whether he could make some broadcasts. It was agreed that he could do so, free for the first few weeks, then, if successful, paying just the weekly transmission cost of $58.[9] Within a decade he would have 40 million listeners across most of the USA and had to employ 145 clerks just to answer his weekly mail. They were an audience who had found a national voice to articulate their concerns about their economic security and their familys' prosperity – bank clerks and small businessmen, shop-keepers and factory workers, all teetering on the brink of personal financial disaster in the early 1930s – and they were not scared about writing to the White House or to their local Congressmen and senators to tell them what sense the radio priest was talking. Indeed he encouraged them to do so. Many of them were not even Catholics: Father Coughlin had broken out of the ghetto.

To start with, Coughlin's sermons were just that: religiously orthodox Catholic teaching and almost entirely non-controversial. He was a success on the new medium, appreciating, unlike many priests and bishops, that he did not have to declaim to the microphone, but could converse with it. He had a voice, the writer Wallace Stegner said, 'of such mellow richness, such manly, heart-warming, confidential intimacy, such emotional and ingratiating charm, that anyone tuning past it on the radio dial almost automatically returned to hear it again . . . without doubt one of the great speaking voices of the 20th Century . . . It was a voice made for promises.'[10]

It was a voice that radiated authority, even serenity, at odds with Coughlin's nervous, chain-smoking and ambitious personality. 'I write the discourse first in my own language, the language of the cleric.

Then I rewrite it using metaphors the public can grasp, toning the phrases down to the language of the man in the street,' he explained. 'Radio broadcasting, I have found, must not be high hat. It must be human, intensely human. It must be simple.'

Soon he secured contracts with stations in Chicago and Cincinnati and then, in 1930, nationally with the Columbia Broadcasting System. By then, he had been able to build a new rectory and an enormous new church, capable of seating 2,600 worshippers (in a parish that had previously had only thirty-two Catholic families), with a gigantic granite tower 111 feet tall and its own radio studio inside. No Klan member was going to prevail against such a building. The church was named after the nineteenth-century French Saint Therese, 'the little flower of Jesus', and Coughlin's weekly talks therefore became *The Golden Hour of the Little Flower*, transmitted at 3 p.m. every Sunday afternoon. Every week the priest struggled to the local post office to bank a sackful of postal orders, at the rate of $55,000 a month by 1935.

But there was nothing particularly gentle, or floral, about his talks. They became aggressive and belligerent. Coughlin's activism appears to have arisen initially out of his concern for Catholic car workers in Detroit, thrown out of employment by the Depression, but it gradually developed from there, his talks becoming increasingly shrill and accusatory. They also became more personal, partisan and politicised, taking up Bryan's old populist solution to economic hardship of leaving the Gold Standard. He attacked the heartlessness of modern capitalism, but then went on to fulminate against Wall Street and after that its bankers and financiers. Coughlin called for the banks to be nationalised. Often he drew attention to the Jewishness of those he attacked most directly.

In 1932 he fawned ostentatiously on the Democratic candidate Franklin Roosevelt because he believed the New Deal would incorporate his ideas. The Archangel Gabriel, he said, was hovering over the White House and the New Deal was Christ's Deal.[11] Once elected, however, although Roosevelt was happy to meet the radio priest, he offered him no support or encouragement. He would not even stoke his considerable ego. Coughlin became disenchanted, his self-esteem affronted, and he began attacking the New Deal instead (now it became the Jew Deal). In 1936 he promoted an independent party, the National Union for Social Justice, a coalition of the populist groups around the USA campaigning for economic relief and offering a series of mutually incompatible and often crackpot solutions to the industrial crisis. His broadcasts proved insufficient to prevent a humiliating result in the landslide for Roosevelt in that year's election, and in response his broadcasts grew increasingly demented and vindictive.

The administration was now denounced as a communist conspiracy and a dictatorship. His newspaper *Social Justice* began reprinting 'The Protocols of the Elders of Zion' and Coughlin started urging supporters to drill (a few, the Silver Shirts, even did so) and expressing admiration for Hitler and Mussolini: 'Had we Christians enforced the discipline and produced the good accomplished by the Nazis for a good end, we would not be weeping at the wailing wall.'[12]

When war broke out in Europe he stridently demanded US neutrality, but it was not until the USA entered the conflict in 1942 that the Roosevelt administration privately pressured the Catholic Church to order its rebellious priest to stop broadcasting. The Catholic hierarchy had censured and criticised Coughlin for years without noticeable success, but by now his devoted following had dwindled and radio stations were giving up taking his broadcasts. He retreated to the role of parish priest at the Shrine of the Little Flower, never again disturbed the air waves, and finally died in 1979.

Coughlin's popularity, though briefly intense in the early 1930s, was entirely based on his broadcasts, which appealed directly to the prejudices of the economically disadvantaged seeking easy solutions. However, his broadcasting franchises never penetrated the Deep South – whose listeners would have been hostile to hearing a Catholic voice with a slight Irish accent – or the Far West.

The radio priest was one manifestation of the political turmoil stirred by the Great Depression in the 1930s, but other than him, the populist, demagogic movements that it inspired were not overtly religious. Huey Long, the King Fish of Louisiana who briefly challenged Roosevelt's hegemony, much more successfully than Coughlin ever did, was distinctly not a religious man. Nor was Dr Francis Townsend, the elderly Californian who came up with the Old

Age Revolving Pension Plan, which required the government to give everyone over the age of sixty $150 a month on condition that they spent it immediately. Those demagogues who claimed a religious background – men like Gerald Winrod, organiser of a band of Christian pilots called the Flying Defenders who made it their business to fly round the Midwest combating the teaching of Darwinism in schools, and Gerald L. K. Smith, a Disciples of Christ minister, who attached himself first to Long and then to Coughlin – soon shaded off into the wilder fringes of anti-Semitism and fascism.

Catholicism was still an outsider, largely working-class faith in the inter-war years, even though its membership was increasingly indigenous, large-scale immigration having been curtailed. It has been calculated that two-thirds of trade union members in this period were Catholics and in the 1940s Archbishop Richard Cushing of Boston could boast that not a single bishop or archbishop of the US hierarchy was the son of a college graduate.[13] The Church's push for a fairer society economically was accompanied by a social conservatism and a fierce opposition to socialism and communism, which may partly account for the two movements' failure to capture a sizeable working-class or union constituency in the USA. In due course, Coughlin's extremism would be succeeded by a more emollient and humane Catholic broadcaster, Bishop Fulton Sheen, whose *Saturday Night Catholic Hour* on the radio in the 1930s was succeeded by his *Life is Worth Living* pioneering television programme in the 1950s. In many ways it was a similar programme to those broadcast by EWTN forty years later, of sermons and homilies delivered straight to camera. Even broadcast in competition with popular shows such as those featuring the comedian Milton Berle and Frank Sinatra, Sheen still managed to corner an audience of 30 million a week. When he preached against the wickedness of Joseph Stalin and his regime in 1953, viewers could hardly fail to be impressed that the Soviet dictator was dead within a month. Sheen's conservative social and theological views attracted converts too: Claire Booth Luce and Henry Ford II among the most prominent.

In time, US Catholicism's arrival as a respectable and influential force would be signified by the narrow election of John F. Kennedy to the presidency in 1960. Even so, in his campaign that year, Kennedy thought it was prudent to assure Protestant ministers in Houston that, as a public servant, he would be governed by the public good, not by the dictates of the papacy, whatever his private beliefs. He told them unambiguously:

> I believe in an America that is neither Protestant, Catholic or Jewish, where no public official either requests or accepts instructions on public policy from the Pope, the National Council of Churches or any ecclesiastical source, where no religious body seeks to impose its will, directly or indirectly, upon the general populace or the public acts of its officials and where religious liberty is so indivisible that an act against one church is treated as an act against all.[14]

He did well to do so, since there were many Protestant and noncon-formist pastors still willing to warn their flocks about the danger of electing a Catholic president. As it was, his Catholicism was probably a lesser factor in gaining the presidency than the perception that he was of a new generation of politicians – though, paradoxically, it was the continuing muscle of the old Tammany Democratic city machines, particularly in Chicago, that ultimately provided him with his majority over Richard Nixon.

The congruence of a young Catholic president and an elderly but reforming Italian Pope, John XXIII, summoning the Second Vatican Council to the Vatican, changed the face of Catholicism in the West, opening it to the possibilities of reform. But Pope John's successor, Paul VI, and the subsequent closing of the door to sanctioning birth control, had a disillusioning effect on many Western Catholics. US bishops would feel the force of this, as would their counterparts in the UK. They would also face vociferous calls for the upholding of 'orthodoxy' in social teaching from a number of Catholic activists on the political Right. This coincided with the revival of the evangelical Religious Right from the late 1970s. In time, the two movements, hitherto mutually suspicious and antagonistic, would find common cause in pursuing their social agenda, to create a formidable voting block. The alliance is by no means seamless. The groups diverge on issues such as capital punishment where certainly Catholic leaders are more hostile than evangelical ones. And, more philosophically, Catholics are generally more supportive of the idea of social collective action and state intervention than evangelicals are.

As I left the EWTN studios in the evening gloom, I looked across at the gift shop, which had long closed for the night. In the darkness all that could be seen were flickering television screens, all showing a re-run of one of Mother's ancient programmes, recorded in the late 1980s when she was still fit and healthy. It may have been one of the shows I caught on the satellite channel in my motel room, dating from 1986. 'We'll have joys in heaven that no one else will have,' Mother assured her flared-trousered audience. 'It's a just reward. We shall all be happy. The rich will have their place if they have never forgot from whence comes their wealth. The poor will be enhanced if they have accepted their lot with joy . . . Material things are not going to matter much so long as you accept the will of God. I will have a different glory and a different joy. I will hear different music . . . we have been glorious in his kingdom. God loves you. *I* love you very much.' Then she pointed her finger at the audience and glared.

10

God Will Make You Better

'To be Spirit filled is the grandest tribute of sobriety and piety one can possess.'

Aimee Semple McPherson

It is hard to comprehend the size of Joel Osteen's Lakewood Megachurch in Houston. Constructed from a converted basketball stadium and looking from the outside like an enormous convention centre, its tiers of seats recede far into the distance and stretch back and upwards into the darkness, row upon row. Some 35,000 people are said to attend on any given weekend, including some who come for a service in Spanish. Outside on the freeway on a Sunday morning, police and uniformed stewards direct the traffic, just as they would have done when the basketball team had a match.[1]

In January 2007, Mr Osteen was named the most influential Christian in the USA. This was admittedly by subscribers to an evangelical magazine, but by doing so they knocked even more famous Christians down the list: Billy Graham came second, James Dobson fifth, President George Bush eleventh, Rick Warren sixteenth, Jerry Falwell fortieth, and Cardinal McCarrick, the only Catholic priest, was in the forty-ninth position. Pope Benedict himself, who'd come forty-fourth the year before, no longer featured at all.[2]

In a land of mega-churches with weekly congregations numbered in the thousands, this is the biggest. Joel Osteen succeeded his father as pastor only seven years ago and lacks his charisma, but his Lakewood Church just keeps on growing. I couldn't see any lakes, or woods for that matter nearby; this was, after all, downtown Houston.

It was unlike any church I have ever been in. Joel's is a non-denominational ministry. There were no religious symbols anywhere that I could see – certainly no statuary, unless you counted the lifesize models of cartoon characters outside the children's crèches downstairs. Behind a lectern in the middle of the stage a large globe turned slowly. Clouds scudded across a bright-blue sky projected on to screens at the back of the stage, behind the banked seats that would be filled by a gospel choir. Waterfalls played down the artificial rocks at each side and a large stars and stripes fluttered overhead, powered by an artificial wind, as theatrical lighting swept around the auditorium. Cameras hovered above us.

Large screens showed people in the congregation greeting each other and chatting, interspersed with advertisements for the church bookshop and meetings of various church groups, for married and for singles. Captive No More! was on Wednesdays for an hour at 6.15 p.m. Help Discover the Champion in You! proclaimed another advertisement. There was also something called Power Classes. You could attend a weight-watching course, coping with divorce sessions, classes in how to do job interviews, even one on how to fill in your IRS tax form.

The church was like an enormous cinema, the padded chairs sloped comfortably back – there was certainly no room to kneel, or kneelers for that matter. While they waited for the service, couples stepped forward to have their photographs taken in front of the empty stage. 'This is one beautiful place,' exclaimed the woman next to me, taking a swig from her bottle of water.

Indeed it is. I was here with my parents-in-law, long-term British expatriates who have washed up in Houston after many years living in Mexico. They live only 3 or 4 miles away from Lakewood, but had never been here before, preferring the impressive, buttoned-up neo-Gothic splendour of a nearby Episcopal church, St Martin's, where former president George Bush senior and his wife Barbara worship when they are in town. That church cost $42 million to build during the last nine years, almost all of it raised directly from the congregation.

Joel Osteen's church, also paid for, had an annual budget of $75 million. The congregation is important, but every week Joel was also beamed out by cable television around the world. 'Yes, ma'am,' said one of the greeters nearby. 'We've come a long ways from the old tin church we used to have.'

I would guess the auditorium was about two-thirds full: maybe 10,000 people, quite big enough to make a crowd, or to fill most cathedrals several times over. Don Iloff, Joel's brother-in-law and press officer, guided us into the second row of seats in the stalls, right in front of the lectern. 'It starts off with a lot of praise. It's quite a bust. Enjoy!' he said. My English mother-in-law, Sheila, stiffened slightly, a rather forced smile on her face and a slight wrinkling of the nose.

Then the music started. It was very loud, with a pounding rock beat and great excitement. 'My God!' exclaimed Sheila in horror under her breath.

After a while, Joel Osteen, sallow and slim, neatly dressed in a dark-grey suit, white shirt and tie and patent leather shoes, his dark hair slicked back and a radiant smile on his face, bounded on to the stage accompanied, hand in hand, by his lovely wife Victoria, a former beauty queen, glamorous with long blonde hair, highly made-up and wearing a green silk blouse, black slacks and open-toed sandals. I was close enough to see her mouth moving rhythmically, as if she were chewing gum. For those old enough to remember, Anthea Redfern, once long ago Bruce Forsyth's partner on the BBC's *Generation Game*, sprang to mind.

There were no cuddly toys as prizes, but there was a cuddly message. Joel told the congregation in what was evidently a ritual chant: 'God is a good God. He is smiling down on each one of you today. We are going to go out for next week, changed by God.' The singers behind him jumped for joy – angels show similar ecstasy in medieval wall paintings – and began a new song:

All things are possible. Nothing's too difficult for you,
Now is the time to worship. Now is the time to give your heart.

By now the entire congregation except for the three Brits in the second row, deep frozen with self-consciousness and embarrassment, were waving their arms in the air. Amid the tumult, the cameras soaring round the arena showed Joel and Victoria taking their seats in the front row and briefly caught my father-in-law standing looking rather sceptical and definitely not ecstatic directly behind them.

Isaiah, the lead singer of the backing group, a tubby black man in a pinstripe suit, suddenly broke off to proclaim: 'You are king over every circumstance in this arena today!' Then he added: 'I will be still and know you are God', before immediately commencing bouncing again and starting at even louder volume.

After they finished, Joel Osteen returned to the stage to lead a chant: 'We are victors, not victims. We will be above, only and not beneath. Lord, we are filled with hope. We know you are a good God, in control of our lives and we thank you – let us have a round of applause – I know you are in control. He has us in the palm of his hand. You gotta show the enemy you have more than he has.'

Then he went into a riff about the frustrations of daily living, the thoughts of a man stuck in a traffic queue: 'I am not going to get frustrated because every way was closed. God is in charge of my life. If God be for us, who can be against us? God can give you $3 a gallon for gas. Don't magnify your problems, magnify your God.'

Members of the congregation wishing to pray or confess were summoned up to the front where, with the cameras and their operators hovering a couple of feet away, they received hugs from Joel and Victoria – her mouth still apparently chewing – and counselling from senior members of the congregation.

Then, the communion part of the service was handed over to Victoria. It was bizarrely like a Tupperware party. She fumbled beneath the lectern and drew out a host to hold up, then again rooted out a tiny wine glass. 'We have so much to be grateful for. If you love the Lord Jesus today you are welcome at His table,' she said by way of a prayer.

Large trays containing thimble-sized cups of wine and hosts were passed along the rows for people to help themselves, while Mrs Osteen made a pitch for the offertory: 'God wants us to make a difference . . . We serve a big God and He owns it all. God is going to continue opening doors for us. He is going to do great things for us. We will do damage to the enemies of the kingdom because of your faithfulness and sacrifice.' It sounded like a slightly paranoid sales pitch. The envelopes for giving that we had been handed contained space for names, addresses, phone numbers and e-mails.

Afterwards, it was Joel's turn, the big moment of the week, his sermon. It was more of the same. Life has a way of pushing people down, but with God's help you can bounce back. If life – or a colleague or neighbour – does you down, don't get bitter, or get even, God will be your vindicator:

'God is in control of your life and He's a loving God. He is a Good God. Your best days are not behind you, they are in front of you. He has promised, if you will keep a right attitude He will restore what has been stolen from you. He will pay you back double. God always makes the enemy pay for what he does to your life. My sister Lisa got divorced in her twenties, but she didn't get bitter. God made the enemy pay. Something new was brought out of her adversity. Life may not be fair but God is fair. Somehow, someway, he will turn your situation around.

'Say to yourself: I am still in control. I am not going to allow my past to prevent my future. God is keeping records: He sees every wrong that has ever been done to you. You will be rewarded. Eventually things will change in your favor. Keep your spirits up because pay day is coming.'

Somehow he made God sound like the Capo di tutti Capi.

Then the peroration: 'God is not mad at you. He has already forgiven you. I want to give you the opportunity to show you are not ashamed of Him. Today is the beginning of a new start.' Beside me the woman with the water-bottle shrieked: 'Yes!' The whole congregation rose to their feet and began to applaud. Joel had timed his sermon to perfection. Twelve minutes and it was over. The closing credits rolled on his cable programme. The show was finished.

Outside, after the service, Joel and Victoria, hand in hand and still beaming, went among their people, greeting those who had waited for them. The small knot of fifty or sixty people – Asian, Middle Eastern and American – were fulsome in their praise. Garth Redman, who had come from Florida to visit the church, said: 'I am a Catholic but we believe in the same God. In fact I was one of the ones who stood up when he called to us. That took a bit of courage.' He conceded that he would probably go back to his own church when he returned to Port St Lucy.

Afterwards, Don Iloff ushered my in-laws and me down some stairs and into a lounge rather at odds with the bare concrete of the former sports stadium. It was furnished tastefully in late Versailles or early Marriott style, with big sofas, bouquets of flowers in vases, bowls of fruit, and large mirrors in gilded frames on the walls. It was clearly the preacher's retiring suite. My parents-in-law sank gratefully into the cushions, exhausted from the service, and were impressed. Victoria's mother wafted through, looking almost as young as her daughter, and greeted us graciously.

Then the man himself appeared, showered and refreshed. He told me:

'We are open to everybody. We believe the relationship with Christ is what is important. We are not beating people down or saying they can only come here if they believe completely, like us. God is doing something new here and people are hungry for faith.

'I try to stay focused, talk about everyday issues in their lives. People don't want a church that tries to find out what they're doing wrong all the time, so they leave feeling beaten up. I tell them to search their own hearts about what they should fight for. There's a new day coming for the church.'

I asked about the lack of religious imagery, which puzzled him. He said: 'Our services are services of resurrection. That's what made it all happen. Churches have to change with the times. We're just trying to help people through their everyday lives. It's like a business we are running here, but I spend 99 per cent of my time on the spiritual side.'

Don said afterwards: 'One on one, Joel knows where the rubber hits the road. He's telling them, God loves you, come on back. When they listen to Joel, they recognise a new face of God.'

I asked him whether Joel did a great deal of pastoral work, visiting the sick, ministering to the dying. 'Oh no,' he said. 'He can't pastor to everyone, he'd have to give up preaching. Writing that sermon every week takes two days.'

It is not hard to see why Joel is so successful. His message is entirely affirming and pain-free. No guilt for him. Some months later, back in England, I caught his programme once again. He was talking – you could not really say preaching since God was scarcely mentioned – on the subject of the importance of sleep and exercise. Houston, of course, is the obesity capital of the USA. He told them how he and Victoria rode their bikes five or six nights a week. 'Make changes for your health's sake and God will make you better…if you get the physical side in balance, you will be rewarded by God. O Lord: teach me the evils of chicken from the South/Lord help me – shut my mouth.'

Osteen is not one of those heavily politically partisan preachers. He comes from a younger generation wary of tangling with politics. 'There are good things in both parties,' he told me. Taking sides might compromise his affirming message. But maybe he's also a bit on the callow side. Up in Washington DC, one conservative evangelical lobbyist had said to me a few days earlier: 'Yeah, but does he ever preach about pain and suffering? How does he deal with grief? Where's the beef?'

A few months later, my father-in-law e-mailed me with slightly unchristian glee. Victoria had just been fined $3,000 by the Federal Aviation Authority for assaulting an attendant on a Continental Airlines flight to Vail. She had apparently become heated with several attendants about cleaning up a drink spillage on the armrest of her first-class seat, jabbing one of them in the chest with her elbow and demanding to see someone in authority in the cockpit. In a statement she had assured the folks back at Lakewood that she had behaved throughout in a very 'Christianlike' manner.

About 250 miles north of Houston, in a windswept suburb of Dallas, where houses and industrial estates fringe off into scrubland, and traffic on the Interstate on the way to Fort Worth rumbles away in the distance, high on a rise sits the Potter's House, a name that does not quite do justice to the immensity of the building, or its surrounding acres of car-parking. It dominates the landscape, a huge, flat-roofed, buff-coloured stone edifice, and is certainly the first church I have ever visited that has security guards on the gate and more security at the door. The newly built main auditorium seats 8,000 – the $35 million mortgage was paid off in three years – and behind it the old hall, now used for youth events, has room for a mere 1,200. Outside, in the burning heat of the summer morning, I parked my car behind a Ford Taurus with the number-plate God LVS Texas.[3]

This is the home of Bishop Thomas Dexter – T. D. – Jakes, currently the most successful and maybe influential black, neo-Pentecostal, preacher in the USA. He has been compared to Billy Graham by *Time* magazine and, although he ranked only fourth in the 2007 Church Report list of most influential Christians (a surprising drop down from first the previous year), he runs a multi-million dollar enterprise. Indeed, the report calls him CEO of the Potter's House which is described not as a church, but as a non-profit organisation. His biographer Shayne Lee estimates Jakes's personal worth at $100 million.[4] It's a long way from where he started in the 1980s, preaching in the tin tabernacles of the poverty-stricken mining settlements of West Virginia.

To catch a Jakes sermon on cable television is a vibrant experience. He's big and bouncy, with a shaven head, a greying goatee beard and a capacious suit as shiny as his perspiring face. He strides the stage, genial and funny, rolling his eyes and bursting with exclamations and whoops of joy – no sermon notes for this preacher. The audience, largely but not exclusively black and Hispanic, jumps too and laughs.

The sermon I caught the day before interviewing him was about the freeing of Lazarus. 'What programme were they showing?' he asked me the next day. 'Oh yeah, I remember that one.' Jakes acted bound up, hands locked by his side and feet together, bouncing across the stage, like a ball – it would have to be pretty substantial winding bands that would keep him in; 'Hey! Hey! Hey!' he squealed. 'I feel a breakthrough in here. God is about to liberate you! I don't know who you are but God's about to free you! I am coming out of this!'[5]

Now he was acting unbound, striding about stiff-legged:

'What God is doing is pulling dead stuff off you! Clap your hands like you are not a slave any more . . . I try and give you sound doctrine and good word. Sometimes I am liberating you and you don't know it. I can pull and pull and pull until you get something loose. Shake hands with your neighbour. Look him in the eye and say: "I am free." I break the habits, the bandages, the psychological disorder. Spread around, untie my mind, my attitude, untie my hopes . . . move into your promised land! Get ready! Get ready! Get ready!'

Jakes's commercial success comes not just from his broadcast ministry but from his ancillary activities: motivational seminars and conferences, books – one is called *Woman, Thou art Loosed!* and another *He-Motions: Even Strong Men Struggled* – and now even films. On the morning when I interviewed him, that was what he was keen to stress, particularly his forthcoming MegaFest, which would attract many thousands to a gala of services, fashion shows, talks on economic empowerment, health and voter registration. The previous fest in 2004 had received 130,000 visitors from fifty-five countries.

'We are spiritual Christians but we are people too: we have issues like anybody else,' he explained. 'We have to pay the grocery bill. We want to get our kids into college.'

And here came the crux: 'I am not partisan. I have served as a pastoral voice both to this administration and the last. If I am invited to the next I will go. It is dangerous to politicise religion. I think when you force them together you can damage both. Faith affects every aspect of our lives and influences our art and literature.'

It was clearly useful for President Bush to invite Bishop Jakes to the White House and for him to be seen with the preacher's gigantic presence looming beside him, but this was something I had also heard from younger preachers, such as Osteen. Rick Warren, one of the most influential, has also steered clear of partisan politics. They believe it damages their ability to preach to a broad congregation. They have their cable channels, but their message is a motivational, not a partisan, one.

I asked the bishop about his range of commercial activities. He replied:

'I am a pastor, that's my calling, but it's not the only thing I do. I can do that independently. Writing's something I really enjoy. I've produced one movie and I've just signed with Sony to do nine more. They'll be family entertainment. I really believe all of us have a diversity of gifts and opportunities. I believe they can be used to spread the Christian message, but also to create revenue streams.

'My focus is more on creating better people and for some of our members that is going to include economic empowerment. This is not about being rich but having the basic things of life. I am not focused on get-rich schemes and prosperity. It is about making Jesus central to our lives.'

I asked him whether everyone was welcome at the Potter's House – what about gays for instance? 'I would consider myself to be a conservative,' he said. 'It's possible to have conservative views and still to respect other people. There have been a lot of people from a homosexual lifestyle who have come here. Those who want to change their lives fit well into the fabric of our church, but if they think their

condition is genetic, no, maybe they would be happier somewhere
else. In our great country there should be a church out there for them
– there is somewhere for everybody.'

Jakes's biographer, Shayne Lee, says he is impacting on
contemporary popular culture in ways older evangelicals cannot:

> [Billy] Graham has never produced a best-selling novel, paper-
> backs on weight loss and financial prosperity, theatrical
> productions and music CDs . . . Jakes's forte is addressing com-
> plex pathologies such as sexual abuse and addictive
> relationships with a blend of scripture, psychology and
> Grandma's folk-wisdom.
>
> Jakes saturates the marketplace with an incessant flow of
> images and products, offers therapeutic religion and mixes
> codes from assorted elements of contemporary and secular
> culture. He obscures traditional lines of distinction between the
> secular and sacred, emphasises personal experience over doc-
> trinal constraints and supports denominational independence
> over church hierarchy . . . What distinguishes Jakes and the new
> black church is their ability to combine an otherworldly experi-
> ence of ecstatic worship and spiritual enlightenment with a this-
> worldly emphasis on style, image and economic prosperity . . .
> Some feel Jakes' brand of Christianity is too commercial, too
> trendy, too self-indulgent and, hence, too American.[6]

A few months later, back in London, I was chatting to Bishop Wayne
Malcolm, who runs Christian Life City in Hackney and whose ministry
is very American in style, as are those of many of the black British
churches. We spoke about wealth. 'It's important for us that pastors
do not give the impression that serving God equals a life of poverty,'
he said. 'Of course, poor people can be very spiritual but so can rich
people. The fact that we love the poor, doesn't mean that we love
poverty. Our people are already poor – they want role models and if
the only ones they have are hip-hop artists and pimps, what sort of
message does that give?'[7]

I asked another spokesperson for British black churches whether
Bishop Jakes might ever come to the UK. 'We'd love it,' she said. 'But

I don't think we could ever afford him.' Well, it turned out they could – T. D. Jakes paid a visit to Britain in July 2007.

If Jakes and Osteen are the future of US entrepreneurial religion, palely imitated by some, mainly black, churches in the UK, then, as we have seen with Billy Sunday, they are treading a long-established path. They are hitting new congregations, new ethnic groups, with a message of self-help, just as Billy Sunday did a century ago. The difference is in their ability to exploit modern communication.

For a movement that has often been suspicious of the snares of modernity in all its manifestations, evangelists have always used the mediums of broadcasting to get their message out with ruthless, not to say, commercial, efficiency. Deprived of early outlets to uncritical secular newspapers and suspicious of the wiles of the cinema, they started their own stations for the use of their flocks and for propagating their arguments in the nineteenth century. When radio came along early in the twentieth century, they appreciated its usefulness as a proselytising tool, providing them with the holy grail of direct access to millions of sympathetic unbelievers sitting in their own homes and now, with cable and satellite television, there are opportunities to reach potentially hundreds of millions across the whole globe. As early as 1932 more than four hundred sponsored religious programmes were appearing on eighty different radio stations nationwide.

Billy Sunday's peak of popularity came just a few years too early for him to exploit the new medium of radio fully, but his successors took readily to broadcasting, none more so than the most exotic of them all, the first great female evangelist (and still just about the only one to gain a mass national following), Aimee Semple McPherson.

McPherson was a force of nature, displaying both the showmanship and the human fallibility – and also giving rise to the same sceptical ridicule – that has dogged broadcasting evangelists ever since. Born in Canada – just like Father Coughlin – to an elderly Methodist father and a much younger Salvationist mother, she was converted from teenaged agnosticism to Pentecostalism by a Scottish missionary named Robert Semple, who would become her first husband when she was still only seventeen. The two departed to the

Far East to convert the Chinese, but no sooner had they arrived in Hong Kong than Semple contracted malaria and died. Aimee, who had also caught the disease when heavily pregnant, recovered and promptly returned to the USA with her baby, where she married her second husband, Harold McPherson, an accountant, and began a career as an 'itinerating' evangelist, accompanying her mother in a Packard 'gospel' car bearing the slogan 'Jesus is coming soon: Get ready' on one side and 'Where will you spend eternity?' on the other. Their conversion services shared space with whatever else was on the bill in towns and cities up and down the East Coast – on one occasion in the middle of a boxing ring, between bouts – and drew large audiences.

Healing was a speciality, so was singing songs such as 'Give me that old-time religion'. So were personal testimonies from penitents. Members of the audiences were each exhorted to go out and find the worst sinners in the city and bring them back the following evening. Arenas were filled with flowers and blossoms to make them a 'fragrant, restful and inviting place' for the returning drunks, gamblers and faithful followers.[8]

Eventually the family wound up in Los Angeles, minus Harold who stayed East and later sued for divorce on the grounds of his wife's desertion, and there in California Aimee founded the International Church of the Foursquare Gospel, evangelical and Pentecostal in character though non-denominational and with a style all its own. Within five years, the church was large and wealthy enough to have built its own headquarters, an enormous domed building in Echo Park named the Angelus Temple, whose $1.5 million cost was funded entirely from donations. It had a seating capacity of 5,300 people and would be filled three times a day, every day of the week, with Aimee preaching at every service.

Sister Aimee was highly unusual in her proselytising and not just because she was female. She was a handsome woman and wore glamorous long white gowns and – what was particularly shocking to contemporary evangelicals – make-up. There was what has been described as an 'unashamed use of low-key sex appeal to attract converts'. Nor did she preach a message of hell and damnation for the unrighteous but, much more welcomingly, one holding out the prospect of a warm, even seductive, greeting eventually in heaven.

She was quick to seize the possibilities of radio, became the first woman to preach a broadcast sermon and, on 6 February 1924, launched her own radio station, KFSG ('Kall Four-Square Gospel'), becoming in the process the first woman to be granted a broadcast licence. It opened with the words of the missionary hymn: 'Give the winds a mighty voice/Jesus saves! Jesus saves!' The channel broadcast Sister's meetings – all her sermons went out live – but also morality plays and contemporary music. She wrote and produced a couple of operas and, on one occasion, made her entrance to the temple by riding a motorcycle down the aisle. Every morning at 7 a.m. she would walk to the studio to conduct a live broadcast called *The Sunshine Hour* and late each evening there would be midnight recitals by the Temple's organist Esther Fricke.

On one occasion in June 1925, the station was even first to broadcast the news of an earthquake in Santa Barbara, after a listener rang in to say their house was shaking. Sister promptly barged into the studio, elbowed a singer off the microphone, and announced a call for listeners to provide emergency supplies and help. Two aid convoys had already been dispatched from the Temple before the *Los Angeles Times* had been able to produce a special edition.

Then, in May 1926, it all went horribly wrong. Sister Aimee went for a swim off Ocean Park Beach and disappeared. It was assumed she had drowned. Mourners held all-night vigils on the beach and at least two would-be rescuers drowned trying to find her body. The news was a sensation, carried with daily updates on the search by the nation's newspapers. After a month a ransom note was delivered (and ignored) and then a few days later, thirty-five days after her disappearance, Aimee herself turned up in a town just over the Mexican border, claiming that she had been kidnapped, drugged and tortured, but had heroically escaped and had walked for thirteen hours through the desert to secure her freedom. She was greeted by ecstatic and relieved, crowds on her return to Los Angeles.

There was, however, a degree of scepticism about her story from those who pointed out that her shoes, clothes and watch (which she had somehow miraculously reacquired following her disappearance, clad only in her bathing costume) showed no sign of her ordeal and that the shack where she had supposedly been held did not appear to exist. Kenneth Ormiston, the radio engineer at KFSG, who had also vanished at the same time, now turned up as well. Witnesses testified that they had been seen together at various hotels and a bungalow in Carmel, some way farther up the Californian coast, during the missing month.

When she preached a sermon back at the Temple about Satan's attempts to discredit her, the spectacle culminated in two costumed angels descending from the Temple dome, one carrying the trusty sword of truth and the other bearing a chain with which to bind the devil.

Charges were eventually dropped for lack of evidence (even Mencken wryly defended her honour, for as a woman, he said, she was incapable of untruth) and the faithful remained loyal, but ever after there was just a whiff of ribaldry around her reputation.

It is not quite true to say that fundamentalism retreated entirely in the aftermath of the Monkey Trial, but that event, and the humiliation of Bryan, had a devastating effect in making fundamentalism seem intellectually backward and provincial. Certainly in eastern and academic circles, in the cities of urban America, even among most churchmen, the supporter of evolution won the immediate propaganda argument. Mencken wrote:

> [Fundamentalists] are thick in the main streets behind the gas works. They are everywhere where learning is too heavy a burden for mortal minds to carry, even the vague, pathetic learning on tap in the little red schoolhouses. They march with the Klan, with the Christian Endeavor Society, with the Junior Order of United American Mechanics . . . with all the rococo bands that poor and unhappy folk organize to bring some new light of purpose into their lives.[9]

In other words, they might still exist but they could be safely ignored and ridiculed as of no account.

Nor did the fundamentalists help their own cause, falling to squabbling and schismatism, liberals trying to oust conservatives and vice-versa. Many of the conservatives did indeed associate with unsavoury fellow travellers, such as the Ku Klux Klan, which enjoyed a revival in the 1920s even in Northern and Midwestern states such as Indiana. Its representatives were elected to office openly and it could even organise a mass rally and parade of white-hooded men through Washington DC. Both the Klan and the fundamentalists shared anti-modernist and anti-evolutionary ideologies and both drew their supporters from the dispossessed and economically disadvantaged of small town America and the rural heartlands.

Both also were drawn to conspiracy theories to account for their puzzling loss of influence over the nation – what the historian Richard Hofstadter was to call the paranoid style in American life – and conjured up far-reaching, foreign-inspired plots that they believed were intended to bring them down. Marsden quotes a publication called the *Crusaders' Champion* in 1926, a fundamentalist organ, outlining a classic example: 'Thirty years ago five men met in Boston and formed a conspiracy which we believe to be of German origin to secretly and persistently work to overthrow the fundamentals of the Christian religion of this country,' it said, leading the USA into moral breakdown: 'a great tidal wave of crime . . . Sunday desecration, an alarming increase in divorces and a tremendous drop in moral standards and ideals'.[10] It only requires a slight amendment to update the language in order to see the same arguments applied by modern members of the Religious Right to similar modern liberal conspiracies to subvert society through gay marriage, abortion, stem cell research and AIDs.

Of course, theories such as evolution had to be the work of such alien forces, foreigners and intellectuals, people who, even if not malign, had no congruence with the sturdy common sense and superior virtue of the horny-handed sons of toil on the farms of rural America, the sort of honest men without whom grass would grow in the streets of sophisticated and corrupt places such as New York City. In the words of Charles Blanchard, president of Wheaton, the evangelical Bible college in Illinois, from 1877 to 1925: 'A common sense people know that it is the Bible and Christian teachings which make their children good . . . unbelief seems never to have originated with the common man.' The reason was obvious: 'It is well known that the critics of our time have been usually men who have poisoned their nervous systems and injured their minds by the use of narcotic and other poisons.'[11]

The most respected columnist and commentator of the day, Walter Lippmann, put it in this way in 1929:

> In actual practice this movement has become entangled with all sorts of bizarre and barbarous agitations with the Ku Klux Klan, with fanatical prohibition, with the anti-evolution laws and with much persecution and intolerance . . . [This] shows that the central truth which the fundamentalists have grasped no longer appeals to the best brains and the good sense of the modern community and that the movement is recruited largely from the isolated, the inexperienced and the uneducated.[12]

Such ideas and associations made it hard to take the fundamentalists as seriously as they took themselves, but in addition they were also splitting into wildly antagonistic exclusivist groups, between those who wanted to work within society and those who wished to withdraw from it, to draw up the drawbridge behind those who accepted premillennarialist dispensationalism and the rest, between the elect and the damned.

Occasionally, internecine quarrels burst out into the open in a way that did nothing to enhance the standing of the fundamentalists among outsiders, but rather reinforced their reputations as fanatics. One such occasion was when J. Frank Norris, a Southern Baptist pastor in Fort Worth, Texas, who had been waging a virulent campaign against the city's Catholic mayor, who he described as being unfit to manage a hog pen (he also fought similar, unrelenting verbal campaigns against the Southern Baptists' leadership), shot dead one of the mayor's supporters, one D. E. Chipps, who came to remonstrate with him in his office over his use of language. Norris was acquitted and not in the least abashed, but his behaviour was scarcely calculated to improve the standing or the dignity of his beliefs.[13]

With sectarian leaders such as Norris and lacking respected national figures, the movement also faced a society that was still changing fast. Americans were now ethnically much more diverse, their attitudes much more heterodox: it was no longer the Catholic

Irish who had to be despised, but the southern European Catholics and Orthodox and the eastern European and Russian Jews who were also changing the USA. They were affecting the USA's image of itself, altering its businesses and infiltrating even its entertainments, especially the new medium of film. Following the upheaval of the Great Depression too, which put a third of the US workforce out of a job and cost the savings of millions, the fundamentalists even lost the one great cause on which they had been united: prohibition, the noble experiment, abandoned as a disastrous failure in 1933. Its abolition and the return of alcoholic drinks were prompted by arguments that were the precise reverse of those that had been used two decades earlier to justify its imposition: that the economy would be boosted, crime would be lowered, tax revenues would be raised, and farmers would have an outlet for their grain production if Americans were allowed to drink alcohol again.

On top of this, by 1933 the USA had a new, Democratic, president, Franklin Roosevelt, whose New Deal, interventionist, policies represented a triumph for the political philosophy of social activism, a secular version of the social gospel in action. In the desperate economic circumstances of 1933, the administration was putting forward the idea that the state had a role in directing economic affairs and ameliorating the conditions of the poor and deprived, giving them socially useful and morally and economically beneficial employment for the advantage of society as a whole. It was a philosophy of government that would have a substantial trial over the next forty years and it was not until the tide eventually went out in another direction in the early 1980s that the Religious Right's resurgence would also come into its own.

What may have saved evangelicalism from retreating too far into introspection and further into internecine quarrels in the immediate post-Second World War years, however, was the revival of public interest in spiritual matters, following the century's second experience of the awesome destructive power of modern technology, which now showed itself capable of destroying whole cities with a single bomb. And there was now also a young saviour in the earnest and attractive shape of Billy Graham.

In the years following the Second World War, Graham became

informally anointed as evangelicalism's foremost preacher. He must have seemed a God-send to the older generation of leaders of the movement: young, personable, charming and, above all, not weird. Ernest Wadsworth, a revivalist promoter, had noted in a book entitled *Will Revival Come?* in 1945: 'God is grieved with many of the older generation who are set in their ways . . . we must look to the young. We need a Whitefield, a Wesley, a young Spurgeon more than ever . . . godly men of the old generation must lay hands on young Timothys.'[14]

Graham may not have been the best, or most intellectual, speaker on the circuit, but he was the most charismatic and he certainly obtained the most conversions – a persuasiveness that may have been partly attributable to a summer vacation selling Fuller brushes door to door. In the words of Joel Carpenter:

> Although Graham was but one of a cohort of talented young preachers and certainly not the most eloquent among them, the other revivalists noticed Graham's remarkable way with an audience. Billy may have talked too loud and too fast and his gestures might have been a bit wild, but people sat up and listened to the tall and slender young man with wavy blond hair, piercing, deep-set blue eyes and a resonant, trumpet-like voice. Graham had developed his preaching style from listening to radio announcers, merging their timing and timeliness with his own passion to save lost souls. [His] intensity and earnestness were contagious.[15]

No wonder then that William Bell Riley, one of the doyens of the circuit, persuaded Graham to take over the presidency of his Bible college and seminary. At the age of twenty-nine he became the youngest college president in the USA, rather against his own wishes or better judgment. Their final, persuasive, encounter took place during a thunderstorm with Riley, on his deathbed, telling Graham: 'Beloved, as Samuel appointed David King of Israel, so I appoint you . . . I'll meet you at the judgment seat of Christ.'

Graham's potential was also spotted as worth promoting by the secular press, most notably the great media proprietor William Randolph Hearst, who ordered his newspapers to 'puff' the young man, so that he appeared daily on their front pages during his first great crusade in Los Angeles. It probably helped that the announcement that the Soviet Union had acquired the atom bomb had come two days earlier. Later, Henry Luce of *Time* magazine would also become a friend and booster of the young evangelist's reputation.

Billy Graham is the figure who bestrides twentieth-century US (and indeed UK and maybe Far Eastern) evangelicalism, both because of the longevity of his career, stretching from the late 1930s well into the first decade of the new millennium, and for the accessibility and even ecumenism of his message of salvation. Although he drew on the techniques of predecessors such as Billy Sunday – and it is a strange coincidence that Graham held his first preaching engagement the night before his seventeenth birthday, on 6 November 1935, which was also the night that Sunday died – Graham's has not generally been an exclusive gospel, much to the aggravation of some of his more fundamentalist rivals.

Graham was brought up on a farm in North Carolina and certainly originally shared some of the prejudices of his fellow Southern Baptists: against blacks, Catholics and Jews. But he consciously worked from the 1950s onwards, as his fame spread, to eliminate the harsher tones of his early rhetoric. He has subsequently visited Popes and cardinals, and apologised after the release of Nixon White House tapes in which he could be heard bemoaning what he called 'the stranglehold' of Jews on the US media during the Watergate crisis.

He supported calls for desegregation in the 1960s and put up bail money for Dr Martin Luther King at a time when other white preachers would not. Graham's support for desegregation and his insistence that his audiences should have no colour bar certainly caused him difficulties in the South, although there were limits: he was not keen on Dr King's civil disobedience campaigns, and declared after the 'I Have A Dream' speech: 'Only when Christ comes again will the little white children of Alabama walk hand in hand with little black children.'

His more progressive later stances do not necessarily exculpate him, but he has at least been prepared to apologise fulsomely for past words and actions, which is more than can be said of some of his fellow preachers. His anti-communism always remained constant, but that did not stop him meeting communist leaders from the Soviet Union, China, and even North Korea. 'Unless the Christian religion rescues these nations from the clutches of the unbelieving, America will stand alone and isolated in the world,' he told his flock in 1947.

Dr Graham's emphasis was however, an orthodox four-pointed message: God loves you; mankind is sinful and separated from God; Jesus Christ mediates man's sin; and we must individually receive him as Saviour and Lord.

As with Sunday, it was leavened, at least in the early years in his missions with the Youth for Christ organisation, with speciality acts and a dash of showbusiness: magicians and ventriloquists, even a horse that would bow at the foot of a cross and tap twelve times when asked the number of Christ's apostles.

Those who came forward at his meetings in their thousands experienced a slick managerial exercise, being sent to one side by trained armies of counsellors, asked to fill in tick-box forms, and directed to churches that were participating in the mission near where they lived.

Graham carefully shied away from direct political partisanship, over particular issues or candidates, though certainly in the early years it did not take a genius to decipher who he favoured. As early as 1951 he was predicting that a voting bloc of religious people could be developed, in much the same way as his successors achieved thirty years later: 'The Christian people of America will not sit idly by during the 1952 presidential campaign [They] are going to vote as a bloc for the man with the strongest moral and spiritual platform, regardless of his views on other matters. I believe we can hold the balance of power.' He said that church members would follow the instructions of their religious leaders and that he might share his personal choice with them as well. Meanwhile he privately urged Eisenhower to stand, ostentatiously praised him as a 'strong spiritual leader', and pointed up the fact that his opponent Adlai Stevenson was divorced. Publicly, Graham estimated he could swing 16 million votes and, a few days before the election, publicised an opinion poll he had organised showing that 77 per cent of clergy and religious editors were planning to vote Republican and just 13 per cent Democrat – a proportion remarkably similar to that won by George W. Bush in 2004.[16] This was about as close to a public endorsement as he could offer. Later, after feeling betrayed by Richard Nixon, he has tended to grow more circumspect about getting too cosy with politicians.

The disavowal of open endorsement of particular candidates (it is always pointed out that Graham for many years was a member of the Democratic Party – hardly a difficult or unusual decision in the South of his youth) and the maintenance of friendships with leaders of both parties, especially presidents, has played in his favour. He has floated above partisanship like an archbishop: the nearest thing to a secular saint that Protestant America has ever known. Most importantly also, no whiff of personal scandal, over money or sex, has sullied his ostentatious image as chaplain to the world.

But there is more than a hint of personal vanity in his boasted meetings and sometime friendships with every US president since Harry Truman, as well as his regular encounters with the British royal family and other leaders around the world – a touch, in the words of a Southern Baptist, of being 'too close to the powerful and too fond of the things of the world'.[17]

Incidentally, Truman, who was a Southern Baptist himself, disliked Graham's brashness – 'I just don't go for people like that. All he's interested in is getting his name in the paper' – but that may have been because of his exasperation when Graham and his colleagues knelt in prayer outside the White House after a visit and were assiduously photographed by the press doing so.[18] All Truman's successors have deemed it convenient to be photographed with the great evangelist, sometimes, as Kennedy did, playing a round of golf with him – the origin of the term 'golf course spirituality' – and several have become personal friends. He it was, who was called in during the mid-1980s to wean the middle-aged George W. Bush back from incipient alcoholism and on to the straight and narrow path that ultimately led to the presidency – he 'planted a mustard seed in my soul', as the president says, 'Billy Graham didn't make you feel guilty, he made you feel loved'. When the president talks of being 'right with God' he is consciously echoing Billy Graham, as his hearers well know.

With his affirming message and his huge crusades, in the USA and abroad, which lasted from the late 1940s to the turn of the twenty-first century, Graham could claim to have converted tens of thousands of people to Christ. More than that, he made evangelical revivalism respectable. He was the man in the suit with the resonant voice and the non-threatening message – the old rhetoric 'I am a Western Union boy. I have a death message! I must tell you plainly – you are going to Hell!' has long been dropped and he has regularly been named as one of the most trusted of prominent Americans. Graham has become, in the words of a recent New Yorker profile, 'the symbol of Protestant Christianity in America – in effect branding evangelicalism as the mainstream American faith'.[19]

The Billy Graham brand remains enormous, even as the old man approaches his ninetieth year, badly disabled with Parkinson's Disease. The Billy Graham Evangelistic Association, however, goes from strength to strength. Its purpose is to 'take the message of Christ to all we can by every prudent means', it employs 500 staff, and last year its annual revenue totalled over $104 million, of which Billy as director and chairman was paid $406,830, and his son Franklin as president and CEO, just under $95,000.

These days Billy Graham is vaguely disdainful of the Religious Right. He told *Time* magazine in November 1993: 'I can identify with them on theology, probably, in many areas, but in the political emphases they have, I don't, because I don't think Jesus or the Apostles took sides in the political arenas of their day.'[20]

In this he is unlike Franklin, who is likely to succeed to his father's mantle, and appears from his statements much less willing to compromise or soft-peddle on political issues. Billy's ecumenism towards members of other faiths, which did much to antagonise conservative evangelicals in the 1950s ('I just loved all those people, whoever they were. They reached out for me and I responded . . . '), has become for Franklin a hardline, blanket condemnation, at least as far as Islam is concerned. In his words: 'The global war on terrorism, let's give it the name – it's Islamic. That's who we're fighting . . . listen, there are millions of Muslims out there who are good people who do want to live in peace. But you have to look at the government of Saudi Arabia; this is what true Islam is. There is no tolerance of other religions or other faiths.' He has taken similarly outspoken positions on abortion and homosexuality: 'Listen, sin is sin, OK?'

When his dad and he appeared together with Bill and Hillary

Clinton for one final crusade at Flushing Meadow, New York, in June 2005, Graham Senior told the crowd: 'They're a great couple. I felt when he left the presidency he should be an evangelist because he has all the gifts – and he'd leave his wife to run the country.'

Of course the Clintons are anathema to Right-thinking people. Within a few days, Franklin issued a statement 'clarifying' his father's remarks. His dad had only been joking, he said. 'President Clinton has the charisma, personality and communication skills, but an evangelist has to have the call of God, which President Clinton obviously does not have and my father understands that.' And, for good measure, he certainly had not intended for his comments to be an endorsement for Senator Hillary Clinton.[21]

11

A Fundamentally Conservative Nation

'Extremism in the defence of liberty is no vice.'

Barry Goldwater, 1964

US conservatives usually date the start of their resurgence as a political force from the time of one of their greatest electoral defeats: that of Barry Goldwater, the Arizona senator who was the Republican candidate in the 1964 presidential election. Goldwater was widely regarded at the time as a rather scary and inept candidate, partly because of his advocacy of the use of nuclear weapons, but mainly because of his resolute refusal to modify his free market and libertarian views to accommodate potential voters. At a meeting with farmers he criticised the farm subsidies they received, and when he visited Tennessee he called for the Tennessee Valley Authority, the federal government initiative that had helped to restore the state economically in the 1930s and was therefore regarded as a great boon, to be closed down.

Yet he is now seen as a prophet, seeking to curtail state power in the interests of individual rights. In the election he won only six states, giving Lyndon Johnson a majority of 16 million popular votes, the largest plurality for any winning presidential candidate to that time. Goldwater's campaign may have been an electoral catastrophe, but it began the mobilisation of a grass-roots conservative insurgency, bred of dissatisfaction with government, that would eventually propel Ronald Reagan to the White House sixteen years later. And it also taught the future leaders of the Religious Right how to become organised.

Goldwater himself was an uncomfortable ally for such a movement. An Episcopalian, he maintained that religion was more to do with ethics than 'how often a man gets inside a church' and he was a doughty supporter of abortion rights for women, on the grounds that the state had no right to intervene in such personal decisions. Many years later, in 1981, he would also express his frustration with the bullying tactics of some on the Christian Right:

> . . . the religious factions that are growing throughout our land are not using their religious clout with wisdom. They are trying to force government leaders into following their position 100 per cent. If you disagree with these religious groups on a particular moral issue they complain, they threaten you with a loss of money, or votes, or both . . . I am even more angry as a legislator who must endure the threats of every religious group that thinks it has some God-granted right to control my vote on every rollcall in the Senate.[1]

Nevertheless, the congruence of his candidacy with a revival in evangelical fortunes and the social disruptions and uncertainties of the 1960s – the era of civil rights agitations, Vietnam, race riots, feminism, student demonstrations, free-love and flower power – helped to energise those who were concerned about the loss of old moral values and the apparent eclipse of religion. As Goldwater himself told the 1960 Republican convention: 'We have been losing elections because conservatives too often fail to vote. Let's grow up, conservatives. If we want to take this party back, and I think we can some day, let's get to work.'[2]

This was a speech made at a time when there had been a Republican in the White House for the previous eight years. It was a call to arms, however, for grass-roots conservatives to seize control of the candidacy from the East Coast patricians who had run the party, men such as Nelson Rockefeller who were used to getting their own way – and who would be shouted down in 1964. Rockefeller had already complained about the party being in 'real danger of subversion by a radical, well-financed and highly disciplined minority', one that would be wholly alien to sound and honest conservatism, but it was the old guard themselves who would be elbowed aside and sidelined in the coming years.

Little noticed at the time was the fact that the states Goldwater won, apart from his home state of Arizona, were all in the South: Alabama, Georgia, Louisiana, Mississippi and South Carolina, which had never elected Republicans since the Civil War, places indeed where 'you never met a live Republican'. Voters there noted that Goldwater had voted against the Civil Rights Act, again on the basis it was not the federal government's job to legislate about how citizens should treat one another. They liked it when he spoke out against the government (actually it was the Supreme Court) for 'banning Almighty God from our schoolrooms', as had happened over the previous two years with court rulings against prayer and Bible reading in state schools.

The constituency especially liked his belief that the national government should be shrunk and its tax-take reduced. Even more, they were impressed by the eloquence of one of the speakers mustered on Goldwater's behalf, the Hollywood actor Ronald Reagan, who first impinged on the national political scene during the campaign with a jeremiad against the moral corruption of US society. As the political commentator George Will noted, Goldwater eventually won his campaign, but not until 1980 when Reagan became President.[3]

William Martin, in his book *With God on our Side*, which chronicles the history of the movement, quotes Morton Blackwell, the youngest Goldwater delegate at the 1964 convention:

> In politics sometimes you win by losing. You lose the battle, but you set up the potential for future winning . . . [the Goldwater campaign] brought a lot of people into politics and we developed expertise . . . The religious leaders who were deeply committed to the values of traditional morality began to say: 'Hey, if we're not careful, this country's going to be changed in ways that we don't like at all.' It was clear that the Republican party was the party that was most hospitable to them.[4]

This was a period when polemical and fringe groups were being set up on the political Right, some of them regarded as eccentric if not plain nutty, or even sinister. Often they were based out in the West, in California or the Mountain states, as if hiding in the wilderness. Just about all of them were united by a fierce anti-communism and it was this that gave them common cause with religious groups who were similarly united, from Catholics to Calvinists, in their fear and hatred of such a godless ideology.

The personnel of such groups was often the same: one of Goldwater's campaign workers, Hal Lindsey, was to go on to write one of the period's most influential and best-selling books, applying the old fundamentalist doctrine of premillennial dispensationalism to current and forthcoming events. It was called *The Late Great Planet Earth*, published in 1970.

The potential influence of the religious vote was not slow to be spotted by politicians. Lyndon Johnson – who grew up in the Disciples of Christ Church – assiduously wooed Billy Graham to keep him away from the Goldwater camp's clutches ('Now, Billy, you stay out of politics,' Johnson is said to have told him just before the election, when he rang to invite him to stay for a weekend at the White House). In 1968, Richard Nixon, as Republican candidate, also played up his friendship with the great evangelist, though with a bit more cynicism than Graham realised at the time.

Martin quotes Charles Colson, one of Nixon's most senior and ruthless aides, who subsequently went to prison after Watergate and emerged as a born-again Christian:

> Sure, we used the prayer breakfasts and church services and all that for political ends. I was part of doing that. But Nixon was an interesting guy. There was an ambivalence about him. There were times when I thought he was genuinely spiritually seeking. The things he'd believed as a young man, he said he no longer believed. He didn't believe in the Resurrection or in Jonah's being swallowed by a whale. He believed those were symbols. But then he'd talk about Catholics and how they had a set of firm beliefs. He'd say he wished he could be a Catholic . . .
>
> At the same time Nixon was a very shrewd politician. He knew how to use religious people to maximum advantage. He noticed that there were voting blocs that were enormously influenced by their religious leaders . . . Early in 1969, he said: 'We want to do something for the Catholics.' We got Cardinal Krol in from Philadelphia and took him out on the presidential

yacht and the cardinal was absolutely mesmerised by Nixon.
Needless to say, we got a lot of help in some of the Catholic
precincts around Philadelphia because the cardinal put the
word out. At the same time Nixon recognised that the
evangelical vote was the key to the southern strategy, so he
began to invite evangelical leaders in and one of my jobs . . . was
to romance [them] . . . They would be dazzled by the aura of
the Oval Office and I found them to be about the most pliable
of any of the special interest groups we worked with.

The strategy paid off. In 1972 when he won the presidential election
by a landslide, Nixon took 86 per cent of Southern churchgoers,
including 76 per cent of all Southern Baptists, an even greater percentage than George W. Bush would achieve three decades later.

Colson told Martin: 'One of the reasons I have written books and
given speeches warning Christian leaders not to be seduced by the
wiles and attractiveness of power in the White House and to keep our
distance and never mix the gospel with politics is that I saw how well
I exploited religious leaders when I was in that job. But that's what
politicians do.'[5]

Billy Graham, like many other evangelical leaders, remained loyal
to Nixon, almost until the end, believing that he could not possibly
have connived in anything as devious as the Watergate conspiracy. It
was not until the release of transcripts of his taped conversations in
the Oval Office that the scales fell from Graham's eyes. On reading
them he was, apparently, physically sick. 'Those tapes revealed a man
I never knew. I never saw that side of him,' he said. In due course
other tapes would implicate Graham too, with publication of the
conversation in which he was disparaging about Jews.

Already by the mid-1970s, even during Nixon's presidency, there
were a number of social and moral causes that were causing disquiet
in middle America and that grass-roots conservatives saw they could
exploit to exert pressure on Washington. Their common feature was
that they concerned sex. There was abortion – though, as we have
seen, the evangelicals were slow to wake up to this, probably because
they saw it as a Catholic issue – there was feminism, a seeming threat
to the stability of the US family, there was for the first time a gay rights

movement, and there was free love and the prospect that the USA's young would abandon all cultural and social norms for ever. As Pat Robertson explained in an interview in 1999: 'There was the introduction of the psychedelic type of music, rock and roll music and excessive freedom in the creative community to bring more and more sensuality and hedonistic types of programmes into television and radio.'[6]

Many people who were concerned about this moral erosion were also resentful about civil rights for black Americans – particularly in the South – about the schooling their children were receiving, or who they might have to mix with if they were bussed to school and, as a spin-off from this, about the role of government in their lives. As we have seen, what originally motivated the evangelicals of the South was the threatened loss of tax exemption from their schools and colleges unless they opened them fully to black pupils – a fight they would eventually win in the Reagan years when the Internal Revenue Service dropped the case.

There was a pool of discontent to fish from. Conservatives could exploit it, because they were outsiders from the governing establishment and saw themselves as such – rebels with causes; liberals could not do this because it was by and large their consensus in office that had produced the discontents in the first place. They were complacent too and slow to respond to voter mutterings, as opposed to their client groups. The conservatives would prove themselves very good at grassroots organisation, at stirring up indignation and outrage – and getting their supporters to do something about it. Soon there would be an interlocking network of conservatively inclined religious and secular think tanks with a range of different interests, skills and priorities, but with many sharing either personnel or close personal ties and friendships based on a common world-view: the Heritage Foundation, the American Enterprise Institute, Conservative Political Action Conference, Concerned Women for America, the Eagle Forum. It was a case, in the words of Connie Marshner, one of the organisers, of getting 'the floating crap game' organised. Or, in the words of another: 'When there's an ice-storm the liberals stay at home, but these guys rent a bus.'[7] Sometimes their world-views were divorced from reality, but at least they all knew which direction they were heading.

There were a number of personalities and groups stirring the pot, people such as Paul Weyrich – incidentally, a Catholic – whose political career started with an attempt to organise a protest against the banning of school prayers and who later went on to found the Heritage Foundation. It was Weyrich who suggested the name for the Moral Majority, the evangelical campaign group that flourished in the 1980s. Described as the Lenin of social conservatism,[8] he has been one of its organising geniuses, giving intellectual clout to the movement.

Another of the earliest and most high-profile champions of the conservative insurgency was a Catholic mother of six, housewife and political activist from Illinois named Phyllis Schlafy, founder of a group called the Eagle Forum, who not only helped to secure Goldwater's nomination but would also prove to be a doughty campaigner in the following decade against the Equal Rights Amendment, making her a considerable hate-figure among feminists. Her enduring significance now is in her abilities as a polemicist – she was one of the pioneers of the raucous and abusive denunciatory techniques against opponents that are often used these days by campaigners on the Right – but also in her organisational skills in rousing and mobilising votes.

In the 1964 campaign, Schlafy produced and circulated a pocket-sized book called *A Choice Not an Echo* on her own intiative, in support of Goldwater, described as mixing 'fact, sensational accusations, commonsensical truths and elaborate conspiracy theories into a compelling but evidently bogus narrative'.[9] At its heart it alleged that Republican kingmakers such as Rockefeller had traditionally wheedled and bribed to ensure the selection of 'America Last' candidates who would be soft on communism. At the 1964 convention in the Cow Palace in San Francisco, 93 per cent of delegates admitted having read the book and 26 per cent said their views had been altered by it. No wonder Rockefeller was shouted down.

In the 1970s Schlafy led the fight against the ERA, a measure meant to establish that equality of rights should not be 'denied or abridged . . . on account of sex', and hence in the climate of the time legislation that was supposedly both timely and politically innocuous. It was supported in turn by Presidents Nixon, Ford and Carter.

Originally three-quarters of the public supported the amendment. Initially 22 of the 37 states (representing three-quarters of the 50 required to ratify it so that it could become part of the Constitution) did so within a year of its passage by both Houses of Congress in 1972.

But Schlafy's campaign succeeded in scuppering the legislation almost single-handed, by a mixture of scare tactics – saying it would lead to unisex toilets, homosexual marriages, women on the front line in battle and husbands being no longer responsible for supporting their families – reasoned argument: claiming it was unnecessary and even harmful; and the mobilisation of an astute grass-roots campaign, playing on supporters' fears and often their religious scruples. She invaded feminist rallies and performed satirical songs such as the following, after *Playboy* donated $5,000 to a pro-ERA group:

> Here comes Playboy cottontail,
> Hopping down the bunny trail,
> Trying to buy votes for ERA,
> Telling every girl and boy,
> You can only have your joy,
> By becoming gender-free or gay.[10]

Supporters were told how to dress when they were interviewed ('Always wear a scarf around your neck . . . ') and Schlafy would start her speeches by saying: 'First of all, I want to thank my husband, Fred, for letting me come. I always like to say that, because it makes the libs so mad.'

This was a campaign that not only initiated some of the tactics later used over other issues by the political and Religious Right and showed them that they could win, but also engaged such groups in a gut issue in contradiction to the spirit of the age. Jerry Falwell, still at his Thomas Road Baptist Church in Lynchburg but shortly to become one of the founders of the Moral Majority, argued patronisingly:

> Of course, Christians believe in equal rights. As a matter of fact, Christians believe in superior rights for their women. We believe in opening the door for our women, helping them with their coats, providing them with their living and protecting them from

their enemies. We are against the ERA because we believe it
degrades womanhood and may one day cause our women to use
unisex toilets and fight in the trenches on the battlefield, where
men belong.[11]

Such arguments carry echoes of those used whenever women have
been engaged in campaigns to improve their rights, as in the
nineteenth century for the right to vote. They might even have been
recognised in kind by Anne Hutchinson in the 1630s. And they
perfectly fit the view of some conservative evangelicals that a woman's
place is in submission to her husband: in St Paul's words in Ephesians
5:24: 'let wives also be subject in everything to their husbands';
1 Corinthians 14:33–5: 'let them ask their husbands at home'; and
1 Timothy 2:11: 'let a woman learn in silence with all submissiveness'.
Thirty years on from the ERA wrangle of course, women are indeed
serving in the trenches of Iraq and may occasionally even have to use
a unisex toilet.

The feminist opponents of Schlafy certainly played into her hands,
appearing both belligerent and threatening, when they weren't being
triumphalist and, somehow, alien to 'ordinary' people, particularly
when militant lesbians appeared openly in a political campaign for the
first time. The feminist Betty Friedan told Schlafy during a public
debate: 'I'd like to burn you at the stake. I consider you a traitor to
your sex. I consider you an Aunt Tom.' None were astute enough to
point out that Schlafy was a pretty fair example of a woman whose
femininity (to say nothing of her family) had scarcely been destroyed
by her campaigning. But that in a sense was Schlafy's point too, that
the amendment was an unnecessary piece of gesture politics.
Gradually, the ERA was stifled.

Schlafy's style certainly has common features with more recent
campaigners on the Right: slashing attacks on conspirators seeking to
subvert and destroy US society for evil, but sometimes unclear
reasons: communists, perverts, East Coast patricians, women's
libbers, even at one time or another such administration hawks as
Robert McNamara, Paul Nitze and Henry Kissinger, for allegedly
being soft on the Soviets. In the words of the *New Yorker*:

Whether Schlafy's paranoia represents actual delusion or just a rhetorical posture is hard to say. Even at its most despairing, her writing has a gleefulness that makes the reader feel she is having fun . . . In the end [her] denunciatory tone, more than any of her actual campaigns, probably represents her most lasting contribution to American life . . . she recognised that deliberation was no match for diatribe and logic no equal to contempt.[12]

In 1976, a genuine evangelical was elected to the White House for the first time, the first such candidate since William Jennings Bryan. He was a Southern Baptist and a lay preacher. He taught in a Sunday School. He ostentatiously paraded his religious views and said he would seek to live up to them. He was even a true Southerner, a peanut farmer from Georgia (and, less often stressed, a trained nuclear engineer and a man with a more distinguished military record than any president since Eisenhower). What was there not to like? The trouble was, he was a Democrat with socially progressive views. And his name was Jimmy Carter.

When he first emerged as a potential candidate, Carter's professions of his faith caused puzzlement to the mainstream media – it is a measure of how far things have changed in US politics over the last thirty years that secular correspondents then had to be told who an evangelical was, or what it meant when he said he had been born again. They thought it was rather quaint, if not quite hilarious, all of a piece with Carter's serious and slightly sanctimonious manner. But evangelicals knew precisely what he was getting at. When he gave an interview to *Playboy* magazine – of all godless journals – and spoke of looking at women with lust, 'I've committed adultery in my heart many times', they understood precisely the reference to the Sermon on the Mount. The fact that the interview appeared in *Playboy* caused criticism from some evangelicals, including Jerry Falwell, who afterwards for the first time gained an inkling that his views might become influential when Carter's adviser Jody Powell rang him to complain about them.

Time magazine described Carter as the 'most unabashed moralist' to stand for election since Bryan. When he spoke of bringing honesty and openness back to the White House – 'I'll never tell a lie. I'll never make a misleading statement' – a public that had been shaken by the Watergate scandal and the calamity of Vietnam responded with relief. It was to his electoral advantage that he was an outsider. He won narrowly, but he also won the support of at least half the white born-again vote as well as ten of the eleven Southern states. It was, *Time* magazine proclaimed, 'The Year of the Evangelical'.

But from an early stage, Carter disappointed that constituency. His causes were not theirs, he did not deliver what they wanted, and he was easy to ridicule. Like his predecessors Nixon and Ford, he supported the Equal Rights Amendment, and it was during his term that the schools tax exemption ruling was initially made, for which he got the blame although the case had actually arisen under his predecessor. Even worse, he refused to ban abortions. When the administration organised a conference on the American Family in Baltimore, it proved far too ecumenical. Gays, feminists, even unmarried parents were invited, so the conservative family group representatives walked out, claiming they were being discriminated against.

Even when Carter invited a group of conservative evangelicals and leaders of the Religious Right to the White House for breakfast in January 1980, the meeting was a disaster. Among those who attended were Falwell; Oral Roberts, the Pentecostal television evangelist and founder of a university in Tulsa, Oklahoma; Jim Bakker, whose days as a television preacher would end in disgrace; D. James Kennedy, another broadcaster and Presbyterian pastor of the Coral Ridge Church in Florida; and Tim LaHaye, who we will meet later and who with his wife Beverley was one of the organisers of Right-wing pressure groups. The delegation quizzed Carter about abortion and found him wanting, and demanded to know why there were not more evangelicals in the administration. LaHaye was not impressed: 'We had a man in the White House who professed to be a Christian, but didn't understand how unchristian his administration was.'

As soon as they got outside, LaHaye bowed his head in prayer: 'God, we have got to get this man out of the White House and get someone in here who will be aggressive about bringing back traditional moral values.'

Falwell concluded: 'Satan had mobilised his forces to destroy America . . . God needed voices raised to save the nation from inward moral decay.'[13]

But by that time anyway they had already founded the Moral Majority in 1979, a body that would be in Falwell's words 'pro-life, pro-traditional family, pro-moral and pro-American'. The name emerged from a conversation between Falwell and Weyrich at the Lynchburg Holiday Inn. Sometimes, pro-Israel was added as well, but essentially the enemy would be – not for the first time in American history – the wicked conspiracy seeking to overthrow US society by stealth.

This time it was the forces of secular humanism, 'the invisible enemy threatening our society' with its so-called 'pluralism, and tolerance and relative values'. Like the communists before them, humanists burrow into the woodwork, operating so subtly that outsiders and opponents don't know what is happening until it is too late. It was not only subversive but, worse, all-embracing and it has remained a potent force in the paranoia of US conservative Christians – and some English evangelicals – ever since. In the words of a Christian magazine article of the period, quoted by Martin: 'To understand humanism is to understand women's liberation, the ERA, gay rights, children's rights, abortion, sex education, the "new" morality, evolution, values clarification, situational ethics, the separation of church and state, the loss of patriotism and many of the other problems that are tearing America apart today.'[14]

It was a theory propounded by an evangelical theologian called Francis Schaeffer, a man influenced by Christian Reconstructionism, who had spent many years running a religious community in Switzerland. There he had advocated a Christian infiltration and engagement in society, much as a mirror-image to combat the humanists and to create Christian theocracy. Schaeffer's books sold 3 million copies and his ideas were taken up by others such as LaHaye, who went on to write not only a best-seller called *Battle for the Mind*, but also an even more successful series, the 'Left Behind' novels, positing the reality of the premillennial End Times. LaHaye estimates there are 275,000 humanists burrowing into US society. The 60 million born-again Christians ought to be a match for them, but you can never tell where the enemy might strike. The great conspiracy throws up an endless list of convenient targets for outrage, from gay marriage to the alleged abandonment of Christmas, and provides an easily understood, over-arching explanation for them all. Salvation is easy: it is not just individual conversion to the true faith that is required, but mobilisation – and the election of supporters to positions of influence.

In 1980, fortunately, the leaders of the Religious Right found the perfect candidate to take on the evangelical Carter. Ronald Reagan was someone whose career had been in the moral cesspits of Hollywood, he was a remarried divorcé whose family relationships with his children had been scarcely exemplary or particularly paternal. Worse, his second wife, a former Hollywood starlet, was, it emerged, keen on astrology and even persuaded her husband occasionally to act on her astrologer's advice. He had been liberal on abortion and tolerant of gays when he was governor of California in the late 1960s.

Reagan was not even particularly religious. He did not go to church regularly and could not be persuaded to do so, as a mark of his religiosity, even when he was in the White House. When during his unsuccessful 1976 campaign for the Republican nomination a reporter had asked whether he was born again, Reagan just shrugged, plainly having no idea what the man was talking about. But he certainly knew how to ring all the right bells for the religious constituency. If he did not necessarily know the biblical buzz-words himself, he could happily deploy moralistic rhetoric about good and evil, particularly when it came to describing Soviet communism. Cleverly, he told a meeting of religious broadcasters and pastors in Dallas in August 1980, just after the Republican convention: 'I know you can't endorse me. But I want you to know that I endorse you.'[15] It was a line suggested to him in the car from the airport by a Texan preacher, James Robison, who would later be one of the first to endorse the candidacy of George W. Bush.

In the November election, Reagan won by a landslide. Several factors played a part in Carter's defeat, but among them was the fact that the white evangelical vote slid by two to one to his opponent. Reagan won ten of the eleven Southern states – a precise reversal of Carter's result four years earlier, with only Georgia staying loyal to the Democrats and its local son. The Moral Majority – which, as Democratic opponents pointed out was neither moral, nor a majority

– understandably played up that part of the victory, but were to become somewhat disillusioned when the new president first did not fill his administration with the born-again in proportion to their numbers in the general population as he had promised (there were relatively few suitably qualified evangelicals who were available to be appointed), and then largely ignored the issues that they wanted tackled, chiefly on abortion and the reinstitution of school prayers. The president could make the rhetorical gestures needed to keep that section of the electorate on side, but did not deliver. In the words of Jack Kemp, his press secretary, as reported by the political columnist E. J. Dionne: 'Whenever Ronald Reagan spoke about abortion or spoke to the Religious Right, his younger yuppie supporters always thought they saw him wink.'[16]

The Moral Majority found itself caught in a bind, pledged to the administration, revelling in its alleged influence as advisers, but taking a partisan political stand on behalf of a movement that was supposedly non-political. It was concerned with moral issues yes, but often voicing opinions that were divisive for its own potential supporters.

When the Moral Majority stepped outside its comfort zone to comment on things it knew little about, it sometimes appeared brash and naïve, or even stupid. Falwell as its figurehead was an engaging and outspoken figure (and, importantly for its core supporters, an ordained minister rather than a political hack), but when he said: 'I don't know why every one of our presidents thinks he has to wine and dine every drunk who comes over here from some other country and dance with his wife . . . if a president is a good Christian, he can offer that foreign head of state some orange juice . . . have a good minister come in and read a few verses of scripture and, if he doesn't like that, put him on the next plane home.'[17] It was certainly populist, but not a particularly sophisticated analysis. Carter's spokesman Jody Powell said: 'Whatever their motivation may have been, I think it's obvious in retrospect that religion either fell into or was delivered into the hands of people who had a rather clear political agenda . . . I remember Mr Falwell and his crowd in the name of Christianity attacking people who had voted against the B1 bomber, for heaven's sake! That's not an issue on which I could imagine the good Lord took a position.'

What the Moral Majority did develop, however, was a grass-roots organisation that could co-ordinate and project the outrage of its supporters, mailing them with newsletters and petitions, based on lists of congregation addresses supplied by local pastors: it claimed to have registered 4 million electors in time to vote in the 1980 presidential election and may have achieved at least half that figure. Its leaders, such as Falwell, Oral Roberts and Swaggart, also had bully pulpits in their television and radio shows from which to broadcast their messages and, even if they exaggerated the number of their viewers, the Moral Majority Report's commentary was broadcast on 300 local stations every day. Also importantly, Falwell persuaded a number of disparate religious groups, including Catholics and Presbyterians, even Jews and Mormons, that they could work together on issues over which they were agreed, such as abortion and homosexuality, despite their theological differences on larger matters of faith.

What the movement lacked, however, was a strategy to achieve its aims, even with an administration that was supposedly sympathetic to it and that it had persuaded its followers to support. With a friendly president in the White House, Falwell and his friends expected results and, when they did not happen, the Moral Majority did not know what to do. As it faltered in the mid-1980s, a new and pointed insurgency was launched, with the ambitious aim of getting its leader, the telly-evangelist Pat Robertson, elected president.

Robertson, the wealthy son of a long-term Congressman, A. Willis Robertson, who had served in Washington for thirty-four years, was, like Falwell, a Baptist minister though one of a more Charismatic, Pentecostal, stamp. But where Falwell had launched a television programme, *The Old Time Gospel Hour*, Robertson had gone one better and started his own television station, the Christian Broadcasting Network, as far back as 1959. He got into the USA's cable expansion early and eventually profited hugely from it.

Understandably, there was a certain degree of rivalry between the two Virginian pastors. Falwell's background was rather less exalted – his father was a drunk who had shot his own brother, and he himself had had to work his way through a Missouri Bible College – while Robertson had attended Yale Law School and New York Theological Seminary. Robertson was not invited to join the Moral Majority.

Robertson's broadcasting was – and has remained – rather more sophisticated than that of other preachers. His nightly 700 Club, so-called from the 700 viewers he originally asked to pledge $10 each a month to keep the station going, mimics the news broadcasts of secular national stations, with Robertson and his fellow presenter sitting behind a studio desk and delivering news, lifestyle advice and improving homilies, often featuring individuals helped by their faith, as well as asides and commentaries on the day's events from the host himself. These have occasionally, particularly as the years have gone by, verged on the extempore, not to say surreal, side as with the gay Scotsmen and their kilts, but also, famously, in 1985 when he called on Hurricane Gloria to veer away from its course towards the coast of Virginia where his television studios are based: 'In the name of Jesus we command you to stop where you are and move north-east, away from land and away from harm!' Gloria did so, and eventually hit Long Island instead – a clear sign of God's viewing habits. Robertson said afterwards: 'I felt, interestingly enough, that if I couldn't move a hurricane, I could hardly move a nation. I know that's a strange thing for anybody to say and there's hardly anyone else who would feel the same way, but it was very important to the faith of many people.'

Robertson had previously shied away from political involvement but as the 1988 election approached, he began to feel that he could mobilise his invisible army of supporters and run for the presidency himself. Many of his potential voters lived under the radar screens of the traditional Republican Party machine, and when he defeated the party's favoured candidate George Bush Senior, who had been Reagan's vice-president, in the Iowa primary – the first electoral test for potential candidates at the start of election year – Robertson was briefly on a roll. He won caucuses, the local equivalent of primaries, in Alaska, Hawaii, Nevada and Washington State, was almost certainly gerrymandered out of victory by the party machine in the subsequent Michigan primary, and thereafter faltered, but there was a brief moment when the established order of things tottered.

Less noticed, another clergyman was also running for the presidency, the Revd Jesse Jackson, for the Democrats, but they were not ready for a black candidate who was also a cleric, even one associated with Martin Luther King. That was not necessarily an attribute for winning white votes in the South, and Jackson ultimately stood no chance of selection for his party either.

Robertson's campaign certainly energised a certain sector of evangelical voters. Randall Balmer, who covered the campaign, reported ecstatic supporters in New Hampshire proclaiming that Satan had controlled politics for too long and that, at last, the Lord was on their side.[18] He also encountered a premillennialist clergyman at a Robertson meeting in Concord telling the candidate that he had no business running against the End Times: 'The next event on the echatological clock is the return of Christ. Things in society should get worse rather than better. If Christians worked to turn our nation around that would be a humanistic effort and delay Christ's return.'

Concerns about Robertson's campaign were not just voiced on the fundamentalist fringe. Opinion polling among religious ministers found that although 43 per cent of Charismatics and Pentecostals named him as their first choice, only 28 per cent of Baptists did so, and 18 per cent of Fundamentalists. While people were happy that their religious views were being taken account of, they did not actually want the country to be run by the Religious Right. In E. J. Dionne's words: 'As long as [it] is a movement of people saying, "Hey, religious America deserves attention. We shouldn't be ignored. We shouldn't be made fun of," then it can be very strong. But as soon as it moves to making the stronger claim that "God's policies should be national policies," an awful lot of people, including religious people, say, "No, that's not how I look at the political process." '[19]

In all this, Robertson was not assisted by two spectacular implosions by fellow television evangelists. First there was Jim and Tammy Faye Bakker, whose 'Praise The Lord' television network and associated Heritage USA amusement park failed, affected by publicity surrounding Mr Bakker's intimate association with Jessica Hahn, a former church secretary, who had been secretly paid $250,000 not to mention their affair. Bakker eventually served six years in prison for defrauding his supporters of $158 million. Hard on the heels of this came news that Jimmy Swaggart, the most popular of all the hellfire evangelists, had been filmed taking a prostitute to a motel room in New Orleans – a story leaked to the network apparently by friends of the Bakkers in revenge for Swaggart's sanctimonious criticism of his erstwhile rival. Robertson had nothing to do with either case, but they scarcely improved the reputation of the nation's would-be exemplars. They did, however, provide something for the nation's gaity.

The man who eventually and ruthlessly won the 1988 election, George Bush Senior, could plausibly present himself as the most religiously observant Republican president for several decades, but that was no longer enough. An Episcopalian, he went (and goes) to church weekly. In the election he won 81 per cent of the votes cast by evangelicals, more than Reagan ever had. But his Christianity was not that of the Religious Right: like the man himself, it was too desiccated and patrician to win their confidence. He had trouble articulating 'the vision thing' in all ways, not least his own religious beliefs. Perhaps realising this, during the campaign the job of liaising with the Religious Right was relegated to his recently born-again son George W., a man who knew how to speak their language. The candidate himself could attend their conferences, even speak about what his faith meant to him, but he just was not one of them. Bush would invite Billy Graham and his wife to the White House on the night he gave the order to launch the first Gulf War, but by his actions closer to home he lost the evangelicals' confidence. In 1990, when he signed the Hate Crimes Bill, the president invited representatives of affected groups to witness the event at the White House, among them gays and lesbians. This naturally appalled and infuriated the Religious Right. Richard Land of the Southern Baptists said such a gesture went far beyond any argument about being president of all the people.

Bush Senior was in a double bind: he never shook off the impression that he was not at one with the Right, so had to fight another distracting and damaging internal challenge to his candidacy for the presidential election of 1992, this time from the Right-wing Catholic polemicist (and isolationist) Pat Buchanan. To the public at large, the Republican Party appeared increasingly in thrall to the influence of the fundamentalists. When it came to the party's convention that year, Buchanan burst forth with a speech for prime-time television audiences of blustering and triumphalist sectarianism (and one that he had not bothered to clear first with the organisers of the convention): 'There is a religious war going on in our country for the soul of America. It is a cultural war, as critical to the kind of nation we will one day be as was the Cold War itself. And in that struggle for the soul of America, Clinton and Clinton are on the other side and George Bush is on our side.' As the liberal columnist Molly Ivins remarked, it probably sounded better in the original German.

Early in the Bush presidency, Pat Robertson recruited a young, fresh-faced supporter named Ralph Reed to organise a new movement, away from Washington, that could establish a more effective organisation to mobilise grass-roots support – handing out voter information cards at elections, often through their churches, to advise which candidates to vote for – and winning power at a local level, in school boards, local councils and commissions. It was to be called the Christian Coalition and for ten years it became a powerful force. Robertson's choice of Reed, who was a twenty-eight-year-old college graduate and political activist, proved to be a stroke of luck. Robertson had found a formidable organiser, lobbyist and manipulator to stir up and mobilise the religious constituency, to push a pre-selected agenda and get them out to vote. Reed was an unusual combination of both a committed Christian and a political obsessive.

Robertson saw the Coalition in strongly sectarian, even messianic, terms: 'When the Christian majority takes over this country, there will be no satanic churches, no more free distribution of pornography, no more abortion on demand and no more talk of rights for homosexuals. After the Christian majority takes control, pluralism will be seen as immoral and evil and the state will not permit anybody to practice it.'[20]

This was verging on Christian Reconstructionism and the establishment of a theocracy – Robertson has clearly been influenced by the views of Rousas John Rushdoony that there should be a reinstitution of biblical punishment and had the prophet as a guest on his 700 Club show – so that the surprise may be that he achieved as much support as he did. That may have been due to the more emollient public stance of Ralph Reed as the face of the movement. Rushdoony and his Reconstructionist ideas have had a pervasive background effect on many leaders of the Religious Right, even though they are aware that they are too extreme to be espoused publicly. In a Reconstructionist America there would be no tolerance for other religions, no public education or welfare and public execution by stoning for a range of 'crimes' such as homosexuality and adultery. Even the restoration of slavery – as mandated in the Bible – could be considered. Nevertheless, 'though we hide their books under the bed, we read them just the same', as one evangelical said.

The Christian Coalition did not immediately transform the nation, but it secured the advance of Religious Right representatives throughout the Republican Party. Many of them were elected both at local level – not always under their true colours as religiously motivated conservatives – particularly to school boards, where they waged campaigns about textbooks, creationism and allegedly Left-wing teaching. The targets were not necessarily overtly religious: 'The pro-family movement must speak to the concerns of average voters in the areas of taxes, crime, government waste, health care and financial security,' Reed said.

Notoriously, in 1991, Reed offered a lurid account of his methods: 'I do guerilla warfare. I paint my face and travel by night. You don't know it's over until you're in a body bag. You don't know until election night'[21] – remarks he later conceded may have been a mistake, though they accurately portrayed his style.

At their first meeting, informally at a dinner marking the Bush inauguration and the awarding of a prize to Robertson as Man of the Year from the conservative Students for America group, Reed chatted to him about how to maximise the defection of socially conservative Democrats to Republican ranks. He told Robertson: 'If the Roman Catholics and the evangelicals could get together and agree on a shared agenda, they would be the most effective political force that the country [had] ever seen.'[22]

In the coming years as the first Bush's presidency slid into the Clinton era, the Christian Coalition was instrumental in stirring up a permanent sense of continuing outrage, against organisations such as the National Endowment for the Arts (for sponsoring exhibitions such as one in which a plastic crucifix was suspended in a jar of the artist's urine). The Coalition grew exponentially: from 125 chapters and 57,000 members in 1990 to 2,000 chapters and 1.9 million members by 1997. At the time of the 1994 election, 88 per cent of white evangelicals cited 'family values' as the major factor in deciding how they voted.

By the time of the 1994 national midterm elections, the Christian Coalition claimed a million members, the annual budget was $12 million and it saw Republican sympathisers elected to Congress in large numbers: 114 members of the House and 26 senators had received perfect approval ratings from the Coalition and an additional 58 Congressmen voted for Coalition positions at least 85 per cent of the time. In all, 60 per cent of victorious Congressional candidates had the backing of the Christian Coalition.

Bill Clinton, president from 1992, provided a target as big as a barn door to his political opponents and not only on the Religious Right. His first significant move as president, within days of coming into office – to announce plans to recruit gays to the armed services – might almost have been calculated to antagonise them, and it did. Clinton's actions, not only in some of his cack-handed political reforms, but also in his private life – his affairs with women during his time as governor of Arkansas and then with the White House intern Monica Lewinsky while he was president – were continuous and running sores throughout his time in office and could only serve to increase the righteous outrage of religious as well as other Americans. This was despite the fact that the president attempted to court evangelical leaders: he saw them at the White House and he made frequent and ostentatious references to his own religious faith – perhaps even more so than George W. Bush, whose need to keep them onside has been less, given that they are unlikely to urge their congregations to vote for anyone else.

Despite that, Clinton's very presence in the office of the presidency served to energise, unite and motivate the Religious Right, some of whose tribunes saw him and his wife quite literally as the anti-Christs. Indeed, Clinton's election – and continuing, mystifying, popularity with the general electorate who continued to accord him 70 per cent approval ratings – were taken both as a sign of the USA's moral depravity and as a symbol of God's displeasure with such a fallen nation. No rumour was too overblown to be believed: in 1994 and 1995 Jerry Falwell happily sold through his *Old-Time Gospel Hour* programme 150,000 copies of a scurrilous video called *The Clinton Chronicles*, produced by an organisation called – presumably without irony – Citizens for Honest Government, which alleged without producing any evidence that Clinton was a drug addict who had arranged murders in Arkansas to protect a drug-smuggling ring.[23]

It may well be true that Clinton was unjustly treated by the raucous tribunes of the Right, the radio shock-jocks, the bloggers of the internet and the polemicists of the Right-wing press, and hounded by his opponents in Congress and the special prosecutor Kenneth Starr, but he certainly gave them plenty of ammunition to fire. The fact that he is a church-going Southern Baptist (and his wife Hillary is a Methodist) did not help in the least to deflect the criticism. He, and in turn in 2000 his vice-president and fellow Southern Baptist, Al Gore, received a smaller share of evangelical votes even than had the markedly less religious Democratic candidate Michael Dukakis in 1988.

The Religious Right joined in the political conservatives' attacks with gusto and helped to provide the background mood music of cultural disgruntlement shared by many white voters. By and large, these targeted discontents have remained the same: schools, abortion, gay marriage – issues that were useful for mobilising support but ultimately unsatisfactory for widening it.

Their tactics – which were often rough and brutal – might be effective, but they were sometimes scarcely Christian. When Bobbie Kilberg, who had served in the Bush White House, ran for lieutenant governor of Virginia in 1993, against a Religious Right opponent, Michael Farris, her Jewishness became an issue. Supporters claimed to have heard Farris delegates shouting 'There's one that Hitler missed' at the party convention.[24]

The Religious Right did not trouble particularly to widen its constituency among more moderate religious groups, those not inclined to buy its whole moral package, or those interested in other issues as well. Still less was it interested in other faith groups. It did not convince either those who believed in the separation of Church and state, or at least the compartmentalisation of personal religious beliefs and secular political allegiances. And, in particular, it made very little effort to win over one conservative religious constituency that it might otherwise have attracted for its moral stances – the congregations of the African-American, black churches.

Reed, who had been brought up partly in Georgia, certainly made some attempts to do so, but they were unsupported and half-hearted. His public stances were sometimes at odds with his private ones too: he had been a supporter of the racist Senator Jesse Helms in earlier days and had opposed the setting up of the annual remembrance day for Martin Luther King. In 1996 he indeed publicly promised that the Coalition would put up a $25,000 reward for information about the identity of the fire-bombers of black churches and in 1997 he promised the Coalition would raise $10 million for black and Hispanic inner-city churches by 2000, but in the event the organisation managed to donate just $50,000.[25]

By then, Reed had gone, moving back to Georgia and entering state politics, his career only marginally set back by the revelation of links both to the disgraced Enron Corporation and to the disgraced influence-peddlar Jack Abramoff. He did secure one dubious triumph, however, in engineering the defeat of the state's incumbent Senator Max Cleland, who had lost both legs and an arm serving in Vietnam, whom Reed had the nerve to accuse of lacking patriotism. Reed's attempt to become lieutenant governor of his home state ultimately ended in failure, either a just comeuppance or an indication of the limits of his political skill.

Following Reed's departure in 1997, the Christian Coalition itself went into decline: losing members and their contributions and having to cut its staff. In recent years, the old leadership has been stale and ageing: Falwell and Robertson have not been supplanted by younger, more dynamic (or sympathetic) leaders.

They remain national figures, to be courted by potential Republican candidates (John McCain gave the speech at a degree ceremony at Falwell's Liberty University in Lynchburg in May 2006), but their rhetoric and bombast have succeeded in alienating many former supporters and they cause others, who might be sympathetic, to edge away. Their lack of self-awareness or even reflectiveness can be extraordinary, as when Falwell attacked the BBC programme *Teletubbies* for promoting a homosexual agenda as he claimed to detect that one of them – Tinky Winky actually – was gay because he carried a handbag. Robertson's most recent foray into controversy was to suggest in August 2005 that the USA should arrange the assassination of its most outspoken South American critic, the

Venezuelan president Hugo Chavez, on account of protecting US access to his country's oil reserves. It would be, he said: 'a whole lot cheaper than starting a war . . . we have the ability to take him out and I think the time has come that we exercise that ability'. Donald Rumsfeld, then the secretary of defence, presumably sighing deeply, replied: 'Our department doesn't do that sort of thing. It's against the law.'[26] As the pollster John Zogby observed, such absolutism scares the hell out of voters in the middle.

As Falwell's and Robertson's stars have waned, a third figure, less widely known abroad, has emerged to make the running. Dr James Dobson, a child psychologist and founder of the Focus on the Family organisation, has come to eclipse them both. Some say he is rather scarier than either.

Dobson, who grew up in Texas and Oklahoma, the son of an itinerant pastor in the deeply conservative Church of the Nazarene, has a doctorate in child development from the University of Southern California and was a tenured professor in the university's medical school when he first came to fame in the 1970s for a wildly popular book on child-raising called *Dare to Discipline*, which has sold more than 3 million copies. As might be guessed from the title, it blends biblical principles, common sense and psychology as a sort of reaction to Dr Spock for conservative Christian parents. Its message is that children need firm discipline as well as love. And that, of course, would include corporal punishment.

He has a noble mission: 'Those who control what young people are taught and what they experience – what they see, hear, think and believe – will determine the future course for the nation.' And, in another book: 'If the salvation of children is really that vital to us, then our spiritual training should begin before children can even comprehend what it is all about . . . I firmly believe in acquainting children with God's judgment and wrath while they are young. Nowhere in the Bible are we instructed to skip over the unpleasant scriptures in our teaching. The wages of sin is death and children have the right to understand that fact.'[27]

Other successful books of populist psychology followed (including one intriguingly entitled *What Wives Wish Their Husbands Knew About Women* and another called *Parenting for Cowards*) and by 1976 Dobson was able to give up his professorship and concentrate full time on writing and lecturing. He set up Focus on the Family the following year and it has grown in the last thirty years into a $150 million a year enterprise, employing over 1,200 people – a third of them answering callers with problems – and based on an 81-acre campus at its headquarters in Colorado Springs, a town that has some claims to being now the Religious Right capital of the USA since it also contains the headquarters of a number of similar organisations, as well as a couple of military bases and Santa's North Pole Workshop.

From Focus's headquarters, Dobson broadcasts daily to an audience of up to 20 million Americans. The headquarters receives 10,000 e-mails, 50,000 telephone calls and 173,000 letters a month and has a mailing list of 6 million names. His empire sends out books and videos of improving literature and there are even guided tours of the premises. Up to 250,000 tourists a year, many of them coachloads of pensioners, are said to make the trek to Colorado to pay homage. Focus on the Family is big enough to have its own postal code and exit from Interstate 25. The radio show is aired over more than 4,000 radio stations and Dobson's syndicated columns are published in at least 500 local newspapers each week. An offshoot organisation, the Family Research Council, forms the organisation's lobbying arm in Washington and is said to have more than 400,000 members. Its first director was Gary Bauer, another strategist of the Right whose motivation was as much political as religious.

Focus on the Family offers its supporters not only advice on child-rearing and family problems – everything from bed-wetting to drugs – but even guidance on what films to see and which to shun. Click on pluggedinonline.com and this is what you will find under, for instance, *Harry Potter and the Goblet of Fire*:

> Crude or Profane Language: Ron has a habit of saying 'bloody h---'and angrily tells Harry to 'p-ss off'. A student exclaims 'oh my God', Harry uses the phrase 'I don't give a d---n'. Other Negative Elements: The audience is made to feel good about Mad-Eye's pragmatic disregard for rules and protocol. Some images (skulls, serpents, headstones etc.) may not be spiritual or violent per se but they convey an aura of wickedness and death.

The review finds the architecture and 'fantastic European locales' Gothic yet charming, but sadly cannot recommend the film for family audiences: 'it is impossible . . . to invest in a series that glamorises witchcraft . . . the film's wall-to-wall sorcery is birthed from a faulty worldview that taps into the occult and never recognises any divine authority . . . the entire series is built on a shaky spiritual foundation'.

So that's a no then.

Dobson's message is inevitably conservative in its morality and this has led him to take firm and increasingly outspoken stances on issues such as abortion and homosexuality.

Although as a psychologist he can claim to be offering disinterested and professional advice, in fact it has become increasingly and overtly politically partisan. Despite his stated reluctance to endorse candidates, he now does so and they are invariably Republicans and those of the Religious Right. Indeed he brooks no dissent from candidates for his full list of demands and rather relishes his position as a would-be king-maker: as the Republican presidential hopeful Phil Gramm, regarded as a hardline conservative, discovered in 1996 after he told Dobson he would not make his campaign a moral crusade: 'I am not running for preacher, I am running for president. I just don't feel comfortable going round telling other people how to live their lives.' In his book *Active Faith*, Reed, who was present, wrote that Dobson stalked out of the room, his cheeks flushed, saying: 'I walked into that meeting fully expecting to support Phil Gramm for president. Now I don't think I would vote for him if he was the last man standing.'[28]

In early 2007 Dobson was making sure he did not favour either of the leading Republican candidates for the 2008 presidential election race, Rudolph Guiliani and John McCain. A third messenger, Mitt Romney – a Mormon no less – was however more than willing to make a pilgrimage to Colorado Springs to court him, presumably spotting a gap in the market.

Dobson's audience base and influence is such that Republicans have been anxious to court him, but he has not been particularly easy to get, rightly seeing his strength and integrity for supporters as lying in his apparent independence. One twitch, though, is enough to send shivers through the party: when a senior Republican was unwise enough a few years ago to suggest that it was big enough to accommodate supporters of abortion, Dobson immediately sent out an eight-page letter to 2.1 million subscribers, 112,000 clergy, 8,000 politicians and 1,500 journalists to announce that a struggle was under way for the soul of the party and he was 'committed never again to cast a vote for a politician who would kill one innocent baby'.

Unlike Robertson and Falwell, Dobson has tended to disown political ambitions, though he clearly likes to wield private influence in the White House and the corridors of Congress. Not exactly reclusive, he does not give interviews easily, probably because he does not take kindly to being cross-examined. In 2004 he finally came out for Bush (a significant moment of triumph for the president).

The Church of the Nazarene is sternly perfectionist and it is said that Dobson himself is not prone to doubts or uncertainties. He is not one to go in for the compromises that make up political life and some say he is politically naïve. In 2005 he was certainly reckless enough to accept President Bush's word that Harriet Miers was a suitable candidate for nomination to the Supreme Court, weeks before she was forced to stand down amid a welter of criticism about her inadequacy.

Dobson dispenses daily jeremiads from Colorado Springs about the 'civil war of values' he sees raging through the USA. There is a slight element of the Wizard of Oz about him, a sense of a large megaphone concealing a small man, but he certainly puts the wind up politicians. And his listeners vote for candidates who they know to share his views at both national and local elections.

Recently Dobson has adopted somewhat of a scattergun approach to his targets, a bit like Robertson. He attacked the children's cartoon character SpongeBob SquarePants as somehow 'pro-homosexual' and Dan Brown's *The Da Vinci Code* as something 'cooked up in the fires of hell', to which the *Economist* magazine commented: 'Wouldn't it have been better written if it had been?'

It is difficult for such an absolutist to mingle in the mucky, compromise-laden world of politics. As he once said:

Tolerance is a kind of watchword of those who reject the concepts of right and wrong. You know, there are no absolutes, there is no right and wrong, there is no eternal truth and we should be tolerant and accepting of everything – anything and everything. It's a kind of desensitisation to evil of all varieties. Everything has become acceptable to those who are tolerant . . . But the Scripture teaches that we are to discriminate between right and wrong, good and evil. And that we are to be intolerant of evil . . . Tolerance is not the greatest good in all contexts as it's being taught in the world of political correctness today.[29]

This is alarmingly close to the Reconstructionist Rushdoony's rejection of pluralism: 'At no point in the Scripture do we read that God teaches, supports or condones pluralism. In the name of toleration, the believer is asked to associate on a common level of total acceptance with the atheist, the pervert, the criminal and the adherents of other religions.' In such a world-view there is no latitude or room for doubt.

In the words of one of his former colleagues, Gil Alexander-Moegerle, who helped Dobson to found Focus on the Family in 1977:

I believe it is accurate and justified and reasonable to say that Jim wants theocracy . . . his perfect president would be someone with a law book in one hand and a Bible in the other, someone who defers to the fundamentalist interpretation. Jim really believes that until that happens, America is on its last legs and is gasping its last breaths. Jim is desperate and fearful and he really believes that only a theocracy can save us.[30]

Clearly such a prophet is doomed to perpetual disappointment with mere politicians. What is startling is his access to millions of listeners every day and the fact that many on the Right, aware of his wealth and influence, continue to seek to court him for electoral advantage. He remains a major, if shadowy, player in US politics, which is just how he likes it. However, his audience is ageing – average age is fifty-two – and so is Dobson, who is now seventy.

I hoped to interview someone from the FRC, or indeed Dobson himself, but was told in no uncertain terms that Focus on the Family had no interest in assisting my research.

*   *   *

As insiders now for many years, the Religious Right still have not secured their goals. Looking back in the late 1990s, Ed Dobson, one of Jerry Falwell's former assistants at the Moral Majority, ruminated:

> The Moral Majority was founded as a reaction against a secular society that was increasingly hostile to conservative Christians. Christians believed they were an oppressed minority and that if they did not stand up, they would be buried by the secularists and the humanists. The Moral Majority was seen as an organisation to stop the rising tide of secularism. It was a fortress to protect, not a battleship to attack. We were not interested in taking over America. We were only interested in making sure we did not get overtaken . . .
>
> Did the Moral Majority really make a difference? . . . Is the moral condition of America better because of our efforts? Even a casual observation of the current moral climate suggests that despite all the time, money and energy – despite the political power – we failed. Things have not gotten better; they have gotten worse.
>
> So were the efforts of the Moral Majority a complete waste of time and money? Absolutely not. The Moral Majority had a profound impact on American life. First, the Moral Majority forced public discussion on moral issues. Abortion became a front burner issue. Jerry would often say, 'Now you can't run for dog catcher in any town in America without having a stand on abortion.' And he was right.[31]

12

The Man of Faith

'I know we are all sinners, but I've accepted Jesus Christ as my personal saviour. I know what it means to be right with God.'

George W. Bush, 2004

There are times when even President George Bush's most fervent admirers admit to his limitations. Stephen Mansfield, the author of one of several books about Bush and his religious beliefs, poses a question in the course of what is generally a hagiographic 2003 volume called *The Faith of George W. Bush:* asking 'Why did Bush win?' the author states: 'He was not the candidate with the widest appeal, nor did he have the broadest experience. In fact he won with one of the thinnest resumés of any president in American history. He very possibly was not, as one columnist sniffed, the "sharpest knife in the drawer". And he made his mistakes.'[1]

Putting aside the fact that in terms of the popular vote, Bush did not actually win in 2000 and that at best his victory was scarcely a ringing national endorsement, the answer David Frum, his former speech-writer, gives is that the electorate wanted someone who was not Bill Clinton. Mansfield adds:

They thought of Clinton in the terms historian Stephen Ambrose once used to describe Thomas Jefferson, as a 'great mind with a limited character'. They wanted a change. They had endured rule by the best and the brightest. Now they wanted rule by the good and they believed that Bush was the man who could make it happen. In a choice between immoral brilliance and the C student with a moral compass, they would take the moral compass.

Mansfield incidentally dismisses the controversy over the election in a couple of sentences.

George W. Bush's life story is very well known: he was an under-achieving, almost wastrel, eldest son of a high-achieving father from a wealthy and ambitious North-eastern political dynasty, who gave up drinking and found God in his fortieth year with the help of Billy Graham. It is the latter part of this story that plays into the traditional Log Cabin to White House presidential narrative – the idea that presidents rise from obscurity, through adversity, to the highest office, a possibility open to each US-born citizen – although in George Bush's case there was no log cabin, but rather a childhood home, in the oil town of Midland, in the bleak and baking flatlands of western Texas. But it is unquestionable that the younger Bush would not have got where he is today without the support, influence, connections and money of his family. Even so, he nearly blew it with a series of mediocre and undistinguished career moves, mainly in the oil industry, until his conversion to Christ in the summer of 1984 or possibly 1985.

Even if the date is a little vague, Bush's is a classic US tale of redemption: a sinner come to repentence, the kind of tale that evangelicals take as the fulfilment of all their aspirations for their fellow men. It is a story they can recognise, sympathise with, and appreciate. Brought up an Episcopalian, Bush became a Methodist in 1977 when he married his wife Laura, a decision made not apparently out of any profound change of religious conviction, but because his wife was already a Methodist. He had always gone to church out of habit, not with marked enthusiasm, and he continued to do so. Mansfield even gives the impression he would sit in his pew making lame jokes about the readings and the preacher.

But in the spring of 1984 Bush was taken to meet an evangelist named Arthur Blessitt who has spent many years carrying a 12-foot cross around the world and was at that time passing through Midland. They got together in the coffee shop of the town's Holiday Inn for what was clearly a momentous meeting. It may, or may not, be significant that Bush's latest financial venture had just failed, but he was also acutely aware of his personal under-achievement as the son of the then vice-president of the USA. Blessitt asked him what his relationship was like with Jesus and Bush said he was not sure. The evangelist then asked: 'If you died this moment, do you have the assurance you would go to heaven?' Bush replied no. He was then asked: 'Would you rather live with Jesus in your life, or live without him?' The answer to such a leading question was obvious. The two men prayed together: 'I love you, Lord, take control of my life. I believe You hear my prayer . . . Lead me to care for the needs of others. Make my home in heaven and write my name in Your book. I accept the Lord Jesus Christ as my Saviour and desire to be a true believer' is how Mr Blessitt remembers it. George Bush remembers 'an awesome and glorious moment'.[2]

Even so, that moment might have passed, but for a drinking and business friend of Bush's, Don Evans, who also got religion at about the same time and who would eventually go to Washington with Bush. Then there was also a meeting the following summer with Billy Graham on the beach at Kennebunkport, Maine, where the Bushes have a holiday home. Having the world's greatest evangelist staying as a friend of the family is not given to everyone, but George Bush appears to have taken full advantage of his good fortune. They went for a walk on the beach and Graham asked him: 'Are you right with God?' 'No,' Bush replied, 'but I want to be.' In his own book, *A Charge to Keep: My Journey to the White House* (2001), Bush says:

> I felt drawn to seek something different. He didn't lecture or admonish; he shared warmth and concern. Billy Graham didn't make you feel guilty; he made you feel loved . . . [He] planted a mustard seed in my soul, a seed that grew over the next year . . . it was the beginning of a new walk where I would recommit my heart to Jesus Christ. I was humbled to learn that God sent his son to die for a sinner like me.

His mother Barbara was overheard telling a friend over the telephone: 'I've got some exciting news. George has been born again.'[3]

Bush started attending Bible classes, with a tutor who had been heavily influenced by reading the works of Francis Schaeffer, and the following year took the second momentous step, on his fortieth birthday, of giving up drinking. The reasons for this are interesting and have varied. In *A Charge to Keep* he says it was because drinking magnified aspects of his personality that didn't need to be any larger: it 'made me more funny, more charming (I thought), more irrepressible. Also, according to my wife, somewhat boring and repetitive.'⁴ A friend, however, told a biographer: 'He looked in the mirror and said, "Someday I might embarrass my father. It might get my dad in trouble." And boy, that was it. That's how high a priority it was. And he never took another drink.'⁵ Given the clannish, driven nature of the Bushes, this seems quite compelling too. Frum recalls him as president in the White House asking a group of clergy to pray for him, saying: 'You know, I had a drinking problem. Right now I should be in a bar in Texas, not the Oval Office. There is only one reason that I am in the Oval Office and not in a bar. I found faith. I found God. I am here because of the power of prayer.'⁶

There seems no reason to doubt the sincerity of Bush's conversion experience. What is more problematic is how it has been deployed in pursuit of office: perhaps more ostentatiously and ruthlessly than any previous incumbent, even though all of his predecessors have also professed to be Christians of various varieties. This has been not only personally helpful to George Bush and his immortal soul, but politically convenient and a good career move for an ambitious man in a party where the Religious Right had become increasingly influential. Bush's ability to apply the language and buzz-words of evangelical discourse, as a signal to followers that he really is one of them, motivated by the same juices and with the same interests at heart, has been extremely useful to him as he has climbed upwards. Without it he would never have become president.

Bush is not alone in this deployment of his religious belief. Many presidents, including his immediate predecessor, have made ostent-atious use of their personal faith. They often employ biblical cadences as rhetorical tools and have frequently learned their oratory from preachers. Perhaps the greatest of them, Abraham Lincoln, used such rhythms himself, even though he was by no means a regular church-goer: the Gettysburg Address shows that with its reference to 'this nation under God'. But Lincoln also enjoyed employing and some-times inventing a range of metaphors drawn from his rural upbringing: country sayings and farmyard observations – he called them 'mighty darn good lies' – that his listeners would have instantly recognised and appreciated.⁷ Sophisticates might deride him as a country bumpkin, but a nation of farmboys could understand his native shrewdness.

George W. Bush – evidently not in Lincoln's league as an orator – appears to employ his phrases almost as coded signs that may elude a general listener, who is no longer well versed in the language and stories of the Bible, but that will certainly ring bells with the evangelically inclined.

This so-called 'God Talk' takes several forms: there is the straight biblical allusion – or rather its seventeenth-century cadences – as in his response to the Columbia shuttle disaster in February 2003: 'Farther than we can see, there is comfort and hope. In the words of the Prophet Isaiah, "Lift your eyes and look to the heavens. Who created all these? He who brings out the starry hosts one by one and calls them each by name" . . . the same Creator who names the stars also knows the names of the seven souls we mourn today. The crew of the shuttle Columbia did not return safely to earth. Yet we can pray that all are safely home.'[8] It is hard to think of another modern politician likely to quote so readily from Isaiah using the language of Tudor England. Again, in a speech about AIDS: 'When we see the wounded traveller on the road to Jericho we will not – America will not – pass to the other side of the road.'

Then there is the biblical-sounding cadence, where scriptural rhetoric is used, as in Bush's address to Congress on 20 September 2001, just after the Al-Qaeda attacks: 'Great harm has been done to us. We have suffered great loss. And in our grief and anger we have found our mission and our moment.'[9]

Repeatedly there is the juxtaposition of good and evil, the language of opposites, to create a moral tension, as in the same speech: 'Freedom and fear are at war . . . Fellow citizens, we'll meet violence with patient justice . . .' Or, in his speech to the UN two months later: 'We're confident that history has an author who fills time and eternity with his purpose. We know that evil is real but good will prevail against it.'

Peter Singer, the Princeton philosopher, has analysed the president's statements and says: 'No other president in living memory has spoken so often about good and evil, right and wrong.' He mentioned the word 'evil' in 30 per cent of the speeches he gave in his first two and a half years in office and furthermore used 'evil' far more often as a noun than as an adjective (914 uses to 182).[10] The language of good and evil, of course, the contrasting choice of opposites, the good way and the bad way, is central to evangelical discourse.

And, above all, there are the textbook-sure, approved answers to standard evangelical questions, references to the importance of prayer, the role of pastors, and particularly the imperative of being born again. An example of this occurred during a meeting in Austin, Texas, with Bishop Keith Butler of the 18,000-strong Word of Faith International Christian Center of Southfield, Michigan, in 1999 when Governor Bush was considering running for president. The bishop asked: 'Governor, are you born again?' When Bush replied 'yes', the bishop asked, 'How do you know it?' Bush answered by quoting Romans 10:9: 'That if thou shalt confess with thy mouth the Lord Jesus and shalt believe in thy heart that God hath raised him from the dead, thou shalt be saved.' Then he added: 'I've been changed inside. My life has been transformed. Jesus is my Lord.'[11] And lo, Butler went on his way rejoicing and pledged his support to the candidate. Compare and contrast Phil Gramm's experience with James Dobson.

During the 2000 campaign, Bush was asked which was his favourite philosopher and did not miss a beat in answering 'Jesus Christ'. He then added by way of explanation: 'because he changed my heart', a simple response that must have caused sighs of relief and satisfaction to Christian souls across the USA. It may even have been the answer that secured his victory. It may be trite, it might even have been anticipated beforehand and been carefully worked up, but it was certainly the only credible answer the candidate could have given – Wittgenstein would not have met the need. And it was mightily effective.

Thus again, Billy Graham's original question in 1985 about being 'right with God', a phrase repeated by President Bush during his re-election campaign in 2004: 'I know we're all sinners but I have accepted Jesus Christ as my personal savior. I know what it means to be right with God.' There are several buzz-phrases at work here, to be recognised and decoded by evangelicals: the acceptance of being a sinner, as we all are, the acceptance of (and conversion by) Jesus Christ, and thus the assurance of being thereby right with God. The words may be formulaic, but they are as transparent to evangelicals as the Catechism used to be to Catholic children – though it's hard to imagine a Catholic candidate these days plucking an answer out of that particular little booklet.

Being able to talk the talk like this was what secured the younger Bush his role of liaising with evangelical groups for his father's campaign for the presidency in 1988. It enabled him to make useful contacts for the future too: 'His father wasn't comfortable dealing with religious types,' one staffer explained. 'George knew exactly what to do.' Doug Wead, an evangelical adviser to the campaign told the *Washington Post* that on meeting the younger Bush he knew immediately 'that I wasn't going to have to write a 20 page memo explaining what "born again" means'.[12]

Such clear identification with a particular brand of Christianity has its drawbacks of course, in occasional errors of tone: as when Bush referred to a 'crusade' against Muslim terrorism, where the word was laden with entirely different resonances, of historic Christian enmity and persecution to the Islamic world, than it has among US evangelicals. There are also dangers in alienating one section of the Christian vote while pacifying another. This was illustrated by his decision in the 2000 campaign to make a speech at the fundamentalist Bob Jones University, a place where they still forbid interracial dating – it was also the college that sued over the loss of its tax-exempt status in the 1970s – and where there remains a tendency to refer to the Pope as the anti-Christ and Catholicism as a satanic cult (it is the place that granted the Revd Ian Paisley his doctorate as well). This caused a crisis in Bush's drive to win both black and Catholic votes and led to him writing a grovelling letter of apology to Cardinal O'Connor of New York. It is a narrow and difficult path, fraught with many pitfalls. As it happens, for a variety of reasons, electorally Bush has won the Catholic vote, though it remains a fickle constituency for Republicans.

Bush's clear sense of divine mission is amply attested, though the White House has found it necessary to deny that he believes he is getting his instructions direct from God, and in October 2004 spokesmen specifically denied Pat Robertson's claim that the president had said he had been guaranteed a low casualty count in Iraq – which, three years on, given what has happened since, may be just as well.[13]

Nevertheless, the president is not only right with God, but is also sure both that God wanted him to run for office and that his precepts are guiding Bush in his daily decision-making. This too is part of the evangelical package. Thus he told the Texan evangelist James Robison in 1999:

> I feel like God wants me to run for President. I can't explain it, but I sense my country is going to need me. Something is going to happen and, at that time, my country is going to need me. I know it won't be easy on me or my family, but God wants me to do it.
>
> In fact I really don't want to run. My father was president. My whole family has been affected by it. I know the price. I know what it will mean. I would be perfectly happy to have people point at me some day when I am buying fishing lures at Wal-Mart and say, 'That was our governor.' That's all I want. And if I run for president that kind of life will be over. My life will never be the same. But I feel God wants me to do this and I must do it.[14]

This aw-shucks folkiness caused Robison to announce later, with no apparent obtuseness: 'Governor Bush doesn't want to use God to get elected. He doesn't want to ride in on a God plank. He just wants God to use him.'[15]

How useful, opponents of evangelicalism sometimes say, for God to prescribe what you are planning to do anyway. But Bush's remarks about his reluctance to run have been a regular refrain to intimates. David Kuo, a special assistant to the president on faith matters between 2001 and 2003, recounts in his book *Tempting Faith* an almost identical conversation when he first met Governor Bush in 1998, when Bush was apparently still deciding whether he would be a candidate: 'He kept rolling on. "I can't do this unless I know that God is calling me to do this . . . the sacrifices are too intense, the strain on Laura, my girls would just be too great." '[16]

The president gets his input from God through prayer: 'People say: "When do you pray?" I pray all the time. All the time. You don't need a chapel to pray, I don't think. Whether it be in the Oval Office, I mean, you just do it. That's just me. I don't say that to try to get votes. I'm just sharing that experience with you." '

Presidents have frequently invoked their sense of the USA's special position, its divine dispensation from God to be a beacon for mankind: Governor Winthrop's shining city on a hill and John Witherspoon's sense in eighteenth-century Princeton that God was bestowing his providence on America still resonate. Very few, however, have asserted they are running by divine command or intention. Presumably God has also sanctioned the compromises and evasions, the ruthlessness and the periodic punch below the belt that George W. Bush, like all successful politicians, has occasionally employed to vanquish his opponents.

The Puritan concept of the special, God-given, nation set above the rest remains strong. It leads to an assumption that the USA's understanding of such concepts as liberty and democracy are self-evident and unchallengeable because they were handed down by God as a special gift first to Americans.

George Bush has often said this, citing them increasingly as justifications for the wars in Afghanistan and Iraq. Thus, in the third presidential debate with John Kerry in Arizona in 2004: 'I believe that God wants everybody to be free. That's what I believe. And that's one part of my foreign policy. In Afghanistan I believe that the freedom there is a gift from the Almighty. And I can't tell you how encouraged I am to see freedom on the march. And so my principles that I make decisions on are part of me. And religion is part of me.'[17]

And again, in a speech in Pennsylvania in October 2004: 'Freedom is on the march in this world. I believe everybody in the Middle East desires to live in freedom. I believe women in the Middle East want to live in a free society. I believe mothers and fathers want to raise their children in a free and peaceful world. I believe all these things because freedom is not America's gift to the world, freedom is the Almighty God's gift to each man and woman in this world.'

President Bush stops short of saying God is an American, but clearly indicates his sense that he is carrying out God's purposes, as in a speech in May 2004: 'Our part, our calling, is to align our hearts and actions with God's plan, in so far as we can know it . . . we cannot be neutral in the face of injustice or cruelty or evil. God is not on the side of any nation, yet we know he is on the side of justice. And it is the

deepest strength of America that from the hour of our founding, we
have chosen justice as our goal.'

This noble aspiration may cause a certain sharp intake of breath
from those recalling the scandal of the Abu Ghraib prison abuse,
which was actually the context for the president's remarks. The divine
mission has its drawbacks in office: a moral certainty that one is
fulfilling God's will is a potentially dangerous assumption to make,
going far beyond the normal politician's conceit that they are
indispensable. It also grates with those parts of the electorate that do
not share the politician's own sense of his manifest destiny. They find
it irksome, if not sanctimonious, and tend to view it as arrogance or
hubris, particularly when things are going badly.

This is not to question the justice of Bush's moral outrage at the
terrorist attacks of 9/11, but it is to query the justifications he has
sometimes used for the decisions he has made in office. Even before
that black day, Bush seemed to be asserting that his administration
would be part of the working out of a divine plan for the USA: as in
his remarks during the 2000 election that 'our nation is chosen by God
and commissioned by history to be a model to the world of justice'.
This was amplified after 2001 in his February 2003 speech at a
National Prayer Breakfast gathering: 'We can also be confident in the
ways of providence, even when they are far from our understanding.
Events aren't moved by blind change and chance. Behind all of life
and all of history, there's a dedication and purpose, set by the hand of
a just and faithful God. And that hope will never be shaken.'[18]

This sense of certainty tends to breed a sort of solipsism, which may
be understandable in a big and powerful country far removed
geographically from much of the rest of the world. It is certainly
something that is still currently widely shared by very many of its
citizens: when in the aftermath of the September 2001 attacks, the
Methodist Church in Belfast felt moved to send a message of
sympathy and fellow-feeling to their counterparts in New York, having
lived with bomb attacks and sectarian violence for more than thirty
years, they were slightly disconcerted to receive back a message saying
that at last the world had woken up to the menace of terrorism.

Americans often appear to see the world filtered through their own
uniquely introspective perspective, assuming in Mansfield's words 'as

though all other nations are somewhere on the road to becoming Americans'. George W. Bush appears to exemplify that. Perhaps it was inevitable given the shocking and devastating suddenness of the attacks on 11 September 2001 that the president should have taken it so personally, but that sense of identification seems to crop up fairly regularly. Briefing reporters in September 2002 on the necessity of removing Saddam Hussein in Iraq, he offered as his concluding reasoning: 'After all, this is the guy who tried to kill my dad,' which as a rationale for committing his country to war may not have been an entirely happy one.

It is also a perspective that limits his ability to deal with a strange and menacing outside world where people do not necessarily act in accordance with the precepts of the Bible or by being motivated in the same way as evangelical US Christians. Nowhere has that been more evident than in his dealings with the Middle East, where, as early as the spring of 2001, he was suggesting that peace would come there when people in the region started to share the USA's philosophical belief in religious freedom. He told a dinner at the American Jewish Committee convention in Washington: 'The Middle East is the birthplace of three great religions: Judaism, Christianity and Islam. Lasting peace in the region must respect the rights of believers in all these faiths. That's common sense. But it is also something more: it is moral sense, based on the deep American commitment to freedom of religion.'

The president often cites this freedom. He has insisted that Islam is a religion of peace and has paid visits to synagogues and mosques. This is not something that finds favour with some fundamentalist supporters, such as the Revd W. A. Criswell of the First Baptist Church of Dallas, one of the largest churches in the USA, who once famously remarked: 'Does God Almighty hear the prayers of a Jew?' to which his answer, confidently on God's behalf, was 'no'.

The president prayed with a group of US Sikhs when they visited the White House in the aftermath of the World Trade Center attacks after an American Sikh was murdered by a gunman in the mistaken belief that he must be a terrorist. This also does not go down terribly well with some in the Religious Right constituency where the essential wickedness of Islam has become an article of faith, beyond debate, since 9/11.

In an interview with editors of religious publications, the president told them: 'My job is to make sure that, as president, people understand that in this country you can worship any way you choose. And I'll take that a step further. You can be a patriot if you don't believe in the Almighty. You can honour your country and be as patriotic as your neighbour.'[19]

Bush retains this ecumenical spirit in his weekly worship at the White House. When in Washington on a Sunday, he usually attends the nearest church, St John's, the other side of Lafayette Square and a minute's drive away. It is part of the liberal Episcopal diocese of Washington, whose bishop John Chane has been a doughty and outspoken supporter of that church's openly gay bishop, Gene Robinson, and a critic of worldwide Anglicanism's more funda-mentalist tendency. The National Cathedral, Bishop Chane's diocesan church high on the hill above Georgetown, dominates the skyline of the capital and continues to provide the setting for important services of national mourning and commemoration, despite the controversies that are currently splitting the Episcopal Church. It was where the funeral service was held for another president, Gerald Ford, a lifelong Episcopalian, in January 2007, with the current president reading the lesson.

George Bush's theology appears to be broad, rather than deep: 'I think he believes the essentials and has no interest in the inessentials,' one contact told David Aikman for his book on Bush called *A Man of Faith* in 2003. Bush has said his daily reading matter before he gets up in the morning includes *My Utmost for His Highest*, which is a book of homilies by Oswald Chambers, a late nineteenth-century Scottish Baptist minister, much influenced by Spurgeon, who held the traditional view that man must not waste his time frivolously, but must use his God-given gifts for the good of others.

Chambers, who died from appendicitis while serving as a chaplain during the First World War, tends to be on the dour side as an inspirational writer. His God demands our unswerving commitment, an 'absolute and irrevocable surrender of the will' with no backsliding: 'If we turn away from obedience for even one second, darkness and death are immediately at work again.' He is a stern God, ever ready to test men's faith and self-control to see how real they are: 'God frequently has to knock the bottom out of your experience . . . to get you in direct contact with Himself,' and so setbacks are merely his way of checking up on you and strengthening your resolve. This is therefore not a God who is particularly keen on letting you evaluate for yourself – or, perhaps, apologise when things go wrong in life – because you (and He) will be vindicated in the end. Chambers's experience in the First World War appears, however, to have modified his views somewhat: 'If war has made me reconciled with the fact that there is sin in human beings, I shall no longer go with my head in the clouds, or buried in the sand like an ostrich, but I shall be wishing to face facts as they are.'[20]

The president has also sidled up to the Catholic vote by lauding the late Pope John Paul II, even though he ignored his outspoken opposition to the war in Iraq. An unnamed White House official told David Aikman about Bush's meeting with John Paul II in 2002, a time when the Pope was already in deteriorating health and scarcely able to speak: 'I think if you asked the president who was a great person in the last 500 years, he'd say the pope . . . He (Bush) was almost without words in Rome. It wasn't just that the president was in the presence of human greatness, but in the presence of a great Christian. [The president] has enormous catholicity of the spirit.'[21]

Despite his attempts to demonstrate his commitment to religious inclusiveness, the president's administration has been seen by its critics as the most ostentatiously theocratic of any in the nation's history, in the sense of claiming to be working in accordance with Christian principles, as perceived by its rhetoric, its courting of the Religious Right, its apparent domestic priorities and in those who have been appointed to senior positions both in its government and in federal agencies.

By several accounts, the atmosphere inside the White House can resemble a prayer meeting (and indeed some offices hold such meetings first thing every morning). According to his memoir, when David Frum, the president's speech writer who is Jewish, first turned up at the White House the first words he heard were: 'Missed you at Bible study'. He was also rebuked when overheard to say 'damn'. Famously, on Palm Sunday 2002, when the president and his colleagues found themselves on board Air Force One coming back from a visit to El Salvador, they held an impromptu service, culminating in the singing of 'Amazing Grace' and hugs all round.[22]

The administration has included a number of figures notable for their religious connections, including Don Evans, the president's old friend from Texas, who helped Bush with his conversion in the 1980s and went on to serve as his Secretary of Commerce, and Karen Hughes, his press secretary in Texas who went with him to the White House as presidential counsel, who is a Presbyterian elder. Kay Cole James, placed in charge of the president's Office of Personnel – essentially overseeing the entire federal workforce – is not only the former dean of Pat Robertson's Regent University, but was also previously a vice-president of the Family Research Council, the Washington lobbyists aligned to James Dobson's Focus on the Family. Christian believers are in post at the Department of Health and Human Services, to promote abstinence and marriage, and the White House has its own Christian Outreach team to liaise with and consult evangelical and conservative groups about the political agenda and every facet of the president's policy.

David Kuo, himself a committed evangelical, who served in the White House during the president's first term, says of the team's leader, Tim Goeglein (a friend of the conservative polemicist William Buckley):

> He talked to religious conservatives about everything: judges, stem cell research, abortion, presidential appointments, health care and anything else they wanted to discuss . . . They held weekly – or more often as necessary – conference calls to update their community on events and announcements while simultaneously soliciting their feedback. Regulars on the call were Tom Minnery, head of public policy for James Dobson's Focus on the Family; Ted Haggard, pastor of New Life Church in Colorado Springs and head of the National Association of Evangelicals; Deal Hudson, conservative Catholic and publisher of *Crisis* magazine; Jay Sekulow, head of Pat Robertson's American Center for Law and Justice; Ken Connor, then head of the Family Research Council; Richard Land, president of the Southern Baptist Convention's Ethics and Religious Liberty

Commission; and Christian talk radio hosts, Janet Parshall and Michael Reagan, among others.[23]

Interestingly, when Haggard was subsequently exposed shortly before the Congressional midterm elections in November 2006 as having had long-term dealings with a male prostitute, including buying drugs from him, the White House quickly denied having had any regular contacts with him at all. Why, they scarcely knew the man. Haggard himself went into counselling in early 2007 for three weeks and emerged to proclaim himself 'completely heterosexual', which, since he had denied having had any gay sexual experiences, was perhaps not surprising. He appeared unlikely, however, to resume his ministry in Colorado's evangelical capital.

Condoleezza Rice, the Secretary of State in the second term, makes much of her inheritance as the daughter of a Presbyterian minister in the Deep South. When she addressed the Southern Baptists' convention in June 2006 it was, understandably, the very first point she made to them:

> I grew up in church. I do pray every day and, in times of heartache I find consolation in the power of prayer . . . Too many people can only whisper their religious faith . . . The Government has no right to stand between the individual and the Almighty.

The convention gave her a standing ovation for that and the choir burst into a rousing rendition of 'God Bless America'.

There are a string of others too of whom, in the first term, John Ashcroft, the Attorney General, who is a Pentecostal and the son and grandson of hellfire preachers, was the most outstanding, some would say notorious. Ashcroft's habit at important junctures of his life, such as his appointment to office, was to have himself anointed with oil (he tended to use Crisco cooking oil as that was most easily available) in the manner of 'the ancient kings of Israel'. He does not dance, sing or drink (of course), but apparently plays a very mean game of basketball, verging on cheating according to his former aide, David Kuo.[24] One of his first acts in office was to order the draping of a cloth over the bare bosom of the statue of the Spirit of Justice at the entrance to his department.

These were mere personal eccentricities, but the identification was palpable: as a critic says, he appears to regard every defeat as a personal crucifixion and every victory a resurrection.[25] Ashcroft made no bones about his priorities as a senator from Missouri, or in government: 'I don't particularly care if I do what's right in the sight of men. The important thing is for me to do right in God's sight,' he has said.

Ashcroft once told an audience at Bob Jones University: 'Unique among the nations, America recognised the source of our character as being godly and eternal, not being civic and temporal'; he believes Jefferson's celebrated wall between Church and state is nothing but a wall of 'religious oppression' because it hinders the creation of the godly nation he seeks. To this end, he expunged the phrase 'there is no higher calling than public service' from the letterheads of his department, arguing that service to God was rather the higher calling.

Many such proclivities were known before Ashcroft's appointment and in office he used his powers in an extraordinary way, particularly over the issue of abortion. He subpoenaed hundreds of hospital records of women who had undergone abortions previously, claiming he needed to access them to check whether they had had partial-birth abortions, which were made illegal by President Bush in 2003. He also attempted to close down a Department of Justice task force which was investigating groups that threatened violence against abortion clinics.

This was all of a piece with other administration initiatives on abortion and other areas of social policy, which will be examined in more detail in the next chapter. Ashcroft left after Bush's first term, but such moves have been echoed by other appointees at a number of levels, including measures of extraordinary pettiness. These include the editing of the video screened at the Lincoln Memorial in Washington DC to cut out a few seconds of footage of gay rights, pro-choice and anti-Vietnam demonstrations and the substitution of a pro-Gulf War rally instead; and the insertion of a provision into the 2004 Defence Appropriations Bill to privatise a 1-acre patch of land in the middle of the 1.5 million-acre Mojave National Preserve in California. This was a spot on which an 8-foot-high cross had previously been erected, in defiance of the Constitutional separation provisions, and privatisation allowed it to be put back in situ.

Such measures are merely silly symbols, but they play into a perception of the administration's priorities and its willingness to pander to a sectarian constituency. As with the stocking of the creationist book at the Grand Canyon bookshop, they are usefully largely cost-free gestures. It is clearly not the sort of thing the president would get involved in personally, but the people the administration appoints do.

Perhaps rather more importantly for the administration's credibility, in late 2006 David Kuo's book *Tempting Faith* appeared. That questioned the White House's commitment to a core objective of its social policy: its faith-based initiative, which has been frequently cited by the president as a special priority. This is the idea that federal funding to aid the disadvantaged members of US society should be channelled particularly to faith groups and charities. As a semi-privatisation project its aims are both to recognise the work that religiously based charities do in society and to underscore the ideas of Christian theorists such as Marvin Olasky that they are actually a better, more effective and efficient way of delivering aid. Olasky, born a Jew, once a convert to Marxism and now a born-again Christian and professor of journalism and another of those attracted to the theocratic ideas of Reconstructionism, has been much criticised even by some conservatives, for suggesting that the small-scale Christian charitable works he espouses could fill national needs for social provision. He believes Christian organisations should: 'teach rich and poor what the Bible has to say about wealth and poverty. Help a poor person negotiate the legal system. Employ a jobless person. Lead a neighborhood association in a poor part of town. Start a crisis pregnancy center. Give a pregnant teenager a room in your house. House a homeless person. Adopt a child' – and that would really form a comprehensive solution to the problems of poverty and deprivation. His picture of a compassionate America, where such things allegedly originally occurred in the days before welfare mucked everything up in its non-judgmental, bureaucratic way, has been described by David

Brooks of the conservative *Weekly Standard* as 'so crude and pinched that one suspects his main effect will be to buttress the stereotypes of those who are prejudiced against religious conservatives'.[26]

Nevertheless, the theory informs a centrepiece of Bush's much vaunted 'compassionate conservatism' policy, a way in the president's words 'to welcome people of faith in helping meet social objectives'. Bush trialled some of this with mixed success when he was governor of Texas, but in the White House he has announced large amounts of federal money for such schemes – over $1,000 million in 2003 alone, to be channelled into mentoring schemes for children whose parents were in prison, and for the treatment of drug addicts.

Yet David Kuo, brought into the White House in 2001 as a true believer to be special assistant to the president in implementing the faith-based initiatives policy, claims they have not worked because the White House has actually been indifferent to the programme and reluctant to fund it. In his angry book, published in late 2006, he claims that much smaller amounts were actually made available – $80 million – and that what there was was given only to Christian groups, rather than to charities from all faiths as the president had promised. Kuo tells of meeting a woman who reviewed grant applications for the Compassion Capital Fund: 'When I saw one of those non-Christian groups in the set I was reviewing, I just stopped looking at them and gave them a zero . . . Was there a problem with that?'[27]

Kuo, a Chinese-American who had worked for John Ashcroft when he was a senator, was employed on the project for two years but left disillusioned. Most attention has been focused on his claims that some senior White House staff thought the Christians were bothersome nuts:

> This strategy wasn't about honor or dignity, it was raw politics of the sort that old-time political bosses would applaud. Even sadder, the Christian community that elected George W. Bush didn't see any of this. They couldn't; they trusted their Christian brother too much . . . No group was more eye-rolling about Christians than the political affairs shop. They knew 'the nuts' were politically invaluable, but that was the extent of their usefulness. Sadly, [they] complained most often and most loudly

about how boorish many politically involved Christians were. They didn't see much of the love of Jesus in their lives.[28]

Kuo has a vignette about his briefing the president in 2003 before a meeting with black pastors. Bush said: 'All these guys care about is money...How much money have we given them?' 'Sir, we've given them virtually nothing because we have had virtually nothing new to give.' 'Nothing, what do you mean we've given them nothing? Don't we have new money in programs like the Compassion Fund thing?' 'No, sir. In the last two years we've gotten less than $80 million in new grants.'

Under pressure from the president's adviser Karl Rove, Kuo says he then admitted that there was technically about $800 million in existing programmes that were now eligible for faith-based groups, but they had been getting money from those programmes already anyway for years. The president replied: 'Eight billion. That's what we'll tell them. Eight billion in new funds for faith-based groups. Okay, let's go.'[29]

Perhaps the only surprise is that Kuo, who had been a political speech-writer for years, was himself surprised at this example of politics as normal:

Christians trust their Christian president. This is true of their evangelical political leadership. But of greater consequence, for Christian moms who home-school their kids and Christian dads coaching soccer and everyone who follows the Dobsons and Robertsons and Falwells, George W. Bush can really do no wrong.

They assume that since he professes Jesus that he won't do the kinds of things other politicians have done – break promises, cover up mistakes, parse words, say half-truths, be a politician. They figure he has surrounded himself with a staff full of other evangelicals to provide him with fellowship and accountability. That, after all, is the image carefully conveyed to them through religious surrogates.[30]

Others may be comforted that George W. Bush is just a politician after all. Would it have been different, would the faith-based initiatives have worked had they been properly funded and if the president and his administration had not been distracted by 9/11 and then the Afghan and Iraq wars, which have swallowed up so much money? Or was the programme always going to be pragmatic? The poor we have always with us, after all, and they will still be there after Bush leaves office. As it is, the rhetoric of the faith-based programme serves both sides: President Bush to demonstrate that he cares about the Christian community and its role in society; and his critics who say it demonstrates the theocratic nature of his administration.

It is impossible to avoid the conclusion that, while the president's religious convictions are perfectly sincere and available for use in pursuit of political advantage, they are not deployed if they are going to cost votes. The evangelical vote is important: one of the triumphs of his re-election in 2004 was the enticing back of 4 million Christians who voted for Bob Dole in a losing cause in the presidential election of 1996, but who failed to turn out in 2000 when Bush was elected by a whisker. But he can't be enslaved to their demands, otherwise he will alienate the rest of the electorate. There are limits to the Religious Right's influence and these are generally where they affect business, such as trade policy. They failed in their attempt to prevent Godless, communist China being granted most favoured nation trading status.

In the third presidential debate in October 2004, George W. Bush told his national television audience:

> My faith plays a big part in my life . . . I pray a lot. And I do. And my faith is a very – it's very personal. I pray for strength. I pray for wisdom. I pray for our troops in harm's way. I pray for my family. I pray for my little girls . . .
>
> That's the great thing about America is the right to worship the way you see fit. Prayer and religion sustain me. I receive calmness in the storms of the presidency. I love the fact that people pray for me and my family all around the country. Somebody asked me one time, 'well, how do you know?' I said, 'I just feel it.'
>
> Religion is an important part . . . I never want to impose my religion on anybody else. But when I make decisions I stand on

principle. And the principles are derived from who I am. I believe we ought to love our neighbor like we love ourself. That's manifested in public policy through the faith-based initiative where we've unleashed the armies of compassion to help heal people who hurt.[31]

Or, possibly, not.

13

Matters of Life and Death

'Stinking, filthy, dirty, rotten sin!'
Pam Stenzel, abstinence campaigner, 2003,
quoted in Michelle Goldberg, *Kingdom Coming*

Every 22 January in Washington DC opposing groups of protesters try to confront one another. They have to be kept apart by the police. One side shouts: 'Murderers!' The other: 'Keep your laws off my body!' It has become almost as traditional as Easter Parades: the commemoration of the date in 1973 when the Supreme Court ruled in the seminal case of *Roe* v. *Wade* that the state had no right to intervene to prevent a woman's private decision to have an abortion. John Ashcroft calls it 'a day in memoriam'. More than thirty years on, when most other Western countries have long since settled the issue politically, usually in favour of allowing women to terminate their pregnancies under certain circumstances, in the USA abortion remains a running sore. This is partly because it was decided judicially rather than democratically: a cause that remains a highly political rallying-point and a vehement and unending argument. In many ways it was the first great modern culture wars issue, because of the accident of the timing of the court's decision, just as unease was growing about the social and sexual hedonism of the 1960s.

More importantly, it was the first prominent issue to twin Roman Catholics and evangelical Protestants, formerly mutually suspicious when they weren't openly antagonistic towards each other, in a united crusade. More than three decades on, it remains the most potent issue, to rally and unite opponents and periodically to incite a few of them to violence. It has indeed been a struggle entirely activated by religious opponents, not secular ones. More than any other single cause, it has been responsible for the mobilisation of religious activism in US politics.

The great cultural and moral arguments in US society – abortion, gay marriages, euthanasia (as raised by the case of Terri Schiavo in

2005), even stem cell research – all hover uneasily around issues of sex and procreation: the fundamentals of life. Liberals say their opponents are motivated by a desire for control – control of other people's bodies and their right to decide how they spend their lives, a desire to reassert social controls, restore the idealised family unit and reimpose male authority, a reincarnation perhaps of that old Mencken definition of Puritans being those who want to stop other people being happy.

If this sounds overblown, consider Pat Robertson getting a trifle worked up while campaigning against equal rights in Iowa in 1992: 'The feminist agenda is not about equal rights for women. It is a socialist, anti-family, political movement that encourages women to leave their husbands, kill their children, practice witchcraft, destroy capitalism and become lesbians.'[1] Phew.

There are certainly conservative Bible-believers in both the UK and the USA who will argue that their belief in male headship – that women cannot be in charge, in the family, in church (hence no women priests or bishops) or in business – is scripturally based. It has not gone unnoticed that some such conservative believers in the USA tend to be rather less concerned about the sanctity of life once it is actually delivered than before it is born: not so worried about health and poverty issues, sexually transmitted diseases, wars, capital punishment (though here the coalition between Protestant evangelicals and many Catholics tends to splinter), not to mention the health of women who undergo illegal abortions.

The irony is that *Roe* v. *Wade* was settled almost in a fit of absent-mindedness by a vote of seven of the nine justices. At the time it was no great cause célèbre, fuelled by a rising public debate or funded by weighty interest groups. 'Jane Roe', the woman in the case arguing for her right to choose (who has since changed her mind and now opposes abortion – a valuable scalp for the Religious Right), was represented in the Supreme Court by two young women lawyers, Sarah Weddington and Linda Coffee, both in their twenties and graduates of the Texas Law School.[2] They were seeking to get the woman's right to an abortion enshrined in the US Constitution and what they got was a Supreme Court precedent, based on privacy and the reassertion of federal exclusion from individuals' decision-making. In other contexts, that removal of state interference is precisely the sort of thing that many on the political Right demand in the name of liberty for citizens. They want to get the state out of their lives, except in so far as it is available to control other people's.

Although the Catholic Church opposed the ruling from the outset, based on its canon law, rather than biblical, understanding of the sacredness of human life and its assumption that every sexual act must be open to procreation, many evangelicals either ignored it, or actually praised the Supreme Court's decision. The Bible does not make a big thing of abortion; indeed, it does not mention it at all in the modern sense except, depending on the interpretation of certain passages – Numbers 31:17 for example – where it suggests that some children might appropriately be killed.

The Southern Baptist convention had already in 1971 called for legislation that would 'allow the possibility of abortion under such conditions as rape, incest, clear evidence of severe foetal deformity and carefully ascertained evidence of the likelihood of damage to the emotional, mental and physical health of the mother'. Greeting the *Roe* v. *Wade* decision, the *Baptist Press* claimed: 'Religious liberty, human equality and justice are advanced by the Supreme Court abortion decision', while W. A. Criswell (the Dallas Baptist pastor who believes God does not hear the prayers of Jews) welcomed it by saying: 'I have always felt that it was only after a child was born and had a life separate from its mother that it became an individual person and it has always, therefore, seemed to me that what is best for the mother and for the future should be allowed.'[3]

The change came over the next few years, as white Protestant groups became concerned that the IRS was depriving them of money for their schools that they began to change their mind about judicial activism. They also began to reconsider when life could be said to begin: and that perhaps it was much further back in the development process than their predecessors, or even the Revd W. A. Criswell, had previously believed. For some it now goes right back to before the moment of fertilisation, which should in no circumstances be prevented. In making common cause with the Catholics, their historic opposition to Catholic schools – and especially state funding for such institutions, which were teaching 'wrong doctrine' – also melted away.

As the movement mobilised, it astutely switched its rhetoric from saying it was anti-abortion to pro-life, or pro-family, a concept that few can be opposed to, bearing with it as it does the imputation that those supporting women's rights to abortion are pro-death. It is a stance that allows for little nuance – what if you hope that abortions should be rare and would be with better advice and contraception, but believe that they should at least be available to women in some circumstances? – and it has wrong-footed the women's movement on the moral argument ever since. Among evangelicals in recent years the argument has tended to revolve around whether abortions should be allowed in any circumstances, even if the pregnancies are the result of incidents in which the mother has been raped or abused, or where her health is in danger. Absolutists like Dr James Dobson believe there should be no exceptions and can point to one of their number, Dr James Robison, the Texas pastor who was one of Bush's first supporters, who himself is the offspring of a woman who was raped.

The abortion issue remains politicised, not only because it has united religious activists, and because politicians including presidents have taken it up in a partisan way, but because it was never settled by political debate, instead of being decided by the Supreme Court. This is the prime reason behind the argument about judicial activism and the Religious Right's campaign to find judges for the Supreme Court who will reverse this particular decision above all others. They want judges who will act on their personal and religious beliefs rather than on the weight of legal arguments presented to them.

For twenty years, since the nomination of Robert Bork in 1987, the focus of questioning of potential justices has centred not on their experience and legal knowledge, but on their personal opinions, particularly about abortion and whether they would seek to overturn *Roe* v. *Wade*. George Bush has said there should be no litmus test for sitting on the Supreme Court, but his nominees to this and other courts have all tended in one direction. Thus Michael McConnell, nominee for the federal appeals courts, says *Roe* v. *Wade* was 'a gross misinterpretation of the Constitution' and Bill Pryor, the former Attorney General of Alabama and supporter of Judge Roy Moore, thought it 'the worst abomination of constitutional law in our history'.[4]

For the first time in the Supreme Court's history, five of its nine members are Roman Catholics, a fact that is of importance only because the justices' religious allegiances are now considered central to their role. The current, recently appointed, Chief Justice, John Roberts, who is Catholic and a conservative, said at his confirmation hearing that he regarded the decision as settled law and he is against overturning precedents, but there is yet to be a test case on abortion that might set a new template.

When, in 2005, the president's nominee for the Supreme Court, Harriet Miers, was under pressure because of her perceived lack of judicial experience, Bush defended her on the basis that she was an evangelical Christian, which seemed to indicate the nature of his litmus test. The White House also dropped the word to Dr James Dobson, who perhaps too hastily broadcast his endorsement too: 'I believe she will be a good justice [who belongs] to a very conservative church, which is almost universally pro-life.'[5] In the end, even this imprimatur was not enough to save her. But the perception is that it is the reliability of one's religious views rather than one's legal reputation that counts.

Or medical expertise for that matter. In December 2002 the Bush administration nominated Dr W. David Hager for chairman of the Advisory Committee for Reproductive Drugs at the federal Food and Drug Administration, the accrediting organisation for contraceptive medicines and devices. He was an interesting choice: a Kentucky obstetric gynaecologist who is a member of the Christian Medical Association and Focus on the Family's Physician Resource Council, who has written and spoken extensively about religion and contraception. In a work entitled *As Jesus Cared for Women*, he suggests that the deciding factor in conception is not a woman's age, position or experience, but that: 'God is looking for people of faith who will trust Him in every part of life . . . Remarkable miracles of conception still occur.'[6] He declines in his practice to prescribe contraceptives to unmarried women, including inter-uterine devices whose function is to prevent conception in the first place: 'My first option for them is abstinence,' he says. In a further book, *Stress and the Woman's Body*, co-written with his wife, he suggests prayer as a treatment for ailments such as headaches and cancer.

In the end Hager was not made chairman, merely a member of the committee, taking his seat alongside two other administration appointees: Joseph Stanford, a doctor who likewise refuses to prescribe contraceptives because they are 'detrimental to marriage' and who believes that the Catholic Church's opposition to the practice is the result of divine inspiration, and Sue Crockett, of the 2,500-member-strong American Association of Pro-Life Obstetricians and Gynaecologists.

In early 2004 the committee came to deliberate on whether Plan B, an emergency morning-after contraceptive pill, should be made available for over the counter sales. The medical advice was that it was a pregnancy preventative rather than an abortion device, that it had passed all its clinical trials, and that it had never been associated with a single serious complication or a death, but a member of the Concerned Women for America group argued that sexual predators might keep stocks of Plan B in their pockets to feed to their victims. Convinced by the medical evidence, the committee voted by twenty-three votes to four to authorise the drug. Normally, that would have settled the matter, leaving it only to be rubber-stamped by the FDA. However, Dr Hager lobbied hard, producing a minority report and, despite the overwhelming vote, the authority declined to give Plan B its authorisation.[7] Given Dr Hager's beliefs and the fact that Plan B is clearly a preventative device, one must conclude that his objection was chiefly a religious rather than a medical one.

Conservative politicians long ago gave up trying to pass a legislative ban outlawing all or most abortions, though Senator Jesse Helms attempted to get a Constitutional amendment to that effect in the mid-1970s. Instead, they have sought to pare away around the edges: regulating to make it more difficult to get access to a pregnancy advice centre – six out of every seven counties in the USA now have no such facilities – limiting funds to voluntary organisations offering such advice, and channelling money instead to pro-life groups. It is easy populist legislation at state as well as national level: in the 2000 legislative session in Michigan alone there were twenty-three Bills seeking to limit women's abortion rights.

Some pro-life groups run Crisis Pregnancy Centers that exist entirely to dissuade women from terminating their pregnancies and that now receive federal funding. There are about 4,000 such centres, often advertising under neutral-sounding names such as resource or 'help centers', and sometimes setting up in the same buildings as abortion clinics in the hope of deflecting their clientele. Indeed the journalist Michelle Goldberg came across a booklet by a group called the Pearson Foundation entitled *How to Start and Operate Your Own Pro-Life Outreach Crisis Pregnancy Center*, which advocates organisations should do just that: 'If the girl who would be going to the abortion chamber sees your office first with a similar name, she will probably come into your center.' Once there, the women are sometimes shown highly graphic videos about abortions and often told what purports to be advice about the health risks of having an abortion – erroneously, that it is likely to cause them to contract breast cancer for example – given to them by unqualified activists dressed in white coats so they look like doctors. The centres, she says, buy ultrasound equipment so that the women can see the foetuses moving. One account on a Planned Parenthood website, quoted by Goldberg, says a woman who wandered by mistake into a centre operating out of the same building as the abortion clinic she was seeking was given a scan and subsequently handed an ultrasound photograph with the words 'Hi Mommy!' typed underneath.[8]

Although several presidents have promised to act against abortions – and Republican presidents have been in power for twenty-two of the thirty-four years since the Supreme Court's decision – the Bush administration has taken more high-profile action than its predecessors. President Reagan at one stage promised an abortion ban but never tried to implement one, and George Bush Senior actually ran as a pro-choice candidate. His son has made up for that, however. In 2003, President Bush signed the Partial Birth Abortion Ban – a measure previously twice vetoed by President Clinton – into law and the following year also signed the Unborn Victims Act. The first prevents the tiny proportion of late-stage abortions where the foetus has to be induced, and the second makes a criminal who murders a pregnant woman also liable for the death of her unborn baby.

In signing the Partial Birth Ban the president proclaimed: 'The most basic duty of government is to defend the life of the innocent. Every person however frail or vulnerable has a place and a purpose in this world . . . this right to life cannot be granted or denied by government because it does not come from government, it comes from the Creator of Life.' He described the process not as the destruction of a foetus but as 'the partial delivery of a live boy or girl and a sudden, violent end to that life'. His performance was greeted with joy by campaigners.[9]

In the overheated debate surrounding abortion, it is usually implied that such late-term abortions (and all other abortions) are a lifestyle choice by a woman deciding (tardily) that she cannot be bothered to have her baby. This is not true at all: it is calculated that in the USA (as in the UK) only 1.4 per cent of abortions are carried out after twenty-one weeks of pregnancy – about 21,000 – and the proportion performed after twenty-six weeks is the equivalent of one five-hundredth of 1 per cent (which would be about thirty in total each year): they are invariably carried out to safeguard the health of the mother or because the baby is so malformed or handicapped that it cannot survive birth. The president's action has therefore had maximum political benefit for a very limited practical effect, except of course to the women having to go through the trauma of a dead birth.

At the same time, the administration has been notably slow in chasing up those opponents of abortions who have targeted clinics and their clients for noisy and sometimes violent picketing. There have been seven murders and more than 200 bomb attacks or death threats directed at such clinics in the last thirty-four years, though, as we have seen, Attorney General Ashcroft tried at one stage to close down the Department of Justice task force tracking those making the threats.

Some of these groups have a fanaticism and fervour quite as zealous as John Brown in the days of slavery: men such as Randall Terry, founder of an organisation called Operation Rescue in the 1980s, another admirer of the theologian Francis Schaeffer, who quite happily compared his violent pickets of clinics and their staff to the civil disobedience of Martin Luther King and the resistance to the Nazis of Dietrich Bonhoeffer: 'Intolerance is a beautiful thing. We're going to make their lives a living hell.' After 9/11, Operation Rescue's website carried an arresting if perplexing image: the World Trade Center on fire and a picture of a bloody foetus, with the caption: 'Join the dots . . .'

Terry has now shifted his attention to campaigning against homosexuals, urging his followers to become 'intolerant zealots of baby killers, sodomites, condom pushers and that pluralism nonsense'.[10] Mr Terry is another whose beliefs are influenced by the Christian Reconstructionist philosophy of restoring biblical punishments and widening the use of the death penalty: 'We are called by God to conquer this country. I want you to let a wave of hatred wash over you . . . Those who love God must hate sin.'[11] Meanwhile, state regulations directed at abortion clinics surround them with restrictive legislation: South Carolina apparently even has a statute ordering that the lawns of clinics must be kept free of any grass that could harbour insects.

Such heightened rhetoric, a discourse of murder and threats of violence, has neither stopped abortions, nor converted the bulk of the nation away from sin and towards the paths of virtue and abstinence. It did not do so either in the mid-nineteenth century, that golden age of rustic rectitude and Protestant family values when abortions were legal and common. Despite all the current restrictions, about 1.5 million abortions continue to take place each year and polls show that about two-thirds of Americans favour its continued availability. A Gallup survey in the summer of 2005 found 65 per cent of respondents saying they favoured the appointment of a justice to the Supreme Court who would uphold the *Roe* v. *Wade* ruling, including 47 per cent of Republicans. At about the same time, a Pew Center poll also found 65 per cent supporting *Roe* v. *Wade* and 29 per cent saying it should be overturned. The same survey recorded 35 per cent of respondents saying abortion should be generally available, 23 per cent saying it should be more limited, 31 per cent saying it should be illegal except in cases of rape, incest or saving the mother's life, and just 9 per cent saying it should never be allowed.[12]

In contradiction of most polls of attitudes to modern mores, those most in favour of retaining abortion rights are older age groups. They presumably can remember what it used to be like in the days when abortions were illegal and between 500 and 1,000 women died each year following illicit procedures. Even in the 1950s and 1960s a million backstreet abortions were carried out each year. As recently as 1967 it was the prime killer of pregnant women, and in 1974, the year following the Supreme Court ruling, the maternal mortality rate in New York dropped by 45 per cent. By contrast, those most opposed to abortions are young, white evangelical Protestants. Research shows that fewer than a fifth of abortions carried out annually are on women under the age of twenty, while a third are on women over the age of thirty. Two-thirds of abortions are performed on women who have never been married and two-thirds also are on women who already have one or more children. Of all women under the age of forty-five, it is now estimated that a third will have had an abortion. Blacks and Latinas have higher termination rates than whites, Catholics account for a quarter of all abortions, and Protestants for nearly a half. There has been a decline in these statistics in the last decade, probably mainly due to the availability of emergency contraception – pace Dr Hager – but of all pregnancies in the USA each year, half are unplanned and half of those are terminated. Since *Roe* v. *Wade* until the end of 2002, 42 million pregnancies have been aborted or, as opponents would say, babies killed.[13]

Clearly, all the propaganda and controversy, all the zeal and all the preaching, has not changed behaviour. And, just as with the prohibition of alcohol, the likelihood is that legal sanctions would not stop the practice either. Even if some sort of national ban could be enacted it is likely that some states would decide to allow clinics still to operate. It is impossible not to conclude that the issue remains so alive because it is politically useful to keep it so: a convenient means of rallying the troops, a source of outrage to make sure they remain mobilised, and a way of pointing up the moral superiority of one's own side against the opposition. Perhaps it is easier all round to retain abortions and to rail against them, than to substantially restrict them or reform the law altogether. Clearly, a political consensus for compromise between greater and lesser evils just isn't there, for otherwise surely it would have been achieved at some point during the last third of a century.

The Bush administration's alternative route instead of abortion has been to promote abstinence education, teaching teenagers in schools not to have sex until they are married. The eight-point code of principles that qualify education programmes for federal funding was originally drawn up by the Heritage Foundation and tacked on to a Welfare Reform Bill in 1996 during the Clinton administration, but the principles have been enthusiastically endorsed by President Bush.

At their heart is teaching about the 'social, psychological and health' gains to be derived from abstaining from sexual activity. Children are to be taught that abstinence is the expected standard outside marriage, the only certain way to avoid unwanted pregnancies and sexually transmitted diseases and other harmful side-effects and responsibilities. They are also to be taught how to reject sexual advances and how alcohol and drug use increases vulnerability. Programmes with titles such as True Love Waits (a Southern Baptist programme), Virginity Rules, Abstinence Clearinghouse and the Silver Ring Thing – which was also introduced in the UK in 2005 – all have an overtly Christian message. The Ring Thing's is that its mission is 'offering a personal relationship with Jesus Christ as the best way to live a sexually pure life'. Its Sexual Abstinence Study Bible, given to participants in the programme, says: 'If you have accepted God's wonderful gift of salvation through his son, Jesus Christ, your name will be found in the Book of Life and you will spend eternity in heaven with God. If you have chosen to reject Christ then your final destination will be the lake of fire. No arguments. Case closed.'[14]

The administration gave $7 million in federal funding grants to specifically Christian organisations between 2001 and 2003, but nothing to non-Christian religious and secular charities working in the same field. Perhaps their applications fell foul of the woman David Kuo encountered from the charities' peer review panel, or one of her colleagues.

It seems that even abstinence may not be the priority for some Christian groups. Michelle Goldberg came across one such campaigner, Pam Stenzel, at a Reclaiming America for Christ conference in 2003, telling her audience that the success rate of the programme was not important to her:

> Does it work? You know what? Doesn't matter, because guess what: my job is not to keep teenagers from having sex . . . Our job should be to tell kids the truth . . . I don't care if it works because at the end of the day I am not answering to you, I am answering to God.
>
>   Let me tell you something, people of God . . . AIDs is not the enemy, HPV (sexually transmitted disease) and a

hysterectomy at 20 is not the enemy. An unplanned pregnancy is not the enemy. My child believing they can shake their fist in the face of God and sin without consequence and my child spending eternity separated from God is the enemy. I will not teach my child that they can sin safely.[15]

Premarital sex, she proclaimed, was 'stinking, filthy, dirty rotten sin'. Stenzel, who runs a company called Enlightenment Communications, which lectures to schools, was appointed by President Bush to the taskforce at the Department of Health and Human Services to help implement the abstinence education guidelines.

The president supported such programmes when he was governor of Texas (where he appointed a health commissioner who opposed condoms 'because it's not what God intended'), with distinctly mixed results – after six years, by 2001, Texan teenage pregnancy rates were one and a half times the national average and were falling at half the national rate, while instances of sexually transmitted diseases were rising – but he has repeatedly asserted his view that they are the only certain way.[16] The president told an audience at West Ashley High School in Charleston, South Carolina, in July 2002: 'You know, I've heard all this talk about abstinence programs and this that and the other, but let me just be perfectly plain. If you're worried about teenage pregnancy, or if you're worried about sexually transmitted disease, abstinence works every single time.'

Such teaching, that abstinence sets the most reliable standard, may be clearly the ideal, but unfortunately it lacks congruence with the real world. And what makes it worse, such programmes are not only forbidden to teach about contraception, at risk of losing their funding, but are also licensed to give out misleading information and to maximise its drawbacks. The intention is clearly to scare, particularly teenaged girls, into submission. The teachers emphasise – in contradiction to medical experts and advocates, or 'the hedonists of Planned Parenthood' as their opponents call them – that condoms don't work. Parents and teachers who say otherwise are branded liars on federally funded television advertisements and pupils are told, falsely, that there is no cure for cervical cancer. In her video *No Screwin' Around*, Pam Stenzel warns pupils that if they have sex outside marriage, even with a partner who has only been with them 'then you will pay'.

There is a burgeoning market for such teaching. In 1988 only one in fifty sex education teachers taught abstinence-only programmes, by 1999 more than a third of all school districts mandated such programmes and a further 51 per cent required it to be taught as the preferred option.[17]

Such research as has been done into the effectiveness of abstinence teaching shows similar findings to the results in Texas. On average, those teenagers making the pledge of abstinence delay having sex by about eighteen months rather than waiting until they are married. But when they do have sex, because of what they have been taught, they tend to have unprotected sex. In the words of the researcher Peter Bearman of Columbia University who conducted a survey of the Southern Baptists' True Love Waits programme in 2001: 'Pledgers are less likely to be prepared for an experience they have promised to forgo.'[18] Bearman found that fourteen-year-olds who took the pledge were the ones most likely to keep it for longest. When he returned to question his survey sample again several years later, he discovered that 88 per cent of the teenagers who had pledged virginity had had sex before marriage. Of the males, 40 per cent who had signed the pledge had used a condom, as against 60 per cent of those who had not pledged to virginity. The pledgers were also less likely to seek help and to be less aware if they caught a sexually transmitted disease: 'Because pledgers make a public pledge, the sex that they have is more likely to be hidden. It is also more likely to be unsafe.'

As others have pointed out: in the USA, the age of physical sexual maturity, now in the low teens, is advancing by three months every ten years, while the average age at which couples marry is now the highest it has ever been: about twenty-five years and three months, and rising, five years later than those marrying in the 1960s. This leaves a gap between puberty and marriage of about twelve years, which is a long time to wait. Many don't make it: the average age of first sexual intercourse is now between sixteen and seventeen.

As Kevin Phillips, the former Republican strategist, points out in *American Theocracy*: 'In the early 2000s the right seems to have taken the lead in promoting unworkable social-planning abstractions.'[19] He describes it as 'apple-pie authoritarianism'.

Abstinence-only education programmes have been described as unsound by the National Institute of Health, the American Medical Association and the American Academy of Pediatrics, but they clearly are politically of no account. All this would perhaps matter less to the world if the policy was confined to the USA, but one of President Bush's first acts in office in 2001 was to reinstitute the so-called Mexico City policy adopted under Ronald Reagan. This denies US government funding not only to American charitable agencies working overseas if they, or agencies they work with, spend money on abortion, and birth control to prevent the spread of sexually transmitted diseases such as AIDS, but also foreign bodies if they do the same, even if the money expended is not American. UN aid agencies such as its population fund UNFPA and bodies as internationally respected as Marie Stopes International and International Planned Parenthood stood to lose substantial funding. The UN agency calculated that it would have a shortfall of $34 million, 12 per cent of its budget, money that it alleged would have prevented 77,000 infant deaths, 4,700 maternal deaths, and 800,000 abortions around the world. If that really was the case, it was averted because, fortunately, the EU made up the money instead.

Instead, the administration's policy is to support programmes advocating abstinence, and it points to the success of Uganda's ABC initiative (standing for Abstinence, Be Faithful, Use Condoms), emphasising the first part of the programme rather than the last. As Franklin Graham, Billy's son, says: 'Dramatic lifestyle changes [are] almost impossible without the moral conviction that sex outside marriage between a man and a woman is contrary to God's law. This crisis will only be curbed when the moral teachings of God's word permeate African society.'[20] Even Catholic aid agencies have pointed out the limitations in this strategy, given that many of Africa's AIDS victims are wives, infected by their husbands, who thereupon pass on the virus to their children. The Ugandan government admits it imports millions of condoms each year to boost the fight against the disease by lowering the risk of infection.

The effect of the Bush administration's policy is therefore likely to exacerbate the AIDS crisis in Africa rather than helping to ameliorate it. This, however, is not something likely to lose the president many votes at home.

More problematic for the administration has been its treatment of gays. The debate about homosexuality has become extremely visceral as secular social mores have changed and gays have emerged from their long social concealment and ostracism. Perhaps the Religious Right sees them, besides being sinful, at one level as an easier target to focus on and simpler to legislate against than women who have abortions, because homosexuality affects a much smaller proportion of the population, maybe no more than 5 per cent. Not everyone consciously knows a gay person, especially those in conservative churches, whereas most of them would know who women are. Gays are outsiders, just as other groups have been throughout US history.

The administration has had to steer a narrow course between its supporters on the Religious Right and an increasing acceptance of gay people by many in the population at large, including Republicans. Many conservative Christians continue to regard homosexuality as a perversion on a par with the worst sexual predations, reaching far into their lexicons to do so. William Pryor, the judge from Alabama nominated by the president for the appeals court, compares it to necrophilia, bestiality and incest (and, incidentally, adultery), and Rick Santorum, the Right-wing Republican (and Catholic) senator from Pennsylvania, compared homosexuality to 'man on child, man on dog, or whatever the case may be' in an interview with the Associated Press. Yet others these days are more tolerant, including the vice-president Dick Cheney whose daughter Mary is gay and has entered into a formal partnership with her companion, leaving her father stoutly defending the right of people 'freely to enter any kind of relationship they want to enter into'.[21] The couple are even hoping for a child.

What particularly annoys and distresses the Religious Right is any treatment or depiction of gays that suggests they might be ordinary, normal, human beings. There is particular outrage when a television character is depicted as gay. When Ellen DeGeneres who was starring in the ABC sitcom *Ellen* came out in 1998 – the first actress ever to do so on US television, nearly thirty years after the start of the Gay Liberation Movement – there were howls of protest, as there were for the gay cowboy movie *Brokeback Mountain* in 2006. When the *Ellen* series was subsequently dropped it was because of falling ratings, not Christian protests.[22] DeGeneres's career did not suffer: she presented the 2007 Oscars ceremony. The Southern Baptist convention organised a long and eventually fruitless ten-year boycott campaign against Disney's Florida theme park because the company gave the partners of gay employees the same rights as heterosexual ones. For some, the only safe gay is a demonised gay. They see any normalisation as extremely dangerous for public perceptions of homosexuality.

The president himself has made a number of appointments of gay people to government posts, including his choice as ambassador to Romania, though most of the appointees have been to AIDS advisory bodies and none has been made without complaints from the Religious Right. The American Family Association demanded that the president should stop 'granting powerful appointments to openly homosexual activists who have been working diligently to overthrow the traditional values of Western civilisation regarding human sexuality, marriage and family'. To keep on side, the administration has endorsed a number of petty acts, such as banning the domestic partners of federal workers from buying into the government health plan, and at one stage in the Iraq conflict, counter-productively, sacked seven gay Arabic-speaking interpreters. It also allows organisations receiving federal funds to discriminate against gay employees on religious grounds.

The language used about homosexuals can verge on the demented and is extraordinary in its intensity. Few on the Religious Right go as far as Pastor Fred Phelps, a Primitive Baptist minister of Topeka, Kansas, who tours the USA in a mobile home, armed with a bull-horn and taking members of his family with him, to shout abuse wherever he suspects homosexuality to be lurking, including the funerals of military personnel killed in Iraq. I came across his party bawling outside the Episcopal Church's general convention in Minneapolis in 2003, standing on the American flag to demonstrate their contempt for their 'sinful, faggot-ridden, fornicatin' nation'. The Phelpses may in fact be the only people in the USA who believe that 9/11 was a very good day, because it demonstrated God's judgment on their nation.[23]

It is over thirty years since the American Psychiatric Association removed homosexuality from its list of mental disorders. Other

Christians may not use bull-horns or, as Phelps has, purchase a plot of ground in a town in Wyoming on which to erect a monument 'celebrating' the murder there of a young homosexual man in 1998, but they still use their bully pulpits to condemn them as 'vile' or to argue, as the Christian Reconstructionists do, that God ordains they should be put to death. For some, the prejudice reaches so far as to be visceral, as when Gary Bauer, sometime Republican presidential candidate and former president of the Family Research Council, claimed he couldn't touch the King James translation of the Bible, normally regarded as unimpeachable and perhaps the most beautifully written of all versions, because it had been commissioned by a seventeenth-century British king who is now fairly widely considered to have had homosexual tendencies. Bauer said: 'I feel uncomfortable that good Christians all over America and indeed the world are using a document commissioned by a homosexual. Anything that has been commissioned by a homosexual has obviously been tainted in some way.'[24]

Incidentally, it was the King James Bible that coined the translation abomination for the Hebrew word *to'ebah* (which actually means ritually or ethnically impure) – the noun most commonly cited by Christians as indicating the vehemence of God's condemnation of homosexuality.

The justification for such contempt is derived from the Religious Right's reading of a select number of biblical passages, mainly in Leviticus ('abomination' is in Leviticus 20:13) which expounds the Jewish holiness code, and in the New Testament exclusively in St Paul's letters. These and others amount to about half a dozen brief passages, which condemn a variety of same-sex practices with varying degrees of severity, though not as strongly as Christ condemned divorce. Jesus Christ was silent on the matter of homosexuality, or at least, if he wasn't, none of the Gospel writers divulged what he said: perhaps they, or he, did not think it sufficiently important. Theologians are still poring over the texts to extract their meaning and – the more liberal of them – to determine whether they have continuing relevance in modern contexts or relate very specifically to circumstances occurring in the time at which they were written.[25]

Several US denominations have struggled with the issue in recent years as their gay members have escaped from the closet of official disapproval and condemnation, but none has been so riven by it as the US Episcopal Church, small in numbers but rich in resources and establishment prestige, following its decision to elect Gene Robinson, an openly gay cleric, as a bishop – as opposed to the privately gay ones it has undoubtedly chosen over the years – to the diocese of New Hampshire at the Minneapolis convention. This effrontery, especially the Church's refusal to repent or reverse its decision, not only convulsed the worldwide Anglican Communion (particularly its more conservative developing world members), but also energised the longstanding conservative revolt within the Episcopal Church's own ranks against the leadership's perceived ongoing and rather patrician social liberalism. The insurgency by a relatively small minority, who had been looking for a united cause to rally behind, has been funded by a number of wealthy members of the Religious Right and incited by conservative think-tanks, including the Institute on Religion and Democracy. The Episcopalians compounded their offence by choosing a woman who is sympathetic to gays, Katharine Jefferts Schori, to be their next presiding bishop – the first ever female primate of a major Christian denomination – at their subsequent convention at Columbus, Ohio, in 2006.

Opponents of gays, both in the USA and the UK, tend to describe something called 'the homosexual lifestyle', as if it is a choice and one that could be changed, through self-discipline or abstinence (the Bush administration's domestic AIDS programme also focuses heavily on this). They speak of a gay 'agenda', though in so far as there is one it seems to be no more than seeking greater public tolerance and maybe social acceptance, and they refer to gays as predatory, as if they will somehow seduce straight people from their natural inclinations. The more moderate opponents insist that they don't dislike homosexuals – that would be prejudice – but hate the sinfulness of their sexual activities.

What currently sharpens the debate are moves in some areas for gays to marry their partners. Decisions in 2004 by the Massachusetts Supreme Court and in San Francisco by the mayor to authorise such unions precipitated the matter as an issue in that year's presidential election.

These followed hard on the heels of a Supreme Court decision,

Lawrence and Garner v. *Texas*, that struck down statutes against sex between two people of the same gender. That case had been brought by a couple who had been interrupted during intercourse in Lawrence's Houston apartment by a police raid (the officers were apparently responding to a neighbour's report of 'weapons' disturbance' rather than sexual activity) and they were subsequently kept overnight in police cells and fined $200. The court upheld their right to privacy, and in so doing undermined the statutes of Texas and a number of other states that criminalised homosexual acts between consenting adults in private.[26]

All this was too good a target for Republicans to miss in an election year, especially as the Democratic candidate, John Kerry, was a senator from Massachusetts and could be satisfactorily tied in knots over his state's decision. Gay marriages were depicted as a threat (for some unexplained reason) to heterosexual marriage, an undermining of the family and an assault on civilisation generally. It is a thin end of the wedge argument: today gay marriage, tomorrow polygamy or incest will inevitably follow.

Similar tactics, endorsed by a number of bishops of the Church of England, have also been deployed in the UK in relation to the Blair government's civil partnerships legislation, which is more careful to distinguish between official, secular, recognition of a same-sex couple's legal commitment to each other and the traditional heterosexual ceremony of marriage, than has been the case in the USA. Gay couples in the UK still see it as a marriage, however, and the legal niceties are lost on most people.

The religious condemnation, both in the UK and the USA, has tended to drown out considerations of whether gay couples' desire to commit permanently to each other and to register their partnerships are beneficial, both to themselves and to society at large; or, for that matter, how precisely their associations deter or undermine heterosexuals' marriage vows. Strident assertions that they destroy the family and threaten children would similarly seem far-fetched: quite apart from the fact that, in the nature of things, gays are unlikely to procreate themselves. Such research as there is for children brought up by gay parents has found no evidence that they emerge more disadvantaged or maladjusted than anyone else.

The USA already had the Defence of Marriage Act (DOMA), passed in 1996 during the Clinton administration, which ensured that states did not have to recognise same-sex partnerships authorised by another state. Heterosexual marriages are recognised across the Union, even those conducted in the sometimes exotic circumstances of Nevada, but a gay relationship legitimised in, say, Massachusetts, has legal recognition only there.

President Bush, in pursuit of re-election, offered the Right the bone it sought early in the 2004 presidential campaign, by saying he supported a Constitutional amendment then before Congress to define marriage as between a man and a woman and to outlaw the legalisation of gay partnerships at state level. He said:

> Marriage cannot be severed from its cultural, religious and natural roots without weakening the good influence of society. Government by recognising and protecting marriage serves the interests of all.
>
> Today I call upon the Congress to promptly pass and to send to the states for ratification an amendment to our constitution defining and protecting marriage as a union of man and woman as husband and wife. The amendment should fully protect marriage, while leaving the state legislatures free to make their own choices in defining legal arrangements other than marriage.[27]

This statement and the placing of proposals for Constitutional bans in eleven states on the ballots for that year's November elections undoubtedly aided Bush's re-election as voters, particularly from black charismatic and Pentecostal churches, turned out to ensure their passage. It provided a useful wedge issue for use against the Democrats and certainly assisted the Republicans to recapture the Christian conservative voters who had not bothered to vote in the 2000 election. The slight rise in Bush's support among black voters was attributed to this single issue.

But Congress had already failed to pass the Constitutional amendment and in January 2005, after he was safely re-elected, President Bush announced that, with DOMA in place, he no longer needed to lobby for a Constitutional amendment. That caused growls of discontent from the Religious Right and so he reversed his policy in his State of the Union Address a few weeks later, though two years on the amendment has not been presented, nor would it be likely to pass through Congress where there are now Democratic majorities. The polling indications are that while two-thirds of the public oppose the idea of gay marriages, they are much less hostile to the legal recognition of gay partnerships. The idea of fiddling with the nation's Constitution at the behest of the politico-Religious Right is also not particularly popular. It seems in the UK, as well as in the USA, the more people get to know gays the less censorious they are about them.

This is a dangerous moment for the anti-gay movement. As Lee Swislow, a lawyer who is also executive director of Gay and Lesbian Advocates and Defenders, told Ray Suarez: 'After a while, if you don't share that strong revulsion for gay people, you say, well actually, why not?'[28]

One feature of the Religious Right's resurgence during the Bush administration has been its leaders' willingness to take partisan stands on issues beyond their traditional sphere of interest in issues of personal morality. Their views have spread to include foreign policy, stem cell research, natural resources, global warming, even petroleum geology and, on most of them, the administration has danced to their tune. There have been some issues on which the Republican Party's traditional business interests have asserted themselves over religious concerns: trade links with China for instance, but not many.

One of George Bush's first gestures towards Religious Right sensibilities was over the controversial issue of embryonic stem cell research, a very new scientific technology about which the president and his advisers characteristically took no expert advice before he made his announcement.

Individual embryonic stem cells were first isolated only in 1998, but have provoked a fierce moral debate in the USA and, to a lesser extent, in the UK because religious opponents of the work claim they have the theoretical potential to develop into human lives, but will not do so because they are destroyed in the course of experimentation.

The reason why embryonic stem cells are enthralling scientists is because, taken from frozen five-day-old embryos which are tiny clusters of about 150 cells, they have the potential to be developed into virtually any kind of cell in the human body and hence could be cultivated into specialised cells or tissues that could then be used to prevent, or treat, a range of hitherto incurable diseases, from cancers to Parkinson's and diabetes. They are actually garnered from frozen embryos from fertilisation clinics which are to be thrown away anyway. So-called adult stem cells, which the Religious Right favours as an alternative technology, are derived from foetuses and infants as well as older children and adults, and so do not even notionally involve the 'death' of the carrier or, in the words of Tom DeLay, former Republican majority leader in the House of Representatives, 'the dismemberment of living, distinct human beings'.[29] Unfortunately, from the scientists' point of view, in the body they have already developed specialised functions so they are much less versatile and useful for research purposes.

On 9 August 2001, the president announced in a televised broadcast that he would permit federal funding on research into adult stem cells and on existing embryonic stem cell lines, which were already being cultivated in laboratories – he thought there were about sixty of these – but would ban all other embryonic stem cell research, because he regarded it as the equivalent of killing potential babies. He told the nation: 'I believe human life is a sacred gift from the Creator. I worry about a culture that devalues life and believe as your president I have an important obligation to foster and encourage respect for life in America and throughout the world.'[30]

The president's advisers believed the speech – which occurred a month before the Al-Qaeda attacks, at a time when the new president's standing was at a low ebb and other parts of his programme had stalled – as a masterly finessing of a problematic issue. It appeased the Religious Right, who regarded the research on embryonic stem cells as akin to abortion, while allowing scientists to conduct at least some research on the adult stem cells, so that US technology would not fall behind work already being carried out in the UK and elsewhere. The speech was duly applauded by the Religious Right: 'Needless to say, I was elated to learn that, contrary to our fears, Mr Bush was planning to act on behalf of unborn life,' proclaimed James Dobson.[31]

The scientific experts in the field were less enthralled. There were not sixty existing cell lines at all – the figure appeared to have been plucked out of the air – but only about sixteen, and only four of those were available for use. The four lines had been left over from IVF treatment, so were in any event probably flawed or unsuitable for use. Furthermore, even then they were obviously from a tiny cell pool so were of almost no use for general research into the wide range of US racial and genetic types. They were almost certainly drawn solely from affluent whites. As it is thought that embryonic stem cell technology could eventually be developed to test drugs and for research into how diseases develop, and also in due course to develop therapies for individual patients, such a limited sample could not possibly provide an adequate source for research.[32]

None of this appears to have been considered by the president or his advisers, but he has anyway consistently ignored the arguments of scientists working in the field, preferring to hear from more religiously inclined scientists, some of them not experts in stem cell research, instead. They do insist adult stem cells could be just as useful, though sometimes their real motivation is revealed. Thus, Professor David Prentice, formerly of Indiana State University, now senior fellow in life sciences at the Family Research Council, appearing before a Congressional committee in July 2004: 'Adult stem cell research is the best science and thoroughly moral at the same time.'[33]

The president's bioethics committee is chaired by Dr Leon Kass, who works for the conservative American Enterprise Institute. Some scientists on the committee have been culled in favour of more conservative voices. One of the departing ones, Dr Elizabeth Blackburn of the University of California, a former president of the American Society for Cell Biology, wrote in the *Washington Post* afterwards: 'The capabilities of embryonic versus adult stem cells and their relative promise for medicine were obfuscated.'[34]

The Religious Right's position, as so often, has been to polarise the debate. Scientists appreciate that both types of cells might have useful capabilities for research but they are pitted against each other as if in competition, with exaggerated claims being made by non-specialists on the adult stem cell side and sometimes over-hasty speculation about the potential of the embryonic cells on the other.

The issue is by no means clear-cut for Republicans or Democrats. Nancy Reagan, whose husband, the former president, suffered from Alzheimer's in his final years, has spoken out in favour of more research, as did the actor Christopher Reeve, paralysed in a riding accident. Opinion polls show that nearly 60 per cent of Americans surveyed believe it is more important to carry out research for medical cures than to avoid destroying embryos with a potential for life. Up to three-quarters oppose political interference by Congress and the White House.[35]

The president, however, has not been swayed from what he sees as a moral argument rather than a scientific one. His first veto of a Congressional measure in office was in 2006, to override the passage of a Bill that would have allowed more federal-funded research into embryonic stem cells and, when the Bill passed again in January 2007, he looked set to veto that one too. Dr Kass commented:

> I don't see the current legislation as being terribly important. I see it as being symbolically important to the scientists who wish to say, 'Get your moral views off our backs,' The president's not going to change his mind. This was fundamentally decided as a matter of complicated moral principle, not to incentivise or reward any future destruction of nascent human life. And if you understood that, you wouldn't expect anything different from him.[36]

Showing the vehemence that characterises so many debates these days, Wendy Wright, president of Concerned Women for America, told the *Chicago Tribune* after the vote: 'Allowing unethical research that kills small human beings is apparently not enough for some. They insist that all Americans must be complicit in paying for it, even though superior alternatives – which are ethical and effective – not only exist but are already treating patients . . . this bill is about playing politics, not helping patients.'[37]

The ban does not, of course, prevent privately funded research, or indeed states providing funding, as California has done. But scientists claim it does inhibit it, as research in other countries that do not have such restrictions, notably India, steams ahead without such moral qualms.

Undoubtedly the most extraordinary intervention by President
Bush and the Religious Right was in the case of Terri Schiavo in 2005.
Schiavo was a young Catholic woman who suffered brain damage
following the accidental loss of oxygen to her brain at the age of
twenty-six. She was left in a persistent vegetative state in hospital for
fifteen years, while her husband and her parents argued over whether
her life support system – specifically the tube used to feed her –
should be removed. Although she had not left a written will or other
evidence of her wishes, her husband testified repeatedly that she had
previously expressed a wish not to be left on life support. Her parents
disagreed.

The Florida courts in whose jurisdiction the poor woman lay found
repeatedly that her condition was irreversible. The District Court of
Appeal noted that it was 'likely no guardianship court has ever
received so much high quality medical evidence in such a proceeding'.[38] When the law failed to uphold their case, the parents turned to
the Religious Right which got into a high lather about her being
allegedly murdered. Videos of the comatose woman were produced.
Pickets stood outside the hospital, ostentatiously praying, and her
likely condition was earnestly discussed on television and phone-in
programmes across the nation by people who had never heard of her
until the day before. Senator Bill Frist, a conservative Republican from
Tennessee who is a heart transplant surgeon, felt confident enough
after watching a video to pronounce that the neurologists who had
constantly monitored her condition were evidently wrong and she was
not in a persistent vegetative state at all. 'I spent an hour or so looking
and she certainly seems to respond to visual stimuli,' he told the
Senate.

Senator John Danforth, a three-term Republican senator from
Missouri who at one stage served as Bush's choice as ambassador to
the UN and who also happens to be an ordained Episcopal clergyman,
viewed the proceedings with distaste. 'I have a high regard for the
ability of Bill Frist, but I cannot imagine a physician making a medical
diagnosis without examining the patient unless he had a special need
to appeal to the Christian Right,' Danforth wrote in his book *Faith and
Politics* in 2006.[39] 'Many, if not most, Americans can imagine a fate
worse than death, and it is the seemingly interminable process of

dying. For them it is frightening that politicians can find ways to interject themselves into this sad process.'

Caught up in the controversy, the Florida legislature passed a law specifically for Schiavo, empowering the governor, Jeb Bush, the president's brother, to prevent the withholding of nutrition and hydration from the patient. In Washington they proposed inviting Schiavo to appear before a committee – so that any doctor who removed her feeding tubes would be in contempt of Congress. When that proved impractical, Congress passed a law instead to give federal court jurisdiction over what had always previously been a state court case. The president ostentatiously flew back from Texas to the capital on Palm Sunday evening to sign the Bill into law.

It was no use, the federal court refused to order the tubes to be reinserted and the poor woman was at last given her release, amid much hyperbole and gnashing of teeth as if she had been wilfully killed when on the verge of consciousness, if not actually alert. A subsequent post-mortem showed that her brain had indeed long since atrophied and there had never been any hope of her recovery.

Public opinion swung as the case developed and the president (and Congress) may not have secured the coup they had anticipated. The majority view was that they had played politics with Schiavo's life, with precious little concern for her welfare or appreciation of what expert medical opinion was telling them. They had not known best after all and their religiously motivated zeal had been distasteful. More than two-thirds of the electorate objected to the politicians' behaviour in the case.

Senator Danforth wrote:

I believe politicians who intervened in the case of Terry Schiavo were not oblivious to the public response, but did so despite the anticipated public response. They intervened to satisfy the demands of their political base: the Christian Right ... They abandoned principle by deciding a medical question without any first-hand knowledge of what they were doing ... the effort to keep Terri Schiavo alive artificially became a religious crusade ... even though it meant abandoning traditional Republican philosophy. It was a clear case of appealing to the

political base at all costs . . . For Republicans, no true believers
are of greater value than Christian conservatives. In the case of
Terri Schiavo, they proved their power.[40]

Someone had told me before I ever went to visit him that Rich Cizik
was feeling clobbered. Cizik, fifty-four, an ordained Evangelical
Presbyterian minister, who grew up in Washington State, has worked
for the National Association of Evangelicals (NAE), the umbrella
body for denominations ranging from the Baptists to the Reformed
and Pentecostal Churches, for many years. He would normally be
counted – indeed sees himself – as a conservative. But he was feeling
out on a limb.

We'd no sooner sat down in the NAE's tasteful offices in the
Washington DC suburbs than he started pouring out his woes. They
rumbled on for the next hour and a half.

Rich's problem was that he had suddenly developed an alarming
concern for the environment. He had not given it much thought
before, but a few years previously he'd happened to attend a
conference in Oxford and the scales fell from his eyes. He'd come
back converted to green issues and saving the planet. The only trouble
was that he could not convince the leaders of the movement to take it
seriously. Worse than that, they had told him to shut up about it – the
environment was not one of 'their' issues compared with abortion and
gay marriage, and so they did not want to confuse or distract the
membership by going on about it. They'd even pressured him to
remove his name a few months earlier from an evangelical petition
signed by a cross-section of fifty senior ministers, calling on the
president to take action on climate change. He took his name off.

'I am a conservative just like them but it's not on their agenda.
They just don't want to talk about it: they don't accept the science of
it. Even those who consider the crisis is serious think it's a distraction
from our main agenda.'[41] Who were they? 'They' were the normal
suspects, leading the Religious Right: the Robertsons and Falwells and
Dobsons, Richard Land and the rest.

Cizik took his stand on the biblical injunction to be stewards of the
Earth: surely that meant looking after the planet? The trouble was, the
premillennialists eagerly awaiting the End Times and the Rapture

could not see any point in saving things – they want it all to come to an end soon.

'The Religious Right say they want to stick to safe issues,' Cizik said. 'This is too much like the Social Gospel all over again. But I don't think they should begrudge me my right to my own conversion on this issue. Some people want to marginalize me and discredit my views on climate change, but once you realise it is human-induced, once you accept that, you have an obligation to God.

'Armageddon doesn't exempt you from your carbon footprint. On the last day, God will not ask you if you are a creationist, he will say: "I gave you life and what did you do with it?" It may cost me my job, but that's fine. I am not going to be silenced. This is the twenty-first-century equivalent of the Civil Rights movement. George Bush senior used to call people like Al Gore, Ozone Man, well no one's laughing now.

'I had my conversion in 2002 in Oxford. I saw the data. I said this takes my breath away. I don't believe I can be a fence sitter but my evangelical friends still say I should not talk about it. Yet this issue challenges our lifestyle in ways other issues don't. We've sold our recreational vehicle. We've redone our heating system. We're recycling and reusing. Read Matthew 6:19: store not up your treasures. Don't we say the prayer: "thy will on *earth* as in heaven"? It's all coming and maybe it's coming a lot sooner than we ever thought it would. Hey, I'm sounding like a preacher now, aren't I?'

A few days later, speaking to someone at one of the conservative evangelical think-tanks, I asked him about Cizik. 'Rich is in a bit of a bind,' he said dismissively. 'I don't think there's a scientific debate going on. The question is whether all this is going to happen in 200 years' time or not. A lot of people think the solutions are currently unwise.

'It's not a Religious Right issue. You're not going to get people active on the environment until they can see it affecting their kids. Sure, they can get their minds around recycling, but it's hard to get movement on electric cars. You can only sustain so many moral movements in a lifetime. Ask yourself: is God going to let it all just burn up?'

I thought Cizik, so amiable, so intense and so battered, had exaggerated when he said evangelicals were starting to get the message about being stewards of the planet, but as the months went on in 2006, it was clear that the environment was moving up the evangelical agenda. Certainly younger evangelical ministers and their congregations were saying the same things as Rich Cizik and the older evangelicals' response was beginning to sound increasingly tired, formulaic and out of touch. In the Spring of 2007 Dobson, Weyrich, Bauer and others once again attempted to get Cizik sacked. In a letter they smeared him by suggesting he supported abortions, condoms and infanticide: 'How is population control going to be achieved if not by promoting (that)?' Cizik complained: 'My wife shows up in church and people ask her: "Is your husband pro-abortion and in favour of abortion as birth control?"' This time the NAE's board supported him, with only a single dissenting voice.

Cizik told the *Washington Post*: 'This tussle over the issue of climate change is part of a bigger tussle over the definition of evangelicalism and who speaks for evangelicals . . . (we) should return to being people who are known for our love and care for our fellow human beings and the Earth. If you put the politics first and make it primary, I believe that is a tragic and fateful choice.'[42]

In his State of the Union address in January 2007, even the president appeared to have got the message. Assailed by the lowest approval ratings in the opinion polls of any president since Richard Nixon at the height of the Watergate scandal, and with Democratic majorities in both Houses of Congress following the midterm elections, the president called for petrol consumption to be reduced by 20 per cent over the next ten years and for an increase in the use of alternative energy sources, such as ethanol, a fuel derived from corn.

But the president remains sceptical about the reality of global warming and continued to insist that reductions in carbon emissions must remain voluntary. Critics point out that ethanol is a problematic source of fuel – it requires vast quantities of corn and, if the 20 per cent target were to be met, an additional 80 million acres of corn cultivation would eventually need to be found. The president and his allies still appear to believe that faith can be placed in the power of technological innovation to stave off disastrous climate changes: among them ideas such as the blocking of sunlight through the placing of giant mirrors in space.[43]

In February 2007 the Intergovernmental Panel on Climate Change, a group of scientific experts set up by the UN, produced the most authoritative and consensual report yet on global warming. Yes, they said, it was real and man-made and temperatures could rise by as much as 6 degrees Celsius by the end of the century. Within hours, conservative Christian websites in the USA were rubbishing the findings. One contribution entitled 'A Necessary Apocalypse' produced for a website called American Thinker described global warming in an interesting choice of words as 'the dominant pseudo-religious tendency of our age in the prosperous West'.

John DiIulio, the first head of the White House's Office of Faith Based and Community Initiatives, the man who recruited the keen young evangelical David Kuo into the administration, grew increasingly frustrated by the lack of meaningful policy discussions in the Bush administration. After he left he complained that everything was political and guided by think-tanks and the Christian Right. It is an increasingly common complaint from former members of the staff. Paul O'Neill, former Treasury secretary, says ideology drowns real-world analysis: 'Ideology is a lot easier because you don't have to know anything or search for anything. You already know the answer to everything. It's not penetrable by facts.' One senior official told a *New York Times* magazine journalist in 2004 how they mocked the intellectual elites, 'what we call the reality-based community . . . [people] who believe that solutions emerge from your judicious study of discernible reality'.[44] What larks. Unfortunately, it has not been so funny in Iraq.

14

Armageddon

'I tremble for my country when I reflect that God is just.'

Thomas Jefferson

For a man so certain that the end of the world is nigh, Tim LaHaye was in a surprisingly benign mood when I called him at his home in California. There had been a power cut in his apartment block and he had just been diagnosed with Parkinson's disease, but he was bubbling over with new projects. There was going to be a film and a computer game and they would help to get his message of the End Times out to the widest audience.

He chuckled: 'I realized from reading *Ben Hur* that to catch fish, you have to go where the fish are. Oh yes, the best is yet to come. I want to see my books made into a blockbuster movie. They're much more powerful than books. That's my big dream: a well-produced movie that does not denigrate Jesus Christ and gives people the opportunity to go home and think about it.'[1]

LaHaye is the man we last saw praying outside the White House after Jimmy Carter's disastrous breakfast for evangelical leaders in 1980, desperate to get 'that man' out of office and bring back traditional moral values, as personified not by a Democratic Southern Baptist Sunday school teacher, but by a Republican former Hollywood actor. LaHaye, himself a Baptist, went on to help found the Moral Majority, while his wife Beverly started another influential conservative pressure group, Concerned Women for America, to fight against the monstrous regiment of feminists and lesbians.

But LaHaye will be remembered probably not for that, but for the astonishing success of the 'Left Behind' series of novels that he co-wrote with Jerry B. Jenkins, which now stretch to fifteen volumes and that are being succeeded by a new series, entitled 'Babylon Rising', the first two volumes of which were co-authored with another writer, Greg Dinallo. The 'Left Behind' books, which came out at a rate of one or two a year between 1995 and 2006, paint a terrifying premillennialist view of the end of the world, with the Rapture spiriting the elect up to heaven while the rest slug it out graphically with the anti-Christ who has come to dominate the Earth, Nicolae Carpathia with his wicked Global Community regime, identified at least partly with the papacy and the UN.

The novels start with the Rapture, with passengers disappearing from a Boeing 747 airliner en route to Europe, leaving just their clothes, jewellery, teeth fillings and surgical pins behind, while on the ground vehicles skid out of control as their owners are spirited up to heaven and people watch their relatives disappear before their eyes. After that, things get interesting. There are battles and earthquakes, a terrifying plague of locusts and a supernatural horde of 200 million demonic horsemen.[2]

The books have sold an astonishing 70 million copies in the USA, where most of the market has been located, and, even accounting for those who have purchased multiple copies to collect the whole series, that is an awful lot of believers for a work that may be fiction but is told with documentary fervour. This audience is the fish he was talking about.

His writing has made LaHaye a very wealthy man and the books were written for a purpose: to warn the faithful, give vision, and to alert them to the warning signs of the approaching End Times on Earth: the moral depravity, the plagues and dislocations, the convulsions of climate and, of course, the wars – especially those taking place in the Middle East where the last, fearful, battle will one day take place on the plains of Armageddon between the forces of the Righteous Christians and the rest, the Unbelievers, the worshippers of the anti-Christ, and the Heathen, whose identity one does not have to look far to find. It is a world-view that tells readers to prepare and to disengage, and it frightens them with what is to come. No wonder, therefore, that 9/11, which coincided with the publication of the ninth volume in the series, seemed to be a dramatic fulfilment of the worst of prophecies. It certainly gave a dramatic boost to sales.

Even in LaHaye's non-fiction, the predictions for the future are pretty terrifying, as well as precise. This is him in a book called *The Merciful God of Prophecy: His Loving Plan for You in the End Times*:

Civilization will descend into chaos. Seven horrific years of Tribulation are going to engulf the world as the Antichrist and his satanic forces devastate the planet. Billions will die through war, persecution, disease, famine and awesome divine judgments. Nevertheless, through it all God will mercifully lavish eternal life on all those who turn to him in repentance and faith. When at last the world teeters on the brink of extinction, God once more will intervene and end those terrible days 'for the elect's sake' (Matthew 24:22). And how will God end those days? By sending his Son to earth, at which time Jesus will set up a kingdom lasting for a 1,000 years. That's the second phase of his return, which we call the Glorious Appearing.[3]

This book, which was published in the USA in 2002, goes on to claim that 62 per cent of Americans believe that Jesus Christ is physically coming back to Earth: 'I consider that amazing, since the same poll revealed that only 41 per cent of respondents have committed themselves to Christ. That means that a quarter of all Americans who believe Jesus is coming again are not ready for his arrival!' Clearly there's still work to do.

Tim LaHaye believes every word of this apocalyptic vision and that God is guiding his hand: 'The Lord led me to Jerry B. Jenkins – he's a great writer. I am afraid Greg Dinallo is an excellent writer but he does not share my biblical vision. He did not have the interior knowledge. How can you work together unless you believe?' Which may be why the third volume in the 'Babylon Rising' series has a third collaborator, named Bob Phillips.

LaHaye said:

'I consider myself the creator of the series. The writer is the one who has the fiction skills. I work up Jesus and the biblical commentaries and that gives the writer the idea how the story line should go. I am not a control freak – once I throw the ball I want him to run for the touchdown with it. Then I get it back and check it carefully and give my approval, or modify it. That's how it works.

'Somehow people seem to be afraid of prophecy these days, but

God uses prophecy to prove he is God. There are 1,000 pages of prophecy in the Bible and 300 of them have already come true. Only God can do that.

'You see, you over there in England, you've got false teaching, you don't believe in the supernatural. You had this migration of Christians who came here and that's stripped England of its religious base. Secularism has stripped Europe of its cultural trappings. The churches there are dead. We've got compromisers on biblical truth here too, of course. What I want with my books is to force people to make decisions, to decide where they want to spend eternity. They have got to wrestle with that titanic spiritual force, it doesn't matter whether they are seven or seventy. We are just laying it out plainly, making it as literal as possible.

'When we die, Jesus comes to the door and asks not whether you are Anglican or Catholic, but why should I let you in? The answer is: I am trusting in eternal salvation. God looks at a man's heart. I see him standing at the gate of heaven, trying to let people in. People want to know about the hereafter, something they can rely on. Most of them have confidence in the Bible, it's like looking at a medical book. This is the word of God – you can trust that.'

Then came the politics:

'The American Civil Liberties Union is the most harmful organization in the history of our country. Socialists took over the education system here in the 1830s and that's where people were led away from God. The great American Christian philosophy made our country what it is, but the Church and the education system, they wanted this country to be socialistic and that's why we have what we have today. A number of us decided we were being disenfranchised: we'd left it up to other people in the '30s and '40s thinking these nice-speaking people would do things right but they were not nice or civil. We don't vote Republican or Democrat: we vote on our moral convictions. We have proved our case, that the Christian people in America can make a difference.

'The majority don't want to live like in Sodom or Gomorrah, like we're getting now. Carter and Clinton weren't interested in this moral turpitude. It took Ronald Reagan to merge the Christian vote. Whether George Bush can do the same remains to be seen but I do know this, when he said the most important philosopher in his life was Jesus Christ, that won him the election.'

The first 'Babylon Rising' book has at the front a message from Tim LaHaye to his readers:

> Bible prophecies and their interpretation are clear signs of what our present and future hold for this world and they are a continuing basis for all of my writing . . . My hope is that the series will help you understand that end times prophecy could be fulfilled in our lifetime and that it will help you make sense of the signs of the times that we see being fulfilled internationally almost every time we watch events unfold on television or read a newspaper . . . my hope is that you will come to feel as I do that Babylon Rising is a real page turning series that manages to be both a totally absorbing story and extremely relevant to our times.[4]

As our conversation drew to a close, LaHaye asked me whether I was a Christian or not. I said I was a Catholic. There was a pause. 'Well, that's all right,' he said eventually. 'But I'd have some differences with you there.'

I think it was when David Parsons, the US lawyer who is the spokesman for the International Christian Embassy in Jerusalem (ICEJ), said that the Holocaust was the carrying out of God's will, that my jaw dropped.

He seemed baffled that we should think it strange that God should not intervene in Auschwitz because it was all part of his plan. The Bible showed it to be so. Look at Ezekiel 5: two-thirds die and one third survives. That proved it: 'God is sovereign. He allowed it to happen. God has preserved the Jewish people but he does not always protect them. We may be uncomfortable with the Bible but the Word of God has proven true.'[5]

It was December 2005 and I and a group of fellow British journalists were at the embassy to talk about Christian Zionism. Over the previous hour, Parsons had grown a touch exasperated at our questioning and our evident sympathy for the plight of Palestinians in nearby Bethlehem, while he was trying to convince us that the embassy was witnessing even-handedly to the working out of God's plan for the Jews.

The ICEJ certainly looks like an embassy. It is housed in a large and tasteful sandstone mansion – rented from the government of the Ivory Coast – fronted by large, cool verandahs and surmounted by US and Israeli flags in a pleasant residential suburb of Jerusalem. Ironically, the building was the childhood home of Edward Said, the Palestinian-American academic and polemicist, before it was confiscated by the new Israeli government in 1948 and given to the Jewish philosopher Martin Buber instead.

Founded in 1980 largely by US Protestants, the embassy is the most visible sign of the working out of the dispensationalist philosophy propounded by John Nelson Darby and his successors. The embassy and its supporters see their job as to give wholehearted and virtually uncritical support for the State of Israel in the run-up to the End Times and the final battle nearby on the plains of Armageddon. It sees itself as a centre 'where Christians can gain a biblical understanding of Israel and learn to rightly relate to the nation . . . to present to Christians a true understanding of what is taking place in the land today so that world events may be interpreted in the light of God's word [and] to take part . . . in preparing the way of the Lord and to anticipate his reign from Jerusalem.'

What is happening in the Middle East, they believe, is a fulfilment of biblical scripture, with the Jews as the Chosen People, returning to occupy the land promised to them by God. It is an inalienable land, they believe, that should stretch right across Judea, Samaria, Gaza and the Golan. Some even believe it should run from the Mediterranean to the Euphrates. Its capital would and will be Jerusalem, undivided, under exclusively Jewish rule. According to a resolution passed by the Third International Christian Zionist Congress in 1996: 'The Islamic claim to Jerusalem, including its exclusive claim to the Temple Mount, is in direct contradiction to the clear Biblical and historical significance of the city and its holiest site.'[6]

Darby saw it first. His heresy was to believe that it was the Israelites who would survive, not the Church, because that had proved itself too fickle and corrupt. For sure, righteous Christians would be taken up in the Rapture, but the Jews were still the Chosen People. Jerusalem was where the returning Christ would establish his 1,000-year kingdom.

This naturally caused a few problems since Bible-believing Christians had always held the Jews responsible for the death of Christ – and weren't Jews planning to take over the world, as 'The Protocols of the Elders of Zion' asserted and weren't most Bolsheviks Jews? – but Darby's followers and successors insisted these were not true Jews: 'not all Jews are liquor fiends, apostates and immoral', wrote one dispensationalist, Arno C. Gaebelein, in an article entitled 'Aspects of Jewish Power in the United States'.[7] Just as surely as the forces of the anti-Christ were massing, the Jewish return to the Holy Land following the 1917 Balfour Declaration was a sure sign of the fulfilment of God's prophecies. The anti-Christ has been variously and sequentially identified as the Japanese, the communists, the UN and, most recently, the Muslims, depending on the sense of the latest threat to the USA and Israel, but the Jewish state remains firmly, indisputably, the manifest sign of God's promise to the world. That is why the USA must ensure that it is saved.

In 1970, this interpretation was given new force by the publication of a bestselling book by the author Hal Lindsey called *The Late Great Planet Earth* – 18 million copies sold, mainly in the USA – which foretold the coming apocalypse in great detail. The book maintains a cast-iron certainty in its judgments for its readers, as do its successor volumes, laden with titles such as *1980s: Countdown to Armageddon* and *The Final Battle*. They warn:

> We are the generation the prophets were talking about. We have witnessed Biblical prophecies come true. The birth of Israel, the decline in American power and morality. The rise of Russian and Chinese might, the threat of war in the Middle East. The increase in earthquakes, volcanoes, famine and drought. The Bible foretells the signs that precede Armageddon . . . We are the generation that will see the end times and the return of Jesus.

And:

You won't find another book quite like this one. We will examine why and how the world is hurtling towards disaster . . . My background as a student of prophecy allows me to place all this information in perspective in a way that is sure to lead many people to the ultimate truth about the coming global holocaust – and, if they are open, to a wonderful way of escaping it.[8]

There would be a nuclear holocaust in the Middle East 'to parallel predictions in Revelation' and an invasion of 200 million soldiers from the Orient. Lindsey was nothing if not thorough:

Messiah Jesus will first strike those who have ravaged his city Jerusalem. Then he will strike the armies massed in the Valley of Meggido. No wonder blood will stand to the horses' bridles from a distance of 200 miles from Jerusalem (Revelation 14:20). It's grizzly to think of such carnage but just to check all this out I measured from the point where the Valley of Armageddon sloped down to the Jordan Valley. From this point southward down the valley through the Dead Sea to the port of Elath on the Gulf of Aqabah measures approximately 200 miles. Apparently this whole valley will be filled with war materials, animals, bodies of men and blood![9]

It is not clear whether it is meant to be comforting that such huge armies appear to be still fighting on horseback, but maybe it is unsurprising with such literalism that Lindsey's readers can see the signs of impending doom everywhere and may interpret those they haven't yet seen as being just around the corner. A Pew Forum poll found that 58 per cent of US evangelicals believe in the coming reality of a Battle of Armageddon.

No wonder the book proved hugely influential – and reached some eminent policy-making quarters. President Jimmy Carter acknowledged his pro-Zionist beliefs, as did Ronald Reagan, who read Lindsey's book while he was still governor of California.

One can never quite tell with Reagan what he believed at any given point, but the book certainly appeared to make an impression. In conversation with a colleague, he asserted: 'For the first time ever, everything is in place for the Battle of Armageddon and the Second Coming of Christ . . . Ezekiel tells us that Gog, the nation that will lead all the other powers of darkness against Israel, will come out of the north . . . Gog must be Russia, now that Russia has become communist and atheistic.

In office, Reagan appointed several Christian Zionists: Ed Meese as Attorney General, Caspar Weinberger, Secretary of Defense, James Watt, Secretary of the Interior, and he also invited Zionists such as Jerry Falwell and Lindsey himself to attend White House seminars. The *Washington Post* reported the president as saying: 'You know, I turn back to the ancient prophets of the Old Testament and the signs foretelling Armageddon and I find myself wondering if – if, we're the generation that is going to see that come about. I don't know if you've noted any of these prophecies lately, but believe me they certainly describe the times we're going through.'[10]

These are not therefore new beliefs: if presidents have been influenced by them for thirty years, so have evangelists such as Falwell and Robertson, who have accordingly given their powerful voices to the Israeli cause. As far back as 1979, just when he was founding the Moral Majority, Falwell was given the use of a Lear Jet by the Israeli government for use in spreading the Word and the following year he received a medal for 'Zionist excellence' from the then prime minister, Menachim Begin. When the Israelis later bombed Iraq's nuclear plant, the first call Begin put in to the USA was to Falwell, not President Reagan, so that he could explain the reasons for the strike to his audience first. In the late 1990s, Binyamin Netanyahu, when he was prime minister, dropped off to see Falwell and fundamentalist Christian leaders on the way to the White House, to ask them to mobilise their congregations and make sure that President Clinton refrained from pressurising Israel to accept the Oslo accords.[11] Robertson too has been a firm supporter and for the same reasons: to defend the land where he expects Jesus's foot to fall when the Second Coming dawns. Dan Cohn-Sherbok estimates there are over 3,250 pro-Israel evangelical organisations in the USA today. They too can pressurise administrations not to place too many demands on Israel.

But the embassy claims to represent much more than that: 'millions' of Christians in over 125 countries, including the UK, 'who share a love and concern for Israel and the Jewish people'. A measure of the scale of the enterprise is the fact that in the last fifteen years or so it has assisted more than 60,000 Jews to return to Israel, including sponsoring more than fifty plane-loads of Jewish immigrants from the countries of the former Soviet Union. The embassy has fifty-five full-time staff.

Each autumn it sponsors the largest annual tourist event in Israel when thousands of Christians descend on the city to celebrate Succot, the Feast of Tabernacles. Every Israeli prime minister in the last twenty-five years has deemed it expedient to attend the dinner it holds and to praise the embassy's efforts fulsomely: 'an act of courage and a symbol of closeness,' Menachim Begin said. 'Thank you for your support in our great endeavour . . . consistent . . . unreserved and very, very, effective,' said Binyamin Netanyahu. 'You see these people? They are part of our army! They are part of our power, they are part of our defence of Jerusalem,' averred Ehud Olmert.[12]

To have such a strong presence of Bible-believing US Christians in the middle of Jerusalem is undoubtedly useful to the Israeli authorities, boosting as it does the US government's traditional support for them in their ongoing confrontation with their Palestinian and Arab neighbours. Some US fundamentalists, including a group quaintly known as the Battalion of Deborah, periodically attempt to start the rebuilding of the Jewish Temple on top of the Muslim Dome of the Rock, an attempt that is equally ritually stopped by the police before they can do any damage, or have damage done to them. The embassy does not do that, but it does provide chapter and verse for the Jewish people's eternal destiny and a narrative that millions of evangelical Christians can believe.

Literalism can even go further than this. Some US dispensationalists have repeatedly attempted to breed a pure red heifer for Israel, in keeping with verses in Numbers 19 so that, when the time comes, the beast may be slaughtered, burned and turned into a paste with which Jews can anoint themselves before entering the Temple site. A couple have been bred in the USA but so far, alas, in the absence of the End Times they have failed to produce a reliable supply of pure red offspring to carry on the line.

Mr Parsons gave us a booklet he had written about Christian Zionism and the Battle of Armageddon which takes the Bible text to be absolutely factually true. Like a preacher's sermon, the booklet is scattered through with biblical references, a verse here, a verse there, Romans jostling with Micah, elbowing Ephesians, Genesis and, of course, Revelation, all accepted as equally and literally accurate. The booklet is scathing of sceptical journalists and attributes any criticism of Israel to distortion and bad faith, suggesting they are all the result of Left-wing scare tactics. It sounds even a little paranoid:

> The traditional alliance between local Arab Christian clergy and their sympathisers in the liberal Protestant churches . . . are being increasingly bolstered by a growing number of professing evangelical Christian leaders, scholars and theologians . . . this alliance in order to further its own pro-Palestinian political objectives is waging a deliberate and increasingly aggressive campaign not simply to challenge Christian Zionism but to discredit and demonise its adherents and to distort and ridicule its true motivations and beliefs.[13]

What is quite extraordinary, however, is the book's implicit belief in the forthcoming battle as a working out of God's plan. The literalism has its comical side: in discussing God's donation of the Promised Land, Mr Parsons writes:

> As a former practising real estate attorney, this author would want to know where the title to the land, given to Abraham's descendants as an everlasting possession, is documented. Normally a deed of title is a written document signed by a granter with a property description, words of conveyance and express warranties . . . In the instance of God's covenant promises with Abraham it would be proper to say that the repository of title to the land was in the loins of Abraham while the Bible is the record that puts the world on notice of that agreement.[14]

For all the world as if it were a land deal in South Carolina.

This all comes down to one thing, however:

To be faithful to our Scriptures, there has to be a limit to political support for the Palestinian agenda if it seeks to deny Israel a place in the land promised to Abraham. Even more anathema to the Church should be the rising Islamic agenda now being preached to Palestinians and their Arab allies that sees the land of Israel as the place where Allah is gathering the Jews for ultimate genocide.

It is clear from Scripture that the promised time of restoration for Israel taking place in our day is the divinely chosen and unmistakeable warning sign openly seen before all nations, that He is coming to judge humanity's continuous rebellion against Him and will be justified in so doing. It is humanity's enduring rebellion against God, His Word and His Messiah that culminates in the Battle of Armageddon, thereby giving birth to the long-awaited Messianic reign of righteousness and peace on the earth ... It is true that God will use the present difficulties in Israel to afflict, save and deliver her and use them to judge the nations, unmask their anti-Semitism and antagonism against Himself. We may not always know the exact timing and manner of God's sovereign acts, but we do know it is the season of favour the Jewish people have long awaited. God's sure promise is one of deliverance for Israel and by doing so He will reveal His existence and character to the nations.

Muslims, of course, are the latest representatives of the anti-Christ, particularly the late Yasser Arafat. When Arafat was invited to attend the annual National Prayer Breakfast in Washington in 1999, the embassy declared that it would be like dining with Satan. There is unfortunately no biblical precedent Christian Zionists can see for accommodating others in the Promised Land. Accordingly, Palestinians in particular must be derided and their claims to ownership dismissed. Why, the land was practically unoccupied when the Israelis took it over. According to Ramon Bennett, one Christian Zionist: 'There never was a Palestinian people, nation, language, culture or religion. Palestine is a hoax! That land was Canaan, inhabited by Canaanites whom God destroyed because of their wickedness.'[15]

Muslims are untrustworthy, they don't play by the same rules – that was shown on 9/11 – they hate the West, and particularly the USA, and they want to eliminate Judeo-Christian culture. Their religious belief is erroneous and inferior and their prophet a paedophile – such is the small change of some US preachers' rhetoric. Therefore they are of no account in the land of Israel and their proxies are doing battle against the Righteous in Iraq, Iran and Afghanistan. Thus are the biblical prophecies being worked out and, in the end, God will be faithful to His promises.

The embassy may be even-handed, as it says, but there is no doubt that the Palestinian occupants of the Promised Land are mere bit-part players in the great drama of the Final Days. Ariel Sharon's enforced evacuation of Jewish settlers from the Gaza Strip a few months before our visit to the embassy had clearly caused some heart-searching. After all, if God gave the Jews the Promised Land, they had no right to give some of it away and Ariel Sharon's subsequent stroke a few weeks later was taken as a sign by Pat Robertson and others that God was not pleased with what had happened and was demonstrating his displeasure directly. He'd done it before too: a decade earlier when the prime minister Yitzak Rabin was assassinated shortly after agreeing to the transfer of territory to the Palestinians. John Hagee, a Texan preacher who later founded a group called Christians United for Israel, wrote at the time that Rabin's murder was the fulfilment of prophecy and his assassin was to be admired: 'to give [the land] away was an act of treason against Israel and an abomination against God,' he wrote in a book called *The Beginning of the End*.[16]

Sharon's decision to pull out of the Gaza Strip in 2005 disconcerted Mr Parsons too, though he certainly did not go as far as Hagee: 'The underlying title to the land is theirs. God gave it to them unconditionally,' he said. 'God is still being faithful to His biblical promises. I put my trust in the Bible as the word of God. We have to be faithful to the teachings of Jesus and the Apostles.'

Then he added: 'The Qu'ran derogates from the Bible. It's not such a significant book. It's nice religion but is it the truth? No, we don't put any stock in the Islamic faith. These times and seasons are in God's hands. We have to expect it in our lifetime. I am not putting my dog to sleep just yet.'

One website in the USA publishes a daily Rapture Index, calculating on a weekly basis from the incidence of natural disasters, wars and inflation, just how close Armageddon is getting. In truth, anything can be accounted a sign that the end is nigh: the Boxing Day 2004 tsunami or Hurricane Katrina could equally be taken as an indication of God's displeasure with the sinfulness of humanity. In one case, there was the hedonism of Christmas holiday-makers, in the other the sinful folk of New Orleans. One website I saw at the time noted that the sea surge on Sri Lanka had petered out under the walls of an inland Christian orphanage, sparing the children inside, though not the presumably godless ones outside.

The Rapture Index calls itself 'a Dow Jones industrial average of end-time activity'. A reading of 85 indicates a time of 'slow prophetic activity', 145 reckons the end is near. In the summer of 2006 when Israel invaded Lebanon during a brief but bloody war, the index shot up to 158. In the month the war started the Rapture Index recorded 250,000 hits, a 25 per cent increase over the previous month.[17]

Some Christian fundamentalists found it difficult to contain their excitement. Jerry Falwell announced in a commentary that the war would serve 'as a prelude or forerunner to the future battle of Armageddon and the glorious return of Jesus Christ'. The evangelical broadcaster Janet Parshall told her listeners: 'These are the times we've been waiting for. This is straight out of a Sunday school lesson.'[18]

It is rather doubtful whether George W. Bush actually accepts the dispensationalist view of the coming apocalypse, though some of his staff may do. The Revd Hagee's CUFI Washington lobbyists have held meetings with White House officials and make common cause with Jewish lobbying groups. Hagee himself is one of those urging the USA to attack Iran: 'The coming nuclear showdown with Iran is a certainty,' he wrote in the Pentecostal magazine *Charisma* in 2006: 'Israel and America must confront Iran's nuclear ability and willingness to destroy Israel with nuclear weapons. For Israel to wait is to risk committing national suicide.'[19]

Four years earlier, the events of 9/11 could not have given End Times folk anything other than additional certainty that the moment they had for so long expected was nigh. With so many of them, with such a hermetically sealed world-view, it is hard for any US politician, let alone a president elected largely by courtesy of their votes, to press Israel for a more equitable settlement with the Palestinians. It is not a question of courting the Jewish vote (which remains largely Democratic) in supporting Israel, but the evangelical Christian one. This is quite apart from any more strategic considerations about the need to support the one democratic state in the Middle East, surrounded by neighbours who make little secret that they wish for her extirpation. But very many Americans believe Israel can do no wrong for reasons quite unconnected with her current situation and most Israeli politicians understandably see no reason to disabuse them. The fact that some Muslims so patently wish the Great Satan ill just reinforces their belief.

President Bush's rhetoric of good and evil plays precisely to the evangelical Christians' perception of what is at stake and what will surely shortly happen. In that sense, the occupations of Afghanistan and Iraq are merely sideshows before the Big Event, portents in the sky before the coming battle. Their absolute certainty of the eventual, bloody, triumph of Good just makes them too sanguine for their own good.

The Middle East is, however, not the only target of the Christian Right's concern and scorn. As we have noted, they are deeply suspicious of international bodies, particularly the UN, and, to a lesser extent, the EU. For premillennialists such as Tim LaHaye, this is because they presage the creation of the anti-Christ's world government, but for most it is more pragmatically because they pose a threat to the USA's freedom of action in the world and create a potential restriction to her ability to take her own decisions. For many evangelical Christians, however, the institutions are also a problem because they don't necessarily subscribe to their views on abortion, AIDS and other moral issues: they believe that the UN's agencies and non-governmental organisations are spending money (often the USA's) in providing the sort of healthcare that Americans don't believe they should. Hence the Bush administration's insistence that money should not be given to organisations funding abortions.

Sometimes such interventions veer between the sinister and the comical, such as the invasion of a meeting of the UN's women's conference in 2000 when a group of young US Christian activists marched into the hall to protest. They were watched by Jennifer S. Butler, an ordained Presbyterian minister and executive director of the group Faith in Public Life, who was her church's US represent-ative to the UN: 'The newcomers were mostly male, white, young conservative and religious while we were female (mostly) middle aged, racially diverse, liberal and (mostly) secular . . . when a group of young . . . men suddenly enters this arena, they can easily cause a stir. They wore professional business suits . . . their hair was short and clean-cut . . . All of them wore bright campaign buttons emblazoned with a single word: "motherhood". One of the young men approached the platform and just glowered at [the speaker] as if the intensity of his gaze might silence her.'[20] When they emerged outside there was no escape for the conference attenders: they found themselves surrounded by monks, praying for them.

Such conferences have been targeted because of the Religious Right's concern that the traditional role of women across the world is being subverted by feminism, undermining the family as part of a deep, secular, liberal and politicised agenda. The women's liberation movement is blamed for drawing women away from their traditional roles, undercutting male authority in the household, secularising society and leading to the unmitigated disasters of sexual licentiousness, abortion and divorce.

As long ago as 1995, James Dobson was railing against the World Conference on Women in Beijing as 'the most radical, atheistic and anti-family crusade in the history of the world', telling his followers that it represented 'breath-taking wickedness'. He explained:

At the heart of the draft document is enormous hostility to the institution of the family. Marriage is seen as the root of all evil for women . . . everything related to traditional male and female relationships is to be despised . . . the radicals want to dissolve the traditional roles of mothers and fathers. They also hope to eliminate such terms as wife, husband, son, daughter, sister, brother . . . being replaced with gender-neutral terms such as parent, spouse, child and sibling. The ultimate goal, though they tried to hide it, is a plan to get rid of traditional sexuality in order to destroy patriarchy.[21]

It's a paranoid old world.

In the current climate, of course, many women, including evangelicals, would resent such an analysis, and so the emphasis these days tends to be laid not on tradition but difference. Women's roles are said to be complementary and sustaining, not subversive. It's little wonder that at the 2000 conference the greying, middle-aged veteran feminist activists in their free-flowing dresses with their book bags 'picked up at previous UN world conferences . . . covered with the symbols and slogans of women's empowerment' felt a little non-plussed to have their gathering so rudely invaded by those who did not share a long-held agenda that had not been challenged for thirty years.

Butler says there have been concerted attempts by the Christian Right to take over some international organisations such as the World Youth Alliance and, what look like standard political tactics, to seize control of their leaderships and agendas. Butler says they did seize control of something called the Youth Caucus before a UN special session on children, and that she saw young activists being coached on tactics by their elders, who sat in on the caucus meeting.

US groups have succeeded in making common cause with conservative Christians from Third World and developing countries, where Pentecostalism is booming and where their social attitudes on issues such as abortion are widely shared. Conservative US Christians, including Mormons and Catholics, can also support much of this agenda.

There is a big, so far largely untapped worldwide potential here and conservative religious groups have spotted it: in Latin America, in Africa and in Eastern European countries – 'new Europe' – such as Poland and maybe one day Russia. These could be the determinants of a conservative international moral agenda in the coming decades. Butler quotes a Kenyan scholar saying: 'The centres of the church's universality [are] no longer in Geneva, Rome, Athens, Paris, London, New York, but Kinshasa, Buenos Aires, Addis Ababa and Manila.' By 2050 it is estimated that there will be 3 billion Christians in the world and only a fifth of them will be white: in the words of Philip Jenkins, the phrase 'a white Christian' may sound as curiously oxymoronic as 'a Swedish Buddhist'.[22]

There is altruism here, as well as calculation, but when US conservative evangelicals turn their attention to an issue they are able to deploy formidable financial resources. In 2006, many churches began to grow concerned about Darfur, not just because of the humanitarian crisis but also because of the perception that Muslims were persecuting Christians (actually, mostly, other Muslims of a different ethnic group). It has been calculated that, in 2006, evangelical US Christians devoted over $2 billion to foreign aid. Some of this effort has been conditional on the recipients being Christian, some has been intended for proselytisation purposes, but much of it has come from a sense of religious imperative.

Clearly, the one socially conservative religious group that these organisations find extremely hard to penetrate in current circumstances are the Muslims, who otherwise might be expected to share their concerns on many moral issues and campaign alongside them. Some of their world-views are strikingly similar. But, arguably, Christianity is spreading faster than Islam, or at least holding its own: by mid-century there are likely to be three Christians in the world for every two Muslims; and they will be religiously conservative.

Butler believes that such conservative beliefs are extremely hard for secular Western liberals to understand and combat because they have got out of the habit of taking religious motivation seriously over the last fifty years. It is a failure of imagination and of understanding: they assumed that God was either dead, or that no one could take him at his word. But they have not spotted that, just as in the USA, demographically across the world religion is becoming increasingly conservative and moving south, among people whose thought-patterns, cultures, traditions and attitudes are not theirs.

In a communion such as Anglicanism, which spread out from England across the British Empire and into North America, this tension has broken into near-open warfare between the rising force of African equatorial, evangelical, Anglicanism and the much more socially liberal English and North American versions of the faith. In terms of numbers, Nigeria is probably now the largest Anglican province and its refusal to accept what it sees as the unbiblical equivocations of the older white churches, particularly over homosexuality – to say nothing of its resentment over white colonialism (although many African churches are happy to take US money) and the white churches' traditionally patronising attitudes towards their black brothers – has brought Anglicanism to the brink of schism. African Anglican leaders now ostentatiously spurn financial aid from the American Episcopal Church because they claim it to be tainted by gay-friendly hands, even though it might help alleviate the sufferings of their people, but they are sometimes quietly happy to receive aid in other ways. When Peter Akinola, the primate of Nigeria, who has led the fight against gays in the Church, consecrated the Revd Martyn Minns, an English white evangelical minister who has a parish in Virginia, to act as bishop for Nigerians living in the USA in 2006, he quietly asked Minns's bishop if he would not mind continuing to support him in the parish.

In an era when orthodoxy is self-defined, the institutional Church's traditional tolerance of regional diversity of worship and government is no longer adequate to hold the worldwide body together. And it is a split that conservative white evangelicals in the UK and the USA have worked together to foment.

It suits these folk to portray Europe and Britain as morally defunct and spiritually dead: infested by relativistic intolerant secular liberalism and overrun by Muslims. There is a certain mutual reinforcement of this prejudice on both sides of the Atlantic. When the Rt Revd Michael Nazir-Ali, the Bishop of Rochester and one of the Church of England's senior evangelicals, attended the US Episcopal Church's general convention in Columbus, Ohio, in 2006 he chose to tell them that they were no longer Christians because of their accommodation with their homosexual members.[23] When the US Catholic writer George Weigel wanted to convey the spiritual emptiness of England, for an article entitled 'Europe's Problem – and Ours' in the conservative journal *First Things*, he chose to claim that St Paul's Cathedral in London had become a museum because it charged tourists such as himself an entrance fee: 'Yes, Christian worship continued at the cathedral church of the diocese of London. But on a Saturday afternoon in January 1995, it had been turned into a museum.'[24] Mr Weigel is a well-known polemicist but he is maybe striving too hard for effect, perhaps ignorant that British museums generally do not charge for admission, or that St Paul's receives no subsidies to maintain its 300-year-old facade.

Such views pass as common currency around the world in hours – sometimes seconds – because of the internet. This is not necessarily, despite the brightest hopes, a means of spreading enlightenment; on the contrary, it can be a reinforcer of mutual prejudice, bigotry and ignorance. When the bishops of the Church of England decided in 2005 not to oppose the government's introduction of civil partnerships for same-sex couples, the blogsite chatter from conservative Episcopalians in the USA was to wonder why the Queen had not blocked such godless legislation – wasn't she head of the Church and didn't she have some responsibility in the matter? And why hadn't the Archbishop of Canterbury opted for imprisonment in the Tower of London rather than accede to the will of Parliament? As I was writing this chapter, the British government committed a further enormity by announcing that no exemptions would be granted from its commitment to introduce regulations outlawing discrimination on the grounds of sexual orientation, a move that particularly annoyed the Roman Catholic Church. From the USA there was instant outrage on the Titusonenine conservative religious website: 'Britain has decided to bring judgment on itself. They are headed straight for hell and are halfway there,' wrote one Paul B. and 'These are folks who affirm the murder of these children up to the point of birth. What a small thing it is to use the already born children to further their aims. Implacable, intractable, evil, there is in this law, now consuming once-lovely England,' added someone signing themselves, presumably without irony, Words Matter.[25]

There is constant, semi-gleeful speculation about when countries such as the UK will wake up to find that Islam is the majority religion. The sub-text is that Europe cannot be trusted because it has lost its Christian faith, as both Tim LaHaye and Judge Moore told me, and been taken over by Muslims and secularists.

In such a climate of daily misunderstanding, rancour and recrimination it is a commonplace that 'liberal' Christianity has failed, just as secular socialism did. The only religious institutions that stand out against the tide of depravity and godlessness in Europe are conservative evangelicals and the papacy, particularly that of John Paul II, for his part in reasserting conservative Catholic values and in opposing communism, though not for his opposition to capital punishment in the USA and war in Iraq.

This internecine squabbling between people who profess the same religious allegiances would be a matter of academic interest except that it has an effect on wider conservative thinking about the world and creates a climate in which a particular world-view can flourish. It is part of the neo-con view of foreign policy that the USA should rightly stand proud on its values and its civilising mission, reinforced by its unilateral military power and scorning those taking a different view. If you know you are right and you have the means, there is no need for consultation or advice – that only leads to weakness or equivocation. In the war against evil, you are either with us or against us.

In other words, it's a faith-based ideology. And if the world can be made to see itself through US eyes, so much the better – and how easier to do that than through the shared moral values of conservative Christianity, since they are already in place and available for mobilisation?

Religious conservatism's political engagement began during the Cold War with hostility towards communism and so did many neo-conservative attitudes. Indeed, many of them were shaped by intel-lectuals and activists who had formerly been communists, understood its absolutist methods and beliefs, and shared its vision of how societies work. They despised liberalism for its wetness and permissiveness and took their contempt for its values as they crossed the political firmament from Left to Right. Liberalism leads only to weakness, appeasement, disorder and a blurring of moral values – and therefore ultimately to tyranny: Weimar becomes Nazism. Or surrender to 'Islamofascism'.

The old Social Gospel was not for them and their belief in state power and its institutions – including the churches (actually many of them, such as Leo Strauss and Irving Kristol were Jewish) – had faded. What they now stood for was individual virtue and self-reliance. This is where neo-con thinking has coalesced with the traditional pieties of evangelical Protestantism – or at least those values it is supposed to have had once, in a Golden Age which may, or may not, have existed in the past. Thus Walter Russell Mead in the *Christian Science Monitor* in 2003: 'the sort of basic values that they are promoting are very much the sort of Protestant, Christian values that were dominant in 19th Century America'.[26]

There is a coincidence of interest, in the words of Joseph Bottum in an article in *First Things* in 2006: 'The opponents of abortion and euthanasia insist there are truths about human life and dignity that must not be compromised in domestic politics. The opponents of Islamofascism and rule by terror insist there are truths about human life and dignity that must not be compromised in international politics. Why shouldn't they grow toward each other?' And William Kristol and Robert Kagan in *Foreign Affairs* in 1996: 'The remoralisation of America at home ultimately requires the remoralisation of American foreign policy, for both follow from America's belief that the principles of the Declaration of Independence are not merely the choices of a particular culture but are universal, enduring, "self-evident" truths. That has been, after all, the main point of the conservatives' war against a relativistic multiculturalism.'[27]

It is a marriage of morality and convenience, clearly made in heaven and, if the war in Iraq was by 2006 causing disenchantment among the US population as a whole, the Christian Right – as exemplified by the midterm elections that November – continued to remain solidly behind the president's crusade.

15

We Are a Different People

'I am not after the votes . . . I am here and I am in this room
sharing concerns because someday I am going to stand before God
and I want to hear Him say, "Well done!" I hope that's why we're
all here.'

President George W. Bush, quoted in Stephen Mansfield,
The Faith of George W. Bush[1]

The Fall had closed in and the day was grey, wet and misty as I drove
for one final appointment, out of Washington DC, past Dulles Airport
and up towards the small town of Purcellville, near the upstream
Potomac River, up by the state line where Virginia, West Virginia, and
Maryland meet. It was midterm election day in early November 2006
– a day on which the president and the Republican Party were due to
lose their control of Congress – and I was to visit at last one of the
most remarkable institutions of the Religious Right: Patrick Henry
College.

I found it a mile outside the town, looking very new, on a bleak,
nearly treeless site of sweeping, sodden lawns and an artificial lake.
The college consisted of a cluster of barrack-like red-brick buildings,
fronted by white, pillared porticos with the odd white decorative
cupola on the roof – the sort of mock ante-bellum architecture that fits
an ancient college or a modern shopping mall. A few students scurried
along under umbrellas, trying to keep out of the rain, but there was
just a smattering of them – most had been given leave to help get out
the vote for Republican candidates that day.

Patrick Henry is a private university mainly for the offspring of
Christian evangelical parents who for ideological reasons of their own
have rejected state schooling as largely immoral, exclusively secular,
woefully liberal and entirely godless – not to say academically
mediocre – and have opted to teach their children at home instead.
Nothing more exemplifies their disillusionment with schools than the

repeated refusal, backed up by the courts on the basis of the separation of Church and state, to permit the saying of prayers before lessons.

There are thought to be about a million such parents now, at least two-thirds of them evangelicals (though US Muslim parents are also choosing the same option in increasing numbers). Christian Reconstructionists are keen on home schooling, since they do not believe there should be public provision of education at all. Maybe 4 per cent of US children are now taught at home and the market for home-schooling teaching materials is approaching $1 billion a year. By the nature of their beliefs about religion and the state, these families form a solid core of conservatism. It has been estimated that three-quarters of home-schooled youngsters vote, compared with a national average among 18–24-year-olds of just 29 per cent.[2]

The college was set up in 2000 to offer higher education to such children, whose families might not wish them to go to a more usual university where they could be tainted with suspect values and beliefs – shades of John Washington Butler who brought in the Tennessee anti-evolution law in the 1920s to stop the state's children being depraved by ideas – and the college now has 400 students, 85 per cent of them home-schooled, each paying up to $20,000 a year for their four-year courses in government, journalism, literature or history. It describes itself as a liberal arts college; when it says it teaches a foreign language, it means Latin, and when it describes a classical curriculum, it means training in the nearly forgotten arts of Logic, Rhetoric and Philosophy.

All the students – and indeed all the academic staff and other employees – have to sign up to a declaration of faith before they join. This includes the statement: 'The Bible in all its entirety (all sixty-six books of the Old and New Testaments) is the inspired word of God, inerrant in its original autographs and the only infallible and sufficient authority for faith and Christian living.' Satan, they must agree, is a personal, malevolent being, and hell is 'the place of eternal punishment where all those who die outside of Christ shall be confined in conscious torment for eternity'. It is non-denominational but non-Christians – indeed many mainstream Christians – might have a difficulty enlisting. If you start to query the college's beliefs, you're out: five of the college's seventeen professors left in the summer of 2006 when they questioned the need to relate the scriptures to every lecture they gave. They were rapidly expunged.

The 2006–7 prospectus goes into exhaustive detail, with full biblical references, about its standards and its vision. It even states that the college expects the biology faculty 'to provide a full exposition of the claims of the theory of Darwinian evolution, Intelligent Design and other major theories while, in the end, teach creation as both biblically true and as the best fit to observed data'. The college's mission is 'to prepare Christian men and women who will lead our nation and shape our culture with timeless biblical values and fidelity to the spirit of the American founding'. Students are told they must integrate a biblical world-view in all aspects of their professional lives. They should, it is said, have 'a winsome appearance, dressed and groomed appropriately in professional and social circumstances'. And, of course: 'the practice of homosexual conduct or other extra-marital sexual relations is inconsistent with our faith position'. The prospectus reassures fathers and mothers that their children will attend church each Sunday and that 'we also support the parents' role in courtship' – in other words, that parental permission must be sought before students go out together.[3]

All this would merely be quaint except that the college has had extraordinary success in its brief life in securing its students' attachments, internships or full-time jobs; at least twenty-two of them with senators and Congressmen in Washington, one for Karl Rove, the president's closest adviser and strategist, at the White House, and others with the military, and even in Paul Bremer's office in the US administration in Baghdad. The college is already able to tell its young people that they can get on an inside track and it can convince conservative Congressmen that they are worth employing. It can also point to Janet Aschcroft, wife of the former attorney-general, on its board of trustees.

I had had some difficulty persuading the college to let me – 'a representative of the ultra-liberal British *Guardian*', as a member of staff described me – in to visit. For months we had performed a stately gavotte while David Halbrook, the director of communications, asked for ever more evidence of my bona fides, copies of articles and even references, but at last, on this election day of all days, they allowed me to see the chancellor Michael Farris and meet some students.

We last came across Dr Farris in this book during his electoral bid to become lieutenant governor of Virginia when some of his supporters were allegedly jeering the Jewishness of his Republican opponent in the primary, but he has a long history of political engagement as a lawyer. He has been with the Moral Majority, was former chief counsel for Beverly LaHaye's Concerned Women for America, and a founder of the Home School Legal Defence Association, set up to defend Christian parents against state attempts to coerce their children into school, a battle that has been won.

The college was Dr Farris's idea. I was led to his office through the administration building, whose walls are lined with portraits of the founding fathers, including at least one – modern – picture of them kneeling reverently in prayer as they worked on the Constitution, an event which had clearly by now achieved actual, as opposed to legendary, status. Patrick Henry, of course, was the polemicist and founding father who famously proclaimed: 'Give me liberty or give me death', and the college's motto is 'For Christ and Liberty'.

Dr Farris was in his study, which was lined with the stuffed and mounted heads of large deer, antlers and signed photographs of Republican luminaries, from the president down, shaking his hand. He was in a relaxed and charming mood and dressed in jeans, cowboy boots and a leisure shirt, sitting in an armchair with his feet on the coffee table as we spoke.[4]

'Sure, they really like us on Capitol Hill. They want someone who is smart and shares their values. Home-schooling families are looking for suitable colleges. I see us meeting the need on both sides of the equation.

'I don't think such another college exists. We wanted to emulate the education received by the Founding Fathers. It is the training of a habit of mind. That's why they study logic, rhetoric and philosophy, and Western civilization and American history and Blackstone and constitutional law. It makes them very adaptive and able to analyse problems. It is contrary to their best interests to educate them in up-to-date fads. Frankly if you are going to get someone into the major leagues you are surely going to have to train them into the mindset of national leadership – just as Harvard does.'

He was particularly proud that he had taken a team of students reading law to Oxford to debate an issue of British contract law with an undergraduate team from Balliol there. They had mugged up on British law and won. When Balliol sent its team over to Virginia to debate US law, Patrick Henry won again. This clearly tickled him: 'I didn't walk away from that thinking we were better than Balliol, that would be preposterous. But it showed we are going in the right direction.'

The right direction is clear. Michelle Goldberg quotes him telling a class of students: 'You in the first row need to be appointed to the Supreme Court and you in the second row need to be in the Senate to confirm him and you in the third row need to be the president of the United States to nominate him . . . I want to train them from scratch to believe in the principles that this nation was founded on.'[5]

And to do that, they need the Bible. Farris said: 'The Bible is the inspired and inerrant word of God. Genesis is literally true. There was a man named Adam and a woman named Eve and there was a talking serpent. That doesn't mean we don't study evolution – we don't do what the Left does to Christians and censor them – we often study things we don't believe, to assess their strengths and weaknesses in pursuit of truth, but we have confidence that God's truth is going to win.'

I ventured to suggest that the students might have a rather limited view of life, but he was having none of it. No, he said, being taught at home made them more independent in their judgment and better able to socialise with a wide range of people than they would have found at school. 'A bigot is someone who makes conclusions without knowing about them. Our students have not been segregated at home by age so they can mix with older people. They have not been subjected to the socialistic herd mentality of American public school education.'

But there was no pretence that these are students who will emerge with a range of views. He said: 'If you take the philosophical positions we take, you are not welcome in the Democratic Party. There probably won't be jobs in the Speaker's Office for a while but there will still be vacancies with Republicans. You can only place a poor candidate once.

I had an Airforce colonel in intelligence write to tell me that the young lady we placed with him was the best person he'd had in his office in 30 years.'

The students I met were indeed dauntingly articulate, if perhaps a little wistful that some career options might be closed to them. Journalism looms large as one of the major courses – students will 'develop a biblical view of the role of a Christian journalist' – and one, Jennifer Carden, from Dallas rather feared that her ambition to work at the *New Yorker*, or for the *Slate* website magazine, might be beyond her grasp:

'I came in thinking I wanted to be in broadcasting but I would probably have ended up as a weather-girl . . . I really admire the journalism of the *New Yorker*, even though it is liberal and I really doubt they'd employ me. I want to be a good journalist and if I do it well, I will be spreading the gospel and using the skills God has given me.'

Will Glaser, a twenty-year-old history student from Oregon, admitted another danger: 'In secular schools I believe there is pressure to conform to the ideology of atheism and humanism. I did not want to be taught things I believe to be completely false.' But he's concerned that won't help him get into Berkeley to do postgraduate work – or indeed whether he would really want to go there.

Dr Farris said: 'The goal of education is the search for truth, but if you try to answer questions about how we got here without God, the answer is difficult to provide . . . We believe that God's truth wins out at the end of the discussion.'

The concerns of the Religious Right sometimes stretch in extraordinary directions, but, however strange, they often spread around the world. Shortly before Christmas 2005 John Gibson, who anchors on Rupert Murdoch's Fox Television News, had an unlikely, though well-publicised, success with a tome called *The War on Christmas: How the Liberal Plot to Ban the Sacred Christmas Holiday Is Worse Than You Thought*, in which he alleged, in defiance of sense and reason and in the face of Christmas decorations illuminating the country from Alaska to Texas, that a co-ordinated attempt was under way to stop people celebrating the birth of Christ.

The basis for this idea – which the Pilgrim Fathers would surely have supported, disapproving as they were of conspicuous celebration – was the fact that some stores had started hanging out banners wishing everyone 'Happy Holidays' and that in New York the mayor (a Republican) had decided to call the city's annual fir a 'holiday tree'. There was also the traditional constipation, based on the founding fathers' separation of Church and state, about whether Christian symbols such as cribs and mangers could be erected on public property (a previous court decision had held that they could, providing they were not the only symbols displayed).

As usual, the issue was characterised as a war. Mr Gibson announced: 'The Christians are coming to retake their place in the public square and the most natural battleground in this war is Christmas ... The war on Christmas is joined.' His colleague, the polemicist Bill O'Reilly, immediately spotted a conspiracy: 'There's a very secret plan. And it's a plan that nobody's going to tell you, "Well, we want to diminish Christian philosophy in the USA because we want X, Y and Z." '[6]

If there was a plot, it's one that has been proceeding with marked lack of success for a very long time. In 1921, Henry Ford, the motor magnate, was going on about how 'the international Jew' wanted to eliminate Christmas: 'The whole record of the Jewish opposition to Christmas, Easter and other Christian festivals and their opposition to certain patriotic songs, shows the venom and directness of [their] attack'; and in 1959, with a different target in mind, the Right-wing John Birch Society warned: 'One of the techniques now being applied by the Reds to weaken the pillar of religion in our country is the drive to take Christ out of Christmas – to denude the event of its religious meaning.'[7]

Well, Christmas came and went, celebrated or not, and everyone got on with 2006. But a strange thing happened. The next Christmas there was a sudden flurry of articles in tabloid papers in the UK about similar alleged attacks on Christmas, this time apparently at the behest of town hall bureaucrats and Muslims. Christmas cards were being amended to 'Happy Holidays', public celebrations banned. Religious folk chipped in their outrage. Very little evidence could be found for any of this, beyond some ultra-defensive memos by odd officials and absolutely no imam came forward to protest that he was offended by the Christian festival. Then everyone settled down to enjoy the break in the normal way. Church attendances were up as they always are on Christmas Day, but most Britons commemorated the birth of Christ as they usually do by ignoring the religious part of the holiday.

The point is that this sort of noisy Americanised protest is growing in the UK too, fuelled by resentment – largely by evangelical Christians, it has to be said – that Christianity is supposedly being marginalised. The tactics of the Christian Right are diversifying and globalising, though in the UK at least they have yet to gather real force seriously to influence a government, even one headed by Tony Blair, who is the most ostentatiously religiose prime minister for at least a hundred years.

There were noisy, sectarian protests outside BBC studios at the start of 2005 when the Corporation showed *Jerry Springer: The Opera*, despite a lobbying and e-mailing campaign by Christian groups. One, by a fringe organisation called Christian Voice, even went so far as to post the home addresses of BBC executives on its website so that its followers could make their representations in person. Unfortunately, the organisation has not yet learned to make ecumenical common cause with Catholics. When a group turned up bearing a plaster statue of the Virgin Mary outside the BBC studio in Glasgow at the same time as their Presbyterian colleagues, the two groups nearly came to blows and ended up with rival demonstrations on opposite pavements. Christian Voice, not unlike the Christian Coalition in the USA – though without its resources or media penetration or, frankly, its public recognition – has embraced a wider, political agenda of eclectic variety, including withdrawal from the EU, the restoration of capital punishment, and the removal of traffic calming speed humps from roads.

Other protests have been more serious, however. There have been protests against the British government's sexual orientation measures, first its legislation to allow civil partnerships for same-sex couples, and then its regulations to outlaw discrimination against gays in the provision of goods and services. In the latter case, in early 2007, the Blair government, not without some anguish, ignored the represent-ations of the Roman Catholic hierarchy and the two Archbishops of the Church of England. In Scotland, the Catholic cardinal warned that Catholics would withdraw their traditional support from Labour candidates if the regulations were enacted, though it remained to be seen how many would actually do so.

These campaigns and others lacked the potency and muscle that they would have achieved in the USA, because the circumstances of national life are very different, but more can be expected. Look out for Christians claiming victim-status as an oppressed minority and demanding special rights by virtue of their beliefs. From the noisier fringes there will be resentment that Muslims are not treated in the same way.

In other, less direct ways, the actions of the US Religious Right do impinge internationally. We have seen how they have influenced the current administration in its distribution of foreign aid and how they have contributed to debates on US Middle East policy as well as its domestic priorities. They can have an effect on areas of policy that seem far removed from religious priorities. And if the president gets told that a certain issue is not a priority for them – climate change, for example – then it's an issue that can be downplayed.

Perhaps more than anything else, however, the Religious Right have affected how the rest of the Western world sees the USA. This will worry them not in the least, since they regard the developed world as godless and effete. In the UK and Europe, there is a lofty tendency to dismiss the influence of folk whose motivations sometimes seem obscure and obtuse and to create a picture not far removed from the one Mencken painted of the inhabitants of Tennessee in 1925: all ignorant and superstitious, credulous, country hicks, and therefore beneath contempt and beyond consideration.

This is seriously to misunderstand and underestimate the potency and range of their influence: the sophistication of their lobbying power, the effect on public opinion about events and issues at home and abroad of their television and radio stations, the mobilisation of a coalition of religious groups – not all by any means Protestant evangelical – and the pervasiveness of their role in the social life of a great swathe of the nation. There are good effects of this as well as bad, in the creation of community cohesion and spirit, altruism, charity, and good works and good behaviour, as well as an insularity of

mind and spirit and an occasional credulousness and sanctimoniousness. Hypocrisy too – considering, for instance, that the divorce
statistics for religious people are above the national average – but that
is by no means a specifically US religious affliction.

What this book has striven to show is that the potency of the
American Religious Right did not begin with the inauguration of
George W. Bush in 2001, or even with the rise of the Moral Majority
in reaction to the licentiousness of the 1960s, the high-water mark of
liberal influence in the USA's government. Many of its features – the
attitudes of mind, the style of its preachers, the role of religion in its
government even its periodic spasms of religious revival and fervour –
have been present in US society since its foundation. They have
contributed to constant and long-running strains in American life: the
idea of the elect and God's special favour, the debate over religious
participation in national life, the racial divide, the place of women –
and the family – the suspicion of outsiders and foreigners, and the
ability, or desirability, of legislating to improve moral behaviour,
whether drinking alcohol or abortion. The USA has not settled these
problems, but it has certainly struggled with them for generations. It
is fashionable now to avoid quoting the nineteenth-century French
observer of American society, Alexis de Tocqueville, but the truth is,
he saw it all in the 1830s: 'There is no country in the world where the
Christian religion retains a greater influence over the souls of men
than in America.'[8]

The irony is that this has occurred in a country whose Founding
Fathers wrestled philosophically with the problem of creating a form
of civil government in which all religions could flourish but none
should have priority. That is a large part of the reason for the vibrancy
of US Christianity: it does not have an established Church to bolster
the social and moral structure of the state, and membership of its
religions is a matter of individual choice. Its churches have to compete
and they rise and fall by the dynamism of their clergy and the
persuasiveness of their message.

The Bush administration has been unusually, maybe uniquely,
ostentatious in its religiosity and in some respects has trialled the ideas
of its supporters in its faith-based initiatives, in its appointments of
supporters to positions for which their qualification is their faith not

their expertise – not that other administrations have not done that – and, most noticeably, in its religious rhetoric. The president has delivered on some parts of the constituency's agenda – on stem cell research and marginally on abortion – and he has placed his evangelical Christianity at the heart of his appeal to the electorate. But he has not given them all they want: abortions are still legal, a constitutional marriage amendment has not been delivered. The Religious Right has learned that the art of government is to compromise, and the closer they get to power the more difficult it is. Compromising on beliefs is especially difficult when your preachers and your president deploy the absolutist language of good and evil.

The administration's defining moment came, of course, on September 11th 2001, with the Islamic terrorist outrages in New York and Washington DC. This and the subsequent wars in Afghanistan and Iraq have shaped the character of the government and convulsed the American people, challenging their sense of well-being and security in the most heart-rending and visceral way. Europeans, used to small-scale, limited terrorism, usually for defined political ends, have underestimated the cataclysmic effect of the destruction of the Twin Towers on the US psyche. Abraham Lincoln's assertion that a foreign enemy could never water its horses on the banks of the Mississippi was proved to be – metaphorically at least – no longer true. If some on the Religious Right saw the signs of the End Times, however, that merely boosted what was already a patriotic imperative to support the president and their country in its crisis.

And they have stuck with him. While the rest of the country has grown disenchanted with the miscalculations and the hubris of the war in Iraq and the president's failure to end it, the Christian Right has remained electorally loyal. In the midterm elections of November 2006, when the Republicans lost control of both Houses of Congress, a result seen as a verdict on the administration's foreign policy miscalculations, the evangelical vote stuck with the conservatives. White evangelicals made up 24 per cent of those who voted in 2006, compared with 23 per cent in the presidential election two years before. Exit polls showed that 70 per cent of the born-again voted Republican: two years earlier the figure had been 72 per cent. What was noticeable was that Catholics did peel away: in Ohio, the

Democrats won 20 per cent more of that group than in 2000, and in Pennsylvania it was 11 per cent more.

The New York Times quoted Bobby Clark, deputy director of ProgressNow, a liberal group in Colorado, saying: 'After 2004, people were saying that the Religious Right owns this country now. Far from it. They have networks and the ability to move quickly and to dominate the airwaves, but they do not represent most Americans. Most Americans are pretty moderate people.' By contrast, the Revd Troy Newman of Operation Rescue, the anti-abortion group, blamed the clergy for not energising congregations in his cause: 'The pulpits of America bear responsibility. I believe God will hold them accountable for that.'[9] To such people, God remains an intimately engaged force in the USA's affairs.

This sort of language exasperates traditional Republicans such as Senator Danforth, ordained Episcopalian though he is. It does not resonate throughout the USA either, otherwise Arnold Schwarzenegger, pro-gay, pro-choice, would never have been elected Republican governor of California. The Religious Right has been written off before, but it has not gone away, or changed. It may periodically overreach itself as in the Schiavo case. It may alienate ordinary Americans with its raucous partisanship and naked politisation. But it is deeply entrenched. All the potential candidates for the 2008 presidential election on both sides are either courting it, or demonstrating their Christian credentials. Even the Democrats, who scorned the religious vote for so long, have started wooing it.

This is because it can now be taken to be a long-term feature of the US electoral landscape. The atomisation of US society continues. Behind the entrance gates and along the neat sidewalks of the middle-class housing estates of Middle America, the churches continue their proselytising mission, providing the enclosed society of shared values and common beliefs that provide security and certainty against an increasingly uncertain and hostile outside world. Against this, there could not be a more visceral threat than Islamic terrorism, which seeks to destroy or convert the non-Muslim world and which presents an almost biblical danger. A hundred years ago, the perceived threats of industrialisation, mass immigration, employment dislocation and the destruction wrought on the Western Front by the weaponry of mass destruction created the insecurities that led some people to cling to the gospel of Christian fundamentalism. Now the international uncertainties of the new millennium create a new sense of fear and they are reaching for the same assurances. The Bible explains everything and provides a framework for belief, so long as its injunctions are followed. It even seems to foresee the unfolding of the end of the world, just as it is happening, if you have the eye of faith. No wonder two-thirds of US evangelicals believe that there really will be a Battle of Armageddon.

There are signs that younger evangelicals are setting their sights on new, less tired targets than their elders: the environment, hunger in the developing world and exploitation. The old rallying cries of abortion and gay marriage may soon, at last, no longer be enough to inspire the troops – and the 2008 presidential election will tell whether this is so.

US society does not stand still. By mid-century it will look different from today. Its Hispanic voters will be more in evidence – and they will be, almost certainly, conservative Catholics or Pentecostals. The only question is whether they will be sufficiently motivated to vote. Richard Land's prediction that the evangelicals will outbreed the liberals may well come to pass and, if it does, the offspring are quite likely to be socially conservative.

As they will be throughout the rest of the world. In Africa, the Far East and Latin America, charismatic evangelicalism and Pentecostalism is flourishing, sometimes in direct competition with Islam. Catholicism too is growing. These are beliefs that are not going to evolve new social insights or modify their moral beliefs in the near future. There is no incentive for them to do so, certainly not from their church hierarchies.

God is not dead. He is flourishing in a mass market. And he is not going to go away. The final question remains therefore: is it the USA which is out of step in the modern world in persisting with its old-time religion, or the UK and Europe? And, if it's the latter, what does that say about us?

My mind went back to something John Bryson Chane, the Episcopal Bishop of Washington, had said to me as we sat in his book-lined study months before, at the start of my journey through the Bible belt.[10]

Bishop Chane sat in his rocking chair and mused:

'I was thinking the other night of the evenings when we used to sit out on the porch when I was a boy, listening to the Dragnet radio programme. It was a quieter life. Divorce was low. Of course, there was segregation. But people were more content with what they had. You could live more in your imagination, there wasn't instantaneous communication. But we've gone through a huge cultural upheaval. It's generated in many Americans a sense of disconnectedness and insecurity. Both parents go out to work, there's low employment for young people . . . gang violence . . . drugs . . . economic issues. People are very frightened of losing what they used to have, what they have now. We have not dealt with the trauma of 9/11. We have not found any closure.

'There's a vindictiveness that has transmitted itself into religion and into foreign policy and they have become partners. We're in shock and we're feeling threatened, not just about terrorism, but gay marriage, abortion. The issues are boiled down to black and white and there's no discussion about them. There's a real cultural revolution. We are seeing a significant struggle and it is not going to go away any time soon.'

Notes

1 From Sea to Shining Sea

1 *Smithsonian Guide to Historic America*, vol. IX, pp. 22 and 437.
2 James Morone, *Hellfire Nation*, p. 35.
3 Gospel of St Matthew 5:14.
4 Michael Northcott, *An Angel Directs the Storm*, p. 24.
5 John Micklethwait and Adrian Wooldridge, *The Right Nation*, p. 263.
6 Michelle Goldberg, *Kingdom Coming*, p. 181.
7 Kevin Phillips, *American Theocracy*, pp. 102–3.
8 Pew Forum poll: Religion and Public Life, a Faith-Based Partisan Divide, January 2005.
9 Micklethwait and Wooldridge, op. cit., p. 187.
10 Thomas Frank, *What's the Matter with Kansas?*, p. 168.
11 Micklethwait and Wooldridge, op. cit., p. 112.
12 Pew Research Center survey, August 2006.
13 Micklethwait and Wooldridge, op. cit., p. 20, citing US Census for 1980, 1990 and 2000 at www.census.gov/press-release/www/releases/archives/census_2000/000717.html.
14 Ronald Green, 'The Diverse Sources and Invented Causes of the Religious Right', in *Conscience: the News Journal of Catholic Opinion*, Autumn 2006, vol. XXVII, no. 3.
15 Goldberg, op. cit., pp. 189–90, citing Steven Hill, *Fixing Elections, The Failure of America's Winner Take All Politics* (2002).
16 Andrew O'Hehir, 'Is the Homeland where America's Heart Is?' in *Salon.com*, posted 28.9.06.
17 Frank, op. cit., p. 26.
18 Phillips, op. cit., p. 175.
19 Micklethwait and Wooldridge, op. cit., pp. 306–7.
20 Interview with Randy Brinson, 17.5.06.
21 *Washington Times*, 28.4.06.
22 www.titusonenine.com, posted 18.11.06.

23 Goldberg, op. cit., p. 18.
24 Goldberg, op. cit., p. 41.
25 Randall Balmer, *Thy Kingdom Come*, pp. 8–9.
26 Interview with Dr Jim Tonkowich, 8.5.06.
27 Balmer, op. cit., p. 175.
28 Morone, op. cit., p. 4.
29 Micklethwait and Wooldridge, op. cit., p. 254, citing Krugman, *The Great Unravelling*, p. 177.
30 Micklethwait and Wooldridge, op. cit., p. 10 and appendix.
31 Morone, op. cit., p. 495.
32 Interview with Michael Cromartie, 11.5.06.

2 Men of God

1 Interview with Dr Richard Land, 13.6.06.
2 *Washington Post*, 11.1.07.
3 Interview with Dr Jim Tonkowich, 8.5.06.
4 'Follow the Money', article by Jim Naughton, published in *Washington Window*, magazine of the diocese of Washington DC, spring 2006.
5 Jim Wallis, *God's Politics*, p. 150.
6 George Walden, *God Won't Save America*, p. 189.
7 Interview with Jim Wallis, 9.5.06.
8 Wallis, op. cit., p. 3.

3 And This Be Our Motto – 'In God Is Our Trust'

1 Jon Meacham, *American Gospel*, p. 42.
2 James Morone, *Hellfire Nation*, p. 35.
3 Morone, op. cit., pp. 40–1.
4 Frank Lambert, *The Founding Fathers*, p. 88.
5 Morone, op. cit., pp. 60–1.
6 Meacham, op. cit., p. 51.
7 Frances Hill, *A Delusion of Satan*, p. 45.
8 Morone, op. cit., p. 88.
9 Hill, op. cit., pp. 172–3.
10 Hill, op. cit., p. 208.
11 Morone, op. cit., p. 94.
12 Hill, op. cit., p. 215.
13 Morone, op. cit., p. 94.

4 No King but King Jesus

1   Roy Moore, *So Help Me God*, p. 231.
2   Roy Moore, *Our American Birthright,* composed 2003.
3   Ray Suarez, *The Holy Vote*, p. 239.
4   Suarez, op. cit., p. 240.
5   Michelle Goldberg, *Kingdom Coming*, p. 26.
6   Interview with Judge Moore, 17.5.06.
7   Noah Feldman, *Divided by God*, p. 175.
8   See 'William Blackstone and the Historians' by Wilfrid Prest, *History Today*, July 2006.
9   Suarez, op. cit., p. 240.
10   David McCullough, *John Adams*, p. 84.
11   Mark. A. Noll, ed., *Religion and American Politics*, chapter by John M. Murrin, p. 23.
12   James Morone, *Hellfire Nation*, p. 102.
13   Morone, op. cit., p. 104.
14   Morone, op. cit, p. 105.
15   Morone, op. cit., pp. 106–7.
16   David Aikman, *A Man of Faith*, p. 180.
17   Samuel Eliot Morison, *Oxford History of the American People*, vol. 1, p. 395.
18   Noll, op. cit., p. 29.
19   E. M. Halliday, *Understanding Thomas Jefferson*, p. 203.
20   Aikman, op. cit., p. 183.
21   Frank Lambert, *The Founding Fathers and the Place of Religion in America*, p. 160.
22   Randall Balmer, *The Kingdom Come*, pp. 52–3.
23   Mark Weldon Whitten, *The Myth of Christian America*, citing Barton, p. 39.
24   Goldberg, op. cit., p. 45.
25   Paul F. Boller Jnr, *Presidential Campaigns*, p. 12.
26   Sister Helen Prejean, *The Death of Innocents*, pp. 185–7.
27   Robert Boston, *Why the Religious Right is Wrong*, p. 67.
28   Boston, op. cit., p. 74.
29   Boston, op. cit., p. 266.
30   Balmer, op. cit., p. 50.
31   Halliday, op. cit., p. 151.
32   Boston, op. cit., p. 78.

5 A Fiery Gospel, Writ in Burnished Rows of Steel

1 Jon Meacham, *American Gospel*, p. 141.
2 James M. McPherson, *Battle Cry of Freedom*, p. 32.
3 Mark A. Noll, *Religion and American Politics*, chapter by Nathan O. Hatch, p. 104.
4 Noll, op. cit., p. 100.
5 James Morone, *Hellfire Nation*, p. 124.
6 Morone, op. cit., p. 127.
7 W. J. Cash, *The Mind of the South*, p. 56.
8 Kevin Phillips, *American Theocracy*, p. 150.
9 McPherson, op. cit., p. 90.
10 Morone, op. cit., p. 186.
11 Stephen B. Oates, *To Purge this Land with Blood*, p. 30.
12 Byron Farwell, *Stonewall*, p. 134.
13 Phillips, op. cit., p. 150.
14 Morone, op. cit., p. 175.
15 Morone, op. cit., p. 182.
16 Oates, op. cit., p. 20.
17 Shelby Foote, *The Civil War*, vol. 3, p. 356.
18 Randall Miller, Harry S. Stout, Charles Wilson, eds, *Religion and the American Civil War*, p. 15.
19 Randall Balmer, *Thy Kingdom Come*, p. 17.
20 William Martin, *With God on our Side*, p. 58.
21 Balmer, op. cit., pp. 15–16.
22 Phillips, op. cit., p. 168.
23 Debby Applegate, *The Most Famous Man in America* (2006).
24 Steve Fraser, *Wall Street*, pp. 122–3.
25 Sydney Ahlstrom, *A Religious History of the American People*, pp. 744–5.
26 George M. Marsden, *Fundamentalism and American Culture*, p. 33.
27 Morone, op. cit., p. 223.
28 Morone, op. cit., p. 235.
29 Morone, op. cit., p. 250, citing James Mohr, *Abortion in America* (1978) and Catherine Clinton, *The Other Civil War* (1999).
30 Morone, op. cit., p. 268.
31 Morone, op. cit., p. 240.
32 Article in *Harper's Weekly*, 22.5.1915.
33 J. C. Furnas, *The Americans*, p. 505.
34 Jacob Riis, *How the Other Half Lives*, p. 159.
35 Luc Sante, *Low Life*, p. 118.

36 Morone, op. cit., p. 304.

37 Morone, op. cit., p. 308.

38 Frederick L. Allen, *Only Yesterday*, p. 213.

6 A Book Dropped Out of Heaven

1   Louis W. Koenig, *Bryan*, p. 63.

2   Koenig, op. cit., p. 465.

3   Garry Wills, *Under God*, p. 99.

4   Koenig, op. cit., p. 465.

5   Diana Preston, *Lusitania*, p. 343.

6   Listen, for example, to Bryan's speeches in 1908, on *In Their Own Voices: Recordings from US Presidential Elections, 1908 and 1912*, *www.marstonrecords.com*. Some of us are sad enough to have bought this.

7   Koenig, op. cit., p. 197.

8   Paul F. Boller Jnr, *Presidential Campaigns*, pp. 167–78.

9   Jon Meacham, *American Gospel*, pp. 147–8.

10 George M. Marsden, *Fundamentalism and American Culture*, p. 132.

11 Marsden, op. cit., pp. 133–4.

12 Marsden, op. cit., p. 92.

13 Mark A. Noll, *The Scandal of the Evangelical Mind*, p. 3.

14 Dan Cohn-Sherbok, *The Politics of Apocalypse*, p. 14.

15 For an account of The Fundamentals, see Marsden, op. cit., chapter 14, and Ahlstrom, op. cit., chapter 48.

16 Sydney Ahlstrom, *A Religious History of the American People*, p. 816.

17 Marsden, op. cit., pp. 118–22.

18 Randall Balmer, *Mine Eyes Have Seen the Glory*, p. 36.

19 Grant Wacker, *Heaven Below*, p. 60.

20 Pew Forum poll, 5.10.06: www.pewforum.org.

21 Ahlstrom, op. cit., p. 823.

22 Robert F. Martin, *Hero of the Heartland*, p. 33.

23 Marsden, op. cit., p. 130.

24 Martin, op. cit., p. 89.

25 Morone, *Hellfire Nation*, p. 335.

26 Martin, op. cit., p. 13.

27 Marsden, op. cit., p. 142.

28 Joel Carpenter, *Revive Us Again*, p. 40.

29 Ahlstrom, op. cit., p. 824.

30 Koenig, op. cit., p. 614.

7 Monkey Town

1   See 'Creating Whoopee' by the author, *Guardian*, 15.7.95.
2   Frederick L. Allen, *Only Yesterday*, p. 178.
3   *Washington Post*, 13.8.05.
4   Chris Mooney, *The Republican War on Science*, p. 36.
5   Edward J. Larson, *Summer for the Gods*, p. 50.
6   George M. Marsden, *Fundamentalism and American Culture*, p. 221.
7   Edward Caudill, *The Scopes Trial, A Photographic History*, p. 4.
8   Larson, op. cit., p. 27.
9   Larson, op. cit., p. 59.
10 Larson, op. cit., p. 111.
11 Caudill, op. cit., p. 5.
12 See John Scopes and James Presley, *Centre of the Storm*, chapter 5.
13 Larson, op. cit., p. 47.
14 Richard Hofstadter, *Social Darwinism in American Thought*, pp. 46–8.
15 Larson, op. cit., p. 198.
16 Marion E. Rodgers, *Mencken: The American Iconoclast*, biography, p. 272.
17 Kevin Tierney, *Darrow*, p. 369.
18 Allen, op. cit., p. 201.
19 Caudill, op. cit., p. 6.
20 Interview with Sonny Robinson, 12.5.95.
21 Marion E. Rodgers, *The Impossible H. L. Mencken*, collected articles, p. 567.
22 Rodgers, *Impossible H. L. Mencken*, p. 579.
23 Garry Wills, *Under God*, p. 98.
24 Rodgers, *Mencken*, op. cit., p. 281.
25 Louis W. Koenig, *Bryan*, p. 651.
26 Rodgers, *Mencken*, op. cit., p. 291.
27 Larson, op. cit., p. 190.
28 Koenig, op. cit., p. 655.
29 Rodgers, *Impossible H. L. Mencken*, op. cit., pp. 606–7.
30 Interviews in Dayton, 11–13.5.95.

8 Creation Men

1   Interview with Ken Ham *et al.*, 6.11.06.
2   Randall Balmer, *Thy Kingdom Come*, p. 126.
3   Roger Patterson, *Evolution Exposed*, p. 10, quoting Ephesians 4:14–15.
4   Patterson, op. cit., p. 25.

5 Patterson, op. cit., p. 220.

6 Patterson, op. cit., pp. 221–2.

7 Patterson, op. cit., p. 26.

8 Patterson, op. cit., pp. 28–9.

9 Balmer, op. cit., p. 110.

10 Balmer, op. cit., p. 122.

11 Chris Mooney, *The Republican War on Science*, p. 180.

12 Balmer, op. cit., p. 121.

13 Balmer, op. cit., p. 123.

14 Michelle Goldberg, *Kingdom Coming*, p. 86, citing Philip E. Johnson, *The Wedge of Truth*, pp. 157–8.

15 Goldberg, op. cit., p. 84.

16 Goldberg, op. cit., p. 84.

17 John Micklethwait and Adrian Wooldridge, *The Right Nation*, p. 159.

18 Mooney, op. cit., p. 173.

19 Goldberg, op. cit., p. 83, citing Center for Science and Culture website.

20 Balmer, op. cit., p. 133.

21 Goldberg, op. cit., p. 86.

22 Goldberg, op. cit., p. 87.

23 Goldberg, op. cit., p. 82.

24 Mooney, op. cit., p. 171.

25 Goldberg, op. cit., see chapter 3.

26 Balmer, op. cit., p. 124.

27 Mooney, op. cit., p. 184.

28 Esther Kaplan, *With God on their Side*, pp. 91–4.

29 Mooney, op. cit., p. 39.

30 Patterson, op. cit., p. 114.

31 See: www.ucusa.org/global_environment/rsi/page.cfm?pageID=1320.

9 The Golden Hour of the Little Flower

1 Visit to EWTN, 16.5.06.

2 Raymond Arroyo, *Mother Angelica*, p. 145.

3 *Sunday Night Live*, EWTN, 14.5.06.

4 Mark Wahlgren Summers, *Rum, Romanism and Rebellion*, p. 282.

5 Paul F. Boller Jnr, *Presidential Campaigns*, pp. 150–1.

6 Robert A. Slayton, *Empire Statesman*, p. 303.

7 Damon Linker, *The Theocons*, pp. 172–3.

8 Kevin Phillips, *American Theocracy*, p. 216.

9   Alan Brinkley, *Voices of Protest*, p. 91.
10   Brinkley, op. cit., p. 92.
11   Conrad Black, *Franklin Delano Roosevelt*, p. 328.
12   Brinkley, op. cit., p. 267.
13   Sydney E. Ahlstrom, *A Religious History of the American People*, p. 1007.
14   William Martin, *With God on Our Side*, pp. 53–4.

10 God Will Make You Better

1   Interview with Joel Osteen, 21.5.06.
2   *The Church Report*, 8.1.07.
3   Interview with Bishop T. D. Jakes, 15.5.06, and visit to the Potter's House, 19.5.06.
4   Shayne Lee, *T. D. Jakes*, p. 83.
5   T. D. Jakes sermon, broadcast 14.5.06.
6   Lee, op. cit., pp. 2–7.
7   Interview with Bishop Wayne Malcolm, 13.12.06.
8   Edith L. Blumhofer, *Everybody's Sister*, p. 158. Information on Aimee Semple McPherson is taken from this biography and others on the web.
9   George M. Marsden, *Fundamentalism and American Culture*, p. 188.
10   Marsden, op. cit., p. 190.
11   Marsden, op. cit., p. 220.
12   Marsden, op. cit., p. 191, citing Walter Lippmann, *A Preface to Morals*, 1929.
13   Marsden, op. cit., p. 190.
14   Joel A. Carpenter, *Revive Us Again*, p. 219.
15   Carpenter, op. cit., p. 217.
16   William Martin, *With God on Our Side*, pp. 32–3.
17   Martin, op. cit., p. 145.
18   Janet Lowe, *Billy Graham Speaks*, p. 146.
19   *New Yorker* article, 22.8.05.
20   *Time* magazine article, 15.11.93.
21   *New Yorker*, op. cit.

11 A Fundamentally Conservative Nation

1   Quoted in *The Tablet* magazine, 11.11.06.
2   William Martin, *With God on Our Side*, p. 74.

3   John Micklethwait and Adrian Wooldridge, *The Right Nation*, p. 59.
4   Martin, op. cit., pp. 87–8.
5   Martin, op. cit., pp. 98–9.
6   Cal Thomas, *Blinded by Might*, p. 249.
7   Martin, op. cit., pp. 175–7.
8   Micklethwait and Wooldridge, op. cit., p. 81.
9   *New Yorker* magazine profile, 7.11.05, p. 136.
10   *New Yorker*, op. cit.
11   Martin, op. cit., p. 163.
12   *New Yorker*, op. cit.
13   Morone, *Hellfire Nation*, p. 453.
14   Martin, op. cit., p. 196.
15   Sara Diamond, *Not By Politics Alone*, p. 68.
16   Martin, op. cit., p. 310.
17   Martin, op. cit., p. 207.
18   Randall Balmer, *Mine Eyes Have Seen the Glory*, p. 170.
19   Martin, op. cit., p. 296.
20   Kimberly Blaker, *The Fundamentals of Extremism*, p. 179.
21   Micklethwait and Wooldridge, p. 111.
22   Martin, op. cit., p. 300.
23   Robert Boston, *Close Encounters with the Religious Right*, p. 150.
24   Martin, op. cit., p. 333.
25   Nina Easton, *Gang of Five*, p. 329.
26   *Guardian* report, 24.8.05.
27   Blaker, op. cit., pp. 7–8.
28   Ralph Reed, *Active Faith*, p. 240.
29   Boston, op. cit., p. 178.
30   Boston, op. cit., p. 197.
31   Thomas, op. cit., pp. 42–3.

12 The Man of Faith

1   Stephen Mansfield, *The Faith of George W. Bush*, p. 114.
2   See www.blessitt.com/bush.html for an account of the encounter.
3   Mansfield, op. cit., p. 69.
4   George W. Bush, *A Charge to Keep*, p. 35.
5   Bill Minutaglio, *First Son*, p. 210.
6   Micklethwait and Wooldridge, *Right Nation*, op. cit., p. 145.
7   See James McPherson's essay: 'How Lincoln Won the War with Metaphor'

in *Abraham Lincoln and the Second American Revolution*.

8   David Domke, *God Willing?*, pp. 1–2.
9   Domke, op. cit., p. 16.
10 Jennifer S. Butler, *Born Again*, p. 107.
11 Mansfield, op. cit., p. 111.
12 Mansfield, op. cit., p. 83.
13 Robert Wright, article in *New York Times*, 27.10.04.
14 Mansfield, op. cit., p. 109.
15 Mansfield, op. cit., p. 111.
16 David Kuo, *Tempting Faith*, p. 113.
17 David Aikman, *A Man of Faith*, p. 205.
18 Demke, op. cit., p. 63.
19 Aikman, op. cit., p. 213.
20 Wright article in *New York Times*, op. cit.
21 Aikman, op. cit., p. 210.
22 Micklethwait and Wooldridge, op. cit., pp. 145–6.
23 Kuo, op. cit., p. 171.
24 Kuo, op. cit., p. 86.
25 Esther Kaplan, *With God on Their Side*, p. 34.
26 Molly Ivins and Lou Dubose, Shrub, *The Short but Happy Political Life of George W. Bush*, p. 66.
27 Kuo, op. cit., p. 216.
28 Kuo, op. cit., p. 229.
29 Kuo, op. cit., pp. 239–40.
30 Kuo, op. cit., p. 229.
31 Aikman, op. cit., p. 207.

13 Matters of Life and Death

1   James Morone, *Hellfire Nation*, p. 454.
2   Noah Feldman, *Divided by God*, p. 195.
3   Randall Balmer, *Thy Kingdom Come*, pp. 12–13.
4   Esther Kaplan, *With God on Their Side*, p. 140.
5   Ray Suarez, *The Holy Vote*, p. 180.
6   Kaplan, op. cit., p. 114.
7   Suarez, op. cit., p. 170, and Kaplan, op. cit., pp. 114–17, both have accounts.
8   Michelle Goldberg, *Kingdom Coming*, pp. 140–1.
9   Kaplan, op. cit., p. 130.

10 Kaplan, op. cit., p. 106.

11 Morone, op. cit., p. 454.

12 Kevin Phillips, *American Theocracy*, p. 374.

13 Suarez, op. cit., p. 164.

14 Goldberg, op. cit., p. 146.

15 Goldberg, op. cit., p. 136.

16 Study by Annie E. Casey Foundation, 2003, cited by Kaplan, op. cit., p. 204.

17 Kaplan, op. cit., p. 211.

18 Kaplan, op. cit., p. 201.

19 Phillips, op. cit., p. 368.

20 Kaplan, op. cit., p. 218.

21 Kaplan, op. cit., p. 150.

22 Robert Boston, *Close Encounters with the Religious Right*, p. 179.

23 Stephen Bates, *A Church at War*, p. 232.

24 Kimberly Blaker, *The Fundamentals of Extremism*, p. 26.

25 See discussion in Chapter 3, Bates, op. cit.

26 Suarez, op. cit., pp. 91–2.

27 Presidential Statement, 24.2.04, cited by Suarez, op. cit., p. 93.

28 Suarez, op. cit., p. 108.

29 Phillips, op. cit., p. 239.

30 David Frum, *The Right Man: The Accidental Presidency of George W. Bush,* p. 110.

31 Kaplan, op. cit., p. 125.

32 See discussion in Chris Mooney, *The Republican War on Science*, chapter 12.

33 Mooney, op. cit., p. 198.

34 Elizabeth Blackburn, article in *Washington Post*, 7.3.04, cited in Mooney, op. cit., p. 200.

35 Pew Forum research finding, July 2005, cited in Phillips, op. cit., p. 372.

36 *New York Times*, 12.1.07.

37 *Chicago Tribune*, 12.1.07.

38 John Danforth, *Faith and Politics*, p. 71.

39 Danforth, op. cit., p. 72.

40 Danforth, op. cit., pp. 76–7.

41 Interview with Richard Cizik, 10.5.06.

42 *Washington Post*, 16.3.07.

43 *Guardian*, 27.1.07.

44 Phillips, op. cit., p. 235.

14 Armageddon

1   Interview with Tim LaHaye, 23.5.06.
2   For analysis, see LeAnn Snow Flesher, *Left Behind?*
3   Tim LaHaye, *The Merciful God of Prophecy*, p. 165.
4   Tim LaHaye and Greg Dinallo, *Babylon Rising*, pp. 10–11.
5   Interview with David Parsons, 2.12.05.
6   Dan Cohn-Sherbok, *The Politics of Apocalypse*, p. 170.
7   Cohn-Sherbok, op. cit., p. 145.
8   Cohn-Sherbok, op. cit., p. 152, citing Lindsey, *Countdown to Armageddon*, p. 11 and *Final Battle*, p. pxxi.
9   Cohn-Sherbok, op. cit., p. 153, quoting Lindsey, *Late Great Planet Earth*, p. 284.
10 Cohn-Sherbok, op. cit., p. 147.
11 Cohn-Sherbok, op. cit., p. 162.
12 International Christian Embassy, Jerusalem, Fact Sheet.
13 David Parsons, *Swords into Ploughshares*.
14 Parsons, op. cit., p. 28.
15 Cohn-Sherbok, p. 176.
16 Max Blumenthal, *Birth Pangs of a New Christian Zionism*, posted online at *The Nation*, 8.8.06: www.thenation.com.
17 Article by Alexandra Alter, *Miami Herald*, 8.8.06.
18 Blumenthal article, op. cit.
19 Blumenthal, op. cit.
20 Jennifer Butler, *Born Again*, p. 2.
21 Sara Diamond, *Not by Politics Alone*, pp. 128–9.
22 Butler, op. cit., p. 27.
23 *Daily Telegraph*, 19.6.06.
24 George Weigel, article in *First Things*, February 2004.
25 See www.titusonenine.com, 30.1.07.
26 Walter Russell Mead article in *Christian Science Monitor*, August 2003, cited by Butler, op. cit., p. 138.
27 Joseph Bottum article in *First Things*, July 2005, and article by William Kristol and Robert Kagan in *Foreign Affairs*, 1996, cited by Butler, op. cit., p. 139.

15 We Are a Different People

1 Stephen Mansfield, *The Faith of George W. Bush*, p. 174.
2 John Micklethwait and Adrian Wooldridge, *The Right Nation*, p. 194.
3 Patrick Henry College, 2006–7 Catalogue.
4 Interview with Michael Farris and Patrick Henry College students, 7.11.06.
5 Michelle Goldberg, *Kingdom Coming*, p. 173.
6 *Sunday Times*, 18.12.05.
7 See *How the Secular Humanist Grinch Didn't Steal Christmas* by Michelle Goldberg, published on Salon.com, 21.11.05.
8 Seymour Martin Lipset, *American Exceptionalism*, p. 62.
9 *New York Times*, 9.11.06.
10 Interview with Bishop John Chane, 9.5.06.

Bibliography

Ahlstrom, Sydney E., *A Religious History of the American People* (Yale 2004).

Aikman, David, *A Man of Faith: The Spiritual Journey of George W. Bush* (W Publishing Group 2004).

Allen, Frederick Lewis, *Only Yesterday: An Informal History of the 1920s* (Perennial Library Classics 2000 edition).

Allsop, Kenneth, *The Bootleggers* (Hutchinson 1961).

Applegate, Debby, *The Most Famous Man in America: The Biography of Henry Ward Beecher* (Doubleday 2006).

Arroyo, Raymond, *Mother Angelica* (Doubleday 2005).

Balmer, Randall, *Mine Eyes Have Seen the Glory* (Oxford 2006 edition).

Balmer, Randall, *Thy Kingdom Come: How the Religious Right Distorts the Faith and Threatens America* (Basic Books 2006).

Balz, Dan, and Brownstein, Ronald, *Storming the Gates: Protest Politics and the Republican Revival* (Little, Brown and Co. 1996).

Bates, Stephen, *A Church at War: Anglicans and Homosexuality* (Tauris 2004).

Bible, Authorised, King James Version (Oxford World's Classics 1998 edition).

Black, Conrad, *Franklin Delano Roosevelt* (Public Affairs 2003).

Blaker, Kimberly (ed.), *The Fundamentals of Extremism: The Christian Right in America* (New Boston Books 2003).

Blumhofer, Edith L., *Aimee Semple McPherson, Everybody's Sister* (Eerdmans 2003).

Bode, Carl, *Mencken* (Johns Hopkins University Press 1986).

Boller, Paul F. Jnr, *Presidential Campaigns* (Oxford 1985).

Boston, Robert, *Close Encounters with the Religious Right* (Prometheus 2000).

Boston, Robert, *Why the Religious Right is Wrong about Separation of Church and State* (Prometheus 2003).

Brinkley, Alan, *Voices of Protest: Huey Long, Father Coughlin and the Great Depression* (Vintage 1983).

Bryson, Bill, *Made in America* (Secker and Warburg 1994).

Bryson, Bill, *Mother Tongue* (Penguin 1991).

Burge, Ted, *Science and the Bible: Evidence-based Christian Belief* (Templeton Foundation Press 2005).

Burleigh, Michael, *Sacred Causes: Religion and Politics from the European Dictators to Al Qaeda* (Harper Press 2006).

Bush, George W., *A Charge to Keep: My Journey to the White House* (Perennial 2001).

Butler, Jennifer S., *Born Again: The Christian Right Globalised* (Pluto Press 2006).

Butler, Jon, *Awash in a Sea of Faith: Christianising the American People* (Harvard 1990).

Carette, Jeremy, and King, Richard, *Selling Spirituality: The Silent Takeover of Religion* (Routledge 2005).

Carpenter, Joel A., *Revive Us Again: The Reawakening of American Fundamentalism* (Oxford 1997).

Cash, W. J., *The Mind of the South* (Vintage 1991 edition).

Caudill, Edward, *The Scopes Trial, a Photographic History* (University of Tennessee Press 2000).

Coffey, Thomas A., *The Long Thirst: Prohibition in America* (Hamish Hamilton 1976).

Cohn-Sherbok, Dan, *The Politics of Apocalypse: The History and Influence of Christian Zionism* (OneWorld Publications 2006).

Danforth, Senator John, *Faith and Politics* (Viking 2006).

Dennett, Daniel C., *Breaking the Spell: Religion as a Natural Phenomenon* (Penguin 2006).

Diamond, Sara, *Not by Politics Alone: The Enduring Influence of the Christian Right* (Guilford Press 1998).

Diamond, Sara, *Roads to Dominion: Right-wing Movements and Political Power in the United States* (Guilford Press 1995).

Domke, David, *God Willing? Political Fundamentalism and the White House, the War on Terror and the Echoing Press* (Pluto Press 2004).

Easton, Nina J., *Gang of Five, Leaders at the Centre of the Conservative Ascendancy* (Simon and Schuster 2000).

Ellis, Joseph J., *Founding Brothers: The Revolutionary Generation* (Vintage 2002).

Farwell, Byron, *Stonewall: A Biography of General Thomas J. Jackson* (Norton 1993).

Feldman, Noah, *Divided by God: America's Church-State Problem and What We Should Do About It* (Farrar, Straus and Giroux 2005).

Flesher, LeAnn Snow, *Left Behind? The Facts behind the Fiction* (Judson Press 2006).

Foner, Eric, and Garraty, John A. (eds), *The Reader's Companion to American History* (Houghton Mifflin 1991).

Foote, Shelby, The Civil War, 3 volumes (Bodley Head edition 1991).

Frank, Thomas, *What's the Matter with Kansas? How Conservatives Won the Heart of America* (Metropolitan 2004).

Fraser, Steve, *Wall Street: A Cultural History* (Faber 2005).

Frum, David, *The Right Man: The Accidental Presidency of George W. Bush* (Random House 2003).

Furnas, J. C., *The Americans: A Social History of the US 1587–1914* (Longman 1970).

Gilgoff, Dan, *The Jesus Machine* (St Martin's Press 2007).

Gingrich, Newt, and Armey, Dick, *Contract with America* (Times Books 1994).

Glad, Paul W., McKinley, *Bryan and the People* (Lippincott 1964).

Goldberg, Michelle, *Kingdom Coming: The Rise of Christian Nationalism* (Norton 2006).

Graham, Billy, *Just As I Am* (HarperCollins 1998).

Green, John C., Rozell, Mark J., and Wilcox, Clyde, eds, *The Christian Right in American Politics: Marching to the Millennium* (Georgetown University Press 2003).

Green, John C., Rozell, Mark J., and Wilcox, Clyde, eds, *The Values Campaign? The Christian Right and the 2004 Elections* (Georgetown University Press 2006).

Halliday, E. M., *Understanding Thomas Jefferson* (Perennial 2002).

Hamilton, Marci A, *God vs The Gavel: Religion and the Rule of Law* (Cambridge 2005).

Handlin, Oscar, *Al Smith and His America* (Northeastern University Press 1987).

Hatch, Nathan O., *The Democratisation of American Christianity* (Yale 1989).

Herbert, David (ed.), *Everyman's Book of Evergreen Verse* (Dent 1981).

Heyrman, Christine Leigh, *Southern Cross: The Beginnings of the Bible Belt* (Chapel Hill 1997).

Hill, Frances, *A Delusion of Satan: The Full Story of the Salem Witch Trials* (Penguin 1996).

Hofstadter, Richard, *Anti-Intellectualism in American Life* (Vintage 1963).

Hofstadter, Richard, *The Age of Reform from Bryan to FDR* (Cape 1968 edition).

Hofstadter, Richard, *Social Darwinism in American Thought* (Beacon Press 1992 edition).

Isikoff, Michael, *Uncovering Clinton* (Three Rivers Press 2000).

Ivins, Molly, and Dubose, Lou, *Shrub: The Short but Happy Political Life of George W. Bush* (Vintage 2000).

Jackson, Kenneth T. (ed.), *The Enclyclopaedia of New York City* (Yale 1995).

Kaplan, Esther, *With God on their Side: George W Bush and the Christian Right* (The New Press 2005).

Koenig, Louis W., *Bryan* (Putnam 1971).

Kuo, David, *Tempting Faith: An Inside Story of Political Seduction* (Free Press 2006).

LaHaye, Tim, and Dinallo, Greg, *Babylon Rising* (Hodder and Stoughton 2004).

LaHaye, Tim, and Phillips, Bob, *The Europa Conspiracy* (Hodder and Stoughton 2006).

LaHaye, Tim, *The Merciful God of Prophecy: His Loving Plan for You in the End Times* (Hodder and Stoughton 2003).

Lambert, Frank, *The Founding Fathers and the Place of Religion in America* (Princeton 2003).

Larson, Edward J., *Summer for the Gods: The Scopes Trial and America's Continuing Debate over Science and Religion* (Harvard 1998).

Lee, Shayne, *T. D. Jakes, America's New Preacher* (New York University Press 2005).

Lerner, Michael, *The Left Hand of God: Taking Back our Country from the Religious Right* (HarperCollins 2006).

Linker, Damon, *The Theocons: Secular America Under Siege* (Doubleday 2006).

Lipset, Seymour Martin, *American Exceptionalism* (Norton 1996).

Longley, Clifford, *Chosen People: The Big Idea that Shapes England and America* (Hodder and Stoughton 2002).

Lowe, Janet, *Billy Graham Speaks* (Wiley 1999).

Macaulay, Lord, *The History of England* (Penguin edition 1983).

Mansfield, Stephen, *The Faith of George W. Bush* (Penguin 2003).

Marsden, George M., *Fundamentalism and American Culture: The Shaping of 20th Century Evangelicalism 1870–1925* (Oxford 1980).

Marsden, George M., *Understanding Fundamentalism and Evangelicalism* (Eerdmans 1991).

Martin, Robert F., *Hero of the Heartland: Billy Sunday and the Transformation of American Society 1862–1935* (Indiana University Press 2002).

Martin, William, *With God on Our Side: The Rise of the Religious Right in America* (Broadway Books 2005 edition).

Matthews, Arthur H., *Standing Up, Standing Together, The Emergence of the National Association of Evangelicals* (NAE 1992).

McCullough, David, *John Adams* (Simon and Schuster 2001).

McPherson, James M., *Battle Cry of Freedom* (Oxford 1988).

McPherson, James M., *Abraham Lincoln and the Second American Revolution* (Oxford 1991).

Meacham, Jon, *American Gospel: God, the Founding Fathers and the Making of a Nation* (Random House 2006).

Micklethwait, John, and Wooldridge, Adrian, *The Right Nation: Why America is Different* (Penguin 2005).

Miller, Randall M., Stout, Harry S., Wilson, Charles R., eds, *Religion and the American Civil War* (Oxford 1998).

Milner, Clyde A. II (ed.), *The Oxford History of the American West* (Oxford 1994).

Minutaglio, Bill, *First Son: George W. Bush and the Bush Family Dynasty* (Three Rivers Press 1999).

Moats, David, *Civil Wars: A Battle for Gay Marriage* (Harcourt 2004).

Mooney, Chris, *The Republican War on Science* (Basic Books 2005).

Moore, Roy, and Perry, John, *So Help Me God: The Ten Commandments, Judicial Tyranny and the Battle for Religious Freedom* (Broadman and Holman 2005).

Moore, Roy, *Our Legal Heritage* (Foundation for Moral Law Inc 2003).

Moran, Jeffrey P., *The Scopes Trial* (Bedford, St Martin's 2002).

Morgan, Edmund S., *Benjamin Franklin* (Yale 2002).

Morison, Samuel Eliot, *The Oxford History of the American People*, 3 vols (New American Library edition 1972).

Morone, James A., *Hellfire Nation: The Politics of Sin in American History* (Yale 2003).

Naughton, Jim, *Catholics in Crisis* (Addison Wesley 1996).

Noll, Mark A. (ed.), *Religion and American Politics from the Colonial Period to the 1980s* (Oxford 1990).

Noll, Mark A., *The Scandal of the Evangelical Mind* (Eerdmans 1994).

Noll, Mark A., Hatch, Nathan A. and Marsden, George M., *The Search for Christian America* (Helmes and Howard 1989).

Northcott, Michael, *An Angel Directs the Storm: Apocalyptic Religion and American Empire* (Tauris 2004).

Oates, Stephen B., *To Purge this Land with Blood: A Biography of John Brown* (University of Massachusetts Press 1984).

Parsons, David, *Swords into Ploughshares: Christian Zionism and the Battle of Armageddon* (International Christian Embassy, Jerusalem, 2004).

Patrick Henry College, Catalogue 2006–7.

Patterson, Roger, *Evolution Exposed* (Answers in Genesis 2006).

Phillips, Kevin, *American Theocracy: The Peril and Politics of Radical Religion, Oil and Borrowed Money in the 21st Century* (Viking Penguin 2006).

Pinsky, Mark I., *A Jew Among the Evangelicals: A Guide for the Perplexed* (Westminster John Knox Press 2006).

Prejean, Sister Helen, *The Death of Innocents: An Eyewitness Account of Wrongful Executions* (Canterbury Press 2006).

Preston, Diana, *Lusitania* (Berkeley 2003).

Rauch, Jonathan, *Gay Marriage: Why it is Good for Gays, Good for Straights and Good for America* (Times Books 2004).

Reed, Ralph, *Active Faith* (Free Press 1996).

Riis, Jacob A., *How the Other Half Lives* (Penguin edition 1997).

Rodgers, Marion Elizabeth, *The Impossible H. L. Mencken* (Anchor 1991).

Rodgers, Marion Elizabeth, *Mencken, The American Iconoclast* (Oxford 2005).

Ross, Shelley, *Washington Babylon* (W. H. Allen 1989).

Rough Guide to the USA (2002).

Sante, Luc, *Low Life* (Granta 1998).

Schlesinger, Arthur M. Jnr, *The Disuniting of America: Reflections on a Multicultural Society* (Norton 1993).

Scopes, John T. and Presley, James, *Centre of the Storm, Memoirs of John T. Scopes* (Holt, Rinehart and Winston 1967).

Slayton, Robert A., *Empire Statesman: The Rise and Redemption of Al Smith* (Free Press 2001).

Smith, Henry Nash, *Virgin Land, The American West as Symbol and Myth* (Harvard 2005 edition).

Smith, Richard D., *Princeton* (Arcadia 1997).

Smithsonian Guides to Historic America (Stewart, Tabori and Chang, 1990).

Stowe, Harriet Beecher, *Uncle Tom's Cabin* (Penguin edition 1986).

Suarez, Ray, *The Holy Vote: The Politics of Faith in America* (Rayo 2006).

Summers, Mark Wahlgren, *Rum, Romanism and Rebellion, The Making of a President 1884* (University of North Carolina Press 2000).

Thomas, Cal, and Dobson, Ed., *Blinded by Might* (Zondervan 1999).

Tierney, Kevin, *Darrow* (Crowell 1979).

Turner, Frederick Jackson, *The Frontier in American History* (Dover 1996 edition).

Victor, Barbara, *The Last Crusade: Religion and the Politics of Misdirection* (Constable 2005).

Wacker, Grant, *Heaven Below: Early Pentecostals and American Culture* (Harvard 2001).

Walden, *God Won't Save America: Psychosis of a Nation* (Gibson Square 2006).

Wallis, Jim, *God's Politics: Why the American Right Gets It Wrong and the Left Doesn't Get it* (Lion 2006).

Warren, Rick, *The Purpose Driven Life* (Zondervan 2002).

Whicher, George F., *William Jennings Bryan and the Campaign of 1896* (Heath and Co 1953).

Whitten, Mark Weldon, *The Myth of Christian America* (Smyth and Helwys 1999).

Wilkinson, Bruce, *The Prayer of Jabez* (Multnomah 2000).

Wills, Garry, *Under God: Religion and American Politics* (Simon and Schuster 1990).

Newspapers and periodicals as cited: the *Guardian*, *The Times*, *Sunday Times*, *The Daily Telegraph*, *New York Times*, *Washington Post*, *Miami Herald*, *Chicago Tribune*, *Los Angeles Times*, *History Today*, *Christian Century*. Also, *Thinking Anglicans*, Titusonenine, Salon.com and other websites.

Index